ZURICH

INVESTMENT & SAVINGS HANDBOOK
2004–05

General Editor:

Paul Wright

Investment Management Director

UK Life Marketing

Zurich Financial Services Ltd

PEARSON EDUCATION LIMITED

Edinburgh Gate
Harlow CM20 2JE
Tel: +44 (0)1279 623623
Fax: +44 (0)1279 431059
www.pearsoned.co.uk

This edition first published in Great Britain in 2005

© Zurich Financial Services Ltd 2005
www.zurichadvice.co.uk

ISBN 0 273 69588 6

British Library Cataloguing in Publication Data
A CIP catalogue record for this book can be obtained
from the British Library

To save endless repetition of 'he or she' we have mainly used
the male gender indiscriminately to denote both genders.

Typeset by Land & Unwin (Data Sciences) Ltd
Printed and bound in Great Britain by Biddles Ltd, Guildford and King's Lynn

*The Publishers' policy is to use paper manufactured
from sustainable forests.*

No responsibility for loss occasioned to any person acting or refraining
from action as a result of the material in this publication can be
accepted by Zurich, the authors or publishers.

The views and opinions of Zurich may not necessarily
coincide with some of the views and opinions expressed in this book
which are solely those of the authors and no endorsement of them
by Zurich should be inferred.

CONTENTS

ABBREVIATIONS

ACD	authorised corporate director
ACT	Advance Corporation Tax
ADR	American Depository Receipt
AGM	annual general meeting
AHA	Agricultural Holdings Act
AIM	Alternative Investment Market
APCIMS	Association of Private Client Investment Managers and Stockbrokers
AUT	authorised unit trust
AVC	additional voluntary contribution
BES	Business Expansion Scheme
CD	certificate of deposit
CGT	capital gains tax
CIS	collective investment scheme
COMP	contracted-out money purchase
CPI	consumer prices index
CTA	commodity trading advisers
CTO	Capital Taxes Office
DCMS	Department for Culture, Media and Sport
DRIP	dividend reinvestment plan
DSS	Department of Social Security
DTI	Department of Trade and Industry
DWP	Department of Work and Pensions
ECA Regs	Open-Ended Investment Companies (Investment Companies with Variable Capital) Regulations 1996
ECB	European Central Bank
EEA	European Economic Area
EIS	Enterprise Investment Scheme
ETF	exchange-traded funds
EU	European Union
FA	Finance Act
FBT	Farm Business Tenancy
FRI	full repairing and insuring
FSA	Financial Services Authority
FSAVC	free-standing additional voluntary contribution
FSMA	Financial Services and Markets Act

PREFACE

Welcome to the 25th edition of the *Investment & Savings Handbook*. Once again, the book has been thoroughly updated to include all relevant changes announced in the 2004 Budget.

Much has happened over the past year relevant to the contents of this book. Stock markets have remained volatile but the slide in UK shares has at least been halted, if not reversed.

Last year's Preface noted that "even the buy to let market remains active" implying but fortunately not promising, a slowdown in the growth of residential property prices. Well, The Governor of The Bank of England was less equivocal, warning that interest rates will continue to rise unless and until house price inflation is brought under control. The Governor's reaction to property prices is interesting (if not worrying) because the broader measure of retail price inflation remains well under control. This highlights the fact that continued house price inflation and the related level of consumer debt poses the greatest threat to the economy – greater even than the $50 per barrel oil price.

In the meantime investors remain cautious in their outlook and nervous of the stock market. This has seen a shift in buying behaviour towards guaranteed and protected products and funds. In turn, product providers have been particularly quick to react to this change in sentiment and, as a result, have developed innovative new products designed to appeal to this new breed of investor.

As ever, my advice to readers considering an investment is to seek advice from a professional.

As usual, I need to point out that, for readers north of the border, although Scottish law varies from English law on many subjects, in most aspects of tax, trusts and domicile, the two systems coincide.

Finally, I'd like to thank all of this year's contributors for their hard work and punctuality.

Paul Wright

CONTRIBUTORS

Geoffrey Abbott, Dip FBA (Lon) FRICS, is Agricultural Investment Consultant in Smiths Gore (Chartered Surveyors) based in their London Office. He was assisted by a number of the partners in their offices throughout England & Scotland.

Sarah Arkle, MA, ACIS, joined Save and Prosper as a graduate trainee and was seconded to the Investment Research Department of Robert Fleming. In 1981, she joined stockbrokers WI Carr (Overseas) Ltd as a Japanese Equity Salesperson and in 1983 joined Allied Dunbar as a Far Eastern Fund Manager. Following the merger of Allied Dunbar Asset Management and Eagle Star Asset Management, she joined Threadneedle Investment Managers as one of its founding directors, and is now Head of Equities & Managed Funds.

Andrew Bull, FRICS, is a European Director at LaSalle Investment Management, the world's largest independent property consultants.

Peter Grimmett is the Retail Compliance Manager for Threadneedle Investment Services Ltd. He has spent a number of years in the industry, initially in marketing and latterly, in regulation, within the Collective Investment Schemes Department of the Financial Services Authority.

David V Hannis, is Director, James Brearley & Sons Ltd and has been with James Brearley & Sons since 1986. He managed the Southport office until 1999, when he became a Director of the firm and founded the Investment Management Division in Preston. He is also the lead manager of James Brearley & Sons' two Unit Trusts, the CF James Brearley High Income Fund and EFA James Brearley Premium Growth Fund.

Peter Howe, LLB, Barrister, is Company Secretary and an Executive Director in the legal department of Zurich Financial Services, UK Life. The legal department provides a complete legal and technical service to companies in the Zurich Group. Financial Services legislation is his principal area of specialisation.

Vince Jerrard, LLB, ACII, Solicitor, is the Legal Director of Zurich Financial Services. He has contributed chapters to other Zurich publications, including the *Tax Handbook, Capital Taxes Guide* and the *Business Tax and Law Handbook*.

Lenny Jordan is the author of *Options Plain and Simple*, published by Financial Times/Prentice Hall. Formerly a commodities options trader at the Chicago Board of Trade, he later traded equities index options at the London International Financial Futures and Options Exchange. Currently he is Global Risk Manager for the London Capital Group.

Malcolm Kemp is the Executive Director in charge of derivatives and quantitative research at Threadneedle Investments Ltd. He gained a first class Honours Degree from Cambridge University in 1981, qualified as an Actuary in 1987 and was a partner in the investment consulting practice of Bacon & Woodrow, Consulting Actuaries, before joining Threadneedle in early 1996.

Brian Mildenhall is a senior member of the Product Management and Development Division at Zurich Financial Services where he is involved primarily in the management of existing products.

John Myers is from Solon Consultants, a specialised research firm that focuses on property and alternative investments. He is also a visiting professor at Sheffield University.

Ros Price started her investment career after business school in in-house pension management in 1979 with Esso Pension Trust, eventually becoming Investment Director for the Civil Aviation Pension Fund in 1985. Since then she has been involved in US ERISA and mutual fund management and, prior to assuming the role of CIO at Seven Investment Management, was a strategist for the Citigroup Private Bank. Whilst managing monies for Metropolitan Life international portfolios in the early 1990s, she was involved in investing in the newly emerging European markets, especially in Russia and the former Soviet Union.

Stuart Reynolds, LLB, is Alliances Director and a Director in the Customer Solutions Division of Zurich Financial Services where his primary responsibility is in relation to the development of new life assurance and pension products for the Company.

Alex Scott (Senior Research Analyst) works with Ros Price in setting the investment strategy and asset allocation at Seven Investment Management. He focuses in particular on the UK, emerging economies and market valuation trends. He has worked recently as an equity analyst, specialising in financial services and consumer sectors, and as a fund manager, and is a popular media commentator on investment markets and strategy.

Mike Wilkes is a Senior Tax Manager in the London personal taxation department of PKF, an international firm of chartered accountants. He specialises in advising foreign domiciled individuals, but also deals with general personal taxation matters of a number of other personal clients, including Lloyd's underwriters.

Paul Wright, BSc (Hons), MBA and Fellow of the Chartered Institute of Marketing, is Investment Management Director for Zurich Financial Services.

1

AN OVERVIEW

PAUL WRIGHT

Zurich Financial Services

The *Investment & Savings Handbook* was first published in 1980 and is aimed primarily at the investment adviser. It is designed to give an annual update on the various types of investment. Most chapters include a section designed to cover highlights of the previous year, a preview of the coming year and a view on the next year or two based on current thinking.

This chapter covers the following topics:

- The investment adviser.
- Types of investor.
- Ways of arranging and holding investments.
- The nature of an investment.
- Investment policy – general principles and special factors.
- Trustees.
- Overseas investors.

In addition, various rates for 2004–05 are provided.

1.1 INTRODUCTION

The basic principles of investment do not change; it is only the influences on investment policy that are likely to alter over the years. These influences are primarily of a political and economic nature, ie the world economic climate and, for the UK investor, the economic and taxation policies of the government of the day.

The investment adviser's task is always to ensure a client's asset portfolio is well balanced and robust in the face changing investment conditions. When interest rates are relatively high, as they have been from time to time over the last two decades, the appeal of short-term deposits can be hard to resist. However, as we have seen more recently, interest rates can fall sharply and remain low, leaving clients with the twin problems of declining real value and declining income. Advisers must always be prepared, if necessary, to lean against the winds of

1

investment fashion to ensure that clients achieve the right balance of risk and reward to suit their personal circumstances.

1.2 THE INVESTMENT ADVISER

Today's investment adviser has the unenviable burden of coping with more and more information about an increasing array of investments. Nowadays, more investment products exist than ever before, described in an ever-growing mass of literature, commented on by experts of varying experience and qualifications in an environment of proliferating legislation, and regulation from the Financial Services Authority (FSA).

Against that background, the investment adviser – solicitor, accountant, stockbroker, insurance broker, bank manager or anyone else – has five main responsibilities:

(1) To know which investment products are available and to establish which are suitable for individual clients (through an understanding of a client's needs and appetite for risk).
(2) To know which questions to ask about investment options and where to find the answers.
(3) To be able to support the investment decision and, if necessary, show that the advice is not influenced by the method of remuneration.
(4) To be able to make arrangements for a particular investment (or disinvestment) to be made on behalf of clients.
(5) To keep up to date on a fast-changing regulatory framework that applies to all those in the business of providing investment advice.

Most importantly, advisers have to recognise their own limitations and to look for advice themselves. That, in the main, is the purpose of this book. It identifies the main investment media, identifies the investor for whom they are suitable or unsuitable (posing the main questions that should be asked about each medium) and provides signposts to the specialist consultants or dealers and to the legal, fiscal and other technicalities.

1.3 TYPES OF INVESTOR

This book aims to help people advising individual investors (including trustees and family investment companies). It is essential that advisers identify the particular category of investor to which their client belongs. It would be impossible to devise a precise, exhaustive categorisation, so it follows that advisers must take into account a number of personal factors in appraising both investors and also the investment and disinvestment situations with which they are concerned. These factors will include the investor's age and health, his intention with regard to place of residence and/or domicile, willingness to accept risk, willingness to participate in the choice of investments and capacity to delegate.

1.4 WAYS OF ARRANGING AND HOLDING INVESTMENTS

All the foregoing assumes considerable sophistication on the part of investment advisers and also a willingness to give their time, for which they will obviously expect to be remunerated. The fact that investors of moderate means are usually unwilling to pay for this level of individual attention has meant that collective investment media have developed hand-in-hand with the relative decline of individually tailored investment portfolios. A corollary of this development is that an ever-growing body of legislation and regulation (see Chapter 21) has had to be developed to protect the small saver against fraud.

For many of the specific investments, comment is made on methods of arranging and holding those investments, although a number of such methods are common to many investment media. It is beyond the scope of this book to give detailed explanations or advice on either the mechanics of establishing and conducting the particular 'vehicle' or its tax implications. The investment adviser will be aware that the principal ways in which investments can be arranged and held are:

(1) by personal direct investment by the individual;
(2) through a trust or settlement (including a Will trust);
(3) in partnership with others; and
(4) through a family investment company.

1.5 THE NATURE OF AN INVESTMENT

1.5.1 Capital and income

The two basic elements of investment are *capital* and *income*. At one end of the scale, the capital remains constant while the income produced may vary (eg bank and building society deposits); at the other end, there are non-income producing assets (eg commodities and works of art) where no income is produced but the capital value fluctuates.

Between the two extremes are many variations. Gilt-edged securities can produce a constant level of income and a known repayment value at maturity. Short-dated securities will have more certainty over the rise (or fall) in capital values to maturity, whereas values of long-dated gilts will vary considerably as interest rates rise and fall. Investments in property or equities will produce variations in both capital value and income. Life assurances, such as single-premium bonds, in theory produce no income while they are held as an investment, but in practice this disadvantage can be overcome by the various withdrawal plans that are available (see Chapter 14).

1.5.2 Inflation

An essential third element in evaluating investments is inflation. For most of the past ten years, governments have viewed inflation as public enemy number one. Although currently under control, high inflation harms investment, damages prosperity and can destroy jobs.

The need for a hedge against inflation has had a strong influence on investment policy since the 1960s. As inflation rates fluctuate, opinions will vary widely on what represents an effective hedge; inflation has different consequences for different people. Commodities, works of art or tangible assets such as 'buy to let' residential property may turn out to be a good hedge against inflation, but the same hope of finding a good hedge often underlies investment in land, commercial property and shares in companies, both domestic and overseas. The list is endless, and investors must take their pick according to their own philosophy or judgement and appetite for risk.

This is an area where fashion can play a part. The current view is that inflation provides only a modest threat to markets. The fact that inflation has been below 3% for the past few years does not mean that higher levels will not return. People with not particularly long memories will recall inflation at four times the current level and the impact this had both on individual savings and the economy.

1.5.3 Time

A fourth investment dimension is the time factor. In most, if not all, of the following chapters, references are made to fluctuations, trends and fashions affecting the various markets. Within a long-term trend, there are likely to be many short-term fluctuations, caused by a myriad of factors. When to buy and when to sell are therefore difficult decisions for the investor. Investors can be guided by professional advisers who have knowledge of the technical factors affecting a particular market, but who can only express an opinion on political factors and the general state of the economy, and who can therefore make only intelligent general forecasts not amounting to precise predictions. For those who invest overseas, fluctuations in exchange rates form a further element in the evaluation of investments.

1.6 INVESTMENT POLICY – GENERAL PRINCIPLES AND SPECIAL FACTORS

1.6.1 Diversification

The first maxim for practically every investor should be diversification. You achieve diversification by investing in varying kinds of investments and also within a particular class of investment.

There will always be investors who have to commit, or to leave committed, a substantial part of their capital in one particular way (eg the person who has built up a substantial business). It might also be thought that the small investor with little money to invest would have little scope for diversification, but unit trusts (see Chapter 8) or bonds (see Chapter 3) indirectly provide significant diversification.

1.6.2 Balance

Investors should, as far as possible, have a balanced portfolio. A part of their capital should be earmarked for security and invested in, for example, building society or bank deposits. However, all investors should also look for a measure of capital appreciation as a hedge against inflation, so a part of their capital should be invested in equity-type investments. The precise balance will depend on the individual circumstances and inclinations of the particular investor.

1.6.3 Advice of specialists

The investor should be guided by the advice of the various specialists in the markets discussed in this book. They all provide a service which, if well performed, is a valuable one, for which they quite properly deserve to be remunerated (either by fees or commissions from the product providers). However, they all wish to sell their wares and another reason for diversification is to avoid total dependence on the judgement and integrity of any one particular specialist.

Any investor investing overseas should pay particularly close regard to the advice of specialists familiar with the markets in the countries concerned. The additional advice required will cover such things as marketability, banking arrangements and (particularly in the case of purchase of property) legal advice to ensure that the investor obtains a good title.

1.6.4 Taxation

The general rule is that, while full account should be taken of likely tax implications, investment policy should not be dictated by tax. For example, it is often the case that decisions tend to be unduly influenced by capital gains tax (CGT) considerations. The investor has to balance the right time to sell an investment that is showing a profit against a loss of use of the money required to pay the tax. In general terms, investors should not be deterred from realising investments simply by CGT considerations alone.

Investments with favourable tax treatment include National Savings certificates (see Chapter 2) and life assurances (see Chapter 14), which continue to have CGT benefits and, in the case of certain trust policies, inheritance tax (IHT) benefits as well. Another tax-efficient investment worth considering is the individual savings account (ISA) (see Chapter 20).

These tax benefits are a good reason for investing in this way. However, there is no guarantee that, over a given period, they will necessarily produce a better return than investments that have no tax benefits at all. Not only may these other investments have compensating benefits (eg better capital appreciation), future tax legislation could alter or even nullify tax benefits that are now available – yet another reason for a policy of diversification.

1.6.5 Commission and expenses of buying and selling

At one end of the scale, there is no explicit cost at all in investing money in a building society or bank deposit. Commission on the purchase of gilt-edged securities is small, while for equities it is reasonable, although stamp duty on purchases will also be payable (see Chapter 3). Commissions on equities vary from broker to broker following the abolition of fixed commissions in 1986.

At the top end of the scale comes the art market where the total commission can be high (in double figures, see Chapter 18). The investor hoping to make an eventual gain must realise that, immediately after purchase, the item may be worth somewhat less than the amount paid (or even less where VAT is taken into account).

1.6.6 Buying and selling prices

On the Stock Exchange, separate buying and selling prices are quoted, the difference between these prices being the market-maker's turn or potential profit. The same principle can apply to other markets and, with certain assets (eg jewellery), the fact that the asset has only second-hand value the moment it has been purchased must be taken into account.

1.6.7 Other benefits

Investments should not be considered only by reference to pure investment criteria. Property may be purchased as a home or, if it is a farm, to provide a livelihood. Life assurance brings with it the element of family protection. Works of art (unless stored away in a safe deposit) bring pleasure to the owner and collector.

1.6.8 Methods of investment

The normal method of investment is for investors, either personally or through an agent, to buy and sell individual investments (and they could give their agent discretionary power to buy and sell on their behalf). Investors can either buy the investment outright or acquire options to buy at some time in the future. Alternatively, they may be able to buy a 'future', which effectively gives full exposure to fluctuations in the value of the underlying asset, but at a much lower cost. Such 'geared' investments carry a commensurate degree of risk.

The same type of investment can sometimes be acquired through different means. For example, investment in property can be by direct purchase of property (see Chapters 9–12), shares in a property company or property bonds. Overseas investment can be through investment trusts, unit trusts or open-ended investment companies (either based in the UK or offshore) holding overseas investments, or in UK companies with substantial overseas activities.

1.6.9 Gearing

For the smaller investor, borrowing to invest is fraught with danger. It should only appeal to investors with free assets who think they can invest these to produce greater capital appreciation. So, it would be pointless for the cautious investor to borrow from a building society and then reinvest the amount borrowed in a building society (or other equally safe investment) because the interest paid would exceed the interest received and the only beneficiary would be the building society itself.

For the wealthy investor, borrowing has often been a case of altering the shape of the asset portfolio. For example, consider an investor (Mr Smith) with £250,000 who buys a house for £150,000. If Mr Smith buys the property without a mortgage, he will have a £150,000 stake in the property market and £100,000 invested elsewhere. If he takes a £100,000 mortgage, he will have an unchanged stake in the property market but £200,000 invested elsewhere.

1.7 TRUSTEES

Trustees are usually appointed by a settlement or a Will. They can, however, be bare trustees, nominees or attorneys for others (under a power of attorney) who might well be infants or persons under some disability. They also include anyone who owes a fiduciary duty of care to others.

For investment purposes their 'bible' is the Trustee Act 2000. The principles that the Act lays down are discussed below.

1.7.1 The Trustee Act 2000

Prior to the Trustee Act 2000, which came into effect in February 2001, trusts which made no specific statement of investment policy fell under the rules laid down by the Trustee Investments Act 1961. This Act restricted investment in equities and did not allow investment in land and property.

The Trustee Investments Act 1961 has been replaced by the Trustee Act 2000. This new Act removes the restrictions imposed by the 1961 Act and allows trustees to make any kind of investment – including investment in land and property. However, in exercising these new rights, trustees must 'obtain and consider proper advice about the way in which, having regard to the standard investment criteria, the power should be exercised'. The standard investment criteria are:

(1) the suitability of the investment to the trust;
(2) the need to diversify investments insofar as this is appropriate to the circumstances of the trust.

1.8 OVERSEAS INVESTORS

1.8.1 Exchange control

UK investors can invest in any country in the world without restriction, although they are subject to whatever restrictions the country in which they plan to invest may impose. Conversely, overseas investors can invest freely in the UK. However, they may be subject to exchange control provisions imposed by their country of residence.

1.8.2 Taxation

Detailed advice on taxation is outside the scope of this book and so the comments made below are necessarily only in very general terms. Overseas investors (and also immigrants and emigrants) must be particularly aware of taxation considerations, which for them depend on domicile and residence.

For tax purposes, a person is regarded as resident in the UK if he or she is physically present there for 183 days or more in any tax year or, if over a period of four such years, present there for an average of three months or more in each tax year.

Individuals are regarded as 'ordinarily resident' if they are habitually resident in the UK year after year and continue to be regarded as ordinarily resident if they usually live there but are in fact physically absent (eg on a long holiday) for even the whole of any tax year.

Inheritance tax (IHT)

Liability to UK IHT depends basically on domicile. UK domiciled investors are subject to IHT on their worldwide assets, whereas investors not domiciled in the UK are subject to IHT on UK property or investments only.

Domicile is a concept of general law and is determined by a range of factors. Broadly speaking, domicile is where individuals have their permanent home. It is distinct from nationality or residence and an individual can have only one domicile at a time.

Individuals would normally acquire a domicile of origin from their father when they were born, though this may change if the person on whom the individual was dependent at the time changed his domicile before the individual was age 16.

Women who married before 1974 automatically acquired their husband's domicile; they may now change it to a domicile of their choice.

Anyone over age 16 has the legal power to apply for a new domicile of choice. However, it is not easy to do and usually requires proof that the individual has severed all connections with his existing country and intends to settle permanently in a new country.

Capital gains tax (CGT)

Liability to CGT depends on UK residence or ordinary residence for tax purposes. The general rule is that the investor ordinarily resident in the UK is subject to CGT and the investor not ordinarily resident in the UK is exempt from it. Investors immigrating to or emigrating from the

UK should take advice on the timing of the sale of assets so as to avoid any CGT liability.

Income tax

Liability to income tax depends on residence, but there are certain concessions for people not domiciled in the UK. Many factors, including the provisions of double taxation agreements, are relevant and the investor must take professional advice.

1.8.3 Other restrictions

Normally, an overseas investor can invest in any form of UK investment without problems. However, difficulties might arise where the investor ultimately wanted to export the investment (particularly where it is a work of art) or where the investment involves a liability in the UK (which could arise with, say, an investment in leasehold property as the landlord might require a UK-resident guarantor).

1.9 CONCLUSION

When it comes to investment, nothing is constant. Continual review and permanent vigilance are essential. The investment strategies appropriate to one investor may not be right for another and those suitable for one particular generation of investor may be wholly inappropriate for the next generation, when the investment climate and the law may have changed. Even a strategy appropriate now may be inappropriate in the future, by which time the investor will have aged and his needs and family circumstances will have changed considerably.

1.10 INCOME TAX RATES, ALLOWANCES, AND NATIONAL INSURANCE RATES FROM 6 APRIL 2004

1.10.1 Income tax rates and personal allowances

Table 1.1 Income tax rates 2004–05

Bands of taxable income £	Rate %	Tax on band £
0–2,020	10	202
2,021–31,400	22	6,463.38
Over 31,400	40	–

Table 1.2 Personal and married couple's allowances

The rates that will apply for 2004–05 (equivalent figures for 2003–04 in italics) are:

Age	Personal allowance £		Married couple's allowance £	
Under 65	4,745	*4,615*	–	–
65 to 74	6,830	*6,600*	5,725	*5,565*
75 and over	6,950	*6,720*	5,795	*5,635*

Note: The income limit for persons aged 65 and over is £18,900. Where the taxpayer's total income exceeds this limit, the age-related allowances are reduced by £1 for every £2 of income over the limit. The allowances are not reduced below the level of the basic personal or married couple's allowances.

1.10.2 National Insurance contributions 2004–05

Table 1.3 Contracted-in

Employer contributions		Employee contributions	
Earnings £pw	% of all earnings	Earnings £pw	% of all earnings
0–91	0	0–91	0
91+ with no upper earnings limit	12.8	91.01–610	11
		over 610	1

Table 1.4 Contracted-out

Employer contributions			Employee contributions	
Earnings £pw	(a)%	(b)%	Earnings £pw	%
0–91	0	0	0–91	0
91.01–610	9.3	11.8	91.01–610	9.4
over 610	12.8	12.8	over 610	1

(*a*) = salary related scheme
(*b*) = money purchase scheme

Self-employed contributions

Class 2 NICs: the flat weekly rate is £2.05 per week.
Class 3 NICs (voluntary) £7.15 per week
Class 4 NICs: 8% on profits between £4,745 and £31,720 per annum, an additional 1% per earnings above £31,720.

These rates take effect from 6 April 2004.

11

1.11 CAPITAL GAINS TAX

CGT is charged on real capital gains. A person who makes a gain is allowed to deduct not only his actual acquisition value (in addition to the costs of acquisition and disposal) but also a proportion of the acquisition value that represents the increase in the Retail Prices Index (RPI) between the month of acquisition and the month of disposal.

Up until the November 1993 Budget, it was permissible to use indexation relief to create or increase a capital loss. From 30 November 1993, indexation relief may only be used in this way for transactions prior to 30 November 1993.

The intention of the new rules was that, in all future transactions, indexation relief should only be used to reduce or extinguish a gain, not create or increase a loss. The rule was relaxed as the Finance Bill made its way through the committee stages; indexation may continue to be used in this way but only for the 1993–94 and 1994–95 tax years and only up to an overall limit of £10,000.

The CGT rates, taper relief, exemptions and retirement relief are as follows:

Individuals taxed:
For individuals, the net gain is treated as the top slice of income and taxed as follows:

The part (if any) up to £2,020 of income plus gains	10%
The part (if any) in the range £2,021–£31,400	20%
The part over £31,400	40%
Trustees and personal representatives	40%

The effective tax rate may be reduced by taper relief as follows:

Tapering scale:
Complete years asset held after 6 April 1998   *Percentage of chargeable gain*

Complete years asset held after 6 April 1998	Business assets	Non-business
0	100.0	100
1	50.0	100
2	25.0	100
3	25.0	95
4	25.0	90
5	25.0	85
6	25.0	80
7	25.0	75

8	25.0	70
9	25.0	65
10	25.0	60

Annual exemptions:

| Individuals | £8,200 |
| Trusts, in general | £4,100 |

1.12 INHERITANCE TAX

Rate %	Band £
0	0–263,000
40	263,000+

2

UNLISTED INVESTMENTS

JOHN SMITHARD
HSBC Investment Management
Updated by
BRIAN MILDENHALL
Zurich Financial Services

2.1 TYPES OF UNLISTED SECURITY

This chapter deals with the most commonly available forms of investment that do not have an official quotation or market price. It includes investments issued by the Government through National Savings, by local authorities, by building societies and by other financial institutions wishing to raise money, which in general can only be redeemed by the borrower.

With some exceptions, these securities provide investors with interest until they mature, whereupon they receive the return of their original capital. Although the rates of return on some of these investments might not always compare favourably with returns on other forms of investment, some have taxation advantages up to a specific amount, particularly for the higher rate taxpayer. Other investments covered in this chapter may produce no income in the course of their lives, but give a guaranteed improvement in capital value on maturity. Premium bonds give no guarantee of income or capital appreciation but offer the holder a chance in draws for tax-free prizes.

Perhaps slowly, savers are adjusting to today's lower interest rates and the expectation of lower future inflation. There remains concern that savers' inertia will leave them with old savings accounts paying less attractive rates of interest. More than ever, savers should regularly review their savings and investments to ensure they are receiving good returns, take advantage of available tax reliefs and, more importantly, strike the right balance for them between short-term savings and longer-term investments.

Many believe that the UK economy has entered a period of long-term low inflation. For most adults this is a new experience. The impact on savings habits is uncertain and may take several years to emerge fully. For now, most savers should be able to find investments that offer returns in excess of inflation. There is much to do to inform savers about 'real rates of return'.

A relatively new type of savings account is gaining wider acceptance. These accounts aggregate all savings and borrowings the individual has with the financial institution, and interest is paid or charged on the individual's net position. This arrangement can offer more than mere convenience – depending on circumstances, the effective rate of return on the savings 'pot' can be considerably enhanced. Such accounts deserve to become far more popular.

2.2 TYPES OF UNLISTED INVESTMENT

2.2.1 National Savings and Investment

The NS&I is guaranteed by the Government. Two types of account – Easy Access Savings Accounts and Investment Accounts – are available.

The current interest rate for the easy access account varies from 2% to 4.55% gross. For the investment account, rates start at 3.25% per annum, increasing to 4.15% per annum for larger deposits. The maximum amount that can be withdrawn daily from an easy access account is £300, and all withdrawals from an investment account require one month's notice, although withdrawal can be made without notice subject to 30 days' loss of interest.

Interest is paid gross (ie without deduction of tax at source). The minimum for each deposit is £100 (easy access account) and £20 (investment account) and the maximum holding is £2 million (easy access account) and £100,000 (investment account).

2.2.2 National Savings certificates

National Savings certificates are guaranteed by the Government. They cannot be sold to third parties. A number of different issues of certificates have been made over the years.

A maximum individual holding is specified for each issue of National Savings certificates. Trustees and registered friendly societies and charities approved by the director of savings can also buy certificates.

No interest is paid, but after a stated period of time the certificates can be redeemed at a higher value than the original purchase price. The total rate at which the value appreciates during this period is indicated on the certificate and in the prospectus and is guaranteed for the duration of the certificate. The current rate is 3.45% compound for five years (78th issue) and 3.35% compound for two years (28th issue). The value builds up by the addition of increments at the end of the first year and each subsequent period of three months. The full table, showing how the value rises more steeply towards the end of the period and levels off after the end of the period, is available from the details issued by National Savings and Investments.

The capital appreciation is free from both income tax and capital gains tax (CGT). The minimum holding is £100 and the maximum £15,000 in the current issues, but holders may have a further unlimited amount of certificates if these arise from reinvestment of holdings of earlier issues.

Holdings should be reviewed from time to time, particularly since new issues may carry more attractive rates of capital appreciation than those already held.

2.2.3 National Savings index-linked certificates

As with National Savings certificates, these certificates are guaranteed by the Government. They cannot be sold to third parties.

The maximum holding is £15,000 in the current issue unless the certificates came from a reinvestment of mature certificates in which case there is no limit. The minimum holding is £100.

If a certificate is encashed within the first year, the purchase price only is repaid, unless it is a reinvestment certificate. If the certificates are held for more than a year, the redemption value is equal to the original purchase price, increased in proportion to the rise in the Retail Prices Index (RPI) between the month of purchase and the month of redemption. In the event of a fall in the RPI, the certificates can be encashed for the original purchase price in the first year, and not less than their value at the previous anniversary otherwise. After a holder's death, indexation can continue for a maximum of 12 months. Certificates can be inherited.

The latest issue guarantees a return above the rate of inflation for a five-year term by offering extra tax-free interest of 1.25% per annum compound as well as indexation (36th issue). For the three-year index-linked certificate, the extra tax-free interest is currently 1.10% per annum compound (9th issue).

As with National Savings certificates, capital appreciation is exempt from income tax and CGT.

2.2.4 National Savings income bonds

As with National Savings certificates, these bonds are guaranteed by the Government. They may be held by individuals, children and some trustees.

Gross interest is paid on a monthly basis but the interest is subject to tax. Investors may cash in part of their holding in multiples of £500, but they must keep a minimum balance of £500.

Six weeks' notice of repayment is required. The maximum holding is £1m. If the investor dies, the money can be withdrawn without any formal period of notice and with interest paid in full up to the date of repayment.

Current interest rates are 4.45% per annum gross for amounts exceeding £25,000 and 4.2% per annum gross for amounts below £25,000. Rates of interest are variable.

2.2.5 National Savings capital bonds

The bonds are guaranteed by the Government. They may be held by individuals, children and some trustees.

Bonds are bought with a £100 minimum and a £1m maximum and give a rate of return fixed for five years at the date of purchase. Although called 'capital bonds', they accrue interest that is capitalised on each anniversary of the purchase date, and this accrued interest must be notified to the Revenue on the individual's tax return (and income tax paid, if necessary, before actual receipt of the capitalised interest at the date of maturity). An annual statement of value, showing the capitalised interest, is sent to the bondholder shortly after the end of each tax year.

The capitalised interest accrues at an increasing rate during the bond's life and the full advertised compound rate, currently 4.7% per annum gross (series 20), is received only if held to maturity. This occurs on the fifth anniversary of the purchase date, before which the bondholder will have been reminded by the bond office of the imminence of maturity.

Repayment can be requested at any time for a minimum amount of £100, provided this leaves at least the minimum holding. No capitalised interest accrues before the first anniversary.

2.2.6 National Savings fixed rate savings bonds

Fixed rate savings bonds offer guaranteed rates for savings terms of one year, three years or five years. The interest rate is tiered, with the highest rate for investments over £50,000. Interest is paid after deduction of 20% tax.

Interest can be paid out annually (a monthly option is available at a slightly lower rate) or added to the bond and paid out on maturity. Current interest rates range from 4.15% per annum gross to 4.8% per annum gross, depending on the amount held and maturity period.

The minimum investment is £500 and the maximum is £1m. Individuals must be over 16 and some trustees can invest.

2.2.7 National Savings children's bonus bonds

These bonds are guaranteed by the Government and are designed to encourage children to save. They can be bought to a maximum of £1,000 per issue for children under age 16, although they can be held to age 21. The minimum holding is £25 and the bonds are available in multiples of £25. A guaranteed bonus is credited every five years and a final bonus at age 21.

All interest, and the bonus, is exempt from income tax and need not be declared to the Revenue. The current return (issue 16) is 4.45% compound over five years, including the bonus.

They may prove attractive to parents wishing to give capital to children, for there is no liability to income tax on the interest which in most other circumstances is deemed still to belong to the parent if it exceeds a token level of £100.

2.2.8 National Savings pensioners bonds

This National Savings product has been designed to produce a competitive income return for older investors who wish to fix a monthly return for a period up to five years despite any change in the level of interest rates during that period.

As well as the five-year bond, one-year and two-year bonds are available, so that pensioners do not need to tie up their savings for such a long period.

Interest is paid monthly without deduction of income tax, although it is subject to income tax. This will be of certain benefit to non-taxpayers, who need not make a reclaim of tax already deducted at source.

The bonds can only be bought by individuals aged 60+, or held in trust for a beneficiary who has reached age 60. The minimum limit for each purchase is £500. The maximum investment across all series of bonds is £1m (either individually or in joint ownership).

Interest is earned on each day that the bonds are held. Repayment is subject to 60 days' notice, although no interest is paid for the notice period. However, there is no loss of interest on the repayment of the bonds on their maturity, or on a holder's death. The amount of each repayment must be at least £500, and there must be at least a £500 minimum holding retained after any withdrawal.

At the time of the bond's anniversary a holder should receive a reminder notifying him of the rate of interest for the next period. The holder then needs to make a decision whether to leave the bonds in place or have them redeemed and reinvest in an alternative investment. This depends on the bondholder's needs at that time and the prevailing level of interest rates, although it is the intention to offer pensioners a competitive return for their savings. Current rates range from 4.35% (one year, series 26) to 4.60% (five year, series 41) gross.

2.2.9 National Savings ISAs

National Savings offer a cash mini Individual Savings Account (ISA) product, offering simplicity, accessability and a current variable interest rate of 4.45% per annum gross. For details on ISAs in general, see 20.2.7.

2.2.10 Premium bonds

Premium bonds are guaranteed by the Government. They cannot be sold to third parties.

Any person aged 16 or over can buy the bonds, and a parent, grandparent or legal guardian may buy bonds on behalf of a child under 16. A bond cannot be held in the name of more than one person or of a corporate body, society, club or other association of persons. Prizes won by bonds registered in the name of a child under age 16 are paid on behalf of the child to the parent or legal guardian.

Bonds are sold in units of £1 and purchases must then be in multiples of £10 subject to a minimum purchase at any time of £100 up to a maximum of £30,000 per person.

No interest is paid, but a bond that has been held for one full calendar month is eligible for inclusion in the regular draw for prizes of various amounts. The size of the monthly prize fund is determined by applying one month's interest at a predetermined rate (3.20% from December 2004) to the total value of the eligible bonds at that time. This rate is reviewed from time to time. Bonds can be encashed at any time. All prizes are free of income tax and CGT. Every month over 500,000 prizes are paid, ranging from £50 to £1m.

Premium bonds are a 'fun' investment for those investors who wish to take the chance of a prize, knowing they can always have the return of their cash investment, and so can be favourably compared to the National Lottery. The odds against winning any prize are currently 24,000 to 1 for each unit.

2.2.11 Government stock

Gilts and gilt-edged or government stock represent a loan to the Bank of England, repayable on a fixed future date and, with the exception of index-linked gilts, on which a fixed rate of annual interest is payable to the holder. By far the largest active market for gilts is through The Stock Exchange, but they can also be bought and sold across post office counters. There are certain benefits to individuals in doing so, although transactions take slightly longer to process.

The full range of gilt-edged stock is now available to individual applicants. Potential investors must decide whether to buy stock that has a high income return with perhaps restricted capital growth prospects, or even a guaranteed fall in value if held to redemption; a low income return and a guaranteed rise in value until maturity; or a balance between the two. In the majority of cases, investment in index-linked stock will protect the capital against inflation until redemption, while providing a low, but inflation-proofed, income.

Gilts can also be bought when offered by the Bank of England through application forms published in the national newspapers.

Interest on gilts is paid without deduction of income tax and so gilts can certainly be considered by non-taxpayers and, depending on their return, by others who normally pay tax. Basic rate and higher rate taxpayers must account for the tax due on the interest. There is no CGT liability on profits made on the redemption or sale of gilts.

The main characteristics of gilts are described at 3.3.

2.2.12 Local authority mortgage bonds

These borrowings are secured on the revenues of local authorities, which have the power to levy the council tax. It is generally assumed that the Government would stand behind such borrowings, although it has no legal commitment to do so.

A minimum investment is usually specified: this varies between authorities.

Local authority mortgage bonds are issued for a fixed term, usually between two and seven years. Unlike local authority negotiable bonds, in which there is a market on The Stock Exchange, they cannot normally be sold to third parties.

Interest is subject to income tax and is paid after deduction of 20% tax. Non-taxpayers therefore have to claim a tax rebate, while higher rate taxpayers are assessed for the balance of tax due.

Deposits are suitable for investors seeking a competitive rate of interest and prepared to tie up capital for a fixed term. Investors who may want to realise their investment more quickly should explore the possibility of negotiable bonds.

Authorities seeking deposits advertise in the national press, stating the period, rate of interest paid and details of where applications should be made. Deposits are acknowledged by the issue to the holder of mortgage bonds.

2.2.13 Commercial banks: current, deposit and savings accounts and certificates of deposit

Deposits with banks carry no government guarantee and their security therefore lies in the reputation and viability of the bank concerned. Certificates of deposit (CDs) are bearer documents and can be sold to third parties, whereas deposit and savings accounts represent a non-assignable debt from the bank to the holder.

There are normally no preconditions to opening a deposit or savings account with a commercial bank. However, the minimum sum for an investment in CDs is usually fairly high.

Interest, which is paid at regular intervals on accounts, can be varied by the bank as the general level of interest rates and the bank's own base rate change. Generally, seven days' notice of withdrawal is required for deposit accounts. The interest on CDs is fixed for the duration of the certificates – normally between three months and five years.

Interest on deposit and savings accounts is paid net of 20% tax, which may be reclaimed by non-taxpayers. Non-taxpayers who complete Revenue form R85 can have the interest credited gross. Higher rate taxpayers are given credit for the tax deducted.

Deposit and savings accounts are useful means of investing funds that may be needed at short notice. Many traditional current accounts do not pay interest, or pay a very low rate, and so are not investments but rather a convenient way to manage cash. Indeed, many deposit and savings accounts pay low rates of interest and investors should review such accounts regularly and compare the returns available elsewhere. CDs are suitable for large deposits and consequently earn a higher return than deposit or savings accounts.

Deposit and savings accounts may be opened, and CDs purchased, by instruction and transfer of cash to the bank concerned. Bank account statements should be kept for reference. Since CDs are bearer documents, they should be held in safe custody.

2.2.14 Building society accounts

Building societies offer share accounts, various higher interest accounts, term bonds and save-as-you-earn (SAYE) contracts. None of these investments can be sold to third parties. Security lies in the reputation and viability of the building society concerned.

The minimum age for entering into an SAYE contract is 16, but any of the other forms of savings may be undertaken by children aged 7+. For younger children, an account may be opened in the name of trustees (normally the child's parents). SAYE contracts are open only to individuals and cannot be undertaken on joint accounts.

Building societies compete for deposits not only with banks but also with each other. On lump sum investments, interest is usually paid every six months, although in some cases monthly. On SAYE contracts the bonus is fixed at the outset and paid at the end of the fifth and seventh years, but other savings plans bear interest rates that, although specified at the time of investment, vary from time to time with the general level of interest rates. A period of notice is specified for withdrawals from share accounts but is in practice seldom required except for large sums. There may be penalties for early withdrawal from term bonds and higher interest accounts.

Income tax at 20% is deducted from the gross interest, which non-taxpayers can reclaim. Non-taxpayers who complete Revenue form R85 can have the interest credited gross.

The simplicity of building society deposit and share accounts and the ease with which small withdrawals can be made on demand, coupled with the sound record of building societies, make them attractive for basic or higher rate taxpayers. Their relative security makes them ideal for short-term cash savings.

The rate of interest offered depends on a number of factors – for example how much is invested, how long the investment is to be held and the notice period for withdrawals, what services the investor requires (eg a cheque book) and whether the account is handled exclusively by post or the Internet rather than through the branch office.

2.2.15 Guaranteed income bonds

These products are issued by some life assurance companies, but their availability has reduced somewhat in recent years. The products are characterised by a fixed rate of return for a specified period, usually one to five years. The quoted return applies to basic rate taxpayers, although non-taxpayers cannot reclaim any tax and higher rate taxpayers have additional tax liability.

Guaranteed income bonds should not be confused with 'higher income bonds' offered by some life assurance companies, building societies and banks. Despite their similar names, the products are very different.

Higher income bonds tend to offer the prospect of a higher return as a regular income or capital sum after three or five years. The return usually depends on the performance of a particular stock market index and is not guaranteed. Generally, the higher the return, the greater the investment risk. If the underlying index does not perform as required, investors may not make any money at all on their investment. In some circumstances, investors may get back less than they invested.

2.2.16 Certificates of tax deposit

Certificates of tax deposit are not strictly speaking a form of investment but a scheme operated by the Revenue whereby future tax liabilities can be provided for in advance. The deposits are therefore guaranteed by the Government.

Certificates are available to any taxpayer – individual, trustee or corporate – and can be surrendered to meet tax liabilities of any kind, except PAYE income tax or income tax deducted from payments to subcontractors.

Interest is paid for a fixed maximum period at a rate specified by HM Treasury when purchased, but the rate varies in line with money market rates. If the deposit is not used to meet tax liabilities but is instead withdrawn for cash, interest is paid at a much lower rate. Interest is paid gross and is subject to income tax.

These certificates are suitable only for taxpayers facing known future tax liabilities, although such taxpayers should consider whether a better return could be obtained by investing elsewhere until such time as the liability has to be met.

Deposits are made by applying to any Collector of Taxes, who issues a certificate specifying the date of receipt and the amount of the deposit. Any request for a deposit to be withdrawn for cash should be made to the Collector, accompanied by the relevant certificates.

2.2.17 Treasury bills

Treasury bills are bearer documents issued by the Bank of England and guaranteed by the Government.

A Treasury bill is initially a 91-day loan to the Bank of England. No interest is paid but bills are issued at a discount. The difference between the discounted price and £100, the redemption price, is the capital gain accruing to the investor, and the annual rate of discount that it represents is called the 'Treasury bill rate'. Although the holder may not encash the bills at the Bank of England before the due date, they can be sold through the discount market at any time at the prevailing market price.

The difference between the discounted price and the price at which the bills are redeemed at the Bank of England or sold in the market is subject to tax. In the unlikely event of a private investor holding a Treasury bill, the gain would be liable to income tax. Treasury bills are suitable for companies rather than individuals and confer total security on short-term deposits.

Tenders for Treasury bills must be made on printed forms (available from the Chief Cashier's Office, Bank of England) and must be submitted through a London clearing bank, discount house or stockbroker. The value of bills tendered for and the price at which the investor is prepared to buy them must be specified. On the day tenders are received the Bank notifies persons whose tenders have been accepted in whole or in part. Since Treasury bills are bearer documents, they should be held in safe custody.

2.3 COMPARING DIFFERENT TYPES OF INVESTMENT

The investor, in making a choice between different types of investment, should take into account not only the relative importance of income and of capital gain but also:

(1) the degree of security against default;
(2) the expected rate of return;
(3) the tax advantages or disadvantages attaching to the investment (see also Chapter 20);
(4) the convenience and cost of dealing in the particular investment;
(5) the ability to realise the investment; and
(6) the prevailing rate of inflation.

2.3.1 Security against default

The British Government has the power to levy taxes and print money, and it is in the highest degree unlikely that it would ever default on any of its borrowings, which include National Savings certificates, National Savings Bank deposits, premium bonds and government guaranteed fixed-interest stocks. It is generally assumed that the Government would stand behind borrowings of local authorities, which in any event have the power to levy local charges. All these securities, therefore, have an intrinsic safety that the private sector cannot emulate.

2.3.2 Rate of return

The rate of return on investments may be specified and fixed, as it is for conventional National Savings certificates, local authority deposits, Treasury bills and fixed interest stocks issued by public and private sector organisations. In other cases the rate is specified initially but may be subject to variation to reflect the general movement of interest rates. Returns on some investments may be linked to the prevailing rate of inflation. Investments linked to a stock market are rarely guaranteed and can rise and fall in value.

2.3.3 Tax advantages

Certain investments carry tax advantages, which may be of particular benefit to higher rate taxpayers. Examples are National Savings certificates, index-linked National Savings certificates, prizes on premium bonds and ISAs. British Government guaranteed stocks are free of CGT (see also Chapter 20).

2.3.4 Convenience and cost of dealing

The investments described in this chapter can (with the exception of certificates of tax deposit and Treasury bills) be negotiated conveniently through high street outlets such as post offices, banks, building societies and, increasingly, the Internet. With the exception of ISAs, in many cases no commission or other dealing costs are incurred. The cost of buying an ISA will often reflect the amount of advice the individual requires.

2.3.5 Ability to realise the investment

With the exception of Treasury bills and certificates of deposit, the investments covered in this chapter cannot be sold to third parties. Thus the investment can be realised only by withdrawing the money from the borrowing organisation. This can be done on demand or at fairly short notice in the case of National Savings Bank accounts and certificates, National Savings index-linked certificates (after one year if indexation is required), premium bonds, government stock, and bank and building society accounts. In other cases the capital initially invested is tied up for a particular period: this applies to local authority deposits and building society term investments as well as National Savings income bonds. If certificates of tax deposit are encashed instead of being used to meet tax liabilities, a lower rate of interest is paid. Early withdrawal in these cases will either be impossible or entail a financial penalty. This disadvantage also applies to commitments to save regular amounts through yearly plan schemes. In the case of ISAs, the investor can usually cash in the investment and receive the proceeds within a few days.

2.3.6 Maintenance

The investor should retain safely all documents (particularly bearer documents) relating to the investments covered in this chapter. If the investor changes address he or she should notify the appropriate body.

2.4 PREVIEW OF 2004–05

Competition for savings will continue to increase. Demand for savings products will tend to rise, so products with the best return and the greatest security will generally succeed. The increasing acceptance of the internet for its visibility as a source of information on savings products will also influence the flow of funds, while the introduction of well-backed internet banking and savings groups will continue to erode older-style across-the-counter high street business. Many of the banks and building societies now have internet banking facilities; their reduced operation costs will allow them to offer better rates in the fight to attract savings. New money should continue to flow into cash savings, but investors need to continually assess the returns they receive and for their longer term savings consider alternative investments outlined elsewhere in this book.

3

LISTED INVESTMENTS

DAVID HANNIS

Investment Director, James Brearley & Sons

3.1 INTRODUCTION

An investment that is 'listed' is one that can be freely bought and sold on a recognised investment exchange (RIE) in the UK or abroad. In the UK the main RIE is the Stock Exchange, London. Other RIEs are Ofex, which specialises in very small companies, and Virt-x, an Anglo-Swiss electronic exchange handling shares in larger European companies. It is also possible, and becoming increasingly common, for investments listed on overseas RIEs to be bought and sold by UK investors.

Listed investments are usually referred to as 'stocks and shares'. However, not all stocks and shares issued by companies are listed. Those that are not are often in companies too small to have sought a listing. Buyers of unlisted shares can be locked in with little or no chance of ever selling them. So take care, particularly if you are approached by someone who encourages you to invest. There are scams, usually conducted by reputable-sounding organisations based abroad, to induce the unwary to pay good money for unsaleable shares.

3.2 REVIEW OF 2003–04

Over the last 12 months, better than expected US economic data early in the reporting period prompted a swift change in the outlook for interest rates. Practically overnight the prospect of higher rates was priced into money markets and a matter of weeks later the Monetary Policy Committee duly increased UK interest rates for the first time since February 2000, an action subsequently repeated over the following months. After the initial negative reaction to this expectancy of higher interest rates, equity markets re-focused on the catalyst of this turn around, namely better than expected global economic growth.

A further driver behind more buoyant markets has been better than expected corporate profits, both fourth quarter 2003 and first quarter

2004 results, beating analyst expectations on the upside. At a time when dividend payments are likely to represent a far greater proportion of total return, the City was particularly cheered by the lack of dividend cuts. In addition corporate activity has picked up with a number of medium and smaller companies falling prey to larger competitors. This tested confidence barometer has equally led to a string of new issues and all in all, investors' appetite for risk has continued to recover.

The progress of the stock market over the first half of 2004 has been less spectacular than that enjoyed in 2003, largely as a result of a re-appraisal of market ratings, which on an international basis appear stretched, particularly in America. The sustainability of the global economic recovery has also been questioned where higher interest rates are now expected in most regions other than continental Europe over the second half of the year. These factors, when combined with an increase in terrorist activity, have induced some profit taking over more recent weeks. Increased geopolitical tensions, the rapid rise in oil prices and the probability of an early US interest rate increase have all been detrimental to investor sentiment.

3.3 WHAT ARE STOCKS AND SHARES?

Traditionally a stock is an investment that pays a fixed rate of return to its holders. Stocks are issued to raise money, usually for a defined period of years at the end of which they are repaid. The British Government issues stocks referred to, not unreasonably, as 'Government stocks' (or 'gilts', as 100 years ago the stock certificates had a shiny gold-coloured edge). Companies also issue fixed-interest stocks. These can be debentures or unsecured loan stocks; the former being safer as the ultimate repayment is secured against a particular asset such as a building owned by the issuing company.

The Government also issues a series of gilts where the interest rate and redemption values are not fixed. These are index linked gilts and were first issued in the days of double-figure inflation. The half-yearly interest is paid at the stated rate but adjusted for the amount of change in the Retail Prices Index (RPI) since the stock was issued. On the stated redemption date the stock is repaid at its issue value adjusted for the change in RPI since issue. These stocks typically pay a meagre income but in times of high inflation, represent a safe home for low-risk cash.

The value of a gilt or fixed-interest stock will fluctuate to reflect the demand for it. In times of rising interest rates a stock paying a fixed rate of return will not be sought after as investors seeking income will prefer to keep their money in the bank and so take advantage of the rising rates. The value of these stocks will therefore fall in times of rising interest rates. Conversely, when rates are falling there is an advantage in holding a stock paying a fixed return so they will be in demand and prices will rise. Bear in mind that most stocks have a fixed repayment date.

The longer the life of a particular stock, the more potential there is for fluctuations in the stock's value. As such, 'undated' or 'irredeemable' issues, where there is no designated redemption point, are the most sensitive to fluctuations in interest rates. Another very influential factor affecting the value of a corporate stock is the issuing company's credit rating. Corporate bonds are classified as being of 'investment grade' or 'high yield'. Dedicated credit agencies scrutinise company balance sheets and trading statements with a view to re-appraising the quality of the company and this in turn is reflected in the credit rating allocated to their stock. This then establishes what rate of interest a company will have to pay on additional loans that they may issue as part of any re-financing.

Shares, technically known as 'ordinary shares', are a means of participating in the fortunes of a company. They are issued by the company to raise capital but, unlike stocks, they do not carry any assurance of either income payments or of ultimate redemption. The rewards for holding shares are twofold. First, a company will allocate part of its profits to be distributed pro rata between the ordinary shareholders and this is known as a dividend. If the company prospers it will be able to increase the dividend paid on each share and the shareholders will be happy to receive a steadily increasing income from their investment. Secondly, the value of the shares will change to reflect both the income currently being paid and the expectations of income growth or otherwise. A relatively young yet acquisitive company is likely to have a fairly limited dividend policy as the majority of profits are re-employed within the business as a means of funding the expansion programme. In contrast, a fairly mature, highly cash generative business is more likely to have a high dividend policy, which in turn will have a more influential impact on the company share price.

There are several types of listed investment that do not precisely fit into either of the above categories.

3.3.1 Convertible loan stocks

These are fixed-interest stocks issued by companies; in addition to the normal income and repayment provisions there is a formula for converting the stock into ordinary shares on a pre-determined range of dates. Such conversions are at the discretion of the shareholder who, if the share price is not high enough, could continue to hold the stock until it is repaid (or sell it in the market). The company will write to each stockholder to remind them of each conversion opportunity.

The value of convertible stocks changes to respond to two separate forces. On the one hand they respond to interest rate movements just like fixed-interest stocks. On the other hand if the value of the ordinary shares that would be received on conversion is greater than that value, then the stock is priced to reflect the post-conversion value. An interesting two-way bet.

3.3.2 Preference shares

Preference shares are shares that pay a fixed rate of dividend. The term 'preference' indicates that the company cannot pay a dividend on its ordinary shares unless it has paid the preference share dividend in full. If the company is wound up, the preference shares are repaid before the ordinary shares. Convertible preference shares are similar to convertible loan stocks. The forces that affect the value of these are the same as for fixed-interest and convertible loan stocks respectively.

3.3.3 Investment trusts

These are listed companies whose business is, usually, to invest in shares in other companies. Investment trust share prices are governed by supply and demand so if the sector in which a particular trust is invested is in favour, the shares could possibly be priced higher than its actual asset value (the value of the trust divided by the number of shares in issue). The converse is also true where a trust could be priced at a discount of more than 15% below its true underlying value.

Over recent years a number of private equity specialist firms have identified the ability to accrue an influential interest in a heavily discounted trust and then press the company's board to propose a liquidation of the company. 'Trust busters' have helped reduce discounts within the investment trust sector while a growing number of trusts now have provisions within their articles of association to liquidate the trust and/or buy shares back for cancellation, should the trust's discount exceed a particular level.

'Split' investment trusts are those that have a capital structure divided (usually) into income shares that receive all the surplus income from the trust's investments and capital shares that on the winding up of the trust receive the entire value of the fund after all other liabilities, including repaying the income shares at their par value, have been discharged. The sector has been a feature of the market for many years but in the late 1990s the managers of some splits borrowed heavily. Their trusts were unable to survive the deep bear market and became insolvent with dire consequences for their shareholders.

3.3.4 Exchange traded funds

These are a relatively new breed of investment trust. They track various indices by investing their assets in a way that reflects the constitution of each index. They are very similar to tracker unit trusts but are more precise in their mirroring of each index. Their cost structure is much lower and, not being incorporated in the UK (Dublin is a preferred 'home'), purchases do not attract stamp duty. Because exchange traded funds are extensively used to hedge institutional positions, their share prices move to reflect accurately movements in the underlying index.

More details about investment trusts and exchange traded funds can be found in Chapter 7.

3.3.5 The Alternative Investment Market (AIM)

This is a part of the Stock Exchange that operates under a different set of rules to make it more attractive for smaller companies than a full listing on the main market. It was set up to encourage new companies and has proved to be a great success. AIM stocks have the advantage over main list stocks of better treatment of profits for capital gains tax (CGT) and inheritance tax (IHT). They cannot be held in PEPs or ISAs and are generally high-risk investments.

3.4 DERIVATIVES

This is a generic term for investments that are not themselves stocks or shares but whose prices are linked to the value of a share or group of shares.

Some companies issue warrants, giving the right to buy shares in the future at today's price, as a sweetener to make an issue of shares, to raise money, more attractive. Warrants are fully listed investments in their own right and give the owner the right, but not the obligation, to buy shares in the issuing company at a set price. They are exercisable on set dates, often several years after issue. The company will write to holders shortly before each exercise date to remind them of their rights.

Warrants (and other derivatives) are priced in the market by the same supply and demand forces that affect ordinary shares but with an interesting twist known as 'time value'.

A warrant that gives holders the right to buy shares at 100p when the shares are worth 110p has an intrinsic value of 10p. However, this simple way of valuing a warrant ignores the fact that the 100p subscription may not be payable for several years. A holder of these warrants will therefore benefit from movements in a share price of 110p whilst only having a much lower sum at risk and with no obligation to pay more if things go wrong. A perception by investors that the underlying shares have good potential for growth over the period to the last subscription date will enhance the warrant's price. This enhancement is known as 'time value'.

If we assume that our warrant is priced at 20p (10p intrinsic + 10p time value) and the shares rise to 130p, it is reasonable to expect the warrants also to rise by approximately 20p. Thus an 18% rise in the share price has produced a possible 100% rise in the warrant price. This is known as the 'gearing' effect and is what makes trading warrants potentially very profitable but also very risky as the gearing effect works in both directions! A warrant may be deemed to be "in the money" if the warrant price is below that of the underlying share price, "at the money" if the prices are around the same level or "out of the money" if the warrant price is above the share price. The "gearing" effect is greatest in "out of the money" warrants. Commission is payable on the value of the warrants as is stamp duty on purchases. Before buying warrants you will have to sign a risk warning form that your stockbroker will supply.

Conventional warrants, as described above, have been a feature of the stock market for many years but have been joined in 2002 by a new type of investment with very similar properties. The London Stock Exchange has begun a new market in 'covered warrants' to extend the range of listed derivatives and in response to the success of similar markets in the US and Europe. The most significant difference between the two is that whilst a conventional warrant is issued by the underlying company as part of its capital-raising programme, a covered warrant is issued by a City institution purely for the purpose of being something to use to gain a geared involvement in the movement of a particular share. It is intended that covered warrants will be issued on a large number of shares and that there will be series of warrants at different share prices and for various terms of up to 18 months. More recently, covered warrants have been issued against other asset types, with it now being possible to take a position in such things as the price of gold, oil and currencies.

Warrants, as discussed so far, have all given holders the right to buy shares, these are known as call warrants. The covered warrants market also deals in put warrants that give holders the right to sell the underlying shares. Investors can simply buy call warrants to speculate on a share rising or buy puts to benefit if it falls. A more sophisticated approach would be that of an investor with a holding of shares showing a substantial profit but where he feels that the price is likely to fall. He could sell the shares but this may give rise to a possible 40% CGT charge. Alternatively, he could hedge his position by buying covered put warrants that would rise in price as the share price fell and so negate the fall in value of this shareholding. The cost of doing this would be less than the tax charge on a simple sale of his holding.

An investor needing income but wanting to take advantage of a hoped-for rise in a share price could put, say, 10% of the allocated cash into covered call warrants on the shares and invest the rest in a high-yielding gilt or bank account. In this way the income would not be substantially reduced, the investor would benefit if the shares rose as expected and, very importantly, only 10% of the capital would be at risk.

Covered warrants are new to the Stock Exchange but look like becoming a major way for investors to take short-term positions in a wide range of shares.

3.5 BUILDING A PORTFOLIO OF SHARES

The establishment and management of an investment portfolio is something often delegated to professionals such as stockbrokers or other investment managers. However, it is possible and often rewarding to build and run one's own portfolio of stocks and shares. This section should be taken as general guidance only and not as specific advice. Part of the skill in building a portfolio is to tailor it to the individual needs of the person whose money is invested in it.

Before any investments are made there are a number of preliminaries to go through:

(1) Read Chapter 1, which gives sensible guidance on the broader aspects of investing.
(2) Decide what part of your investment portfolio you wish to be in the stock market.
(3) Decide what you want from your investments – income, capital growth or a balance of the two – and make an assessment of your likely income needs over both the short and the longer term.
(4) Decide what level of service you want to receive from your stock-broker. He will be able to offer you various levels of service, for example a full discretionary management package, where they make all the decisions, or an advisory service, which will respond to your requests for advice and will supply you with investment recommen-dations. A stockbroker will also have an execution only service that simply carries out your instructions without being able to offer advice. All stockbrokers should be able to supply you with portfolio valuations on request; many have an internet service to give clients online valuations. It is always useful to have a chat with your stock-broker to see just what can be done. If a particular stockbroker is not

prepared to talk to you at this stage then find one that will. The commissions they charge should reflect the level of service you have chosen.

(5) Consider using an ISA (see 20.2.7) for part of your portfolio. Most stockbrokers offer a self-select ISA in which you can hold virtually any listed (but not AIM) investments as well as most unit trusts and OEICs. PEPs are closed to new money but both they and existing ISAs can be transferred to a stockbroker and used to hold at least some of your investments in a tax-free way. The long-term value of transferring assets into tax-protected areas cannot be overestimated.

(6) Decide what level of risk you are prepared to take. This is often difficult without talking to a professional. High-risk investing is only for the foolhardy who can afford to lose. For most investors a cautious, balanced approach is the best way forward.

Having climbed through these six hoops you can begin.

As income is what you live on and capital is what your family hope to inherit, it is best to sort out the income-producing investments first. At this point you should assess all your current and future income, including your pensions (both state and private), and any property or family trust income. If you have a retirement date in mind then you will want your portfolio income to become substantial at about that time. You will also want your income to be likely to increase as the years roll on.

Someone in their twenties or thirties can look at their portfolio as a means of accumulating capital with no regard for income as there is plenty of time to switch into income-producing assets later. There is also a tendency for beginners to confuse investment with speculation and to concentrate on high-risk equities. Too often investment is seen as a 'fun thing' and enormous risks are taken which may be successful on occasion but will inevitably lead to losses being made. Everyone who invests must realise that their income in later life is directly related to the amount of capital that can be accumulated and that placing capital at risk in the early years can have a dramatic effect on income in retirement.

For those who are no longer batting from the nursery end this is a receding luxury, and as the years roll on the balance of a portfolio should change to reflect the need to protect earlier gains rather than put them at risk. Portfolios, like people, should get more boring with age!

Government stocks and other fixed-interest investments will provide a high and constant level of income for a fixed period. Upon redemption the income will cease and you will have to reinvest to secure a future income. If interest rates are lower then than now, this reinvestment will secure a lower income than before. Should interest rates have risen, then a higher return will be seen. Either way, it is likely that prices will have advanced over this period.

This uncertainty of a long-term flow of income from even the most secure of investments is a dilemma when assembling a portfolio that has to provide for someone who will be dependent upon it. An alternative source of income could come from holding equities. These pay dividends that can be reasonably expected to rise even though the initial income is lower than that obtainable from fixed-interest stocks. A yield of 3% that doubles every ten years is better than a fixed yield of 6% when assessed over a 15- to 20-year term.

One answer is to assess the future income need carefully and to strike a balance between fixed-interest and equities to give a reasonable expectation of an adequate income flow.

When choosing the individual investments the risk factors should be borne in mind. A higher yielding equity is not necessarily the best to go for. A share will often have a low yield simply because it is expected that dividends will rise sharply, a typical example has been pharmaceutical shares. Others, such as utility shares, may have a high yield because it is thought that growth prospects are slight. Experience has shown that a cautious approach is best.

3.6 KEEPING YOUR PORTFOLIO IN BALANCE

This word, 'balance' keeps cropping up – it is a fundamental part of investment management but what do we mean by it? A well-balanced portfolio is one that is constructed to best fulfil the requirements of the investor. It does this in two ways – by meeting the needs of the investor in terms of the proportions of the various types of investment within it and by managing the risks involved in the chosen mix.

3.6.1 Investment strategy

Your first decision is fundamental; do you want income, capital growth or a mix of the two? Table 3.1 gives a suggested split of investment types for each kind of investor.

Table 3.1 Suggested split of investments

	Income	Growth	Mixed
Gilts	30	0	20
Corporate fixed-interest	30	0	20
Convertibles	20	10	10
Equities	20	80	45
Warrants	0	10	5
	100%	100%	100%

Table 3.1 shows a possible, rather bland, split of investments in each type of portfolio. This needs to be refined to meet the personal criteria of the investor. For example, the equities in the income portfolio would normally be high-yielding solid shares such as those of utility companies or banks. In the growth portfolio one would expect to find lower yielding pharmaceutical and electronics shares as well as the middle of the road engineering, food and retail shares. A sprinkling of smaller companies could also be accommodated. The mixed portfolio should contain elements of each but with a bias away from the more speculative sectors and stocks.

3.6.2 Portfolio risk

Every investment has a risk. There is no such thing as a risk-free investment. The skill is in managing the risk so that, as far as possible, no one perceived risk will affect your entire portfolio. Table 3.2 gives some idea of how risk affects different sectors within classes of investment.

Table 3.2 is intended to be a guide only and not a comprehensive table of risk. Every investment decision should be viewed as a risk-based action and should not be made without careful thought. The table reads horizontally rather than vertically so as an example, an Undated Gilt is a high risk government stock, rather than being a high risk investment.

Table 3.2 Degrees of risk

Risk	Low	Medium	High
Gilts	Index-linked	Conventional dated	Undated
Corporate bonds	High interest cover	Adequate interest cover	Interest not covered
Convertible stock	Conversion price lower than share price	Conversion price near but above share price	Conversion price well above shares
Equities	Investment trusts, utilities	Engineering, foods, stores, pharmaceuticals	Media, electronics Telecommunications AIM
Warrants	In the money	At the money	Out of the money

3.7 INVESTMENT ADVICE

Once the fundamental decisions mentioned above have been made, it is time to consider the specific shares to be held in your portfolio. How do you find them? Where can you go to find out about them? What tools do you need – a computer, a chart, or a pin?

There has never been as much information circulating about investments as there is today. The traditional source of the quality daily and Sunday press is now augmented by an incredible volume of facts and opinions available on the internet. It is likely that your stockbroker will make his 'buy list' available to you; often this is available on the internet and includes his reasons for liking each share. The London Stock Exchange has a website with links to each company's own site. There are many investment websites that can be subscribed to but which often make basic information available free of charge. Usually they have 'chat rooms' where opinions can be aired about shares, brokers and companies.

There is no feeling quite like having picked a sound investment and reaping the rewards. Often you will notice how much better a particular company seems compared to its competitors. A glance at the share price charts may show that its shares have not risen as much as the (inferior) others. This could be the one to go for. After some thought, and maybe bouncing the idea off your stockbroker, you make an investment. Suddenly you feel involved in the company. Do not get carried away for there will come a time to say goodbye to the shares. Many people find selling more difficult than buying. It is almost as if they have fallen in love with the shares. There are no records of this feeling ever being returned! Do not be sentimental.

3.8 MEASURING YOUR PERFORMANCE

Assessing how well, or badly, your homespun portfolio has performed is an important way of measuring your success as an investor. It is difficult to buck the trend of a market but it should be possible to do marginally better than average over a period of time.

So that you are, as far as possible, comparing like with like, it is best to measure your portfolio movement against an appropriate benchmark index. For example, if your portfolio comprises mainly leading equities, its performance can be compared to an index such as the FTSE-100 index, also known as the Footsie. There are many indices and you should choose one that most closely resembles your portfolio. Possible indices to use are:

APCIMS (Association of Private Client Investment Managers and
Stockbrokers)

- Growth – For a portfolio with a spread of investments, focused on growth with a yield of less than 2.5%.
- Balanced – For a portfolio designed to provide a mix of income and growth with a yield of between 2.5% and 5%.

- Income –   For a portfolio focused on non-speculative investments, where the resulting yield is above 5%.

FT-SE (Equity portfolio benchmark)

- 100 Index –   For an equity-based portfolio where at least 70% of the positions are constituents of the 'Footsie'.
- All Share Index –   For a wider equity based portfolio where the emphasis on 'Footsie' constituents is less than 70%.
- World Index –   For a globally based equity portfolio where the UK content is less than 50%.

All the above indices can be found in the *Financial Times* and other quality daily newspapers.

If your performance does not compare well with the chosen index there are several options:

(1) change to a more appropriate index;
(2) change your investing style; or
(3) hand over your investments to a professional.

3.9 TAXATION OF YOUR PORTFOLIO

The various taxes are covered in more detail elsewhere in this book. Here is a brief outline and some of the ways of minimising taxation on your investment income and profits.

Tax is charged on the interest paid on fixed-interest investments at the current standard rate and each payment is accompanied by a certificate that details the amount of tax deducted. Thus a standard rate taxpayer will have no more tax to pay whilst a higher rate payer will simply pay the excess. A UK non-taxpayer can reclaim any tax deducted on interest received.

Dividends on shares are different. They are paid as a net amount per share but come with a tax credit certificate. This tax credit, currently 10% of the dividend paid, is deemed to be equivalent to standard rate tax so that a standard rate taxpayer will pay no more. A higher rate taxpayer will pay the excess over standard rate. A non-taxpayer cannot claim any tax back.

Capital gains tax is charged on the net gain made per individual each year in excess of £8,200, as detailed in Chapter 1.

3.9.1 Avoiding taxation

There are ways of (legally) mitigating the tax charge on the income and capital gains from your portfolio:

(1) **Spread the portfolio between husband and wife** This is particularly useful if only one is a taxpayer or a higher rate taxpayer. It also takes advantage of two annual CGT allowances.
(2) **Use ISAs and PEPs** Individual Savings Accounts (ISAs) are the successors to Personal Equity Plans (PEPs) and are described more fully in Chapter 20. Your broker will probably offer a self-select version of each which can be used to shelter all or part of your portfolio from taxation. Gains made in an ISA or PEP are not subject to CGT.

   The tax deducted from interest received on fixed-interest stocks (including unit trusts and OEICs) can be reclaimed in full. Unfortunately, the tax credit on corporate income arising within a PEP or ISA may no longer be reclaimed from April this year.

   When planning to use ISAs or PEPs bear in mind that:
   (a) you can transfer all existing PEPs and ISAs to your stockbroker;
   (b) you can subscribe £7,000 each year to an ISA;
   (c) husband and wife can each subscribe;
   (d) in the short term it is better to have fixed-interest stocks in your plans, as a full tax reclaim can be made;
   (e) in the longer term you should aim to build up as much value in your plans as possible – they can be switched to hold fixed-interest investments to get a greater, tax-free income in later life.
(3) Consider investing in a Self-Investing Personal Pension (SIPP). Investments held in a SIPP have the same tax advantages as money held in ISAs and PEPs. The downside is that whereas money can be removed from ISAs and PEPs at will, with no tax clawback, any money invested in a SIPP will remain there until it is used to provide a retirement income. This said, the SIPP administrator will reclaim basic rate tax on any contributions made to a SIPP and add this to the account. A higher rate taxpayer may additionally claim marginal tax, typically as part of his annual tax return.

If saving for retirement is important you should consider SIPPs, ISAs and PEPs. This is an area where specialist advice should be sought, particularly before committing to a SIPP.

3.10 DOWN TO BUSINESS

So far we have covered the theory of investing. Now we need to look at the practicalities of actually dealing and managing your portfolio. What you will need are:

(1) a dealing facility;
(2) a source of advice when you need it;
(3) a means of holding your investments; and
(4) a way to monitor your portfolio.

All of these can be obtained from independent sources. However, by choosing your stockbroker carefully it is possible to get all of them as a package.

3.10.1 Choosing a stockbroker

Most stockbrokers will take on private clients who wish to manage their own portfolios. You can be an 'execution' client or an 'advisory' client. Both types can deal as they wish but an advisory client will be able to receive advice from the broker. The broker will need to hold certain information about you, your financial situation and your investment aspirations before he can offer advice to you.

Instructions to buy or sell can (usually) be placed by telephoning the broker's dealing desk where you will be given the current price of the share and you can place an order to buy or sell. You can tell the broker to 'deal at best' which means he will deal as quickly as possible at the best price he can get. Alternatively you could place a 'limit order' which instructs your broker to watch a share until your specified price is reached and then to do the deal (or 'bargain' to use the correct term) without further reference to you.

To do the deal the broker will check his screen which will show him the selling and buying prices being made by the Retail Service Providers (RSPs) who deal in that share. He will, if you are a buyer, telephone the RSP that is offering the shares at the cheapest price and, after persuading him to deal at a marginally better price, do your bargain. Shares are bought and sold over the telephone with no paper confirmation. Deals so done are binding on all parties and cannot be ignored or overturned. 'My word is my bond' applies to everyone in the system, including the client.

Increasingly, the telephone call to the RSP is being replaced by a computer link. The modern stockbroker will put your instructions into his system, which will check around the market, find the best RSP and often get an improved price.

The large institutional dealings are done using a system known as the Stock Exchange Electronic Trading Service (SETS), a form of electronic auction. However, nearly all dealings for private clients are done via the RSPs, as this is a more satisfactory way of achieving a complete execution of clients' instructions.

Once the bargain has been done the broker will send you a contract note, which gives you the full details of the transaction. It is, effectively, an invoice and shows the cost of the shares, commission, stamp duty, etc and confirms the date and time of the deal.

The bargain done for you is settled with the market by your broker a few days after dealing. Traditionally, clients have held shares in paper form, ie they have received a share certificate showing their ownership of the investment. When the shares are sold the broker sends the client a transfer form to sign and return to him with the certificate. This paper chase takes up to ten days to complete.

The modern way is to hold shares in electronic form through a service known as CREST. Your broker will have an account at CREST into which your shares will be registered. They will not be in your name but that of the broker's nominee company. Your broker will look after your interests by collecting dividends and either accumulating them for you in a deposit account or sending them out to you. He will also handle 'corporate actions' such as scrip issues, takeovers, etc on your behalf. Brokers are governed by very tight rules on shares held in a nominee account. These include monthly reconciliations and periodic confirmation to the client of just what is being held.

Brokers generally charge a fee for their nominee service but, by using it, a client will often save the extra charge the broker applies to deals settled on paper.

To monitor your investments you need to be able to see their value on a regular basis. This can be done by maintaining records yourself and updating them from prices available in newspapers or on Teletext. Most brokers will supply valuations on request, sometimes for a fee. Others will make your valuation available on the internet for you to view, in real time, whenever you want. Typically, this is a free service.

3.10.2 Internet share dealing

There is a new breed of stockbrokers that only offer execution dealing and which use the internet to allow their clients to deal themselves. Some traditional brokers have added this to their range of services.

Using an internet broker is very simple; switch on and log on to see your current portfolio. In a couple of clicks you can have sold any share you own or invested any cash held. Deals are done as you click (so be careful) and settlement is done using the broker's CREST account with your money being held by the broker in a deposit account for you. Outside market hours, orders can be placed for execution the next day. Limit orders can usually be placed in the system to be done when the price comes into line.

Internet dealing is the future of execution stockbroking, with many systems now handling overseas shares and even unit trusts and OEICs being dealt in. Commissions are lower than those a traditional broker would charge but you must be aware that neither advice from nor chats with a sympathetic broker are available.

3.10.3 Costs

When dealing in shares there are possibly several costs to pay:

(1) commission – usually based on the value of each deal;
(2) stamp duty – 0.5% of the value of shares you buy (some investments such as gilts, exchange traded funds and covered warrants are not subject to stamp duty; overseas shares are usually liable to different rates);
(3) settlement fees – often levied by a broker, particularly on 'paper deals';
(4) PTM levy – £1 to the Panel on Takeovers and Mergers on each deal worth over £10,000.

3.10.4 Alternative ways of dealing

Instead of dealing directly with a stockbroker, you can do so via an intermediary who is authorised by the FSA to conduct investment business, such as an independent financial adviser, solicitor or accountant. Be sure that they are adding to the broker's services, not impeding them.

Shares can be bought directly from a company via an initial public offering (IPO) of the shares. This is usually a one-off occasion but can be a useful way to get in at the start of a company's life on the Stock Exchange.

Dividend reinvestment plans (DRIPs) are offered by some companies and are a way of investing the cash dividends into more shares in the company. This is an interesting but messy way of acquiring shares. Working out the CGT on a sale of shares acquired by a DRIP is not a simple matter. There is no tax advantage in buying shares this way.

Rights issues are one of the ways by which a company will raise money by issuing more shares to existing shareholders at a price below the current market price. This is not such a bargain as it might at first appear. For example, consider that you have 1,000 shares worth 100p each and the company gives a one for one rights issue at 50p. To your shares worth £1,000 you add the same number at a cost of £500, a total of £1,500. On the first day of dealing after the issue the share price will be about 75p, valuing the 2,000 shares held at £1,500.

Scrip issues, properly known as capitalisation issues, are made by a company to increase the issued share capital without raising any money. If the basis of the issue is one for one, the share price will halve on the first day of dealing after the issue.

Some investment trust companies have a monthly subscription scheme whereby people can commit to a sum that the company invests in its own shares by buying them in the market. This is a useful way of saving. Often an ISA is offered and charges are low. However, it suffers from a lack of flexibility and as only one ISA can be subscribed to each year there could be a shortfall in contributions.

3.11 PREVIEW OF 2004–05

Our analysis still indicates that underlying corporate fundamentals remain sound. Companies are more than coping in a low inflation world by sustaining productivity growth at a higher rate than has been the case in previous business cycles. The upshot is that earnings look set to surprise investors again by their strength in the rest of 2004, and provide the confidence for companies to engage in another round of expansion.

Whilst this can be seen as a positive – in that policy makers appear to have confidence in the recovery, as supported by the increase in interest rates – it could lead to greater volatility as we progress through the rest of the year, when economic disappointments are likely. This leads us to expect interest rates generally to remain lower for longer than widely anticipated and as currently reflected in money markets.

We believe a greater focus on a balanced investment strategy, rather than the traditional equity portfolio will be required. We equally believe it is necessary to have a more dynamic approach to portfolio management than in the past, where the use of derivatives, on a controlled and cautious basis, will in our opinion, help in achieving out performance and a greater consistency of return.

In conclusion we look forward to a steady advance in the UK equity market over the coming six-month period but believe volatility will increase as we move ever nearer to the US presidential election, which may well coincide with the peak in US economic growth.

USEFUL ADDRESSES

The Public Relations Department
The Stock Exchange
Old Broad Street
London EC2N 1HP

Tel: (020) 7797 1372
Web: www.londonstockex.co.uk
www.share-aware.co.uk

Director of Savings
National Savings Bank
Boydstone Road
Glasgow G58 1SB

Tel: (0141) 649 4555

The Director
Department of National Savings
Bonds and Stock Office
Preston New Road
Blackpool FY3 9XR

Tel: (01253) 766151
Web: www.nationalsavings.co.uk

The Director of Savings
Savings Certificate and SAYE
Office
Milburngate House
Durham DH99 1NS

Tel: (0191) 386 4900
Web: www.nationalsavings.co.uk

The Building Societies
Association
3 Savile Row
London W1X 1AF

Tel: (020) 7437 0655
Web:www.bsa.org.uk

Bank of England
Threadneedle Street
London EC2R 8AH

Tel: (020) 7601 4444
Web: www.bankofengland.co.uk

The Association of Investment
Trust Companies
3rd Floor, Durrant House
8–13 Chiswell Street
London EC1Y 4YY

Tel: (020) 7282 5555
Web: www.aitc.co.uk

The Panel on Takeovers and
Mergers
PO Box 226
The Stock Exchange Building
Old Broad Street
London EC2P 2JX

Tel: (020) 7382 9026

Association of Unit Trusts and
Investment Funds
65 Kingsway
London WC2B 6TD

Tel: (020) 7831 0898
Web: www.investmentfunds.org.uk

Association of Private Client
Investment Managers and
Stockbrokers
112 Middlesex Street
London E1 7HY

Tel: (020) 7247 7080
Web: www.apcims.org

The Financial Services
Authority
25 The North Colonnade
Canary Wharf
London E14 5HS

Tel: (020) 7676 1000
Web: www.fsa.gov.uk

4

MAJOR OVERSEAS MARKETS

SARAH ARKLE

Threadneedle Investments

4.1 INTRODUCTION

Although domestic equities and bonds still form the lion's share of UK portfolios, investors have increasingly looked to diversify their portfolios into overseas markets over the past 25 years. It is possible to distinguish two drivers for the long-term growth in overseas investment: first, the desire to diversify the risk in a portfolio by reducing its dependency on one country's market alone; and secondly, the belief that overseas assets may generate better returns than those in the UK. The burgeoning demand for global assets has prompted investment houses to extend their expertise and ensure coverage of all the world's major markets and, in many cases, emerging markets also. As a result, the market has seen a proliferation of new unit trusts specialising in overseas investment, thus making it easy for the investing public in the UK to gain international exposure.

4.2 OPPORTUNITIES OVERSEAS

The range of possibilities when investing overseas is wide, from the large, well-developed US markets to the fledgling entities of the ex-Soviet Union states. Excluding the 'emerging markets' (see Chapter 5), the UK-based investor can divide the world into five main regions. The relative size of each of these markets within the global stock market at the end of June 2004 is as set out in Figure 4.1.

4.2.1 United States

The US stock market is the largest and most important in the world. It also has a good track record of outperformance against the UK. This is partly due to favourable demographics and partly a result of the entrepreneurial spirit that embodies American culture. This spirit provides a conducive background for companies to develop, for example, by pro-

Figure 4.1 World market capitalisation weights

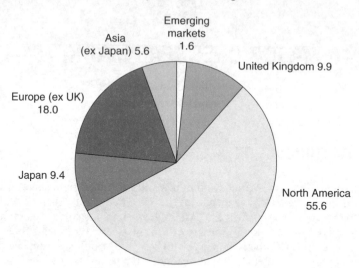

Figures based on the FT-SE World Index as at 30 June 2004.

Source: Factset.

viding relatively easy access to capital. The US is also the 'home' of technology. From IBM in the 1960s and 1970s, to Intel in the 1980s, Microsoft in the 1990s and a host of internet and communications equipment stocks since, the US has provided many of the world's leading technology companies. The sharp appreciation of technology share prices worldwide at the end of the 1990s and the high valuations reached has been well documented. The subsequent fall in share prices as investors realised that the corporate profit growth of a number of these companies was not going to be as strong as had been anticipated and was not immune to an economic slowdown was equally savage. The US market is also well developed in other areas. Many US companies are household names across the globe. Coca-Cola drinks, McDonald's hamburgers, Colgate toothpaste, Heinz beans and Ford cars reach into the lives of families in countries too numerous to count.

There are several stock exchanges in the US. In the case of the New York Stock Exchange (NYSE), companies quoted are generally large and to obtain a quotation they must have sound finances and a good record. The National Association of Securities Dealers Automated Quotations (NASDAQ) has also emerged as an important market in the US with many of the largest capitalised stocks, particularly within the technology area, choosing to stay within this market. NASDAQ is the major method of electronic trading.

Apart from being the largest in the world, the US stock markets are arguably the most sophisticated. A great deal of company information is published and is readily available in printed form or on screens. That being said, authorities have further tightened the regulation of markets after various scandals in the last few years. Business is regulated by the Securities and Exchange Commission. There are well-developed options and futures markets, though these are principally designed for the institutional investor.

4.2.2 Continental Europe

Stock markets in continental Europe were traditionally unimportant in comparison to those of the UK and the US. Companies preferred instead to turn to banks to provide them with the finance they needed, with these banks often then taking strategic stakes and sitting on the board.

It was the advent of the European Single Market in 1992, followed seven years later by the arrival of a common currency, the euro, that really provided the impetus for change. The single market entailed the deregulation of a host of industries ranging from electricity to airlines, exposing formerly protected state industries to the rigours of competition and the market. Governments, typically heavily indebted and facing the prospect of providing for ageing populations, moved towards privatisation, tax reduction and an acceptance of the role of the private sector in pensions provision.

As a package this proved a heady cocktail for equity markets. Although the first half of the 1990s saw sluggish economic growth exacerbated by the need to comply with the Maastricht criteria for economic convergence, the latter part of the decade saw a swift turnaround. In the run up to the introduction of the euro, growth was particularly strong among the more peripheral European economies, notably Spain and Ireland. Subsequently, and aided by the European Central Bank's policy of 'benign neglect' towards the euro which boosted exports, growth picked up in the core economies of France and Germany. The inflationary outlook remained benign, labour unions were quiescent and several European companies were at the forefront of technological changes to the 'new economy'.

A unified capital market had far-reaching implications for the European corporate world. Competing for capital, managements became much more concerned with creating shareholder value. Disclosure, accounting practices and standards of corporate governance improved. In particular, the need to be pan-European placed a premium on size and forced restructuring, mergers and takeovers even in areas where governments had wanted previously to preserve 'national champions'. Initially largely domestic, but eventually extending across borders, the apotheosis of this restructuring trend was the hostile takeover of Mannesmann by Vodafone at the turn of the century. The bursting of the 'TMT' bubble in early 2000 eventually called into question the rationale for 'mega mergers' such as this, however, and slower economic growth in the early years of the new century saw companies focusing more on strengthening their balance sheets than pursuing growth via acquisition. This proved more helpful to bond investors than shareholders but, with economic growth now starting to recover, companies have begun to return once again to more expansionary strategies.

4.2.3 Japan

Low interest rates, low inflation, a strong currency and financial deregulation created a substantial pool of liquidity in the mid-1980s. Much of this money found its way into the property market, though substantial sums were also invested in the stock market, giving rise to the now notorious 'bubble' of 1986–89. The bubble finally burst when the authorities began to worry about asset inflation feeding through into more general price increases and, indeed, the stability of the whole financial system.

The ensuing period of monetary retrenchment caused a sharp slowdown in the rate of economic activity, which, owing to compounding corporate and government policy errors, persisted throughout much of the 1990s. A particularly pernicious feature of this long recession was deflation, not only in assets but in general wholesale and consumer prices. The chief culprit was the retention of excess supply in the economy. Encouraged by government subsidies and futile public spending artificially sustaining demand, companies repeatedly ducked harsh decisions to cut capacity or reduce their workforces.

In the last years of the 1990s the balance sheet deterioration and accumulated competitive disadvantage caused by these policies started to claim high-profile victims. Yamaichi Securities' failure at the end of 1997 catalysed a near-collapse in the banking system. Nissan Motor, one of Japan's largest employers, also reached the end of its road and was forced into an unprecedented (but ultimately very successful) merger with foreigner Renault. Government policy began to move to a less interventionist, market-orientated stance. In the first quarter of 1999 industrial firms started to restructure in earnest, rekindling interest in Japanese stocks from foreign investors. At the same time new companies with entrepreneurial management in growth areas like mobile telecommunications, the internet and finance started to receive more prominence. To many people's surprise, in the last year of the decade Japan's stock market was the best performer among the developed economies, but it did not escape the significant market falls of the early 2000s. Today, there are still obstacles to be overcome (eg a large number of companies that should be allowed to go under are still being artificially kept afloat) but economic data have started to improve and company restructuring has continued. These trends have helped Japan to return to a more normalised economic cycle.

There are several stock exchanges in Japan, but the one in Tokyo is by far the biggest, handling more than 90% of transactions. The market is split into three categories: the first section, the second section and the over-the-counter market. In general, companies graduate from the over-the-counter market to the second category and then to the first category as their sales and profits reach the appropriate levels.

An unusual feature of the Japanese stock market has been the presence of large 'cross shareholdings' in which one company will hold shares in a selection of other companies with which it has business or other relationships. In the past this has accounted for as much as 30% of the market. Restructuring pressures and consolidation in the financial sector are now eroding the rationale for these relationships and many cross shareholdings are being unwound.

From 2002, a change in pensions regulations has allowed companies to hand back a significant amount of pension fund assets and obligations to the Government. Though a lot of this money will be reinvested in equities in time, it has caused some temporary liquidation, particularly for large-cap stocks.

4.2.4 Other Far Eastern markets

The performance of the Asian stock markets has been characterised by considerable volatility over the last few years. The year of the Asian financial crisis, 1997, saw the majority of the region's markets sharply lower in local currency terms, while returns for sterling investors were depressed further by local currency weakness. After a bias on the downside in 1998 the Asian markets registered stellar gains in 1999 on the back of an impressive V-shaped recovery in economic growth combined with strong earnings momentum. Over the next three years the countries where the domestic economy showed greater resilience tended to see their stock markets outperform, for example the Australian and Thai markets. Those countries where trade is a relatively higher proportion of GDP, namely Hong Kong, Singapore and Taiwan, tended to see their stock markets perform according to the ebb and flow of sentiment towards the global economy during this period. Indeed, with Asia being a higher risk/higher return region, all of its stock markets have been subject to the fluctuations in risk appetite that have characterised recent years.

The scope of the Far Eastern markets covered by dedicated funds includes Australia, China, New Zealand, Hong Kong, Singapore, Malaysia, Taiwan, Korea, India, Indonesia and the Philippines and Thailand. Although Australia is still the largest constituent of the regional indices, many of the other markets have received considerable coverage thanks to their potential to provide superior growth. None has had a higher profile in recent years than China, with reams of superlative statistics proving the growing importance of this regional powerhouse as both a producer of goods and a consumer of commodities. There is little doubt that China's share of the world economy will grow over the coming decades. In the shorter term, however, worries remain as to the sustainability of growth following several years of rapid expansion. Whatever happens, long-term investors are finding it increasingly difficult to ignore China as an investment theme.

4.2.5 Emerging markets

In addition to these well-established targets for a UK investor wishing to branch out internationally, there are emerging markets such as Brazil, Russia and Turkey. The specific opportunities and issues around investing in these markets are covered in Chapter 5.

4.3 THE MECHANICS OF INVESTING OVERSEAS

4.3.1 Direct investment

While investment in UK Listed Securities is a relatively straightforward process, and one familiar to many members of the public, investment in overseas markets can be more difficult. However, it is important to draw some distinction between the major investment markets, where provision of information and execution of transactions may well be quite straightforward, and less mature markets where this is not the case.

Consider first the information needed to make an investment decision. Many large companies in major developed countries now produce their Report and Accounts in English as well as in their local language, and this and other company literature can be obtained quite easily from the company or through a stockbroker. Indeed, a listing on a major stock exchange will in itself oblige a company to make available key information with some reliability. However, the ability to make sense of the information will depend on the investor's knowledge of the accounting practices in the country and the domestic markets in which the company operates in order to assess the company's future prospects. It is perhaps this question of understanding the environment in which the company operates, its market and competitors, the economic conditions of its home country, and the business culture driving profitability that makes it most difficult effectively to analyse a foreign company as an investment proposition.

In less developed markets, the difficulties of obtaining and analysing information are far greater, through differences in language, accounting standards, cultural understanding or simply the lack of emphasis placed on shareholders.

Then comes the question of buying, selling and holding stock. In major developed markets, stock is often held in dematerialised form. This means that stock certificates are no longer issued and the investor's holding is recorded on a central system. An example of this is CREST in the UK. Furthermore, the practice of holding stock for investors in nominee form by a recognised custodian (often a major international bank) commonly is understood and recognised to be secure. This does require, however, that the investor make use of the services of a stockbroker and a custodian bank to effect all the administration of dealing, execution, corporate actions and dividends, and eventually remittance of the proceeds of the sale to the investor. Clearly this implies a cost for the investor.

In less developed markets, the process is essentially the same, but in practice is more often fraught with complications, delays and additional costs. It may be necessary to employ the services of a major international bank as custodian, which then takes responsibility for a subcustodian in the particular country of investment. A subcustodian will not only hold the stock and effect corporate actions and dividend transactions, but will also handle any issues of local taxation, exchange control, monitoring of restrictions on share ownership and the impact of any legal, fiscal or regulatory changes in the local country.

However, ultimately the responsibility and risk for the investment rests with investors, and their ability in practice to resolve issues of title, value or the repatriation of funds from overseas investments may be severely stretched.

Because of these mechanical difficulties that investing overseas may present, and indeed the additional risks presented by exposure to foreign economies and currencies, investing internationally through the direct route can be time consuming, costly and risky.

For this reason, it is useful to consider the alternatives to direct investment, in the form of investment in collective investment schemes, that are available.

4.3.2 Collective investment schemes

Buying and selling overseas investment through a collective scheme is as simple as buying domestic funds. The investor is presented with a rich choice of funds for investing overseas. First there are country-specific funds (eg a US fund) that will invest in companies from that country; thus the investor has a concentrated exposure to the economic and political climate, and the business sector of that country. The fund may offer a particular specialisation within the chosen country (eg US Smaller Companies or European High Yield Bonds).

Then there are funds that invest worldwide. Here, the decision of how much weight to give any one country is taken, and reviewed regularly, by the fund manager backed up by the investment company's expertise, including up-to-date economic research. Such funds might typically invest in a selection of the world's major companies, or may offer specialist investment in a particular sector or theme such as pharmaceuticals, choosing the best companies throughout the world in that particular sector.

Collective investment schemes and the characteristics of each type of investment scheme – unit trust, OEIC, offshore fund or investment trust – are discussed in detail in Chapters 7 and 8. Many such schemes offer the opportunity to invest in overseas markets so that the investor can gain exposure to those markets without any of the difficulties of direct overseas investment mentioned above.

Furthermore, the investor still has the assurance and protection of the UK's regulatory environment just as much as if he were investing in a fund exposed only to the UK market. The burden of getting hold of company information, interpreting it, making the investment decision and handling the administration of holding the stock is all borne by the fund management company.

4.4 CONCLUSION

To summarise, investing overseas presents significant opportunities for the UK-based investor. Exposure to these markets is most easily achieved through one or other of the collective investment schemes that give the opportunity to invest in country-specific funds, global funds, or worldwide sector-based funds. A key factor to remember is that the returns on investment overseas can be significantly affected by fluctuations in exchange rates.

5

INVESTING IN EMERGING MARKETS

ROS PRICE
(Chief Investment Officer)
and
ALEX SCOTT
(Senior Research Analyst)
Seven Investment Management

5.1 INTRODUCTION

Investors are used to the concept of risk in investing their assets, and usually address the issue when selecting the right asset array to meet their strategic investment objective and reflect their risk profile. However, when they consider investing in emerging markets they are often frightened by the apparent real increase in the various risks associated with these markets. Others are seduced by the romance and appeal of the new and relatively unknown. Of course investing and trading with the unknown has been an alluring prospect since time immemorial, and perhaps so much more exciting than investing in the domestic market. The rewards for patience can be exceptional, but so can the losses when getting it wrong, as many investors will attest to. The sharp sell-off in emerging markets equities in April and May 2004, as investors seriously began to fear the implications of a possible economic 'hard-landing' in China was painful for those exposed to it, but was a relatively small move compared to many more severe emerging market crises in the past. Latin America provides examples of this, such as the economic collapse of 2001–02 in Argentina and the mid-1990s 'Tequila Crisis' in Mexico.

5.2 DEFINING EMERGING MARKETS

Definitions vary over exactly what constitutes an 'emerging market' – and of course the boundaries are flexible. The term is generally used to describe the capital markets of less economically developed nations. The World Bank has a formal classification of emerging markets based on GNP per capita, under which most of Asia, all of Africa, all of Central and South America and parts of southern and eastern Europe are regarded as 'emerging'. Other states with higher income per head may be included in the definition, such as the Middle Eastern Gulf States (due to the uneven distribution of wealth) and Israel. Standard & Poors, which calculates a range of indices (including emerging markets indices) allows another general criterion, in its classification of emerging equity markets; namely, that a country's investible market capitalisation is low relative to its most recent GDP figures. Under most definitions, the largest and most important emerging markets would include: Brazil, Mexico, China, India, Korea, Taiwan, Israel, Russia, Turkey and South Africa. Debate continues as to how some Asia-Pacific markets such as Hong Kong and Singapore – which have quite mature economies and well developed equity markets – should be regarded. In practise, these regions are included in many emerging markets investment portfolios.

The term 'emerging markets' implies that change is taking place, in terms of economic and social development, as well as financial markets. Over time, as progress is made on these fronts, former emerging markets can come to be regarded as more mature, mainstream, developed markets. Such a change in investors' perception will be a gradual process for certain, but it can and does happen. Forty years ago, Japan was regarded as an emerging market; more recently, Greece has made the shift in many investors' minds from emerging market to mainstream – a corollary of its accession to the EU. Other markets – Korea, Taiwan and Mexico perhaps – have shifted from being regarded as rather exotic outposts to being perfectly normal areas for investment in an institutional portfolio. Perhaps in another decade or so, today's exotic, frontier markets (Croatia, say, or Vietnam) will be regarded as acceptable emerging markets – and some of today's emerging markets in central Europe will be part of the continental mainstream. With an enlarged EU already a reality, and an enlarged Eurozone only a few years away, the time may come when UK investors regard an investment in Komerční Banka or Telekomunikacja Polska as no more outlandish than a holding in Barclays or BT.

5.3 WHY INVEST IN EMERGING MARKETS?

We will examine the particular risks and rewards of investment in emerging markets later. First, some consideration of the context – and hence the opportunity – may be valuable. The world's population today is around 6 billion people – around five billion live in a country that might be classed as an emerging market. The other one billion, the population of the developed world, have around 80% of global GDP; the five billion in emerging countries have around 20% of global GDP.

It is not therefore surprising that the focus of most investors has been and continues to be on the developed world. But the balance is shifting. In 2025, the world's population will be around eight billion – of which, seven billion will live in today's emerging economies. By 2050, current projections estimate a global population in the region of nine billion – with around eight billion in developing countries.

The point should be clear. Population numbers in the mature economies – of western Europe, North America, Australasia and Japan – is expected to be stable overall, in round numbers. By contrast, over the next 50 years, today's emerging markets could see population growth of perhaps 60%. Even if there were no relative improvement in GDP per head, and no improvement in living standards in the developing world relative to the West, then simply the shift in population numbers would see a significant increase in the share of world GDP accounted for by emerging economies.

Figure 5.1 A shifting balance: share of global population and GDP accounted for by developed and emerging economies

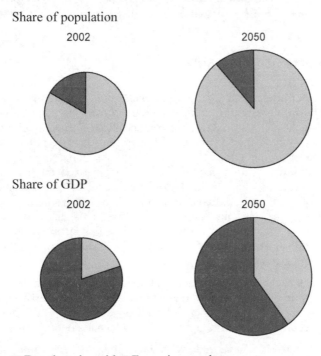

■ Developed world ▨ Emerging markets

Source: World Bank

Figure 5.1 represents this shift in graphical form. These trends could mean that a materially higher proportion of global GDP may be accounted for by today's emerging market economies. In essence, the 'pie' of global GDP will be substantially larger than today; and the 'slice' accounted for by today's emerging economies will also be a higher proportion than today. Though their share of global GDP will of course still be much smaller than their share of global population, it will be significant. This increase of significance implies the existence of a long-term structural trend that should not be ignored by investors today.

However, this is more subtle than simply a numbers game; population growth alone does not translate to GDP growth. Indeed, the opposite may well be true. Unchecked population growth in the poorest countries arguably holds back development; spending per head on education and health is lower, land and other assets are split between too many heirs in younger generations and large numbers of unskilled and unemployed workers drive down average wages. As we shall see, however, there are reasons to suppose that GDP per capita in many developing economies could rise – that the gap between 'rich and poor' could narrow to some small degree. These depend more on the 'positive demographics' of some emerging markets countries than on sheer population growth.

5.4 RISKS AND REWARDS

The risks of investing in emerging markets may be higher than those of investing in more mature equity markets. Over time, investors may anticipate these higher risks being compensated by the potential higher returns. However, the likelihood of higher than average volatility may mean that emerging market investments are not suitable for all investors. For the majority of investors, the risks implied by exposure to emerging markets mean that they are likely to form a relatively small element of their portfolio allocation. Economic crises have often featured in frontier markets over the years, and these present a special risk to investors – one that may be regarded as a low probability risk in most developed economies, but a real danger from time to time even in some of the leading emerging economies.

So, as well as the usual risks facing all investors – for example, the risk of buying overvalued assets that subsequently underperform, or of company-specific risks associated with owning securities – investors buying securities in emerging markets may face many other risks.

Some of these risks have to do with the resilience of emerging markets economies and their institutions. In some cases, developing economies may be quite poorly diversified, reliant to a high degree on relatively few commodities or industrial sectors. We would note the high importance of semiconductor manufacturing to Taiwan's economy, for example, the reliance on oil of the Gulf States, Venezuela, Nigeria or even Russia, and the significance of a small number of agricultural cash crops to many sub-Saharan African states. Such economies – and therefore their currencies and perhaps their quoted markets – can be vulnerable to a global downturn in demand, or to local factors affecting a key sector (eg climate affecting harvest of a key commodity). Financial institutions in emerging markets are likely to be less robust than in many developed markets; banks' credit controls may be looser, their reserves and ability to lend may be weaker. It is possible that (as in the case of the Asian contagion following the collapse of the Thai Baht in 1998) the availability of foreign capital going into emerging markets could dry up, with serious consequences.

Experience has shown that flows of overseas capital into and out of emerging markets can be extremely volatile. The resilience and conduct of government is also a consideration for investors in emerging markets, as those who have watched the struggle between Yukos and the Russian government will be aware. The norms of western market-led democracy are clearly not applicable in all emerging countries, where other models of government may be evident. Investors must be aware of the likelihood and implications of government change on countries or companies, the stability of the existing regime, the prevalence of electoral violence or corruption, the risks of extremism or terrorism affecting countries and investors' attitudes towards them and the risks to physical and intellectual property rights.

Other risks are connected with the conduct of investment business in emerging markets – with the legal and regulatory framework. Investors must be aware that regulation is less stringent in some emerging markets than it is in their domestic market and that shareholder rights may be less well-defined. Liquidity in some markets, or particular securities, may be very poor, or dealing costs expensive. Settlement may be less clear-cut than is the case with deals in most western markets.

Although there are fine examples of best practice in some emerging markets, behaviour at a company level may differ from expected norms in the West; investor expectations regarding corporate governance and the application of accounting practices may be at odds with local practices. On the other hand, it might be argued that the record of corporate governance and institutional integrity in more mature markets has also left something to be desired in recent years.

Investors may also need to take into account the nature of the technical and social structure of countries in which companies are conducting their business, and attempt to understand the implications of these factors on companies' operations. This may be just as much a consideration for global multinationals operating in developing economies as it is for local companies in those markets. Weak infrastructure – from transport to communications networks and power utilities – can have an impact on a company's ability to operate its business. Social instability, or the impact of disease and climate, which might also be expected to play a larger role in less-developed economies, may have a similar impact on businesses. Any of these factors could therefore undermine the market's assessment of a companies' valuation.

This list of risks and problems is not exhaustive, but it summarises some of the main issues. Investors in emerging markets clearly have much to consider at a country and currency level, as well as at the level of individual securities. It seems perhaps a daunting proposition, but not an insurmountable one, and may be justified by the possible rewards and by the risk management benefits of holding non-correlated emerging markets as part of a well-diversified portfolio (see 5.7).

In practical investment terms, these potential rewards are, as yet, unquantifiable. Recent performance is discussed in greater detail below, but clearly it is the possible future performance of these markets, rather than the past, which should be of interest to investors contemplating an investment in emerging markets. As ever, the past is unlikely to be a reliable guide to the future. Most serious investors would accept, however, that over the long-term there is likely to be a strong link between the real returns on equity investments and the real economic growth experienced by the markets in which those investments are held. If this is the case, then there is a clear attraction to investors in having some exposure to regions and markets where economic growth is likely to be highest over a sustained period.

It is possible to consider the forces at work in the demographic and economic development of emerging markets and surmise that although the uncertainties will be great, investors who are prepared to direct some of their risk capital to firms in emerging markets will be exposed to some of the most significant structural economic growth stories in the world today.

5.5 THE SHIFTING BALANCE – DEMOGRAPHICS AND INDUSTRIALISATION

'There is solid evidence, based on two generations of experience and research, that there is a "population effect" on economic growth. Since 1970, developing countries with lower fertility and slower population growth have seen higher productivity, more savings and more productive investment. They have registered faster economic growth.' – United Nations Population Fund (UNFPA), *State of World Population 2002: People, Poverty and Possibilities*

5.5.1 The demographic window

Most of us are familiar with demographic challenges facing the developed world. With the notable exception of the United States, most OECD[1] nations are experiencing a quite dramatic aging of their populations. This is the consequence, broadly speaking, of significantly rising life expectancy and falling birth rates (often to below the 'replacement level' of around 2.1 births per woman). The impact of birth rates on overall population structure is felt not just in the numbers of births per woman, but also the mother's age at which the first child is born, which is rising, and the longer spacing between births. The so-called 'baby boom' generation is also getting older. The shift in population structure can be illustrated with reference to the median age of a society. In the EU today, the median age throughout the population is around 39 years. By 2050, it is forecasted to be around 50 – in other words, half of the EU's population will be over the age of 50; 28% will be over 65 (currently just 16% are over 65). (See Figure 5.2.)

Figure 5.2 EU population projections, 1950–2050 (year 2000 = 100)

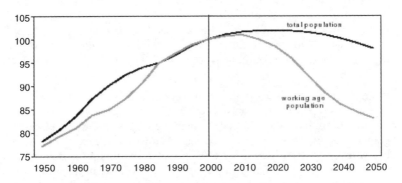

Source: Citigroup Smith Barney/United Nations Population Database, 2002 Revision

As most individuals experience their most economically productive years between the ages of 16 and 65, this dramatic aging will have an impact on the economic growth potential of Europe, and other OECD countries with a similar profile, such as Japan. The rising median age will have material consequences on spending patterns across a population, and on the demand for financial assets from the savings industry. Simply put, youthful spenders will be outnumbered by middle-aged savers and then – between 2010 and 2050 – by pensioners, whose numbers will grow dramatically relative to the working population. Between now and 2050, while the proportion of the population aged over 65 is expected to almost double, the numbers of working age Europeans are expected to go into a small absolute decline. This story – familiar perhaps, but fascinating nonetheless – lies behind the increasing urgency of European governments' attempts at pension reform. Figure 5.2 illustrates the severity of the problem, highlighting the dramatic decline anticipated in Europe's working-age population.

Some of us may be familiar too with the particular challenges of unchecked population growth in much of the developing world. The historical consequences of low levels of education, poor health and nutrition and high mortality can be seen in the large families still common in many developing regions. Considerable progress has been made; fertility in developing regions has halved since 1960, from 6 births per woman to 2.9 now, as education and health improvements have become more prevalent. In the least developed countries, however, birth rates still stand above 5 births per woman.

High fertility and rapid population growth in isolation is more likely to impede economic development than advance it. As the UNFPA points out: 'High levels of fertility contribute directly to poverty, reducing women's opportunities, diluting expenditure on children's education and health, precluding savings and increasing vulnerability and insecurity.' This does not portray an attractive environment for international or local investors. Capital formation is uncertain, incomes per head are stretched by the high growth in absolute numbers – which keep wage rates for the uneducated low – and consequent social unrest may hamper the conduct of business.

From an investment standpoint, then, neither of these demographic scenarios looks particularly attractive. Things can change of course – population migration could subtly alter the trends in European demographics, as is the case in the United States. However, the expansion of the EU, after the entry of ten new states in 2004, is unlikely to be a major boost to the European demographic picture; very low birth rates in the accession countries mean that in aggregate their demographic structure is even less attractive than that in Western Europe. In the fullness of time, accession to the EU by Turkey, which has a young and growing population, could ease the pressure of the EU's aging demographic profile.

There is of course another demographic scenario, applicable to some emerging economies, which can bring about the 'population effect' on economic growth mentioned in the passage quoted at the beginning of this section. This phenomenon has been witnessed already in some countries, especially in East Asia and a few in Latin America. The link between demographic shifts and economic growth can be seen as a result of improvements and investment in health, including nutrition and the treatment of disease, and education.

Improving health, including lower infant mortality, removes the requirement for individuals in developing countries to have large families to ensure enough children survive to adulthood to support their parents in old age. Faced with a realistic choice, many families do choose to have fewer children. Across a society, total fertility rates can drop quite markedly. Education can further improve the understanding of such choices, and also increases the employment opportunities for the younger generation.

In the slow-moving dynamics of population structures, a fall in fertility (from the very high levels associated with less developed countries towards the low fertility of more developed countries) can bring about a significant change over the course of a generation. The resulting structure – a larger cohort of working age people, in the most economically-productive 16–65 age group, relative to their younger and older dependents – can create the conditions for much stronger economic growth. National health and education resources are then stretched across slightly fewer younger people, increasing their potential efficacy, and perhaps reinforcing the process of demographic change once it is underway. Fewer young, unskilled people entering the labour force can help increase wage levels. Rising income levels, in combination with smaller families, can reduce the pressure on wage earners at a survival level and drive an increase in disposable income. In turn, this can help the development of a consumer economy and an enlarged urban 'middle class', and allow savings (creating greater stability in the event of financial or economic shocks) and capital formation.

These factors can help countries achieve quite rapid levels of economic growth over the course of a generation. Such an optimistic outturn as that described above is of course far from assured, and in practise poor governance, civil unrest, disease prevalence, dramatic social inequality or a host of other factors can and do limit the extent of the benefits that reach the poorer echelons of a developing country. This can mean that the potential benefits outlined above are not fully realised. But they can be achieved, at least in part, and real advances can be made. According to the UNFPA, the economic benefits of falling family sizes alone has translated to economic growth of around 0.7% per year per head over a sustained period, and similar benefits have been observed in some other Latin American countries.

In population terms, then, there is a sharp contrast between the economically developed nations, with (in most cases) aging populations of stable or falling size, and the less developed nations, with generally much younger and more rapidly growing populations. But in economic terms, the benefits to developing nations are to be found in directing health and education spending such that population growth slows, largely through a declining birth rate. Although it may take a generation to achieve this transition, and can generate significant economic benefits, it is a process that clearly cannot be repeated; the demographic window opens once and is then closed again. Investors may benefit from exposure to these demographic trends, particularly as they are observed in an increase in household disposable income and the development of local consumer sectors.

5.5.2 Industrialisation – growth and jobs

In many cases, countries have already opened the demographic window and enjoyed the boost to economic growth from this population effect – and yet their trend economic growth rates, though volatile, may still exceed those of more mature western economies. The chart alongside highlights some of these, showing countries which have already experienced many of the benefits of declining fertility and its impact on economic growth, and yet are still enjoying growth rates in excess of more developed economies for extended periods.

Figure 5.3 Real GDP growth comparison 1982–2002

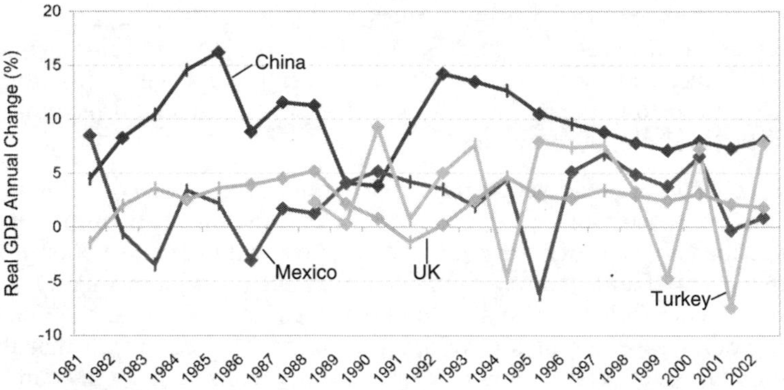

Source: Reuters

This positive picture of growth in emerging economies can be ascribed at least in part to the coincidence of rapid adoption of technology and industrialisation with the changing population structure. Globalisation – evident in constant improvements in global transport and communications – has made it easier for multinational corporations to source products and services from more remote markets, either through locating their own operations in these markets or by building relationships with local suppliers. Many emerging countries have embraced this trend, developing free-trade zones or preferential terms for multinational firms, in an effort to boost employment and exports, thus stimulating broader economic growth.

At the same time, intense levels of competition in many industries have also encouraged western firms to look for the cost savings that may be available by moving operations into emerging economies. Although income levels may be rising in some developing countries as they experience falling birth rates, labour is still likely to be considerably cheaper than in the west – including educated, skilled workers. This has led to a trend of manufacturing industry relocating its operations eastwards, with south east Asia, and to a lesser extent Eastern Europe, benefiting from this 'export of jobs' from the factories of western Europe and North America. It is a continuing trend, but one that has perhaps been intensified by the corporate difficulties of the weak economic cycle of the past few years. Investment bank Société Générale estimates that the weakness in western industrial production has led to the evaporation of perhaps 5 million manufacturing jobs in developed economies in the last two years alone. The industrial cycle is clearly to blame for some of these losses, but it seems a remote prospect that – as in previous cyclical upturns – the next upturn will bring back many of these jobs. Structural forces are at work here too; it is estimated that over the same period, foreign enterprises in China alone have taken on around 2 million new workers.

We have long been used to the shift eastwards in manufacturing. The inscription 'Made in Taiwan' (or China, or Korea) has long seemed more common on many consumer durables than has 'Made in Germany', let alone Britain. This is not to say that western companies are no longer producing the goods we use every day; on the contrary, many are, but – from refrigerators, to cars, to training shoes – they are increasingly likely to be manufactured in the Far East, and (since 1991) in Central and Eastern Europe.

However, there is another development apparently underway in this process. However long western manufacturing has been vulnerable to lower cost operators in the developing world, service industries have until recently seemed more secure. There has always been migration of populations to the developed world to meet the demand for labour in many service industries, but the recent advances in communications technology (and particularly the sharp falls in costs of international communication) have given rise to new trends. The evidence so far is anecdotal rather than compelling, but the export of service jobs from the economically developed to the developing nations appears to be well underway. From call centres and back office processing to software design and specialist financial research, more and more western companies are looking to relocate or outsource services to lower cost operations in the emerging market countries. This may cause short-term disruption to their businesses, but the lower operating costs are likely to help defend margins in a world where low pricing power means that profit margins are constantly under pressure.

As the adoption of modern technology continues, as standards of education, health and infrastructure improve, and as urban populations in developing countries continue to grow, we may expect the growth in employment to continue. Incomes per head will no doubt remain well below levels seen in the developed world, but increased employment and reduced numbers of dependents are likely to see disposable incomes rise. Local propensities to save or spend vary widely form country to country and between different age and social groups within countries, but it seems certain that rising per capita income will stimulate the growth of local consumer economies in a form that we in the west would recognise. Retail, leisure, financial services, energy, telecommunications, media, transport and other sectors have scope to develop in such a scenario, as do the producers of goods – both domestic and international – destined for household and industrial use within these countries.

The nature of the risks that exist, and the dramatic speed of social change that is taking place (dramatic in the context of the generational clock of demographics) should underline that progress will not be as smooth as optimists might hope. Financial crises, social unrest, poor government, disease and extremes of climate can all hamper economic development – not to mention the vagaries of the global economic cycle and the wild swings of sentiment that can direct capital flows into or out of particular markets. The risk of asset price bubbles, or of desperate sell-offs, remains. But the combination of economic and demographic development is a powerful one, and underwrites the potential, at least, for those emerging markets with the requisite elements of good governance, international investor and donor support, receptiveness to change in local populations, industrial and technological infrastructure and luck to generate higher than average levels of economic growth for a sustained period.

5.6 THE INVESTIBLE UNIVERSE

There may be quite general acceptance of the potential for above average GDP growth in emerging markets. What is perhaps less obvious is the route for international investors seeking to build exposure to this growth potential. In some cases, local restrictions make investment in a country's equity market either difficult or impossible for international investors. Currency controls may also prevent the easy repatriation of funds once invested in an emerging market. In other markets, it may be the case that the quoted sector accounts for a very small or unrepresentative element of a particular country's GDP – the opportunity for equity investors to buy into the economic growth potential of that country may therefore be hampered by the low availability of appropriate quoted enterprises trading on that country's market. China is perhaps a case in point here; the opportunities for overseas investors to take stakes in mainland Chinese companies had been very limited, and hampered by quite poor liquidity. Liberalisation of the regulations regarding domestic and overseas share classes on the Shanghai market in 2001 have improved liquidity, and new listings of mainland Chinese companies in Hong Kong (so-called Red Chips) have also recently widened the investible universe for overseas investors. Nonetheless, these are serious issues still for investors contemplating exposure to these markets.

Of course, investment in securities listed on stock exchanges in emerging markets is not the only way to gain exposure to economic growth in the region. Early emerging markets funds directed a significant element of their investment into those global or multinational companies with material exposure to developing economies in their revenues or profits, or their future profit potential. Emerging markets exposure may therefore be a prime factor in investment decisions concerning securities listed on western exchanges. In the UK alone, the possible rewards and risks of emerging markets exposure are key considerations for companies as diverse as Tesco (with its growing portfolio of stores in SE Asia and Central Europe), Prudential (with its growing long-term savings business in the Asia Pacific region) and Unilever (whose products sell in developed and emerging markets worldwide). For some investors, simply favouring those domestic companies, which derive a meaningful element of their current or future profits from emerging markets, may be a preferred method of gaining exposure. Of course, the downside to this approach is that other issues – unrelated to the operating performance of their emerging markets businesses – may dominate the share price performance of such firms.

5.7 PORTFOLIO CONSTRUCTION

The bubble – and subsequent bust – in global equity markets has contributed to two important developments in international stockmarkets. Just as the inflating bubble was observed in almost all markets, so was the bust that followed. This appears to have had an impact on the psychology of major equity markets, such that the correlation between the major western markets has reached unusually high levels. At the same time, the violence of these movements has driven equity market volatility (the common expression of investment risk) to unusually high levels. The implication from this is that in a world of generally higher investment risk, the benefits of diversifying across different equity markets have diminished; of course, the benefits of diversification, in terms of managing risk in a portfolio, are strongest when investing across assets with a low degree of correlation.

Figure 5.4 depicts this increase in correlation between the US and European markets in graphical form. It can be seen that the markets have rarely moved more closely in alignment. (This chart uses data to the end of 2002.)

Figure 5.4 Global equity market correlations

■ Three year rolling correlation, US vs Europe equity

Source: Citigroup Smith Barney

There has been a similar rise in correlation between western markets and Asia-Pacific markets in the first half of the 1990s, but since the Asian crisis of 1998, this correlation has begun to reverse and has actually fallen. Furthermore, the correlations between individual emerging markets have also fallen over the last two to three years, while correlations between western markets have been rising. So, while the benefits of diversifying a portfolio across western equity markets have diminished, due to the rising correlations between those markets, the potential benefits of introducing some exposure to emerging markets in a globally diversified portfolio may have increased. Even the allocation of just a few percent to emerging markets equities within a portfolio can bring some diversification benefits. The high expected volatility of these markets may mean that allocations of more than 10% of a portfolio to emerging markets could be suitable only for the most risk-tolerant investors.

At the very least, the consideration of emerging markets equities as part of the investment universe increases the 'decision space' available to investors, making possible a much greater range of risk-reward combinations than that provided by a mainstream equity portfolio alone, or even by a combination of mainstream equities and bonds. Figure 5.3 illustrates the theory behind this point. The relatively limited combination of risk-reward profiles that is possible from a portfolio combining only mainstream western equities is shown in the centre of the chart.

Figure 5.5 Risk–reward curves: the decision space for asset allocation

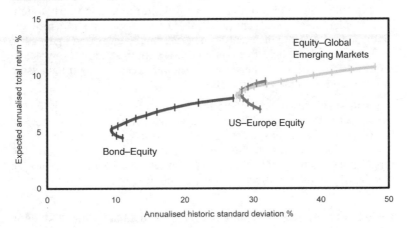

Source: Citigroup Smith Barney

Modern portfolio theory demonstrates how combining assets with low correlations will produce a return that is simply the weighted average of the two assets, but with a level of risk, measured by standard deviation, that is lower. This can be seen in the two other curves in the chart above. Towards the lower end of the risk-return spectrum, portfolios combining equities with bonds allow a much wider range of possible portfolio combinations; as do portfolios which combine global equity with global emerging markets equity at the higher end of the risk-reward spectrum. The implication from this observation is that investors who are prepared to tolerate a higher level of risk (as measured by the volatility of annual portfolio returns) in the hope of higher total returns should consider holding a higher proportion of emerging markets equity in their portfolio.

5.8 PERFORMANCE

The potential attractions of investing in emerging markets in theory are clear. The different risk/return combinations and low correlation of emerging markets equities with mainstream western markets offer a useful tool in portfolio construction. The social, demographic and technological changes in progress in some emerging markets look set to drive stronger than average economic growth potential for some years; in theory, this could support attractive returns from equities in emerging markets.

Has this played out in practise? In some senses, we must fall back on the legendary response of Chairman Mao's deputy, when asked about his assessment of the impact of the French Revolution: it's too early to tell. The demographic, social and political shifts that provide much of the rationale for investing in emerging markets can be measured in decades, or even generations. Investors prepared to accept the trade-off of risk and reward that emerging markets involve should accept a longer than usual time horizon for these investments.

Stock markets clearly have a shorter perspective, revising the prices of individual securities in real-time, based on anticipation of uncertain future events. Returns from emerging markets over periods of much less than a decade are of limited use in any analysis, as they allow too little time for the volatility inherent in these markets to be diluted, and for the population trends that affect long-term economic growth to play out.

Table 5.1 Major emerging markets: Compound annual growth of index price returns by country 1996–2003 (GBP % per annum)

		Country Index Price Return CAGR 1996 – 2003, GBP
Russia	RTS Index	24.9%
Mexico	MXSE	8.2%
Turkey	ISE 100	7.0%
Brazil	Bovespa	5.3%
Israel	TA25	4.8%
China	Hang Seng China Enterprises	3.5%
India	BSE Sensex	2.9%
UK	FTSE All Share	2.6%
South Africa	Johannesburg All Share	−1.8%
Taiwan	TWSE	−2.8%
Korea	KOSPI	−7.9%

Includes UK FT-SE All Share for comparison

Source: Reuters, 7IM Calculations

Nonetheless, performance over shorter periods can clearly have a material impact on portfolios holding exposure to emerging markets assets. Table 5.1 presents the returns observed on the major emerging markets over the eight years from 1996–2003, with the FT-SE All Share return included for comparison. This may be a relatively short period of analysis in the context of demographic and economic shifts taking place over decades, but the table does hint at the startling returns that emerging markets investment has the potential to deliver – as well as the painful losses that can result, even over quite long periods. The sharp divergence in returns between these countries also hints at the importance of country and regional selection within an emerging markets strategy. This point is discussed at greater length below.

Of course, investors will want to measure progress on shorter timescales too, looking at calendar year returns. For most emerging markets, as well as the majority of mature equity markets, 2002 was another disappointing year in performance terms. By contrast, 2003 was more spectacular, with the majority of emerging markets handsomely outperforming the strong returns of more mature markets, as they benefited from the resurgence in investors' risk appetites as it become clear that the global economy was experiencing a synchronised economic expansion. Some of these markets also benefited from their perceived exposure to two of the strongest investment themes of 2003: the growth in Chinese imports of both capital and consumer goods; and the dramatic rises in many industrial commodity prices. Table 5.2 presents the price returns (in sterling) for selected individual emerging markets over the last seven years as well as the returns for the global MSCI Emerging Markets (Free) Index.

Table 5.2 Major emerging markets: returns by country by year (GBP %)

		1997	1998	1999	2000	2001	2002	2003
Brazil	Bovespa	40.2%	−38.8%	72.5%	−10.6%	−22.8%	−51.0%	117.8%
Mexico	MXSE	58.1%	−38.6%	92.7%	−15.8%	22.1%	−23.4%	19.6%
India	BSE Sensex	12.7%	−23.4%	63.4%	−19.9%	−18.3%	−6.0%	63.9%
Korea	KOSPI	−70.1%	109.6%	97.9%	−52.3%	36.0%	−9.4%	15.8%
Taiwan	TWSE	3.9%	−21.3%	38.0%	−42.4%	14.0%	−26.9%	21.8%
South Africa	Johannesburg All Share	−8.4%	−24.7%	63.4%	−14.8%	−16.5%	10.0%	29.4%
Israel	TA25	32.4%	−14.1%	61.0%	15.8%	−14.3%	−39.1%	47.4%
China	Hang Seng China Enterprises	−23.5%	−45.1%	16.2%	−11.3%	11.3%	2.2%	128.7%
Russia	RTS Index	105.8%	−85.2%	204.1%	−11.6%	84.3%	29.3%	39.2%
Turkey	ISE 100	90.6%	−50.5%	246.0%	−45.7%	−29.8%	−40.9%	89.7%

Source: Reuters

This volatility of returns is a key element in investment decisions regarding emerging markets. Although some more mature markets – such as Germany – have recently tended to exhibit higher volatility (as measured by beta) than emerging markets, there is clearly still scope for quite volatile returns from the less developed markets, including very significant upswings when markets are in favour (e.g. most markets in 1999, especially Russia and Turkey; Russia again in 2001; Korea in 1998 and 2001, all emerging markets, especially Brazil and China, in 2003); and correspondingly vicious sell-offs when they move out of favour (e.g. Korea in 1996-1997; most emerging markets in 1998, 2000 and 2002; and, to a lesser extent, in the sharp sell-off seen in the second quarter of 2004). Many of these swings may be driven as much by shifts in sentiment and rapid changes in fund flows (so-called 'hot money' in global investment portfolios) as by changes in the fundamental worth of companies in an index.

This volatility therefore creates an opportunity for an active asset allocator to increase or decrease emerging markets allocations in a global portfolio on a tactical basis. This may require an investor to swim against the tide, selling those markets where optimism and valuations have become overstretched – or reducing exposure to emerging markets as a whole – and buying into markets which are fundamentally sound long-term prospects, but where sentiment is depressed by short-term factors. The market's reaction to the appearance of the SARS virus in Greater China in Spring 2003, which interrupted progress in many South East Asian equity markets, looks as if it was one such opportunity. Whether the sell-off in most emerging markets, particularly in the Asia-Pacific region, in April and May 2004 was a temporary loss of sentiment caused by passing fears over the strength of Chinese demand, or whether it was just the initial fall in one of the periodic more serious reversals will become clear in time. Uncertainties such as these simply underline the need for a longer than usual time horizon and a robust attitude to investment volatility for any investor contemplating exposure to emerging markets in their portfolio.

5.9 COUNTRY SELECTION

In mature markets, country selection has been a declining influence in determining the variation in investment returns over most of the past two decades. Indeed, correlations between major western equity markets have rarely if ever been higher. However, the pattern of data in emerging markets is very different.

Here, the impact of country-specific factors on equity market returns appears to be much greater, on the upside and downside. Whereas total returns in more mature markets have become more closely correlated, there remain wide differences in performance between the many emerging markets and, in fact, correlations between emerging markets have actually fallen in recent months.

Some emerging markets crises in the past – notably the Asian crisis of 1998 – have seen an element of contagion, with financial pressures transmitted from one country to another. In this instance, almost all equity markets fell, whether directly related to the crisis or not, as international investors' risk appetites collapsed, and funds flowed out of all emerging markets into 'safer' assets. In more normal conditions, of course, the links between emerging countries may be regarded as less strong, and correlations between their equity markets may remain low. There is a perfectly rational explanation for this of course. Country-specific factors (positive and negative), whether related to government or legal developments, exchange rate fluctuations, sentiment of international investors, or system-wide economic issues, can have a proportionately greater effect on a country's equity market performance than is the case in more mature equity markets, which may be sensitive to a far more diverse range of factors.

The upshot of this is that in emerging markets investment, country allocation decisions are of paramount importance. Table 5.3 provides a few examples to illustrates this point. It shows the performance of the best and worst markets in aggregate from 1995 to 2001, and then compares the performance of the worst stocks in the best performing market with the performance of the best stocks in the worst performing market. In almost every case, the worst stocks in the best market have outperformed (often quite considerably) the best stocks in the worst market. It is noteworthy too that individual countries can swing from best performer to worst, or back, in a very short period of time.

If this pattern is to be repeated, then its message is clear; focusing on country allocation is likely to bring the greatest benefits – far more so than focusing on stock selection. This suggests that an emphasis on the analysis of macro-economic, currency and political factors is likely to have a significant impact on investment returns.

Many investors may be unwilling to tolerate the high potential volatility of returns associated with investments in single emerging market. For these people, a diversified approach, spreading investment across a range of emerging markets – perhaps in a single fund vehicle – may help reduce the expected volatility.

Table 5.3 Best and worst performing equity markets in contrast

	Best Market	Performance %	Performance of worst stocks in best market %*	Worst Market	Performance %	Performance of best stocks in worst market %*
1995	Peru	23.3	–31.8	Pakistan	–36.5	–28.1
1996	Russia	152.9	136.6	Korea	–38.1	32.2
1997	Turkey	118.1	–13.2	Indonesia	–74.1	–55.2
1998	Korea	141.1	–36.7	Russia	–83.0	–67.1
1999	Turkey	252.4	79.8	Colombia	–13.7	–10.3
2000	Venezuela	4.5	4.5	Indonesia	–61.9	–35.0
2001	Russia	55.9	47.8	Egypt	–41.3	–32.7

* Weighted average performance of ten best/worst stocks; in markets with less than ten stocks, weighted average of five best/worst stocks is used
NB: Index data used here are MSCI, and will differ from index returns on Table 5.2 earlier.

Source: HSBC/MSCI

5.10 EMERGING MARKET DEBT

Most investors, when considering emerging markets, automatically think of emerging markets equities. This would be to ignore a large and increasingly well-accepted class of investment opportunities in the shape of emerging market bonds. This grouping encompasses debt securities issued by sovereign, public sector and corporate entities in emerging countries.

Because of a history of credit default and the risk that future repayments could also be missed, many emerging market borrowers, including governments, labour under low quality credit ratings. These borrowers are often a far cry from the AAA-rated UK and US governments, where the risk of default may be counted as minimal. The corollary of this low quality credit rating, of course, is that emerging markets debtors generally expect to pay higher costs to borrow than would their developed markets counterparts – they pay a premium or 'spread' over similar borrowings for other borrowers with higher credit ratings. This yield differential is often quoted as the spread over US Treasuries. For investors prepared to contemplate the real risks to capital that exist in holding emerging market debt, the potential of very high income yields may be sufficient compensation. It has not been unusual for emerging market debt issues to offer a yield 5%, 10% or even more above US Treasury yields at a similar maturity, although current spreads are generally narrower.

We are in the unusual situation that two of the three largest emerging market debtor nations, Mexico and Russia, are currently rated as investment-grade borrowers by the independent ratings agencies; in other words, they are regarded by these agencies as relatively good credit risks, buoyed in both cases by the strength of oil revenues to their respective governments. This perception could, of course, change, leading to a drastic reassessment of the risks of holding their debt and a widening of spreads.

Investment in an emerging markets debt security demands analysis of all the factors which would be considered for any other fixed interest investment – including credit risk, interest rate risk, duration/maturity profiles of the bond – plus a range of other considerations. Credit risk analysis needs to take into account not only the risk of an individual company defaulting, or experiencing a credit rating downgrade, but also the risk of a government default or system-wide crisis affecting repayment of interest and principal. Currency and exchange rate analysis also takes on new dimensions. This remains the case even if an investor is looking for emerging markets debt denominated in sterling, euros or (more likely) dollars; although the debt issue may be priced in dollars – theoretically removing currency risk for a Dollar investor – it is possible that the revenue base of the debt issuer (government or corporate) is in the local currency. A dislocation of the local currency exchange rate against the Dollar, as happened in Argentina in 2001–02, could lead to a default on payments if local currency revenues are no longer sufficient to service dollar-denominated debt.

In practice, the market's pricing of emerging market debt is driven as much by sentiment and liquidity as it is by changes in the fundamental creditworthiness of the borrower. Emerging market debt yields may be driven down (i.e. prices driven up) by comparison with yields on debt securities in mature markets. If yields, for example, on US Treasuries are driven down, then investors seeking income may be tempted to increase allocations to higher yielding (and of course higher risk) securities, including junk bonds and emerging market debt. The strong performance of both asset classes for most of 2003 and 2004 to date may be in part ascribed to this. In the search for income in a world of low-yielding assets, investors have (perhaps unwittingly) taken on considerably more risk to generate what they consider adequate returns, chasing prices higher (and yields lower) on high yield and emerging market bonds. Of course, the risk exists that market perceptions could change and the spreads of emerging market bond yields could return to more familiar territory; this would imply quite substantial price reversals. Potential investors must judge whether the yield premium currently on offer on emerging market debt – ie the spread over corresponding Treasury bonds – is adequate compensation for the additional risks in holding the asset, primarily the risks of a default by, or a downgrade of, the issuer.

5.11 INVESTMENT VEHICLES

Investors who wish to build exposure to emerging markets – whether equity or debt – within a diversified portfolio have a wealth of alternatives to help them implement such a strategy. The following sections consider the implications of some of these.

5.11.1 Direct investment

Although it is possible in theory, most investors will find it difficult in practice to invest directly in emerging markets securities. Markets like Hong Kong and Singapore (arguably not strictly in the emerging markets category), and perhaps Mexico, may be reasonably accessible for individual investors. However, it could be somewhat challenging locating a private client stockbroker equipped to undertake deals in most emerging markets. Some emerging markets companies will have American Depositary Receipts (ADRs) or Global Depositary Receipts (GDRs) listed on recognised stock exchanges (such as New York or Tokyo), and these may be expected to trade in line with the underlying stock. Direct dealing in the ADRs or GDRs where they are available may be rather more straightforward than attempting to deal directly in securities listed on emerging markets' stock exchanges.

The alternative of purchasing the securities of international companies listed on mainstream western stock exchanges, which have significant emerging markets operations, is clearly more straightforward. The limitations of this approach to building true emerging markets exposure into a portfolio have already been discussed.

It is likely that most investors – apart form those with the most aggressive attitudes to risk – will want to limit emerging markets exposure to a relatively small proportion of their portfolio. Therefore, only very large investment portfolios are likely to be of sufficient size to take on direct emerging markets exposure, encompassing a well diversified selection of individual emerging markets equities. Compressing an allocation to emerging markets into too few individual securities is likely to give rise to a high degree of security-specific volatility, as well as the volatility associated with the market as a whole.

5.11.2 Pooled

The challenges posed by direct investment in emerging markets – not least the need to have an extremely large portfolio in order to be able to achieve effective diversification across a wide enough range of emerging markets securities – mean that a pooled fund solution could be appropriate for most investors.

There is a wide variety of such vehicles available for private investors in the UK, both closed-ended (investment trusts) and open-ended (unit trusts, OEICs). (See Chapters 7 and 8 for a broader discussion of the particular qualities of these two types of investment vehicle.) Some classes of UK investor may also be able to purchase overseas-listed exchange-traded funds, of which a number exist that track individual emerging market indices.

Funds available in the UK include a number of individual country funds, regional funds and global emerging markets funds. Investors may also be able to buy exchange traded funds (ETFs), listed in the US or elsewhere, which track country, regional or global emerging market indices. The effect of country selection on investment returns must be a key issue for investors deciding which approach to take. Those who are prepared to undertake the necessary research and accept much higher volatility in the hope of identifying a single country that can perform strongly may select one or more individual country funds. Although the choice of managers in any given category may be rather limited, there are single-country funds available in the UK specialising in Brazil, Chile, China, India, Indonesia, Israel, Malaysia, Russia, South Africa, South Korea, Thailand, Vietnam and others, plus ETFs listed in the US which track large-cap indices for Brazil, Hong Kong, Malaysia, Mexico, Singapore, South Africa, South Korea and Taiwan. These may provide a solution for investors hoping to select a number of strongly performing markets from the range of global opportunities.

Many investors will prefer to take a more diversified approach, reducing the risk of making a wrong country selection and being overexposed to a single, poorly performing market. Investing through a diversified vehicle can provide exposure to the positive demographic and economic themes associated with emerging markets, whilst reducing the short-term risks associated with overexposure to individual securities or countries. Funds are available in the UK that invest on a regional basis (eg Eastern Europe, or Latin America) or across global emerging markets. In each case, fund managers may be prepared to take active positions regarding countries or regions in their universe. There may be some attractions to non-specialist investors in delegating the regional level allocation decisions to a specialist investment manager focusing on emerging markets, who may be well-placed to make top-down country selections (based on macro-economic research and strategy) as well as bottom-up security selections (based on rigorous analysis of companies' financial statements, valuations and product/market strategies).

5.12 CONCLUSION

Rational investors should always be driven by two main and related desires; either to limit the amount of risk they must take to achieve a desired level of return, or to maximise the amount of return they may expect from a given level of risk. Used correctly, a measured allocation to emerging markets equities (and, perhaps, debt) within a diversified and correctly asset-allocated portfolio can help meet either of these ends.

The particular social and economic factors at work in many emerging markets combine to create a more favourable demographic background than may be evident in some developed markets – creating an environment in which a faster pace of economic growth may be sustained for an extended period. There are many and various risks to the most optimistic scenarios being realised, but for investors who accept that there must be a long-term link between the growth rate of an economy and the returns delivered by equity investment in that economy, then the potential for higher than average economic growth demands attention and can justify an allocation within a portfolio, albeit only for investors with a reasonably robust attitude to risk and a fairly long investment time horizon.

On the other hand, although the risks of investing in emerging markets in isolation may be quite high, the relatively low levels of correlation they have tended to display against more mature financial markets can provide useful diversification benefits. Combining non-correlated assets within a portfolio can reduce the level of expected risk for a desired level of return (or increase the expected return for any given level of risk). This characteristic may justify modest levels of exposure to emerging market assets in a range of portfolios.

Main sources and note

Bank for International Settlements, Bloomberg, BNP Paribas, Citigroup Smith Barney, Goldman Sachs, HSBC, JP Morgan, Merrill Lynch, Morgan Stanley, Reuters, Société Générale, United Nations Population Fund (UNFPA), World Bank.

Note

This document has been issued by 7IM, a division of Killik & Co, on the basis of publicly available information, internally developed data and other sources believed to be reliable. Whilst all reasonable care has been taken to ensure the facts stated and the opinions given are fair, neither 7IM, Killik & Co, nor any partner or employee shall be in any way responsible for its content. Partners of Killik & Co and their employees, including those within 7IM, may have a position or holding in any of the above investments or in a related investment. The value of investments and the income from them may vary and you may realise less than the sum you invested. Part of the capital invested may be used to pay that income. In the case of higher volatility investments, these may be subject to sudden and large falls in value and you may realise a large loss equal to the amount invested. Some investments are not readily realisable and investors may have difficulty in realising the investment or obtaining reliable information on the value or risks associated with that investment. Where a security is denominated in a currency other than Sterling, changes in exchange rates may have an adverse impact on the value of the security and the income thereon. The past performance of investments is not necessarily a guide to future performance. The investment or investment service may not be suitable for all recipients of this publication and any doubts regarding this should be addressed to your advisor. 7IM is a division of Killik & Co, who are members of the London Stock Exchange and are authorised and regulated by the Financial Services Authority.

Principal place of business: 46 Grosvenor Street London W1K 3HN.

6

DERIVATIVES DE-MYSTIFIED

MALCOLM KEMP

Threadneedle Investments Ltd

6.1 INTRODUCTION

The aim of this chapter is to set out what futures, options and swaps are, indicate how they are priced and give a few examples of when they are used. Derivatives enable asset management decisions to be undertaken cheaply and quickly. They offer fund managers the ability to tailor the risk/return profile of a fund in many different ways.

The topics covered are:

(1) why the reputation of derivatives for being inherently 'risky' may be inaccurate;
(2) how futures contracts work and how they can help fund managers;
(3) what sorts of options and contracts exist and how they can be priced; and
(4) the characteristics of swaps and other 'over-the-counter' derivatives.

6.2 'SURELY DERIVATIVES ARE VERY RISKY?'

In some quarters, derivatives have acquired a reputation for being risky, and have been blamed for some large losses, for example at Barings. However, this reputation is often misguided. The important thing is to consider the derivatives not in isolation, but *in conjunction with other assets in the fund*. Some derivative positions will add risk to the portfolio, but others can actually reduce the risk being run.

For example, a fund invested in equities might buy put options, which give the fund the right (but not the obligation) to sell the equities at a fixed price, even if the equities have fallen further than this floor. Put options such as these effectively provide insurance against large falls in the values of these equities. Viewed in isolation, they have speculative characteristics because they will rise in value very substantially if the market falls. Buying a put option in isolation is a little like buying insurance on a property you do not own. But viewed in conjunction with the rest of the portfolio, such options make much more sense. In the above example, the rise in the value of the option compensates the fund for the fall in the value of the equities it owns, just like other sorts of insurance.

A key way to control risks that derivatives might introduce is to avoid gearing. It is gearing that could cause a modest market movement to lead to insolvency. It is gearing that is dangerous, not derivatives *per se*. This was vividly displayed by the collapse of Barings Bank in February 1995. It had two large positions relating to the Japanese equity market that doubled up on each other, rather than cancelling out each other. This introduced massive gearing, which went badly wrong when the market moved adversely. However, it is important to bear in mind that gearing is not specific to derivatives. Dangerous gearing can be entered into by borrowing and investing in blue chip stocks or gilts, without going anywhere near an option or a futures contract.

6.3 WHAT IS A FUTURES CONTRACT, AND HOW DOES IT WORK?

Futures contracts are quick and efficient ways of increasing (or reducing) exposure to a particular market. There are many different exchanges around the world where they are traded. Futures are based on or derived from (hence *derivatives*) an underlying asset. When futures contracts began trading in 1848 at the Chicago Board of Trade, the underlying assets were agricultural produce. Farmers wanted to fix in advance a selling price for a specified quantity for a specified date in the future. More recently, however, contracts on commodities like these have been eclipsed by financial futures. In these sorts of futures, the contract is linked to some underlying financial asset or variable, for example stock market indices, bonds, currencies or interest rates.

Perhaps the most important future for a UK investment manager is the FT-SE 100 Index futures contract traded on LIFFE. It is a contract based on the FT-SE 100 Index of 100 leading UK equities. It is by far the most liquid futures contract relating to the UK equity market (indeed the amount of equity exposure traded using FT-SE 100 Index futures contracts usually exceeds the amount traded on the underlying stock market).

The exposure to the equity market represented by one FT-SE 100 Index futures contract is £10 times the price of the futures. Thus with the FT-SE around 4400, the value of the market exposure represented by one futures contract would be around £44,000. This is the amount that would be lost by a buyer of one futures contract if the equity market fell to zero, the same as for an investor who bought actual stocks in line with the index for £44,000. Similarly if the market doubled, any investor who had bought/sold one contract would gain/lose £44,000.

A *buyer* of one FT-SE 100 futures contract will therefore gain/lose £10 for every point that the futures price rises/falls between the time the contract is entered into and the time that the contract expires. At any point in time there are four separate futures contracts potentially tradable, with expiries in March, June, September or December. Most of the trading actually takes place in the month with the nearest expiry, which is known as the *front month* contract.

Conversely, a *seller* of one FT-SE 100 futures contract would lose/gain £10 for every point that the futures price rises/falls over the same period. It is possible to sell a future without holding the underlying stocks (indeed it is easier to do this than to short sell the stocks themselves), but it is potentially risky to do this since it introduces a form of gearing.

Every futures contract will have a buyer and seller. However, when a futures contract is effected, no cash or stocks are transferred between the two parties. Instead the futures contract behaves as if the buyer and the seller commit to buy/sell equities at expiry date. Perhaps a good analogy is the exchange of contracts prior to purchase of a property. Once contracts are exchanged the investor becomes exposed to the implications of owning the property (eg if the house burns down, the investor will on completion pay a large sum to acquire a worthless asset, which is why it is important to insure a property from exchange of contract and not just from completion). Legal ownership, however, only transfers on completion.

In any sort of contract in which two parties commit to do something in the future, each becomes exposed to the risk that the other will default on the contract. This is why a deposit is paid on exchange of contracts in a property transaction. Most of the complexities of futures arise from the need to introduce a procedure protecting either side from default of the other. Derivatives exchanges try to limit these exposures by use of a central clearing house and a margining system.

When a futures contract is entered into, both parties put up what is merely a returnable good faith deposit, called *initial margin*, to the clearing house. For example, the current level of margin per contract on a FT-SE 100 Index future is £1,500, but this figure can be increased in periods of high volatility. The clearing house for LIFFE is the London Clearing House, owned by several of the leading clearing banks. The clearing house then interposes itself between the two parties by replacing the original contract with two separate equal and opposite contracts, one between itself and the first party and one between itself and the second party. To avoid additional credit exposures arising as the futures price moves up or down, the contracts are *marked to market* at the end of each day, with any capital gain or loss being paid from or to the clearing house. These payments are called *variation margin*.

When the contract matures the initial margin is returned to each party. At expiry the FT-SE 100 future is cash settled, ie the seller transfers only the cash value of the shares rather than the shares themselves to the buyer. This means that the contract is legally classified as a *contract for differences*.

6.4 DEALING IN FUTURES AND STOCKS COMPARED

Futures contracts enable exposures to be bought and sold much more cheaply, quickly and efficiently than dealing in the underlying shares.

If FT-SE futures did not exist, an institutional fund manager moving in and then subsequently out of the UK equity market might typically incur the following expenses:

(a) *on buying*
middle price to offer price (spread)	0.2%
commission	0.1%
stamp duty	0.5%

(b) *on selling*
bid price to middle price (spread)	0.2%
commission	0.1%
Total	**1.1%**

Thus if the FT-SE were about 4400, it would need to move by roughly 48 points merely to compensate for the expenses incurred in such a 'round trip'.

In contrast, with FT-SE futures, the bid-offer spread on each leg of the round trip is around one index point, as is the total round-trip commission. Also, no Stamp Duty should be payable under current tax rules. Hence for each £44,000 that is 'round-tripped', dealing in futures might cost roughly £30 compared with approximately £480 – a vast reduction in cost!

In addition, consider what would need to happen if the fund manager wished to change exposure quickly. With futures the trade could be done in a few minutes, with just one deal ticket. Effectively all the stocks would be dealt in at the same time. In contrast, the problems posed by dealing in 100 individual stocks at times of rapidly changing prices – plus the effort of booking, checking and settling all these trades, registering and perhaps claiming dividends, scrip issues, etc – are obvious.

Moreover the required change in UK equity exposure might involve a compensating change in exposure to gilts or some specified overseas equity market(s). Appropriate futures contracts can also be used for the other side of such asset allocation switches.

6.5 PRICING FUTURES CONTRACTS

Investors who buy FT-SE futures will make or lose money depending on market movements in much the same fashion as investors who buy actual stock. However, purchasers of the futures will be able to earn interest on the cash they do not need to use to invest in the market, although they will not receive the dividend yield that holding the shares would generate.

If the interest on cash is 4% per annum and the dividend yield is 3% per annum then the use of futures saves what is known as the *cost of carry* of:

$$4\% - 3\% = 1\% \text{ per annum.}$$

For FT-SE futures with, say, three months before they expire (and if, say, dividend payments on the index are spread uniformly over the year), the cost of carry would then be 1% divided by four, ie 0.25%. So if the FT-SE index were, say, 4400 then the *fair value* of the futures contract, allowing for this cost of carry, would be 4411. The futures contract will in general trade at a price which differs from this fair value, but not normally by very much, because otherwise arbitrageurs would become active bringing the actual price back closer to the contract's fair value.

6.6 WHAT IS AN OPTION?

Options are more versatile than futures contracts, but this also makes them more complicated.

There are two main types of options, called *calls* and *puts*. Again, it is possible to both buy and sell either sort of option – indeed for every buyer there must also be a seller of the relevant option.

A *buyer* of a call option has the *right*, but *not the obligation*, for a specified term to buy an agreed quantity of a particular asset at a stipulated price (from the option seller, otherwise known as the option writer). The stipulated price is called the *exercise price* or the *strike price*.

A *buyer* of a put option has the *right*, but *not the obligation*, for a specified term to sell an agreed quantity of a particular asset at a stipulated price.

An investor who buys an option, whether a call or a put, will not lose more than the option premium paid because he does not need to exercise the option if the asset price moves in the opposite direction from that anticipated. Potential profit from the option in isolation can be virtually unlimited.

Conversely, an option writer will not make more profit than the option premium received, unless the option buyer behaves irrationally. Potential losses from the option in isolation can, however, be virtually unlimited. At first sight writing options would appear to be a very risky strategy. However, if the option is 'covered' (see 6.2) then losses from the written option should be compensated for by profits on the asset used to cover the option. For example, if an investor holds stock and writes a call option on that stock then if the market rises a loss arises from the option, but it is counteracted by a gain on the stock held by the option writer. In effect the writer has foregone market upside (since the option buyer can buy the stocks off the writer at a fixed price even if the stocks rise above this level in value). In return, the option writer receives some premium income.

Two principal classes of options are recognised:

(1) 'American-style' options, which can be exercised at any time up to the expiry date of the option; and
(2) 'European-style' options, which can be exercised only at the expiry date.

These terms no longer have any relationship to the geographical area to which the options relate or from which they originate.

6.7 PRICING OPTIONS CONTRACTS

Calculating a fair value for an option is more difficult than calculating a fair value for a futures contract. The reason is that the value of an option depends in part on how likely it is for the option to be exercised. The price of an option also depends, *inter alia*, on the time to expiry, interest rates, volatility of the stock to which the option relates and the current stock price in relation to the option's exercise price.

By far the most important tool used to value and price options is the Black-Scholes option pricing formula. This provides a theoretical fair value, C, for a European-style call option that depends on the sorts of factors described above. The formula is:

$$C = S.N(d_1) - X.\exp(-rT).N(d_2)$$

$$where:\quad d_1 = \frac{\ln(S/X) + (r + \sigma^2/2)T}{\sigma\sqrt{T}}$$

$$d_2 = d_1 - \sigma\sqrt{T}$$

S = current stock price
X = exercise price of option
T = time to expiry of option
r = risk-free interest rate (ie return on cash)
σ = standard deviation of stock price (measuring how volatile the stock is)
$\exp(x)$ = exponential function
$\ln(x)$ = natural logarithm function
$N(x)$ = cumulative probability density function for a standardised normal distribution*

* We should expect there to be some dependency on a probability distribution since the fair price depends in part on how likely it is that the option will be exercised.

Although these mathematical functions look complicated, they are all available within modern spreadsheet packages such as Microsoft Excel. It is therefore reasonably straightforward to calculate the Black-Scholes price within such a package, as long as suitable estimates of the parameters on which it depends are available, for example the rate of return available on risk-free investments and the volatility of the underlying stock price. The formula requires the stock not to be dividend paying, but there are reasonably straightforward adjustments that can be made if the stock does provide dividends.

There is a similar formula for the fair value, P, of a European-style put option. It can also be found using a relationship called 'put–call parity', ie:

$$S + P = C + X.\exp(-rT)$$

Put–call parity recognises the equivalence between buying a stock and a put now, and holding cash and buying a call now to be exercised at the same specified future date. The ultimate pay-off from either strategy at expiry is the same, and therefore the two should also have the same value.

Although the Black-Scholes formula provides the conceptual basis for a large number of option pricing approaches, it is widely accepted within the market that it does not in isolation provide a complete explanation of actual market prices. For example, call options that are out-of-the-money (ie would not be exercised immediately, ie $S<X$) tend to trade at prices that require a higher volatility assumption (implied volatility) than call options that are at-the-money ($S=X$) or in-the-money ($S>X$). Also, the Black-Scholes formula applies only to European-style, not American-style, options. For more complicated options it is nearly always necessary to modify the formula in some way, usually increasing the complexity of the mathematics involved. Indeed, derivative pricing experts are often jokingly called rocket scientists by others in the investment field, because of the high level of mathematical skills they often possess.

6.8 OVER-THE-COUNTER OPTIONS

Options traded on recognised exchanges are restricted to specified assets, strike prices and expiry dates. The sorts of assets on which options are available range from specific shares (eg BA) or market indices (eg FT-SE). Usually there will be a range of strike prices and expiry dates available for any given asset, but most of the liquidity, ie dealing, would be concentrated in contracts which have the shorter periods to expiry and have strike prices quite close to current market levels.

Options not traded on recognised exchanges are called over-the-counter (OTC). These permit much greater flexibility in contract design, including the ability to incorporate more complicated pay-off characteristics, and thus permit the option to be tailored to the investor's precise requirements.

Often, options will be used purely as a way of implementing an investment view. However, option activity may be driven more by concerns over liabilities than assets. For example, a fund manager or insurance company may launch a retail guaranteed equity fund or bond that provides to the investor a guarantee of no capital loss, but also promises to give the investor a set percentage of any rise in the market over, say, a five-year period. The provider of the fund/bond can then match this liability (and thus avoid the risk of not being able to provide the stated guarantee) by buying a suitable option from an investment bank.

6.9 WHAT IS A SWAP, AND HOW IS IT PRICED?

The most common equity derivatives are futures and options. The exposures bought and sold via equity derivatives often exceed those bought and sold via transactions in the underlying equities. However, even these volumes are relatively small compared to the volumes transacted in the swaps markets.

In a swap, one party agrees to pay the other one sort of cashflow stream, receiving a different sort of cashflow stream in return. The most common sort of swap is a fixed for floating rate swap. In this contract, there will be some agreed principal sum, for example £100m. The first party will then agree to pay the interest receipts receivable were this sum to be invested in cash, which for large sums will vary up and down in line with what is known as LIBOR, the London Interbank Offered Rate. In return the second party will pay a fixed rate, for example 5% per annum (ie £5m per annum) for the lifetime of the swap, which might be up to 40 years, say.

For example, a corporation might be willing to enter into this sort of transaction in order to help it fix more precisely its likely borrowing costs. It might borrow money at today's variable interest rate, but avoid the risk of this interest rate rising substantially by swapping fixed payments in return for the floating rates it needs to service this debt. Fixed for floating rate swaps are also used extensively by building societies and the like if they are offering fixed rate mortgages to their customers (since they will generally need to pay floating rates to their depositors).

Practically any sort of cashflow can be swapped in this fashion. For example, the swap could involve paying away the return achieved on the FT-SE Index in return for the (floating) return available from cash. By entering into such a swap, the investor would shed exposure to the UK equity market and gain exposure to cash instead, much like the result of selling a FT-SE futures contract.

Not surprisingly, the fair price of such a swap can thus be calculated in a manner similar to that used for futures contracts. Swap contracts that contain *optionality*, i.e. some element of option-like behaviour, are more complicated to value and require techniques of the sort mentioned at 6.7.

6.10 THE USE OF SWAPS FOR 'LIABILITY DRIVEN INVESTMENT'

Over the coming years pension funds and insurers are likely to increase their use of derivatives. Regulatory changes for insurers and accounting rule changes for pension funds are, amongst other factors, encouraging such institutions to invest their assets more closely in line with their liabilities. However, their liabilities often contain guarantees and other characteristics that are not easily replicated by readily available *physical* investments. So institutions are increasingly investigating whether bespoke derivatives might help them match their liabilities better. For example, final salary pension fund liabilities extend so far into the future that it is difficult to buy bonds with a sufficiently long term or *duration* to match these liabilities. The derivatives market has a history of enormous innovation and it is now possible to buy derivative instruments that more closely match these sorts of liability characteristics.

6.11 CONCLUSION

The difficulties of Barings, Sumitomo and Orange County among others have shown what can happen when the fundamental principles of trading in derivatives are forgotten by operators. However, when sensibly used, derivatives are a useful investment management tool, providing quick, cheap and efficient ways of shifting between different asset categories and managing risk exposures.

SOURCES OF FURTHER INFORMATION

The London International Financial Futures and Options Exchange (LIFFE)
Cannon Bridge
London EC4R 3XX

Tel: (020) 7623 0444
Fax: (020) 7588 3624
Web: www.liffe.com

7

INVESTMENT TRUSTS

Updated for this edition by
PAUL WRIGHT
Zurich Financial Services

7.1 INTRODUCTION

Collective investment media enable investors to pool their resources to create a common fund for investment by professional managers. The two great benefits of this collective approach to investment are:

(1) more efficient and economical investment management; and
(2) greater security through the spreading of risk over a diverse range of investments.

To meet these needs, various different media, eg investment trusts, unit trusts, OEICs and offshore funds (see Chapter 8) and insurance bonds (see Chapter 14) have evolved from separate legal and financial origins, subject to varying regulation and tax treatment. In practice, the choice between the different media may depend on the investor's convenience as much as the features of the collective media, which are increasingly given a 'level playing field' by regulations. Nevertheless there are still some marked differences in the ways these investments are marketed, priced and taxed, quite apart from the management of the underlying assets.

The most straightforward and flexible of these media is the investment trust, which is actually not really a trust but simply a limited company in which investors buy shares and other securities so as to benefit indirectly from its assets and income. An investment trust is constrained by its authorised capital, which cannot readily be changed or repaid to shareholders, and the shares are generally bought and sold by investors on the Stock Exchange at market prices determined only by supply and demand.

7.2 HISTORICAL BACKGROUND

The first investment trust to be established in England was the Foreign and Colonial Government Trust, created as a trust in 1868 and, owing to doubts concerning the legality of its original structure, reorganised in 1879 as a public limited liability company under the Companies Act 1862. The Trust's original objective was, in the words of its initial prospectus, to provide '. . . the investor of moderate means the same advantage as the large capitalists in diminishing risk in foreign and colonial stocks by spreading the investment over a number of stocks'. By the early twentieth century, a number of other investment trust companies had been incorporated in England and Scotland and the investment trust had become firmly established in the UK as an investment medium. Some of these early trusts (including The Foreign and Colonial Investment Trust plc which is now a constituent of the FTSE 100 index) still exist today despite two World Wars and many serious economic crises. During the last 100 years, investment trust companies have provided much new capital for UK businesses by underwriting or subscribing for public issues of securities and accepting private placings, thus giving important support to capital investment in the UK.

Investment trusts are probably the most flexible of the collective media, free to invest in any kind of assets, and the individual companies and the securities that they issue vary widely. In comparison with the other media, two distinctive characteristics are their ability to 'gear up' their sensitivity to the markets by borrowing, and the fact that the shares are generally priced by supply and demand in the market at significantly less than the value of the investment trust's underlying assets. Both these factors tend to make these trusts more sensitive to movements in the markets as a whole, while still spreading the specific risks of investments in individual stocks.

As explained in 7.7, certain CGT concessions are given to those investment trusts that have been approved by the Revenue. To obtain approval the investment trust must, among other requirements, be resident for tax purposes in the UK and have its ordinary share capital listed on the Stock Exchange. This chapter deals primarily with investment trusts that have been so approved for tax purposes and have been incorporated in the UK. Unapproved investment trusts can generally be treated like any other company.

7.3 RECENT DEVELOPMENTS

The recent bear market for equities has been a difficult period for investment trusts with net asset values falling. Prices of trusts have generally fallen even more as the discounts to assets which most trusts trade at has typically widened. Those trusts where the asset value performed particularly poorly have also seen the greatest widening of discounts confirming that performance is the key determinant of discount changes.

The split capital sector has gone from bad to worse with 19 trusts suspending trading in their shares by the end of 2002. Of these nine have called in receivers. A combination of high gearing (see 7.6.5) and cross-shareholdings in other split capital trusts has proven to be a disastrous combination in a falling market.

In recent years a number of split capital trusts have tried to enhance their returns by investing in classes of securities issued by other split capital trusts. This is a risky business at the best of times and introduces an element of systemic risk. During periods of market turbulence, if one trust should fail it would have a knock-on effect on those trusts which had invested in it and so on.

The main lesson to be learnt from these recent developments is that the quality of the underlying portfolio is crucial (see 7.4.4) and that each class of security will have its own profile of risk and reward which an investor needs to be aware of when making an investment.

The difficult market conditions of the last few years has resulted in the boards of investment trusts taking a more critical view of their managers' performance and in some cases this has led to managers being replaced.

7.4 LEGAL NATURE

7.4.1 Constitution

An investment trust is a limited liability company with a share capital, and is a legal entity separate from its shareholders or managers. In practice the trusts are often promoted and managed by fund management groups who run a number of investment trusts and other funds that, in some cases, own the management group. All trusts must now have a majority of non-executive directors, according to AITC (Association of Investment Trust Companies) guidelines. However, the shareholders are always entitled to vote to replace the management, and there has been much takeover activity in the industry.

Like any limited company, an investment trust company is constituted by the contract with its shareholders contained in its memorandum and articles of association. The memoranda of investment trusts usually contain wide powers to invest the company's funds in securities and property and to borrow, but, for tax reasons, commonly prohibit trading (as opposed to investing) in securities or property; and their articles of association normally contain a provision prohibiting the distribution of capital profits by way of dividend. However, approved status for tax purposes (see 7.7) requires certain practical limitations on the exercise of these wide investment powers.

An investment trust itself, like any limited company, is not permitted to advertise its shares for sale except by reference to Listing Particulars, registered with the Registrar of Companies and complying with the Financial Services Act. However, managers will eagerly respond to enquiries, and increasingly advertise schemes to facilitate investment. Further advice and information are available from stockbrokers, through whom the shares are often bought, and from the AITC (see Useful addresses at the end of this chapter).

7.4.2 Investment trust securities

Investments are made by buying stocks, shares and warrants of the trusts. Apart from ordinary shares, a trust may issue debenture stock (secured by a charge on its assets), unsecured loan stock, preference shares or warrants. The holders of such securities are entitled to receive interest or preference dividends at the applicable rate before any dividends are paid to the ordinary shareholders. These securities may, in the long run, prove less profitable, but are more secure since, on a winding-up of the company, the ordinary shareholders are entitled only to any surplus assets remaining after payment of all other liabilities, including the repayment of principal and income due to holders of loan capital or preference shares. If an investment trust has a high proportion of its capital in the form of loan capital and preference shares, major fluctuations in the value of the underlying assets attributable to the holders of its equity share capital can result. This topic is discussed in more detail at 7.6.5. (Debenture stocks, loan stocks and preference shares are discussed at 3.3.)

Warrants are securities that give the holder the right (without obligation) to subscribe for shares subsequently on fixed terms: in the meantime the warrants are themselves listed investments the market price of which will change rapidly according to the prices of the underlying shares, but in most cases without yielding an income. For example, suppose a warrant entitles the holder to subscribe for certain investment trust shares at 95p each. If the shares are currently worth £1, the warrant will trade at about 5p. In practice the majority of warrants will trade at a premium to their intrinsic value, because of time value. If the shares rise by 10% to £1.10, the warrants should rise 200% to 15p; conversely, if the shares fall by 10% to 90p, the warrants would be practically worthless. Warrants, through their gearing, clearly offer a more volatile capital investment in the success of an investment trust than its ordinary shares (see also 3.4).

7.4.3 Split capital trusts

As well as issuing all the usual company securities, investment trusts can also go further and, instead of ordinary shares, issue their capital split into different issues tailor-made for different kinds of investors.

In most ordinary companies, directors generally have considerable freedom over how much dividend to distribute out of profits, and are only expected to manage their dividend policy to provide growing dividends indefinitely; such companies are not expected to be wound up, and shareholders' rights in a liquidation are largely academic. Investment trusts must distribute most of their income and none of their capital profits for tax reasons, although to some extent they can manage what proportion of profits are receivable as income.

However, some 110 split capital trusts are constituted with separate classes of shares that will be repaid (or at the least, the question will be put to a vote of shareholders) at a fixed date. Each class of share capital has specified entitlements to dividends in the meanwhile and to capital distributions, in a stated order of priority between the classes of shares, and the directors have very little discretion over the application of whatever profits they make. While the total performance of the investment trust will always depend on the success of its investment managers, each class of shares will have relatively more or less predictable expectations, designed to be particularly valuable to certain kinds of investors. These benefits can make the total value of the trust's securities higher than if it simply issued one class of ordinary shares.

The earliest split capital trusts have capital shares, which provide no dividend income at all but the right at liquidation to all capital gains within the trust, and income shares, which distribute the entire trust's net income but will be repaid at the liquidation date normally at their issue price. The prices of each share will reflect the demand from investors, taking account of the specified rights of *all* prior classes of shares and other securities. Thus, the income shares offer a very high running yield, suitable for ISAs or for trustees paying a widow's annuity, while the capital shares would attract a higher rate taxpayer approaching retirement.

7.4.4 Specialised split capital investment trust securities

Investment trusts are free to create any kind of securities for their investors, and the principle has been used to design shares with sophisticated characteristics that require individual analysis of exactly what is offered and the security that will be obtained. These securities can be superbly efficient investments, but it is quite inadequate and highly dangerous merely to rely on the names of such specialised securities, and investors must consider the rights of both their own intended shares and all other securities that will have priority in any situation, together with current circumstances that change after the securities are issued. Some kinds of income shares have little or no capital entitlement, and other preference shares can have index-linked or other formula-based income. Each class of security will have its own profile of risk and reward, ranging from a preferred stock many times covered by assets, to highly speculative zero coupon shares. The latter should not be confused with zero dividend preference shares or zero coupon debentures, which are actually relatively 'safe' (see below). Needless to say, the value of these securities will depend ultimately on the success of the managers' investment policy, but to very differing extents. The only real rule is that, inevitably, the sum of the rights of all classes of issued capital is equal to the trust's total net capital and income. Thus, at the end of the queue on each distribution, one class of shares will have the most uncertain outcome, in effect securing all the prior entitlements; and naturally such risky securities will be priced to earn, on average, the highest expected rewards.

Among these more sophisticated securities are the following.

Zero dividend preference shares

This is a relatively low-risk investment suitable for financing future capital sums without income tax liability in the meanwhile, such as school fees. The risk can be assessed by measuring how many times the capital repayment is covered by net assets, ie how much the managers can lose without affecting the repayment at all.

Capital entitlements: a fixed capital return payable on liquidation.
Income: nil.

Income shares and annuity shares

It is essential to check exactly what type of share is being considered. These shares can be particularly appropriate for non-taxpayers, in ISAs, or for non-working spouses. In many cases, a gross redemption yield can be calculated and compared with that on the nearest equivalent gilt-edged securities, taking account of the different levels of risk.

Capital entitlements:

(1) the original split capital trusts repay a fixed amount on liquidation, and their income share price will fall towards this value as this date approaches, eg traditional income shares that are issued at £1 and repaid at £1 would normally see their share price increase in the early years, as dividend growth increases the yield, before falling towards their final value in the latter years;

(2) some more recent issues are also entitled to part of any capital appreciation, after prior classes of shares are satisfied;

(3) a very different type, sometimes called annuity shares, have little capital entitlement that may be as low as 1p, or even less.

Income: these shares have exceptionally high running yields, benefiting from the income gearing probably by other classes of capital such as zero coupon shares and capital shares that do not rank for dividends.

Stepped preference shares

Another relatively low-risk security having priority over ordinary shares and most other classes, giving a known growing income and capital return if held to redemption (hence redemption yields can be calculated and compared with government securities).

Capital entitlements: a fixed capital return payable on liquidation.
Income: a predetermined dividend rising at a specified rate (eg 5% pa).

Geared income shares

Otherwise known as highly geared ordinary shares, or income and residual capital shares. These shares are typically in structures with zero dividend preference shares or RPI-linked debentures. They are, effectively, a combination of income shares and capital shares and offer a high level of running yield and geared capital exposure.

7.4.5 Flexible investment vehicles

The flexibility of investment trusts to issue innovative securities using sophisticated financial structures should enable them to continue competing effectively against less flexible investment media. This flexibility in the hands of professional managers should ensure they remain efficient and attractive investment vehicles for small and large investors alike.

The last few years have seen a stronger level of activity in venture capital trusts (VCTs). VCTs are not really typical of investment trusts generally, but merely happen to use the flexible form of an investment trust for a special purpose vehicle. A VCT, like any investment trust, is exempt from CGT, so that VCTs themselves will be broadly tax neutral. However, in addition, investment in a VCT is free of income tax and CGT, like an ISA; investors will receive income tax relief on subscriptions into new VCTs, and capital gains on other investments which would otherwise be chargeable to tax can be rolled over into a VCT investment within six months before or after realisation. Note that CGT rollover is a deferral, not a cancellation of the tax liability. The limit of

£100,000 investment pa is far more generous than for ISAs, but tax relief is only available if held for three years.

A VCT, like an investment trust, is a listed public company specially approved by the Revenue, which must derive its income 'wholly or mainly' (in practice, at least 70%) from securities; but which must also within three years of approval invest at least 70% of its assets in 'qualifying holdings' in unquoted UK trading companies. At least 30% of a VCT's investments overall must be in ordinary shares, with the balance in other share capital or long-term debt. A VCT may invest a maximum of £1m pa in any one trading company, which may not be larger than £11m immediately after the investment, and must not be controlled by the VCT or anyone else. No holding may exceed 15% of the VCT. The detailed requirements for the trading companies are comparable to those for the Enterprise Investment Scheme, such as the requirement for the investment to be used in trading within 12 months.

All the VCT's investments must be new, ie initial subscription of shares or debt (although listing on the AIM is allowed, as is subsequent admission to listing). Like an approved investment trust, a VCT must retain 15% of its income, but it may also choose to distribute capital profits (see 7.7.1).

7.5 CONDITIONS FOR PURCHASE

There are in general no limitations on the purchase of UK investment trust shares. Investors must satisfy any restrictions imposed by their own powers (eg as trustees) or any foreign laws to which they are subject. Investment trusts are normally a wider-range investment under the Trustee Investments Act, and collective investment media generally help to satisfy trustees' duty of diversification.

7.6 CHARACTERISTICS

All investment trusts have the same legal structure in common, but its flexibility gives an enormous range of very different investment vehicles, both as to the underlying investment management of the trust and the interests that investors can take. As well as traditional general trusts directly comparable with conservatively regulated unit trusts and insurance bonds, there are highly specialised issues tailor-made for particular purposes and suitable only for sophisticated or expertly advised investors of the appropriate type (see 7.4.4).

7.6.1 Spread of risk and flexibility

An important feature of investment trust shares, like other collective investments, is the spread of risk that can be achieved by the investor. Investment trust shares represent an indirect interest in all of the trust's underlying assets, which can give the small investor a well-balanced portfolio with a good spread of risk that would be too expensive and impracticable to obtain and manage by direct investment. But larger investors (personal or corporate) also invest through investment trusts in order to obtain professional or specialised investment management, currency management or gearing, and their attention to the trust's management of their interests may benefit all shareholders.

The wide investment powers of most investment trusts enable them, subject to the limitations acceptable for tax purposes, to follow a reasonably flexible investment policy. In response to changes in investment or fiscal conditions, they can adjust the emphasis in their portfolios on income or capital appreciation or on a particular sector of the market or geographical location. In addition, they are able, within limits, to invest in real property (although usually through the securities of listed property companies), in shares of unlisted companies and in other assets and, although they do not trade in securities themselves for tax reasons, they may establish dealing subsidiaries to take short-term positions in securities. Owing to FSA regulations, an authorised unit trust must necessarily have a less flexible investment policy than that of an investment trust.

The basic investment characteristics of any investment trust are stated in its prospectus and may be indicated in its name. However, since investment trusts are flexible vehicles and investment conditions are constantly changing, a better indication of an investment trust's current policy can be obtained from its latest report and accounts.

As well as its investment objectives and financial record, another vital characteristic of an investment trust is its size. A small investment trust may be able to outperform a larger one by adopting a more flexible investment policy, but its shares could be less marketable than those of a bigger trust, with a greater spread between buying and selling prices.

7.6.2 Income and capital gains

The total returns from an investment traditionally are assessed as income and capital gains, but in an age where the marginal rates of tax on income and capital gains are similar the distinction is rather artificial, and the balance between the two can be adjusted deliberately (eg by selling securities cum- or ex-dividend). However, in general, dividend income is usually more predictable than capital performance, not least because it is often managed actively for consistency. Income and capital gains from investments are taxed differently and may be owned separately, so the balance between the two is very significant to many investors. Some markets, for example in the Far East and continental Europe, offer negligible dividend yields and correspondingly greater expectations of gains, but investment trusts may be chosen with a wide range of dividend policies.

As previously mentioned, the majority of warrants yield no income at all, which can be useful, for example to parents who would otherwise be liable to income tax on investments given to their children.

Most investors are free to adjust the 'income' they draw from their investments, either by reinvesting surplus net dividends or by regularly selling shares to supplement the dividend yield. So far from being improvident, this is often a very sound strategy: up to £8,200 capital gains pa can be taken free of tax, in addition to the income tax allowances. Provided the withdrawals do not exceed the capital gains (often profits retained within the trusts), the value of the investment will not be eroded. Note that if one sells discounted assets to realise a capital gain and provide a running income, then one can erode one's capital base markedly.

7.6.3 Investment overseas and currency management

Although most investment trusts adopt a flexible investment policy and are not rigidly committed to maintaining a particular proportion of their investments in any one geographical area, some of them specialise in one or more overseas area in which they maintain special knowledge and investment expertise. These trusts provide a useful medium for overseas investment that often presents practical difficulties for direct investors.

Many trusts use foreign currency loans for overseas investment, so that the trusts' exposure to the foreign exchange markets can be managed independently of the investments made in any country. At the same time the trust may be geared-up (see 7.6.5), but whenever the managers choose to reduce the trust's exposure to the market they can simply make a sterling deposit to remove the gearing.

For example, a foreign investment that gains by 20% in local currency terms would still show a 20% sterling loss if the exchange rate fell by a third. However, if the managers borrow the amount of the investment locally and the exchange rate falls, the liability to repay is reduced along with the assets. At the same time the trust's original capital remains intact, and could also be invested in any market.

Another, sometimes cheaper way of hedging against exchange rate exposure is the 'currency swap' under which a UK investment trust swaps an amount in sterling with, say, a US company for an equivalent amount of

US dollars. The US dollars received by the investment trust are used for portfolio investment. At the end of the agreed period the investment trust simply hands back the same amount of dollars to the US company in return for the sterling amount agreed at the outset. The risk of a default by the other party is limited to the possible exchange loss and attributable expenses, and both companies avoid the expenses of using a bank as intermediary.

The investment trust has always been a useful medium for overseas investment by UK residents because such investment is a difficult matter for most private investors, having regard to the distances involved, foreign market and settlement practices and the taxation and other problems that may arise in the overseas territories concerned. The average UK investor does not have sufficient resources to manage his UK investments effectively, let alone a portfolio of overseas investments.

7.6.4 Stock market price and underlying net asset value

The market prices of investment trust shares are dictated by supply and demand and for many years have generally stood at a discount to the value of their underlying net assets. These discounts and valuations are published regularly for most trusts. Investment trusts still often stand at a price in the stock market that is 10% or 20% lower than the estimated amount per share that would be paid to shareholders on a liquidation of the company. The obvious explanation for these substantial discounts is a lack of demand for investment trust shares in the market. It is owing, in part, to lack of publicity, competition from pension and insurance funds and unit trusts (whose managers are free to advertise their units for sale and to offer commissions to selling agents) and the fact that investment trust shares are often held by long-term investors. All these factors have contributed towards a comparatively low level of regular dealing activity in investment trust shares and so reduced their marketability. It also seems that as institutional fund management has become more sophisticated, their appetite for investment trust shares has diminished.

To realise the profit inherent in the discount on net asset value (NAV), a number of investment trust companies have been reconstructed by their managers, taken over by other companies, placed in voluntary liquidation or 'unitised'. Unitisation is a scheme under which the shareholders pass a special resolution to wind up the investment trust and transfer its investments to an authorised unit trust or OEIC in exchange for units or shares, respectively. Subject to Revenue clearance, unitisation does not of itself involve the investment trust shareholders in any liability to CGT and on a subsequent disposal of units in the authorised unit trust, the acquisition cost of those units for CGT purposes is the original acquisition cost of the shares in the investment trust from which the units arose. Following uni-tisation, the former shareholders in the investment trust can sell their new units in the authorised unit trust at a price based on the unit trust's under-lying assets (see Chapter 8) and so the discount effectively will have been eliminated, although one needs to be aware of dealing costs and the bid/offer spreads.

The discount on NAV has also been eliminated for some investment trust shareholders by takeover offers being made for their shares at prices near their underlying NAV. Some of these takeover offers have been made by predator companies, while others have been made by institu-tions (eg pension funds) that see the acquisition of an investment trust company as an inexpensive means of acquiring a 'ready-made' invest-ment portfolio and perhaps eliminating a competitor. However, a takeover, unlike a unitisation, may unexpectedly crystallise a CGT lia-bility, though most will offer a tax-efficient rollover.

If the discount is eliminated in one of these ways, or simply narrows as a result of increased market demand, it will be beneficial to holders who bought their shares at a discount and can sell at a price nearer to the NAV. When investors come to sell their shares, so long as the discount is not larger than when they bought them, they should not suffer loss solely by reason of its existence, and in the meantime will have benefited from the income on the undiscounted or gross assets.

Another factor that will affect the stock market price of investment trust shares is the market-maker's turn, ie the difference between the higher offer price (at which the market-maker is prepared to sell to the investor) and the lower bid price (at which the market-maker is prepared to buy from the investor). The spread between the market-maker's bid and offer price will usually be wider in the case of shares of the smaller, less mar-ketable trusts. Note that spreads are actually very narrow, and much narrower than bid/offer spreads on unit trusts.

This assumes that there is a sufficient market for the shares to enable them to be sold at all. In practice, a small investor in most of the larger investment trusts should not experience any difficulty in disposing of his or her shares at close to current market prices.

7.6.5 Gearing

In addition to its equity share capital, an investment trust may raise fur-ther capital by issuing debenture or loan stocks or preference shares and borrow money in sterling and foreign currencies. On a liquidation of the investment trust, holders of such stocks or preference shares and lenders of funds to the investment trust are entitled to repayment of fixed amounts of capital or principal from the trust's assets in priority to equity shareholders. Only the surplus assets remaining, after discharge by the investment trust of all its other liabilities, are distributable to the equity shareholders. In effect, any increase or decrease in the value of the investment trust's assets is attributable primarily to one or more classes of its equity share capital. An overall increase or decrease has a greater effect on the underlying value of its equity share capital in the case of a trust that has raised most of its capital in the form of loans or preference shares than in the case of a trust that has raised most of its capital by issues of equity shares. In UK securities terminology, if the proportion of a company's capital that has been raised in the form of loans and preference shares is large in relation to its equity capital, the company is described as 'highly geared' and, if small, the company's gearing is said to be low; the US term is 'leverage'. Gearing levels of 10–15% would normally be regarded as moderate for an investment trust. For conventionally structured trusts (ie excluding geared ordinary or capital shares in splits), gearing in excess of 30% would be considered high.

The following examples illustrate the consequences of gearing; taxation and other factors have been ignored in the interests of simplicity.

Example 1: Ungeared trust

A new ungeared investment trust raises £1m by an issue of equity shares and invests the proceeds of the share issue in a portfolio of securities. If the portfolio's value doubles to £2m, the trust assets attributable to the equity shareholders will increase 100%. If the portfolio halves, the net value for ordinary shareholders will, likewise, decrease by 50%.

Example 2: Geared trust

Suppose a new geared investment trust raises £1m by (a) issuing 500,000 preference shares at £1 each and (b) issuing equity shares at an aggregate price of £0.5m, and then invests the total proceeds of £1m in a portfolio of securities. If the portfolio doubles in value to £2m, on liquidation the investment trust will have to pay £0.5m to the preference shareholders; but, after this payment, the amount attributable to the trust's equity shares will have increased by 200% from £0.5m to £1.5m. On the other hand, if the portfolio's value halves, the preference shareholders will be repaid £0.5m, leaving nothing for the ordinary shareholders – a 100% loss.

The ability of investment trusts to gear their portfolios in this manner is one of the principal differences between investment trusts and unit trusts. The latter have only very limited powers to borrow money without gearing up.

Examples 1 and 2 illustrate the effect of gearing on an investment trust's capital assets but, if the lenders of money to an investment trust or its preference shareholders are entitled to payment of interest or dividends at a fixed rate, gearing will also have an effect on the income of the trust from its investments that is distributable to its equity shareholders. An increase (or decrease) in the income arising from a geared trust's investments will have a greater impact on the amount of income available for distribution to equity shareholders of the trust by way of dividend than will a similar fluctuation in the income of an ungeared trust.

Equity shareholders of investment trusts will benefit from investing in highly geared investment trusts when the assets in which those trusts have invested are rising in value, but they are at greater risk when such assets are falling in value. One of the more difficult tasks of a professional investment manager is to utilise gearing successfully. The investment manager must decide when to gear up the trust and when to undertake a rapid 'de-gearing' exercise by repaying borrowings or turning substantial portions of the investment portfolio into cash or assets that are not likely to fluctuate significantly in value.

7.7 TAXATION: APPROVED INVESTMENT TRUSTS

7.7.1 Approval of investment trusts

Only 'approved' investment trusts (and authorised unit trusts) attract the CGT exemption outlined below. An approved investment trust is one that is not a 'close company' and that, in respect of an accounting period, has been approved by the Board of Inland Revenue. The Revenue appears to have discretion to withhold approval, even in the case of an investment trust that would otherwise qualify, but it will approve a company that can show that:

(1) it is resident for taxation purposes in the UK;
(2) its income is derived wholly or mainly (which in practice means approximately 70% or more) from shares or securities, or from eligible rental income, or from any combination of the two;
(3) no holding in a company (other than another approved investment trust or a company that would qualify as such but for the fact its shares are not listed as required by (4) below) represents more than 15% by value of its investments;
(4) all its ordinary share capital is listed on The Stock Exchange;
(5) the distribution as dividend of capital profits on the sale of its investments is prohibited by its memorandum or articles of association; and

(6) not more than 15% of its income from securities is retained unless legally required.

It is expressly provided that an increase in the value of a holding after it has been acquired will not result in an infringement of the 15% limit referred to in (3) above. However, the holdings of an investment trust in its subsidiary companies are treated as a single holding for the purposes of this limit, as are its holdings in other companies that are members of the same group of companies. In addition, any loans made by the trust to its subsidiaries are treated as part of its investment in the subsidiaries for the purposes of ascertaining whether the limit has been infringed.

7.7.2 Capital gains

Investment trusts are corporations and their income is subject to corporation tax in the same manner and at the same rates as other corporations, but capital gains accruing to approved investment trusts are wholly exempt from CGT in the hands of the trust. Thus active management of the trust's investments need not be constrained by tax on realising gains and the investor may only be subject to tax on disposing of his investment trust shares.

7.7.3 Income

The taxation of the trust's own income, and of the income and gains of investors in the trust, is exactly the same as for other limited companies (see Chapter 3). The corporation tax system is complicated and a detailed explanation of it is outside the scope of this book, but a brief summary may help.

Income

Franked investment income

This is income received by a trust in the form of dividends paid by a UK company. Franked investment income is not liable to corporation tax in the hands of the trust.

Unfranked income

This is all other income (eg interest on bonds, rental income, bank deposit interest and dividends paid by foreign companies). Interest paid by the trust and the fees paid to its investment managers are set primarily against unfranked income, reducing the amount liable to tax.

7.8 TAXATION: UNAPPROVED INVESTMENT COMPANIES

Unless an investment company has the status of an approved investment trust (see 7.7.1), it is subject to ordinary forms of corporate taxation and will not qualify for the CGT exemption mentioned at 7.7.2. Thus both the investment income and capital gains made by such a company will be taxed, under the terms of FA 1987, at the corporation tax rate. Under TA 1988, a close investment holding company does not qualify for the small companies rate. In addition, if an investment company disposes of its assets and is then liquidated there is effectively a double CGT charge, because:

(1) the company will be liable to corporation tax on capital gains realised by it on the disposal; and
(2) its shareholders will be liable to CGT for any capital gains realised by them on the disposal of their shares in the investment company, which will occur by reason of the distribution of cash proceeds to them in the liquidation.

(Considerations affecting investment in a private investment company are discussed at 13.4.)

Having regard to these disadvantages and to the fact that, so long as the investment company continues in existence, profits on the sale of investments may only be distributed to its shareholders by way of comparatively highly taxed dividends, the investment company has become unpopular as an investment medium. In fact, in order to mitigate this unsatisfactory taxation position, many unapproved investment companies have been 'unitised' (see 7.6.4). The advantage of unitisation is that it defers the capital gains liability on the company shares until the ultimate disposal of the units issued on unitisation, which may be spread over several years to take full advantage of the annual CGT exemptions.

7.9 SUITABILITY

Investment trusts are a suitable investment medium for small and large investors who are resident in the UK for tax purposes, who wish to spread their investment risk and who do not have the expertise or the resources to make direct investments. However, the investor in investment trusts should be aware of the possible advantages and disadvantages that may result from the existence of the discount on NAV (see 7.6.4) and from the ability of investment trusts to gear their portfolios (see 7.6.5). If the investor is unwilling to accept the risk involved for the sake of the possible greater rewards, the unit trust or OEIC is probably a more suitable investment medium. Yet investment trusts have frequently shown better long-term returns than unit trusts. Split capital trusts are highly suitable for the investors for whom they are designed, but more care must be taken accordingly.

7.10 MECHANICS

Investment trust shares may be bought in new issues or acquired on the Stock Exchange through stockbrokers, banks and other investment advisers. A number of stockbroking firms specialise in the investment trust sector and will be able to provide detailed information relating to individual trusts, including analyses of past performance, level of discount on underlying NAV and investment policy. The AITC freely offers excellent literature on investment trusts generally, and its members in particular. Information on individual trusts can be obtained from Extel cards (available in large public libraries), on the internet at www.trust-net.co.uk, or directly from the managers, who may also offer shares for sale through 'savings schemes'.

Investment trust savings schemes are operated by managers to avoid some of the restrictions on marketing shares. Typically they offer lump sum, regular savings and dividend reinvestment options. The contributions are pooled by the managers and used to buy shares on the Stock Exchange, and the saving in transaction costs may reduce the investor's brokerage to as little as 0.2%, although some schemes provide for the payment of substantial commissions to intermediaries, the cost of which is ultimately borne by the investor.

Costs of both acquisition and disposal on the Stock Exchange will normally include stockbrokers' commission, which is subject to negotiation, but for a private investor is likely to be something between 1% and 1.65%, depending on the extent of the service the client requires from the broker; there will usually be a minimum, perhaps £25, and a lower rate for large deals. On purchases, there will also be stamp duty at 0.5% and the spread between bid and offered prices may be around 1.5%, though it will usually be less on the freely traded shares of large companies. There is no initial charge payable to the managers, but further brokerage will be payable on final realisation of the shares by sale.

7.11 MAINTENANCE

Running costs vary from one investment trust to another, but management fees, often in the region of 0.5% pa on the portfolio value, are usually payable by the trust at half-yearly intervals in addition to its day-to-day operating expenses. New and converted specialist trusts, for example those involved in providing venture capital, often pay higher fees, perhaps 1.5%. Economies can often be achieved in cases where managers act for several investment trusts and are therefore able to spread the burden of management and administrative expenses among a number of different trusts. These management fees and expenses are normally deductible from the trust's income for corporation tax purposes, whereas the management fee of a private portfolio manager generally has to be found out of the client's after-tax income. In the case of investment trusts, the level of management fees and the extent to which operating expenses may be charged to the trust are not controlled by any external regulation and generally trusts are lightly regulated without the expensive compliance arrangements required of unit trusts.

Like any other investment, the investor or the adviser should periodically review holdings in investment trusts. A trust's performance may be monitored by observing its quoted stock exchange price in the daily newspapers and the changes in its underlying NAV, and by reading the half-yearly financial statements and annual directors' reports and audited accounts, which will be sent to registered shareholders and are generally available free on request. The annual report and accounts will contain detailed financial and other information relating to the trust and will usually include details of its investment portfolio as at the date of its balance sheet. The trust will also convene an annual general meeting of shareholders to adopt the annual report and accounts and to conduct other business. Registered shareholders may attend and vote on the resolutions proposed at these meetings or, if they do not wish to attend, may appoint a proxy to vote on their behalf.

USEFUL ADDRESSES

Association of Investment Trust
  Companies (AITC)
8–13 Chiswell Street
London
EC1Y 4YY

Tel: (020) 7431 5222
Web: www.aitc.co.uk/

(The AITC has undertaken a substantial advertising campaign to educate the public about the benefits of investment trusts.)

UBS Warburg
1 Finsbury Avenue
London
EC2M 2PP

(This firm does not deal directly with private investors, but publishes an annual *Private Investor Guide to Investment Trusts*, which includes a list of some suitable brokers.)

8

OEICS AND UNIT TRUSTS

PETER GRIMMETT

Retail Compliance Manager, Threadneedle Investments

8.1 INTRODUCTION

Another form of collective investment medium (see Chapter 7) is unit trusts, a trust fund in which the investors hold direct beneficial interests. It is normally open-ended, meaning that units are created or redeemed at the current fair prices, and so the managers buy and sell units as required by investors (see 8.7).

The honesty and competence of the managers of such trusts is of fundamental importance, and the constitution, management and marketing of trusts are all regulated in the UK, primarily under the Financial Services and Markets Act (FSMA) 2000. These powers are exercised by the FSA with delegated powers over member firms. Only authorised persons may conduct investment business. The European Community Directive on Undertakings for Collective Investment in Transferable Securities (the UCITS Directive) requires all member states to assimilate their regulations for certain collective investment schemes, which may then be sold throughout the European Economic Area.

In 1997 a further form of authorised collective investment scheme (CIS) was introduced into the UK – the open-ended investment company (OEIC). It is often described as a unit trust in corporate form and, while this is true, there are differences between the two products. In fact, the FSA OEIC regulations are very similar (and identical in some cases) to the unit trust regulations. They are combined in one document called the CIS Sourcebook and more recently in 2004, the New CIS Sourcebook. The OEIC is considered to be a modern form of collective investment scheme (and a form that is very common in Europe) that provides some more flexibility to the industry than previously available under unit trust regulations. It has proved to be an extremely popular form of CIS with many fund launches now using the OEIC route (as at 2002 there were over 70 management companies with over 900 sub-funds in existence).

See 8.12, which outlines the key differences to unit trusts.

8.2 HISTORICAL BACKGROUND

Units in the first unit trust in the UK were offered to the public in April 1931 by the M&G Group, which still exists today as one of the leaders of the industry. Allied Investors Ltd, now Threadneedle Investment Services Ltd, followed in 1934 and remains one of the largest unit trust groups in the UK. The first trusts were 'fixed' trusts and offered virtually no flexibility in investment policy once the trust deed had been executed. Each new subscription was invested in the fixed portfolio and each unit was thus unchanged in its composition. Each unit was normally divided into sub-units for sale to the public.

The first 'flexible' trust (the type of trust that is marketed today) was not offered to the public until 1936. When the Prevention of Fraud (Investments) Act 1939 came into force, supervision of the new industry was made the responsibility of the (then) Board of Trade. Under that Act, revised and re-enacted as the Prevention of Fraud (Investments) Act 1958, the Department of Trade and Industry (DTI) laid down regulations for the conduct of unit trusts, supervised charges and 'authorised' unit trusts complying with its requirements until 1988. The power of authorisation for new unit trust schemes then passed from the DTI to the FSA.

The Open-Ended Investment Companies Regulations 2001 (the 'OEIC Regs') lay down the structural elements of the OEIC (essentially the formation, supervision and control, and the corporate code). The FSA adds the flesh in the Collective Investment Schemes Sourcebook which came into operation originally on 16 January 1997. These Regulations deal with the matters that an OEIC is required to comply with on an ongoing basis.

The first company to launch an OEIC was Global Asset Management in mid-1997. This was set up as an umbrella company, but at the time had only one sub-fund when it was authorised. The next and arguably the first major OEIC to be launched in the UK was by Threadneedle Investments in August 1997. Again it was set up in an umbrella format, but initially had 23 sub-funds making up the company. Threadneedle was also the first company to take advantage of regulations permitting unit trusts to be converted into OEICs and to market an OEIC successfully into Europe.

8.3 AUTHORISATION

The main requirement for authorisation of a unit trust by the FSA is that a trust deed conforming with the FSA's regulations is executed between a company performing all management functions for the trust (the managers) and an independent trust corporation (the trustee) to hold the trust's investments and supervise the managers. Both the managers and the trustee must be incorporated under the law of, or of some part of, the UK or any other EU member state, must maintain a place of business in Great Britain and must be authorised persons to conduct investment business and so subject to the regulators' rules for conduct of business. The persons who are to be directors of a unit trust management company must be approved by the FSA. The trust deed and regulations must provide for, *inter alia*:

(1) managers' investment and borrowing powers and limits on investment of the trust's assets;

(2) determining the manner in which prices and yields are calculated and the obligation of managers to repurchase units at the 'bid' price;

(3) setting up a register of unitholders, with procedures for issuing certificates and dealing with transfers;

(4) remuneration of the managers and trustees;

(5) periodic audits of the trust and the issue of financial statements to unitholders, with reports by the managers, trustees and auditors;

(6) meetings of unitholders under certain circumstances.

Authorisation makes it possible for unit trust managers to advertise units for sale to the public and carries with it tax privileges for the trust. Here we deal only with unit trusts that have been authorised by the FSA; 'unit trust' here means an authorised unit trust unless otherwise indicated. (For discussion on unauthorised unit trusts, see 8.13.)

Authorisation of OEICs runs along a very similar line and is created by virtue of the OEIC Regulations. To market its shares to the public the OEIC must be authorised by the FSA. It is governed by its instrument of incorporation, rather than a trust deed.

8.4 HIGHLIGHTS OF THE PREVIOUS YEAR

Sales of unit trusts and OEICs in 2003, compared with the previous two years, were as follows:

	2001	*2002*	*2003*
	£bn	*£bn*	*£bn*
Industry sales	51.1	47.6	46.9
Industry repurchases	39.3	39.6	37.2
Net new investment	11.8	8.0	9.7

Source: IMA.

At 31 December 2003, the total funds invested in authorised collective investment schemes were £241bn (up from £195bn in 2002).

The number of authorised schemes was 1,924 compared to 1,957 in 2002. There were 201 investment fund managers compared to 201 in 2002 (including 72 OEIC providers). Unitholder accounts numbered 19.1m (18.9m in 2002).

UK corporate bond fund retail sales dominated in 2003 with 22% of total gross sales (the UK All Companies sector with 23% was the most favoured sector for institutional gross sales).

8.5 PRICING OF UNITS

Since 1 July 1988, unit trust managers have been free to choose whether to deal on 'forward prices', ie at the next price to be calculated, or at prices already calculated and published, as had been the norm. Most management companies have availed themselves of this opportunity. With forward pricing, a buyer does not know exactly how many units he will receive, but he does know that he will deal at a fair, up-to-date price. If, on the other hand, a management company is dealing on historic prices and the value of a trust is believed to have changed by more than 2% since the valuation on which the company is offering to deal, a new price must be calculated, and indeed a forward price must be given to any customer who requests it.

The bid and offer (or selling and buying) prices can be found in the newspapers, with additional information available if the customer asks the management company for it. Regulations now permit unit trusts to calculate their prices on a single price basis.

The Financial Services Act 1986 became effective in 1988, superseding the Prevention of Fraud (Investments) Act 1958. As a result, much of the regulation of unit trusts, including authorisation, was transferred from the DTI to other bodies. More recently the Financial Services and Markets Act 2000 replaced the 1986 Act. The regulation of borrowing powers and permitted investment and the constitution, as well as the management, of unit trusts is regulated by the FSA.

The pricing of shares in an OEIC is different, in that shares must be single priced and the OEIC regulations generally express a preference to deal at a 'forward price'. Therefore there is one price at which an investor can buy or sell shares in an OEIC and he or she may not know that price until it is next calculated. The underlying mechanism in determining the price of a share is, however, similar to that of unit trusts.

An additional concept for OEICs is the dilution levy or dilution adjustment. In some instances the actual cost of buying and selling a company's investments may be higher or lower than the mid-market value used in calculating the share price (eg because of dealing charges or through dealing at prices other than the mid-market price). Under certain circumstances this may have an adverse effect on shareholders' interest in the company. This is called 'dilution', and to prevent this effect the directors/ACD (see 8.6 below) have the power to charge a dilution levy on the sale and/or redemption of shares or to swing the price up or down. Any charge made is paid back into and becomes part of the company. The directors/ACD must declare under what circumstances a dilution levy or adjustment may be charged in the prospectus.

8.6 LEGAL NATURE

A unit trust scheme is constituted by a trust deed that is made between the managers and the trustee. The managers are the promoters of the scheme and are subsequently responsible for the conduct of the investment and for administration. The trustee (usually one of the clearing banks or major insurance companies) is responsible for ensuring that the managers act in accordance with the provisions laid down in the trust deed. The trustee holds the trust's assets on trust for the unitholders. Regulations determine the content of the trust deed and other binding requirements, and both the trustee and the management company are subject to the FSA Conduct of Business Rules.

The underlying securities are registered in the trustee's name or, if in bearer form, held in the custody of the trustee, which also holds any cash forming part of the fund. The trustee, as the legal owner of the underlying assets for the unitholders, receives on their behalf all income and other distributions made in respect of such assets.

The trust deed and regulations also lay down a formula for valuing the trust to determine the prices at which units may be sold to the public by the managers and at which units must be bought back by the managers from the public (see below). Additional units may be created to meet demand from the public or existing units may be cancelled as a result of the subsequent repurchase of units from the public. A unit trust is thus 'open-ended' and can expand or contract depending on whether there is a preponderance of buyers or sellers of its units.

Two prices are quoted for unit trusts although some have switched to a single price. These are the 'offer' price, at which units are offered for sale to or subscription by the public; and the 'bid' price, at which the managers buy back units. The offer and bid prices are, broadly speaking, ascertained in the following manner:

(1) The offer price is calculated by reference to the notional amount that would have to be paid to acquire the underlying assets held by the

trust, to which are added the notional acquisition costs (eg brokers' commission and stamp duty) and the preliminary management charges (see 8.11.1).

(2) The bid price is calculated by reference to the amount that would be received on a disposal of the assets held by the trust, from which are deducted the notional costs of the disposal, ie brokers' commission and contract stamp.

Investors must never be required to pay more for their units than the offer price as calculated under the trust deed, nor may unitholders on a sale of their units be paid less than the bid price as so calculated. When an investor buys units, the managers may either create them or sell units that they have previously repurchased and are holding in the manager's 'box'. The spread between the offered and bid prices can be between 8% and 11%, but in practice most unit trust managers quote spreads for their own dealings in units between 4.5% and 6.5%, which may be positioned anywhere between the maximum offered and minimum bid prices applicable on subscription for new units and cancellation of existing units.

Managers normally base their buying price for units in a particular trust on the full bid valuation if they are buying back more units than they are selling, since this is the price at which units must be cancelled. Conversely, if the managers are selling more units than they are buying, their selling price is normally based on the full offer price, at which units must be created.

A unit trust cannot 'gear' its portfolio by borrowings, either unsecured or secured, on the trust's assets. The only circumstances in which borrowing is permitted are to anticipate known cashflows (such as dividends due).

The trust deed, which takes effect subject to any regulations under the FSMA 2000, may make provision for the trust to be terminated and also specifies circumstances in which the approval of unitholders at a general meeting needs to be sought. Such approval is required, among other things, for proposals to vary the provisions of the trust deed, to change the trust's investment objectives or to amalgamate the trust with another trust. Unitholders' interests are thus protected despite the fact that no AGM is held, since certain material changes affecting their interests may be effected only with their approval in general meeting.

As mentioned earlier, an OEIC is constituted under a form of company/corporate law as opposed to trust law for unit trusts. It is governed by its instrument of incorporation and its prospectus – the OEIC and FSA Regulations lay down what is required or permitted to be disclosed in these two documents.

The two main parties in the OEIC are the directors (similar to a manager of a unit trust) and the depositary (similar to a trustee). Where there is only one director, it must be an authorised person (the 'authorised corporate director' (ACD)). Most OEICs have been launched on this basis. The depositary has similar, but lighter, regulatory duties than a trustee, but maintains the essential requirement to have safe custody of the company's property and ensure that the company is managed in accordance with certain parts of the FSA regulations.

8.7 CONDITIONS FOR PURCHASE

Any individual, corporate body or trustee may acquire and hold unit trusts without any condition or restriction, subject to any limitation that may be imposed on its own investment powers.

Unit trusts are mentioned specifically as approved 'wider range' investments under the Trustee Investments Act 1961. Unit trusts the portfolios of which consist exclusively of investments suitable for 'narrow-range' investments under the same Act may themselves be included in the narrow-range investments. Trustees should, however, satisfy themselves of their powers to invest in unit trusts by reference to their trust instrument.

Nearly all unit trust managers specify a minimum investment, usually in the range of £500–£2,000. Certain specialist funds have higher minima. These minima do not apply to monthly saving schemes, where amounts from £20 pm may be invested on a regular basis.

Since a unit trust is open-ended, there is no maximum holding, though a corporate or trustee unitholder may be restricted by his own investment limitations.

The position for OEICs is very similar.

Persons resident outside the UK may acquire and hold unit trust units, subject to the local exchange control rules in their country of residence or domicile. However, for reasons of taxation, it is usually preferable for such people to invest in 'offshore' funds.

8.8 CHARACTERISTICS

OEICs and unit trusts must invest the greater part of their portfolios in securities listed on recognised stock exchanges. Each manager (or ACD), with the trustees' (depositaries') approval, will determine a list of 'eligible markets' for each trust. These will be markets that are considered to meet basic criteria of investor protection such as having regulatory authorities, high accounting standards and no restrictions on the repatriation of funds. Up to 10% of the trust's property may be held in 'non-eligible markets'. Note that the determination of eligibility is not made by the FSA.

The investments of the majority of unit trusts are usually in equity shares.

Authorised OEICs and unit trusts may, in general, invest only in securities, although some classes of OEICs and unit trusts are now authorised to invest in other financial instruments, for example futures and options, warrants or property. These new schemes have separate regulations of investment and borrowing powers, and may have a separate tax regime. All schemes may use derivatives within the constraints of Efficient Portfolio Management for hedging purposes. With the exception of GFOFs (geared futures and options funds), all derivatives must be fully covered by cash, stock or other derivatives.

The specific investment characteristics of unit trusts and OEICs will vary depending on the stated objective of any particular scheme. However, all schemes share certain general characteristics.

New CIS rules implementing new UCITS Directives now permit certain types of funds to invest in a mixture of equities, bonds, cash, other funds and derivatives within the same fund. This is a welcome flexibility for fund managers. Additionally, it is also possible to limit the issue of shares and to provide guarantees. In 2004 the FSA introduced a new type of non-UCITS retail fund that has yet further flexibility in where and what types of assets it can invest.

8.8.1 General characteristics

Spread of risk

By acquiring an interest in a portion of all the investments in the underlying portfolio of a unit trust or OEIC, an investor can achieve a much wider spread of risk than could be achieved economically with limited resources. By spreading their investments across a large number of companies in a wide variety of industries in a number of different countries, investors can much reduce the risks inherent in a holding of shares in only one company or a small number of companies. The result is likely to be a much more even progression of capital and income growth. Regulations covering the maximum investment of a fund's assets in a single company or issue ensure that a wide spread of risk is achieved. In practice, funds usually hold something between 25 and 150 investments, considerably more than the required minimum.

Professional management

By committing investment funds to the purchase of a holding in a fund, the investor is in effect delegating the day-to-day management of his portfolio to the scheme's managers. Virtually all management companies employ a team of investment specialists whose aim is to maximise capital and/or income performance, and who are given a wide discretion within the limitations imposed by the trust deed or instrument of incorporation to increase or decrease the scheme's liquidity or to switch investments as they consider appropriate. The advantage to the investor is that the investments are under the continuous supervision of people whose business it is to keep abreast of economic, political and corporate developments at home and abroad.

Simplicity and convenience

The sometimes tedious paperwork associated with owning a portfolio of securities is largely eliminated. Day-to-day decisions on such matters as rights and scrip issues, mergers and takeovers are all taken by the managers. Dividends are received by the trustee and distributions of the scheme's income are made, usually twice a year, to investors together with a report on the progress of their scheme during the preceding accounting period.

Marketability

In view of their open-ended nature, as a result of which units and shares can be created or cancelled to meet investors' requirements, unit trust units or OEIC shares can be regarded as an almost totally liquid investment, with none of the constraints on marketability sometimes encountered in connection with investment in some of the smaller listed companies. As a result of the pricing structure, referred to in 8.5, purchases and sales of units or shares take place at prices that reflect the underlying value of the trust's assets.

8.8.2 Types of unit trust and OEIC

While all schemes share the investment characteristics listed above, there is a very wide range of funds that offer different investment objectives designed to suit different categories of investors. The main types are described below.

Balanced funds

These invest in a portfolio that is usually composed of leading 'blue chip' shares with the aim of achieving a steady growth of both capital and income. These funds are designed for the investor who wishes to invest in a wide spread of ordinary shares. They may be suitable for the first-time investor in equities, who wishes to hold the units for longer-term investment or saving.

Income funds

These aim to achieve an above-average yield to the investor whose primary need is for a high and growing income. Normally, such funds give a yield between 1.2 and 1.5 times that available on shares generally. These funds are more suitable for retired people, widows, or others who depend on investment income. Such funds may purchase convertible shares as a way of achieving their yield objectives.

Capital growth funds

These are designed to seek maximum capital growth. The income from such funds is usually low. These characteristics make them particularly suitable for those who want to build up a nest-egg.

Fixed interest funds

These generally invest in a portfolio of government bonds, corporate bonds and convertible shares and may be either income or capital funds. Such funds may be suitable for those requiring a high income, although prospects for income growth are unlikely to be as good as in equity funds.

Overseas funds

These aim to provide the investor with an opportunity to invest through stock markets in other countries. Investment overseas is a particularly complex and difficult task for the private person, but can be rewarding in times when sterling is weak against other currencies or when economic conditions in a region overseas are particularly buoyant. The sharp depreciation of sterling in 1992 proved again the merits of investing in these funds as a hedge against devaluation.

Specialist funds

Certain funds, sometimes referred to as 'specialist funds', are promoted to invest in particular sectors of the securities market (eg commodities, technology, health care or smaller companies). These funds are suitable for the larger or more sophisticated investor who wishes to focus on a particular sector while still achieving a spread of risk. The specialist nature of such funds means that the investor may be somewhat more at the whim of fashion.

Accumulation funds

Certain funds within all the categories referred to above are structured and promoted on the basis that they will accumulate the net income within the fund rather than distribute it to unitholders. This income is nonetheless subject to taxation as if it had been received by unitholders.

Limited issue funds

These can limit the issue of shares to a fixed amount after which it can close to new investment (or issue further tranches of shares at a later date). However the investor always retains the right to redeem his shares.

'Tracker' funds

Certain funds are structured to imitate a stock market index and so achieve a performance matching that market. Because of their essentially passive nature, with investment managers taking fewer active decisions, such funds normally have lower management charges. These funds are also referred to as 'indexed' funds.

OEICs

A key advantage of OEICs is that these funds can be made up of different classes of shares. For example, an umbrella company can be made up of several subfunds, which in turn can have classes of shares such as net income, net accumulation, gross accumulation and even currency classes of shares. There could be a situation where, for example, the subfund is marketing in different countries and would like to market it in the currency of that country. Recent FSA regulations have aimed to level the playing field by allowing unit trusts to have a similar structure.

8.9 TAXATION

Authorised unit trusts (AUTs) and OEICs have their own taxation regime. They are treated as companies for tax purposes but with important differences. No liability to corporation tax arises on capital gains derived by the AUT or OEIC, the chargeable profits being limited to unfranked investment income less management expenses and charges on income. The rate of corporation tax levied on the profits is limited to 20%.

Distributions by AUTs and OEICs are treated as dividends unless, under special circumstances (see below), they are treated as interest distributions. Distributions by way of dividend are treated in the same way as distributions by other UK companies, in that until 5 April 1999 ACT at the rate of 25% of the dividend paid had to be paid by the dividend payer. For individual unitholders in the AUT or shareholders in the OEIC resident in the UK, a tax credit was available on the dividend distribution equal to the amount of advance corporation tax (ACT), which they could set off against their total income tax liability and, in appropriate cases, reclaim in cash. The tax credit satisfied the total tax liability of basic and lower rate taxpayers. Higher rate taxpayers were liable to an additional tax liability. On 6 April 1999, ACT was abolished and dividends can now be paid without the need to account for ACT to the Revenue. However, individual recipients of dividends continue to receive a tax credit that has been set initially as 1/9 of the amount of the dividend. This tax credit is sufficient to cover the liability of starter rate and basic rate taxpayers, but is no longer repayable except for individuals holding their units or shares through a PEP or an ISA who may continue to receive repayment of tax credits until 2004. Higher rate taxpayers may still be liable to an additional tax liability.

The amount of distribution received by a unitholder or shareholder subject to corporation tax (and not dual resident) is separated into franked and unfranked components of the dividend. The unfranked component is deemed to be an annual payment received under deduction of income tax at the rate of 20%; the franked component is treated as a dividend and usually not subject to further tax liability. Whether unitholders or shareholders who are resident in countries other than the UK are entitled to payments from the Revenue of a proportion of the tax credit attaching to the dividend depends in general on the existence and terms of any double tax convention between the UK and the territory of residence.

AUTs and OEICs that meet a qualifying investment test may make distributions by way of payments of interest rather than dividends. Such interest is paid under deduction of income tax at 20%. The qualifying investment test is satisfied provided the market value of qualifying investments held by the AUT or OEIC exceeds 60% of the market value of all the investments held. Qualifying investments include money placed at interest, securities excluding shares in companies, and shares in a building society. The tax deducted satisfies the tax liability of starter rate and basic rate taxpapers. Higher rate taxpayers may still be liable to an additional tax liability. In appropriate cases, individual and corporate unitholders and shareholders may be able to obtain repayment of the income tax deducted. Non-resident unitholders and shareholders may be eligible for interest distributions to be made gross. When they are not paid gross, all or some of the income tax credit may be recoverable from the Revenue. This depends on the provisions of any tax convention or agreement that exists between the relevant country and the UK. If a UK corporation is the beneficial owner of the interest, it can, if they certify their tax position to the managers, ask for interest to be paid gross. As from 1 October 2002, pension schemes, charities, PEP and ISA managers will also be able to be paid gross.

No taxation will be withheld from payment made to unitholders on redemption of units or shares. However, the redemption, sale or transfer of units may constitute a disposal (or part disposal) for the purposes of UK taxation of capital gains.

8.10 SUITABILITY

Unit trusts and OEICs can be suitable for investors, large or small, whether trustees, corporations or private individuals who wish to invest in a portfolio of either general or specialist securities in the UK or overseas, but who do not wish, or are not investing sufficient sums, to run their own investments. They can also be available as tax-free investments, eg through ISAs.

Because the income from and the value of all securities can fluctuate, investors should understand that collective investment schemes are risk investments. 'The value of the units as well as the income from them may go down as well as up' is the caveat that must appear in all collective investment schemes' advertisements and literature soliciting purchases and never has it been more true than in the last three or so years. However, the facts that collective investment schemes cannot generally gear up, that present regulation ensures a reasonable level of diversification within the scheme, and of the overseeing function of the trustee or depositary, considerably reduces the inherent risk of the investment.

8.11 MECHANICS AND MAINTENANCE

8.11.1 Mechanics

Unit trust units and OEIC shares may be acquired through any professional adviser (stockbroker, bank, accountant, solicitor or insurance broker). Many have departments specialising in advice on the selection of collective investment shares. There are also several firms that offer portfolio management and advisory services. If there is any doubt about the suitability of unit trusts or OEICs to the investor's needs, professional advice may be desirable in any case.

Alternatively, units or shares may be acquired directly from the managers on either telephoned or written instructions. The disposal of units and shares can be achieved in exactly the same way.

The names, addresses and telephone numbers of unit trust managers and OEICs are given in many leading newspapers, together with a list of the current prices of the schemes they manage. All managers supply more comprehensive information and copies of recent reports on particular funds on request.

The Investment Management Association can supply a comprehensive list of members and other general information about collective investment schemes on request. (See end of chapter for details.)

When units or shares are purchased, an initial charge is payable and is usually included in the price. Initial charges are normally in the region of 3–6%.

Most managers pay commission to accredited agents. This is borne by the managers from the permitted initial charge.

The investor receives a contract note giving details of the purchase and may subsequently receive a certificate showing the number of units or shares held. Payment of the proceeds of sale is normally made by the managers within a few days of their receiving the certificate signed on the reverse by the investor.

8.11.2 Maintenance

Annual management fees based on the fund's value are deducted by the managers normally from the scheme's income. As in the case of investment trusts, these fees are deductible from the fund's income for tax purposes. From the annual charge the managers must meet the costs of trustees' (or depositaries') fees, audit fees, administration and investment management. If managers wish to increase the fees, holders must be given notice in writing. Fees charged usually vary between 0.75% and 2% pa, although management charges for certain indexed funds may be as low as 0.5%.

Certain other costs, including agents' fees for holding investments in safe custody overseas and the cost of collecting foreign dividends, may be charged to the scheme's income. These costs are usually small in relation to the total income.

The stamp duty and brokerage on the purchase and sale of underlying investments are borne by the scheme but are reflected in the pricing structure (see 8.5).

Like any other investment, the investor or adviser should periodically review fund holdings. The investor should be able to monitor the managers' performance by reading the half-yearly (or annual) reports they are required to send. These reports should contain:

(1) a statement of the scheme's capital and income performance during the period, compared with appropriate indices;
(2) an assessment of portfolio changes during the period or any change in investment philosophy;
(3) the managers' view of the forthcoming period;
(4) a list of the current investment holdings;
(5) the figures for the income distribution; and
(6) a capital and income record.

8.12 OPEN-ENDED INVESTMENT COMPANIES

It is fair to say that OEICs are very similar beasts to unit trusts, but because of the structure of the overarching legislation there are differences. Significant differences have been highlighted in the sections above (eg AGMs, flexibility in classes of share, directors, and its legal structure).

Those used to the concept of unit trusts will recognise the many similar features (production of a prospectus, the investment and borrowing powers, income, report and accounts and other features listed above). Therefore, it is possible in most instances to read across to OEICs where the text refers to unit trusts.

Some of the terminology will have changed (eg shares rather than units, prospectus compared to scheme particulars, directors/ACD instead of manager and depositary for trustee) but the roles, although not identical, are in general very similar.

A further difference to note is the requirement for an OEIC to hold AGMs of shareholders, in much the same way as a conventional company. Two essential elements of the AGM are that the directors must lay copies of the annual report before the company and that the auditors must be reappointed at each meeting. Other business that the company/ACD wishes to conduct with its shareholders may also be carried out at an AGM.

The tax treatment of an OEIC is identical to that of an authorised unit trust: see 8.9 above.

8.13 UNAUTHORISED UNIT TRUSTS

Unauthorised unit trusts are unit trusts that have not been authorised by the FSA (see 8.3). Their income is liable to ordinary income tax at the basic rate (22% from 6 April 2000), the payment of which is reflected in distributions to the unitholders.

An unauthorised unit trust does not benefit from the CGT exemption of authorised unit trusts. CGT is therefore payable in full, putting such a trust at a disadvantage in comparison with an authorised trust so far as CGT is concerned, unless the unauthorised trust is an exempt trust.

8.14 EXEMPT UNIT TRUSTS

Exempt unit trusts are unit trusts designed for particular types of unitholders. While many such funds exist, their rationale was destroyed by the exemption of unit trusts from tax on chargeable gains in FA 1980. Exempt unit trusts may be in authorised or unauthorised form.

8.15 PREVIEW OF THE YEAR AHEAD

The FSA has issued new rules that completely overhaul the current CIS sourcebook. Among the new rules are a merging of all non-UCITS type funds into one category 'non-UCITS mixed funds', new non-retail type funds with a lighter regulatory regime, performance fees, limited redemption and flexible charging. The FSA will look further at the pricing regime for CISs over the coming months.

8.16 CONCLUSION

For the private investor who wishes to participate in the historically greater returns available from investment in the world's stock markets as compared to deposits or savings accounts, the unit trust and OEIC are ideal vehicles to mitigate some of the inherent risks. Prime examples include the role of the trustee/depositary who will protect the customer's assets in the event of the manager's default, and the ability to gain the skill of an entire investment team of professionals for as little as £20 a month. Having decided on the vehicle, the choice, although initially daunting, of manager and fund type should be enough to satisfy the requirements of almost every private investor.

If not, one can be sure that product development teams are already working on the next evolution in the market.

SOURCES OF FURTHER INFORMATION

Legislation

Capital Gains Tax Act 1979
Companies Act 1985
Finance Acts 1980–2004
Financial Services and Markets Act 2000
The Collective Investment Schemes Sourcebook and the New CIS
  Sourcebook
Income and Corporation Taxes Act 1988
Open-Ended Investment Companies Regulations 2001
Prevention of Fraud (Investments) Act 1958

USEFUL ADDRESSES

Investment Management
  Association
65 Kingsway
London
WC2B 6TD

Tel: (020) 7831 0898
Web: www.investmentuk.org

Department of Trade and Industry
Companies Division
10–18 Victoria Street
London
SW1H 0NN

Tel: (020) 7215 5000
Web: www.dti.gov.uk

Financial Services Authority
25 The North Colonnade
Canary Wharf
London
E14 5HS

Tel: (020) 7066 1000
Web: www.fsa.gov.uk

9

REAL PROPERTY

GEOFFREY J ABBOTT
Dip FBA (Lon) FRICS
Agricultural Investment Consultant of Smiths Gore (Chartered Surveyors)

9.1 INTRODUCTION TO REAL PROPERTY

This chapter is a general introduction to the subject of real property and to Chapters 10 (residential property), 11 (agricultural land and woods) and 12 (commercial property). Readers should appreciate that the subjects covered are vast and complex. All matters covered have been condensed and investors must take independent professional advice.

Real property is a legal interest in land and/or buildings of four principal types:

(a) residential;
(b) commercial (offices, shops/retail warehouses and factories/storage warehouses);
(c) farmland;
(d) woodlands.

In the case of vacant farmland and woodland, it may also include growing crops as well.

Investment in property normally falls into two main categories:

(1) direct investment – by purchase of an interest in a property;
(2) indirect investment – by purchase of units in property bonds and other unit-linked schemes, or by the purchase of shares in a property company or timeshare.

Chapters 9, 10, 11 and 12 deal with direct investment only.

Property is generally considered one of the most secure forms of investment as it is almost indestructible and immovable (it cannot easily be lost or stolen) and usually can produce an income. However, an investment in property is complicated and a thorough understanding of all its implications is necessary to ensure optimum results are obtained from the investment selected.

Today, ownership of land and property is in many hands. The principal types of owner are:

(a) private individuals;
(b) trust funds;
(c) public and private investment and trading companies;
(d) traditional (Crown, church, colleges, etc) and financial (insurance companies and pension funds) institutions;
(e) national and local government and various bodies under them;
(f) numerous official and semi-official 'conservation' bodies such as the National Trust, the RSPB, etc.

Property owners or freeholders (superiors in Scotland) may have others under them with lesser interests in the whole or parts of their property. The owner of these lesser interests is normally either a lessee, a tenant or a licensee (vassels/feuers) depending on the nature of his interests. There can also be third-party rights over property. These may vary from a right of the general public to use a footpath, or a statutory undertaking to lay a water pipe or electricity cable on, under or over the owner's or lessee's land, to a personal right to cross another person's land for some specified reason.

An interest in property may satisfy three separate needs: enjoyment, investment and security. Enjoyment in its broadest sense might be considered as the actual use of that land, whether agricultural or as a place to live, to manufacture or trade, from which to extract minerals or of employment or entertainment. Enjoyment and investment are commonly combined, for example owner-occupiers of residential property rarely consider their home as an investment, although for the great majority it is the largest single investment that they will ever make.

Many forms of ownership of an interest subject to a letting do not entitle the investor to any direct enjoyment of the land, but simply to participate in an agreed share of the income or produce obtained from it, usually in the form of a cash rent.

All readers must appreciate, however, that where investments are made for maximum financial gain the most important factor is timing. All markets are cyclical. Whatever the care in initial selection and subsequent management, if a purchase is made at the top of a market cycle, short-term performance will inevitably be disappointing. Alternatively, almost all purchases made at the bottom of a cycle will ultimately perform well. Investment based on this strategy is known as 'counter-cyclical' – but, at a time when short-term considerations are driving the markets, it is an unfashionable strategy amongst the investment institutions which may create opportunities for private investors who can take a longer-term view.

9.2 LEGAL, TAXATION AND COST FACTORS OF REAL PROPERTY

9.2.1 Legal

The legal root of English and Welsh property law is fundamentally different from that in Scotland. While legislation originating from the Palace of Westminster is commonly drafted to give similar effects, it does not always do so in practice and, with the Scottish Parliament, it will evolve even more independently in the future.

Historically, the main purpose of property laws and legislation was to establish ground rules by which owners, landlords and tenants should behave to each other and their neighbours. However, recent legislation to protect the wider community's interests with planning and other legislation has tended to restrict the owner or tenant's right to do what he likes with his property. The body of law is substantial, but its application to any individual property varies. An experienced property lawyer is therefore an essential member of any property investor's team.

9.2.2 Taxation

As with all forms of investment, owners of real estate are liable to pay revenue, capital gains and inheritance taxes in one way or another. The impact of these taxes on the owners of different types of property varies significantly and may determine the type of property invested in and even whether to choose property or non-property investments. Business rates apply on occupation of most commercial property and council tax on residential property.

The body of taxation law is again substantial, detailed and complex. An experienced property tax adviser should be consulted.

9.2.3 Costs

The purchase, ownership and the eventual sale of any interest in real estate will normally incur costs. When property is held for investment it will affect the net yield achieved. The level of costs will reflect the particular nature and circumstances of the property or portfolio held and will typically be in the form of acquisition, management and/or disposal costs.

Acquisition costs

The purchaser of any real estate should be prepared for costs of 2.5–5.5% on top of the purchase price (costs associated with a lease may be substantially different). These costs are made up of 1% stamp duty on properties having a value of £60,001 (£150,001 in certain 'disadvantaged areas') rising up to 3% on properties worth more than £250,000 and 4% on those worth more than £500,000. Additionally, 1% should be allowed for agents' fees and 0.5% or more for solicitors' fees. There may be an additional charge on the solicitors' account for search fees and VAT is payable on both agents' and solicitors' fees. The VAT status of many forms of property investment should also be checked out before an offer is made.

Investors should consider certain other additional costs, for example a structural survey on older buildings or a planning appraisal for potential development situations. The investment may also involve a mortgage or other form of borrowing and the associated valuation and commitment fees are normally paid by the borrower/purchaser.

Finally, the purchase of vacant farmland usually also involves the purchase of growing crops and the payment of tenant right. Professional fees for the valuation and negotiation of agreement on these will normally be in the 2.5–5% range.

Management costs

Stocks and shares are essentially a passive investment, whereas most forms of property investment call for active management. Property management costs are variable. Over the years most property will need to be repaired, insured, altered, re-let, improved or perhaps redeveloped. It is only by good management that the asset can maximise its rental and capital value in a changing marketplace.

Examples of typical management costs are:

(1) fully let office on full repairing and insuring (FRI) lease: 2–3% of gross rent;
(2) small market town shop on standard repairing lease: 5% of gross rent;
(3) substantial arable farm on FRI lease: 7% of gross rent;
(4) complex traditional let estate: 10% of gross rent;
(5) short-term furnished residential letting: 20% of gross rent.

Agents' property management fees are usually agreed at the outset, as a package to reflect the range of services needed, and paid out of rental income when received. Fees for farm and forestry management services depend on whether the agent is merely used on a consultancy basis or is responsible for the day-to-day running of a trading business. Where a surveyor is instructed to negotiate or advise on a rent review, lease renewal or re-letting fees range from 7.5–10% of either the first year's rental obtained or of the increase over the previous rent, depending on the circumstances of each case, plus VAT and expenses.

Disposal costs

The costs of selling are as variable as the types of property involved. Agents' fees vary from 1% of the price achieved for a large commercial property investment up to 2.5% for a smaller residential property, with the associated solicitors' fees normally in the 0.5–0.75% range. VAT is also payable on professional fees.

Local advertising costs at the lower end of the residential markets are normally borne by the agent. National advertising and higher quality particulars, professionally printed, are usually met by the vendor, who also carries the cost of all advertising and printing for most other forms of property sale.

An owner may wish to dispose of just part of his property interest for a certain period. This would normally be dealt with by granting a lease, tenancy or licence. Agents' fees are typically up to 10% of the first year's rent plus VAT and direct expenses, including marketing costs. Solicitors' fees depend on whether a standard lease/agreement is used or whether a document has to be specially drafted to meet the circumstances.

9.3 PROPERTY VALUATION

The diversity of property types and reasons for ownership produce a wide range of approaches to property valuations. The location, accessibility and setting of a property will always influence its value.

The capital value of a vacant house is an equation of demand and supply in the relevant market at the time. Reference to sales of comparable properties is the only guide. However, specific purchasers may pay a premium for a particular property for no better reason than that they want to live in it or it has a marriage value to their adjacent property. They are often referred to as 'special purchasers' and may be prepared to pay a premium price.

In other sectors (eg sporting estates), the market seeks to quantify a purchaser's potential pleasure of ownership by relating value to past bag or catch records. Similarly the value of amenity woodlands is linked to the purchaser's anticipated pleasure in ownership. In commercial softwoods, however, the value is based on capitalisation of future anticipated income flows from timber sales, perhaps many decades ahead.

It is only in the markets for let properties that value is linked to the capitalisation of rent passing. Indeed, in many sectors of the commercial property markets a well-let property is worth significantly more than its vacant equivalent.

In most commercial property markets the rental income is capitalised over a term of years or in perpetuity (depending on whether the property is leasehold or freehold) at an investment rate set by the market for comparable properties at the time. This rate will reflect the risks associated with that property (security of income, obsolescence of the building, economic factors and the cost/inconvenience of management). The capitalisation rate also reflects the expectation of future rental growth.

Most forms of professional valuation today are covered by the Royal Institution of Chartered Surveyors recently substantially rewritten Appraisal and Valuation Manual (the Red Book).

9.4 ROLE OF ADVISERS

Real property should never be acquired, sold or developed without the investor first obtaining competent professional advice. For most investors the advisers will comprise:

(1) **A chartered surveyor**: for knowledge of the relevant market, ability to appreciate and value potential properties, negotiating skills and ability to manage the property over the years to maximise its end value.
(2) **A solicitor**: with appropriate property experience to advise on legal matters generally, to convey properties on purchase and sale and draw up leases and other legal documents throughout the life of the investment.
(3) **A chartered accountant/financial adviser**: to advise generally on funding/sources of capital and methods of minimising the impact of revenue and capital taxes over the years.

Dependent on the nature of property investments actually made, some investors may also require the services of other advisers from time to time. They might include architects, quantity surveyors, and farm and/or forestry management consultants.

RESIDENTIAL PROPERTY

GEOFFREY J ABBOTT
Dip FBA (Lon) FRICS
Agricultural Investment Consultant of Smiths Gore (Chartered Surveyors)

10.1 HIGHLIGHTS OF THE PAST FEW YEARS

After the decade of housing recession from 1988, the more recent boom clearly showed signs of having run out of steam in some areas, including Central London/smart Home Counties, in the spring of 2003. However an influx of overseas money, seeking multi-million pound houses, and improved City bonus prospects, benefiting the next tier down, restored confidence and values although, given the diversity of markets and sub-markets up and down the country, generalisations should be treated with care. The best advise currently is to think of the markets as a three-dimensional model with the most expensive areas in the South having seen little growth over the last year and previously less fashionable areas further west and north continuing to grow at up to 30%. This phenomenon also happened in the last cycle when the 'north/south divide' closed quite significantly for a time.

Ignoring the inevitable local variations, the overall shape of the national housing market over recent years is conveniently summarised by the Halifax National House Price Index. It fell away from 222.5 (or 4.66 times the national average wage) in the last quarter of 1989 to 197.8 in the third quarter of 1995. It then started to recover again through 225.4 in 1997 to 312.1 in 2001 and 394.4 in 2002 with a further rise in 2003 of 20%.

10.2 THE ALTERNATIVES

10.2.1 Personal homes

The purchase of a home is probably the largest investment that the great majority of us make without ever considering it an investment. It is the only form of property investment where capital gains are normally tax free. The owner, if he has more than one home, may elect which is the 'principal residence' and may vary this from time to time subject to notifying the Revenue. A person required to reside in employer-provided accommodation may acquire a house and enjoy capital gains tax (CGT) exemption on it, provided he intends in due course to live in it.

The CGT exemption usually applies to a house and an appropriate area of grounds (normally up to one acre), but exceptions exist above and below this amount and professional advice should be sought.

The purchase of a home has long been considered the safest and soundest form of property investment, with the purchaser theoretically enjoying absolute control over his investment. Traditionally, funds for purchase are obtained on mortgage from building societies, insurance companies or the major clearing banks.

Houses are normally sold by private treaty, but investment or let houses and mortgage repossessions, are sometimes sold by auction. Factors to consider, against your personal objectives, on house purchase include:

(1) style, location and potential planning factors;
(2) structural condition;
(3) availability of main services (gas, water, electricity, telephone, drainage);
(4) the local rate of council tax and the quality of schools.

Bearing in mind the recent problems on the railways, the length and cost of journeying to work is an increasingly important factor. Unmodernised houses may be eligible for local council improvement grants.

However, the most important question is whether you and your family actually wish to live in the house. First and foremost, it is to be your home.

Insurance of property should usually be on the estimated cost of replacement (equivalent reinstatement cost), which may bear little direct relationship to the property's market value. It should normally be index-linked to increase the sum insured in line with inflation of building costs between periodic reviews.

10.2.2 Let houses and flats

Let houses and flats are occupied by tenants and produce a rental income. They are often referred to as 'investment' houses or flats and most post-war legislation was viewed as favouring tenants. As a result the market shrank dramatically, though legislation in the 1980s to restore the market has had some effect, with the London market showing signs of being overdone.

Rent Acts

Many let houses and flats are still covered by the old Rent Acts (commonly referred to as 'regulated tenancies'). Under them the tenant has security and the rent is fixed from time to time by the Rent Officer (an official of the local authority) at a 'fair rent' level – which is generally well below market levels. Increases set by the Rent Officer may only be phased in over a period of years and will be influenced by the Rent Acts (Maximum Fair Rents) Order 1999.

Protected shorthold tenancies (one to five years)

Protected shorthold tenancies were introduced by the Housing Act 1980 for new lettings of more than one year but less than five years under which the landlord could regain possession upon expiry, provided certain conditions were fulfilled. While the initial rent may have been agreed between the parties, the tenant could apply to have the rent fixed by the Rent Officer at any time.

Assured and assured shorthold tenancies

These were introduced under the Housing Act 1988 for new lettings after 15 January 1989 at market rents, subject to a right of appeal to the Rent Assessment Committee, which will look to comparable market lettings in the area. Both give the landlord greater rights to possession at the end of the term, but in the case of assured shorthold tenancies the landlord or his successors have the right to a court order for possession.

Corporate tenants

Corporate tenants are excluded from the security of tenure provisions of all the Acts, though tenancies predating 15 January 1989 are subject to the Rent Officer's assessment of a fair rent. Care must be taken to ensure that all sublettings to company employees are genuine, as 'sham' arrangements may result in a secure subtenancy.

Long leasehold houses (over 21 years)

Houses or flats let on long leases were common, particularly in the major cities. Under the Leasehold Reform Act 1967, the lessees of the majority were granted the right to enfranchise or purchase their freeholds.

Under the Leasehold Reform, Housing and Urban Development Act 1993, these rights of enfranchisement, subject to a number of conditions and exceptions, were extended to higher value leaseholders previously excluded from the 1967 Act.

General

In the case of old regulated tenancies, a 100% or more increase in capital value can be released if vacant possession is gained. This situation attracted some experienced investors but supply is now inevitably starting to dry up.

Let houses and flats are considered a safe and secure form of investment if the location is selected carefully, management standards are high and the investor understands the nature of the tenancy. Subject to the inevitable political risk of a change in legislation reversing the more favourable 1980s legislation, let houses and flats are worthy of consideration as investments. There are growing signs, however, that short-term supply may be increasing ahead of demand in certain parts of London and elsewhere. If interest rates continue to rise into the 5 to 5.5% range, as currently forecast, rents may no longer cover mortgage payments and some 'buy to let' investors may be forced to sell.

10.2.3 Blocks of flats

The investment considerations for blocks of flats are similar to those for let houses and flats. However, the market in blocks of flats has tended to be determined by their 'break-up' value rather than by the income produced. This break-up value arises through an investor being able to acquire a complete block of flats at a figure that will enable him subsequently to dispose of the flats, either to the occupying tenants or with vacant possession if obtained, at a profit.

In the late 1980s the competition for blocks of flats having a break-up value was dramatic. However, it is a high-risk form of investment, as there is no guarantee of obtaining vacant possession. Also tenants now often form their own associations to try to control their landlords' operations and the political risks and social problems for an investor operating in this market can be considerable.

The tenants of flats let under the Landlord and Tenant Act 1987 also now have a right of first refusal if the landlord should decide to sell his interest. Further, under the Leasehold Reform, Housing and Urban Development Act 1993, tenants have the right, subject to complex rules and criteria, to initiate either the purchase of the freehold of their block of flats or the extension of their leases.

There have been a number of highly publicised abuses of the rules by certain landlords and further restrictive legislation may eventually result.

10.2.4 Holiday homes and time sharing

With increasing leisure time, the demand for holiday homes in the UK (which vary from a site on which to park a caravan to a substantial secondary house) has increased considerably. The value of these properties is very much related to the personal choice of the purchaser, who is usually greatly affected by the ease of access to and from the major conurbations and the environment when he gets there. They can be good investments, with the added advantage that they can provide holiday accommodation for the family as well.

Holiday homes may also be purchased abroad. Specialist advice must be taken on such matters as local exchange control, the purchase of a clean title, the practical mechanics of purchase/sale and the availability of services. Good agents and lawyers are even more essential abroad than in the UK.

Partly as a result of this, the concept of property ownership known as 'time sharing' evolved in the late 1980s. In essence, this provides for the investor to acquire an interest for a stated period (a week or a month) in each year in perpetuity or for a period of years. It effectively widens the spectrum of investment to encompass the smaller investor who can secure holiday accommodation with the added potential of capital growth.

Beware, however. It is often associated with questionable sales techniques (and sometimes even fraud), but it is an interesting concept for those who have limited funds that would otherwise be insufficient to purchase a holiday home. If the owner does not wish to use the accommodation each year, the property can often be exchanged if the location is in a major resort.

The method of sale varies, some properties being sold freehold and others on long leaseholds. An annual service charge is payable by the owner, together with the cost of electricity, water and other services used during a vacation. There are a number of companies specialising in this market who advertise nationally.

Holiday homes can be a sound investment, but location is critical. If abroad, there are many possible pitfalls, not the least of which can be guaranteeing sound title.

10.3 PREVIEW OF THE YEAR AHEAD

The immediate future will almost certainly be driven primarily by interest rate trends – with even the Governor of The Bank of England ringing warning bells. Currently, opinion seems to be that we are going to see interest rates rise from 4.5 towards 5.5% over the next 12 months.

To those of us brought up through the years of double-digit interest rates and inflation, this may not seem a lot. However in reality most buyers have to budget to their limits and, allowing for the increases which have already occurred, a 20 to 33% increase in interest rates will be very painful for many.

Another potentially useful guide to the overall health of the country house market is, making due allowance for the season of the year, the weight of property advertising in the *Country Life* magazine. On 3 June 2004 there were 84 pages of property adverts, with 93 on 10 June and 109 on 17 June. Nationally both the number of pages and the increasing trend seem to be indicating some combination of increasing supply and slowing down of turnover. A further pointer may be that mortgage application levels are starting to fall away. In other words 'beware'. One of those characteristically uneven phases of periodic downward adjustment may well be starting.

11

AGRICULTURAL LAND, WOODLANDS AND MISCELLANEOUS

GEOFFREY J ABBOTT
Dip FBA (Lon) FRICS
Agricultural Investment Consultant of Smiths Gore (Chartered Surveyors)

11.1 INTRODUCTION

During World War II and in the post-war period up to the late 1970s, the pressure to increase self-sufficiency in both agricultural and forest products led to significant changes in crop and livestock selection/husbandry and the rapid incorporation of modern technology into the rural industries. The last 30 years have been more about changing perceptions of desirable land uses generally and the pressures on rural land of our predominantly urban population.

The issues underlying these pressures for change are complex, yet the problems in the countryside are often seen in over-simplistic terms by our predominantly urban population.

Currently, the theoretical implications of laboratory created Genetically Modified Organisms (GMOs) 'escaping' continue to cause concern and the market for expensive, organically grown produce grows among the more affluent.

Few yet seem to recognise that controlling the perceived threats of global warming and the like will ultimately have a more dramatic effect on the lifestyles and work practices of our urban areas. The majority of the world's undesirable gases and waste products emanate from urban chimneys, heating/cooling systems, exhaust pipes and dustbins. Similarly, much of the pollution in our rivers is the result of discharges from urban factories and sewage works. It is ironic that the cleanest potential source of future power on a sufficiently significant scale is the harnessing of wave power – yet the various power groupings are still managing to protect their existing investments in 'dirty' hydrocarbon burning systems, thus avoiding the commercial development of this exciting option.

The countryside is also covered by an ancient web of footpaths and bridleways that historically served the practical daily needs of local communities. In their present form they are not ideal for the recreational purposes they primarily serve today. The recent imposition of what I regard as ill-considered legislation in England and Wales granting additional 'rights to roam' over 'open land' to the general public has done nothing to help and generated much squabbling over the detailed plans now being issued. An overall proposal to rationalise the whole footpaths/bridle path system to serve modern needs better would have been welcomed by most landowners and farmers – and been of far greater value to the general public.

The countryside is still essentially about diversity. An investment primarily in one form of land use will often directly or indirectly involve other land uses as well. Houses and woods are an integral part of farmland and all often overlay mineral deposits and are the natural habitat of the sportsman's quarry. Redundant farm buildings are increasingly being converted to commercial uses.

Politically, probably one of the most important lessons that has come out of the recent foot and mouth crisis was that farming and forestry, whilst essential to the formation and maintenance of the countryside we all love, are no longer necessarily the driving forces of the local rural economy. For instance, in many areas rural tourism is now economically far more important.

Throughout this chapter we seek to indicate typical cash yields on the various forms of land use, but obviously many of the benefits of owning country property, which influence its value, do not come in the form of annual income. These other benefits are very diverse. For instance, many purchasers of a vacant farm also get a nice house to live in and perhaps an interesting shoot as well. Development possibilities (whether in the form of houses, alternative uses of traditional farm buildings, leisure uses or mineral workings) or favourable capital or IHT treatment in the future have a value today even if they do not currently earn any income. The surrender of a secure tenancy of a house or farm in due course can release significant latent capital value and the mere ownership of a certain stretch of countryside can give the owner great personal satisfaction.

It is these factors, and the post-war investment track record of country property, that explain the historically relatively low initial yield typically earned on most forms of investment in land. In the context of agricultural support, the much maligned Common Agricultural Policy in Europe used to be about product price support but, in line with domestic policy, is increasingly about subsidising conservation objectives.

11.2 AGRICULTURAL LAND

11.2.1 Background

Usable agricultural land in Great Britain totals approximately 45m acres of which about 66% is owner-occupied or vacant, and 33% is subject to secure Agricultural Holdings Act (AHA) tenancies. They form two very separate markets with significant valuation and yield differences for otherwise physically similar properties. Within these overall totals there is an enormous diversity of soil types, topography, climate and physical location to which individual farmers apply their financial resources and technical/managerial skills. The result is the diverse range of land uses and end products still found in the countryside today.

Potential investors are strongly recommended initially to reflect on Table 11.1 (overleaf). Whatever the financial resources and skills investors bring to bear on the property they buy, its many physical and climatic characteristics will rule the uses to which it is suited. Field scale bulb growing is only economic on the better soils and hardwood trees simply will not survive on solid rock at high altitudes. A good livestock farmer is seldom a good arable farmer and vice versa.

Within both the vacant and let (often referred to as 'investment') land markets there are therefore many submarkets within which properties suited to different principal agricultural uses are grouped.

Investors should also appreciate that a farmer runs a business. Like any other business, the actual financial results on any individual farm, however well the farming system is suited to the property, will reflect the farmer's managerial/technical skills and commercial judgements. As reflected in the rental market, the profit potential of a good farm is significantly greater than that of a poor farm. However, managerial skills on the individual farm remain critical to that unit's actual profitability. There will always be examples of poor farmers on the best land going out of business and good farmers on the poorest land making good money.

All investors should review the future of each property in their portfolio regularly to decide whether each should be retained, sold or passed down to the next generation. Also the potential of each piece of land for a more valuable alternative use should be considered – together with any actions which might expedite or maximise such potential.

Could that droughty field cover potentially valuable gravel deposits, or might the field by the village be developed in 20 years' time? If the answer is 'Yes', consideration should then be given of whether you will need that money in due course or whether it would make more sense to pass the land down to the next generation at purely agricultural value.

Table 11.1 Approximate distribution of soil grades and land uses

Soil Grade	England		Wales		Scotland		Great Britain		Principal Farming/ Forestry Uses	Principal Alternative Uses
	Percentage	Acres 000s	Percentage	Acres 000s	Percentage	Acres 000s	Percentage	Acres 000s		
I	3.3	806	0.2	8	0.3	49	1.9	863	Intensive arable cropping eg bulbs, vegetables, roots & cereals. No forestry.	Coarse fishing in drainage channels and lowly valued pheasant shooting. Principally 'dull' flatland but greater potential on poorer Grade II land out of Fens and similar areas
II	16.7	4,083	2.3	96	2.3	383	10.2	4,562	Arable cropping/intensive grassland eg cereals with roots and/or dairy cows. Limited forestry.	
III	54.0	13,203	17.5	729	13.6	2,175	36.1	16,107	Extensive arable cropping, rotational grassland eg cereals, oilseed rape & beans or grass leys for dairy cows, beef, sheep. Hardwood forestry mainly.	Pheasant/partridge shooting/roe deer stalking. Game fishing if suitable rivers/ streams. Limited B&B, pony trekking etc.
IV	15.7	3,838	44.2	1,842	10.2	1,631	16.4	7,311	Permanent grassland/rough grazing eg beef and sheep rearing with limited dairying & cereals. Commercial softwood forestry.	Grouse shooting, Red deer stalking on open hill. Roe deer stalking in softwood plantations. Game fishing where suitable water. Extensive B&B, pony trekking, hill walking, rock climbing etc.
V	10.3	2,518	35.8	1,491	73.5	11,775	35.4	15,784	Rough grazings often with rock outcrops, eg principally summer grazing with hardy sheep breeds & hill cattle. Limited softwood forestry.	
TOTAL	100	24,448	100	4,166	100	16,013	100	44,627		

Note: MAFF Grades for England and Wales with Scottish equivalent.

138

Finally, a well-screened site is more likely to receive planning consent in due course than a prominent one out in the open. Should a belt of trees be planted now?

11.2.2 Highlights of the previous year

After a period of strong profits and rental/land value growth in the mid-1990s, the vacant possession land markets have remained resilient through the recent period of economic uncertainty for almost all the traditional rural industries. 2003–2004 actually proved to be a very much better year for most farmers with healthily increased product prices. However, grain prices were looking a bit soft again as we approached the 2004 harvest which itself suffered from wet weather.

The fall in supply of land to the market has continued from around 500,000 acres per annum 30 years ago down to 230,000 acres in 2002 and only 150,000 acres in 2004. During that period the residential/amenity/alternative use elements of properties offered has become an increasingly powerful influence on a property's value. However, at current low levels of market turnover, the superficially volatile quarterly average value figures published by the RICS and others should be treated with some caution.

In the investment or let farmland market, supply to the open market also continued to fall from almost 36,000 acres in 1996 down to nearer 5,000 acres in 1999 to a negligible acreage in 2001, 2002 and 2003. Average gross yields on the few open market transactions recorded show an excess of demand over supply with interesting properties showing yields down to 2.5% and around 3.5% for the rest.

In the vacant farmland market, overall values were 'wobbly' during the spring/summer of 2003. They then grew strongly through the winter with confidence being underwritten in the spring of 2004 with the announcement of the outlines of the EU's Mid Term Review. This allowed the market to take a view on likely the pattern and form of future subsidies.

11.2.3 Vacant possession land

As vacant farmland represents over two-thirds of all farmland in Great Britain, it is obviously the principal land market. By definition it is freehold land offered for sale with vacant possession or available for the purchaser to physically occupy. Traditionally between 1– 2% have been offered for sale each year in packages from five acres of bareland to 5,000-acre units fully equipped with houses and buildings. However, offerings in recent years have fallen consistently to well below these historic levels.

Well-funded farmers seeking to achieve economies of scale from farming increased acreages are only part of the equation, as many others also buy farmland for a variety of reasons.

The ownership of land in the UK has always been used to demonstrate commercial success and been treated as a storehouse for wealth. The market for particularly attractive stretches of countryside with high-quality houses or for Scottish sporting estates is therefore dominated by the wealthy, and in some cases the international wealthy, for reasons unrelated to the income that they may be able to earn from ownership of the property. In the case of land overlying potentially valuable minerals or that may be developed in the future, the more imaginative investors or mineral operators and developers will normally compete to purchase.

Vacant possession land has been a very satisfactory investment since World War II, but values have fluctuated over the years and timing, as in all investment, has been a major factor for the most successful.

Given the diversity of the markets and understandable regional variations over time, reliable statistics about past land value trends are very difficult – and potentially dangerous if used for short-term comparisons. The only published annual average value figures that stretch back over the whole of the post-war period is the now suspended Oxford Institute/ Savills series. It, however, was based on averaging vacant land sales at auction. It could not therefore make allowance for properties withdrawn 'in the room' and subsequently sold privately or for the evidence of private treaty sales generally. Further, it probably disproportionately reflected grassland value trends as auction is a more common method of sale in the livestock areas. The series remains, however, the best guide to value trends over time and is set out in Table 11.2 – though the further in time we get away from its supension in 2000 the even less valuable it will become.

When selecting the part of the country in which to buy, most private investors will be influenced by their background. As a general rule, investors in straight farmland should seek to acquire the best land in the chosen area because history shows that, given a competent level of farm management, the best land generates the greatest profits over the years. Being the most adaptable land it also allows for the greatest range of potential crops for the future in an increasingly uncertain world.

Further, outside of the wholly commercial areas of farming, such as the Fens, farmland with an attractive appearance has always tended to sell for a premium value. As conservation considerations become more influential, the land markets should increasingly reflect the conservation value of otherwise well-farmed land. Enhancing the wildlife potential of a

Table 11.2 Average vacant land values at auction (Suspended in 2000)

With Possession £/acre		With Possession £/acre	
1951	88	76	734
52	76	77	991
53	73	78	1,327
54	75	79	1,769
55	80	1980	1,726
56	78	81	1,729
57	73	82	1,844
58	85	83	2,082
59	101	84	1,978
1960	123	85	1,935
61	124	86	1,697
62	134	87	2,001
63	168	88	2,178
64	214	89	2,654
65	235	1990	2,568
66	242	91	2,431
67	258	92	2,202
68	280	93	2,208
69	299	94	2,333
1970	245	95	2,484
71	262	96	3,560
72	596	97	3,263
73	757	98	2,934
74	636	99	2,478
75	539	2000	3,196

property, by well-planned hardwood tree planting, pond maintenance and sensitive management of ancient pastures, should be an ongoing management consideration of all investors.

In recent years an increasing level of grants and subsidies has been available for conservation policies, which are often based on the poorer quality soils. Increasing levels of such reliable 'high-quality' income from government sources may distort the short-term value of such inherently poor soils in the future.

It was thought that the overall shape of future EU CAP reform had been established in the 1990s with subsidies that encouraged ever-increasing levels of output per acre with fixed payments per arable acre cropped or breeding animal kept being replaced by allegedly conservation-friendly policies. These included set aside on arable land and lower stocking densities on grassland.

However, the recently published outline of the EU's Mid Term Review proposed Single Farm Payments scheme (to be calculated slightly differently in Wales and Scotland from England) changes most of that – rather more favourably than many had forecast. Whilst 'the devil will no doubt prove to be in the detail', which has yet to be announced, the markets at least now have a basis for making assumptions about probable future forms and levels of subsidy which may be available.

There are many options open to investors for the management of vacant farms or land and they should take professional advice. For instance they may manage a farm personally, farm in partnership with another farmer or have a contractual or profit-sharing arrangement with another farmer. Following the passing of the Agricultural Tenancies Act 1995, some of the land previously 'let' on these complex arrangements is being let on new Farm Business Tenancies in England and Wales (currently averaging around 200,000 acres each year) but the recent Scottish Agricultural Holdings Act has complicated the situation north of the border.

The method chosen will depend on the investor's income requirement, managerial ability and capital situation. The choice will affect the amount of farming capital required, the level of return obtained and the extent of involvement in the day-to-day running of the investment.

Generally, 'intensively housed livestock' enterprises are a specialist form of farming restricted mainly to pigs, poultry (chickens and turkeys), veal, barley beef and salmon or trout. They are usually capital intensive in their use of buildings and equipment, but occupy little land (say 2–20 acres). As any pig farmer will confirm, they are very volatile enterprises.

11.2.4 Let or investment land

'Let' or 'investment' land normally means land let under the old Agricultural Holdings Acts (AHA lettings) and comprises about 33% of the total usable agricultural acreage of Great Britain, having declined from around 90% at the turn of the last century. AHA lettings are lettings of land or equipped farms to secure tenants in occupation who pay rent, thus the investor will usually be unable to live on the property or farm it himself.

Traditionally, let land was worth two-thirds or more of its vacant possession value. However, in the post-war period up to 1995, most legislation affecting the landlord–tenant relationship was seen as favouring the latter. Taxation policies also tended to favour the owner-occupiers. As a result, AHA let land is now generally worth only half of its vacant value.

From September 1995 all new lettings of farmland in England and Wales (not being succession tenancies under the old Agricultural Holdings Acts) are in the form of Farm Business Tenancies (FBTs) covered by the new Agricultural Tenancies Act. Subject to the length of the tenancy granted, the value differential between vacant and FBT land should be less, although this new market is still relatively untested.

In Scotland, the Scottish Assembly passed a new Agricultural Holdings Act in 2003 that comes into effect by Statutory Instrument. It was introduced with the stated intention of bringing to Scottish land tenure the practical flexibility that the Agricultural Tenancies Act 1995 did for England and Wales. Sadly the Act as passed is expected to have exactly the opposite effect.

Investment opportunities vary from single let farms to large residential estates, from 10 acres up to 5,000+ acres.

AHA lettings are technically annual tenancies, but actually give security for life with rights of succession, subject to certain rules, for up to two further generations. Under most of them, the landlord is responsible for insuring and for a major part of the cost of repairs to the houses and buildings, though full repairing and insuring tenancies became increasingly common from the early 1970s. The tenancy agreement must be examined by a professional adviser, as it will form the basis for most matters affecting the investment in the future.

Rental levels vary. Rents fixed under the old Agricultural Holdings Acts are typically 50% below those obtainable in the open market for FBT lettings.

Three-yearly rent reviews on AHA lettings had been showing between 7% and 10% compound annual growth and agricultural investments had outperformed commercial property in the decade 1989–99. However, the recent sharp decline in farming profitability had brought rental growth to a halt, with sitting tenant rents tending to show a fall on review in the short term.

Most AHA let land is owned by private families as part of substantial estates passed down through the generations, or by traditional institutions such as the Crown, the church and numerous colleges and charities that tend to hold for the long term.

Tenanted land may be one-third of the total stock of farmland in Great Britain but, because of this ownership pattern, only represents a very small part of the total farmland market each year. Supply to the market obviously varies from year to year but has shown an overall decline from around 50,000 acres per annum in the early 1970s to a negligible acreage in recent years.

Currently, most buyers of let farms are tenants buying in their farms and a small but broadly based group of private investors, family trusts, certain charities, traditional institutions and some foreign investors. Management is normally undertaken by professional firms of chartered surveyors with land agency departments or by resident agents on larger estates.

Investors should be aware that there is no fixed relationship between gross and net yields. A typical gross yield today of 3.5% on the rents passing might net back on a full repairing and insuring let farm to 2.5%, whereas on a traditional landlord repairing and insuring let estate it might be under 2% in the short term. However, that rare multilet estate may well have latent potential to be released by active management to compensate for the lower initial net yield. Each investment opportunity must be viewed on its own merits.

11.2.5 Redundant farm buildings

The last Conservative Government's White Paper 'Rural England – A Nation Committed to a Living Countryside' pointed out that only 1.3% of those living in the countryside actually earns a living off the land. However, 31% of manufacturing and 25% of service sector employment (and an even higher proportion of business start-ups) were based in the countryside. A recent government Cabinet Office Discussion Paper reinforced this thinking.

More and more planning authorities are sympathetically viewing well thought-out schemes for business-related uses of redundant traditional farm buildings. They are proving to be an increasingly common and attractive diversification for farm and estate owners.

11.2.6 Finance

The basic rule for investors in farmland is that they should have the majority of the funds available in cash. Except in special circumstances, farmland investments should not be made on the back of borrowed money. The initial gross yield of a let farm is currently only around 3% and the price of a similar vacant farm is typically twice as high, so the return on an investment in vacant land (being that land's rental value) is currently only around 1.5%. A significant proportion of the purchase price as borrowed money, at possibly variable rates of interest, cannot realistically be funded by the farm.

Within the agricultural industry, short-term borrowings for working capital are provided by the clearing banks. Merchants' credit can also be taken but, when allowance is made for the discounts foregone, it can prove very expensive. Medium-term finance for machinery purchases, etc is also provided by the clearing banks and various specialist finance/leasing houses.

All long-term finance to the industry was traditionally provided by the Agricultural Mortgage Corporation and the Scottish Agricultural Securities Corporation, but all the main clearing banks also now participate. Subject to the borrower's ability to service the loan, up to two-thirds of a farm's agricultural value can usually be borrowed at competitive rates, which may be variable or fixed and be for up to 40 years. Interest is normally tax allowable and repayment of principal can be by way of linked life policies.

11.2.7 Preview of the year ahead

With continuing relatively low inflation, volatile product prices, interest rates rising and a relatively strong pound sterling the agricultural and rural business sectors face uncertain times.

The excessive levels of demand of a year or two ago for vacant and investment farmland have thinned so with signs of increasing supply, values look at some risk.

11.3 WOODLANDS

11.3.1 Background

Woodlands cover just over 5 m acres (about 10%) of the surface area of Great Britain. This compares with between 20% and 30% in most EU countries. Of UK timber consumption, 90% is imported, at a cost of £7.2bn in 1990. Annual timber production in Great Britain grew from about 3.5m cubic metres in 1980 to 5.35m cubic metres at the end of the decade and nearer 10m cubic metres currently. Consumption is also rising.

Of the national forest, some 25% is made up of hardwoods (often referred to as 'deciduous woodlands') and 75% is made up of softwoods (often referred to as 'coniferous' or 'evergreen' – but note the deciduous larch). Woodlands and forests take three principal forms.

Amenity and sporting woods and copses

These are normally found in lowland Great Britain in the form of hardwood mixtures. They are usually relatively small and can be politically sensitive locally, often being covered by Tree Preservation Orders. While individual trees may be substantial, and of significant value if they could be felled, these woods were planted for amenity/sporting purposes and have little to do with commercial timber production. However, they can provide great enjoyment and satisfaction to the buyer.

Larger blocks of hardwoods

Typically found in lowland Britain, these can have a significant value, but day-to-day management is often influenced by sporting and conservation considerations. Originally they formed parts of larger estates and can prove a very worthwhile investment.

Commercial softwood plantations and forests

These are commonly found in the higher rainfall areas of the country, principally in the South West, the hills of Wales, the North of England, Scotland and in other pockets such as the Breckland Sands around Thetford on the Norfolk/Suffolk borders and the New Forest in Hampshire. Being based on fast-growing trees, well suited to both the pulp industry and the saw-wood market, they have become the backbone of commercial forestry. Conifers grow in western Britain almost twice as fast as in Scandinavia, Russia and most of North America, thus providing shorter rotations and, theoretically, a long-term competitive advantage.

Of the national forest, approximately 40% is owned by the Forestry Commission and 60% by private investors/estates. The Forestry Commission was established in 1919 to encourage private owners to restore the productivity of their 3m acres of woodland ravaged by fellings during World War I and to create a State Forest of 1.75m acres. The Commission's current estate is just over 2m acres and is made up principally of softwoods.

The privately owned forest is more balanced overall between hardwoods and softwoods. The former tends to be owned by farmers and estate owners in lowland Britain. Much of the latter is in the hills, having often been established during the 1960s, 1970s and 1980s by investors with substantial incomes from other sources motivated by the tax planning benefits available at that time.

Forestry planting still attracts substantial grants, though forestry costs can no longer be offset against other income. The ownership of woods also has other valuable advantages:

(1) income from productive woodlands is tax free;
(2) assets comprising forestry business qualify for 100% relief from IHT after two years' ownership; and
(3) the land element can attract CGT rollover relief.

Investment in woodlands is essentially about buying usually relatively low value land with a growing crop on it, the rotation life of which may typically range from 40 years for young fast-growing conifers to 100–200 years for slower growing hardwoods. Normally, the first 20 years or more are about outgoings to establish the crop and manage it through to production age. From the commencement of thinnings, income may be expected to pick up from humble beginnings every five years for softwoods and ten years for hardwoods, through to the bulk of the income from the felling of the final crop for softwoods. Management of hardwoods is currently being converted to a policy of 'continuous cover forestry'. Ultimately the success or failure of this new hardwood strategy will be about achieving good natural regeneration and that will be closely linked to deer and grey squirrel control. A softwood crop planted today may be expected to show an internal rate of return of around 5% per annum over the life of the crop.

Alternatively, an investor may acquire an established plantation already in production and obtain a tax-free income. Such a wood is typically valued on the basis of a discounting of the expected net income stream in the 5–7% range.

The underlying economic argument for investing in forestry is that the world has been consuming its forests at well in excess of sustainable growth rates for many decades. A significant shortfall of timber is therefore likely in the future. However, as much of the world's timber reserves are in the Third World and the old Communist Empire, which are primarily concerned with short-term economic survival, the supply of timber on to the world markets may well continue at in excess of growth rates for some time yet. Further the current high value of sterling is very damaging to the domestic forestry industry as timber imports are so cheap.

11.3.2 Market trends

Demand for attractive, well-located amenity/hard woods remains very strong, with values underwritten by numerous conservation bodies and wealthy private investors.

Well-roaded areas of good, commercial softwoods in production and close to markets are also sought after, with plantations in the 'golden triangle' in south Scotland often achieving premium prices even in the current depressed woodland markets.

Poorer areas of commercial softwoods in isolated areas with bad access or younger plantations many years away from production have been heavily discounted for some time and remain very difficult to sell.

11.4 MISCELLANEOUS LAND USES

11.4.1 Accommodation land

'Accommodation land' refers to small areas within a farm or estate that do not naturally fit in with the main land uses. They are often held for alternative use at a later date or as grazing land for conservation purposes (eg a small area of permanent grassland). The expression can also be taken to mean those small areas of farmland that come up for sale from time to time, typically on the edge of a village or town.

Because of the limited acreage, accommodation land often appeals to the smaller investor, although it is usually more expensive to buy per acre than normal farmland. For the investor prepared to take on the problems of management and supervision, they can sometimes generate a significant income from pony grazing. A portfolio of such units can give outstanding performance over the years if planning consent for an alternative high value use (eg residential development) is granted on parts.

Accommodation land with vacant possession is sometimes held unused, but more often let on short-term arrangements.

Grazing for ponies and horses is normally done on a per head/per week payment basis and often generates a premium income. Horses are, however, choosy grazers and pasture deterioration usually results from horse grazing over the years.

On specialist dairy/beef farms, other people's sheep are often bought in 'on tack' during the winter months to tidy up the pastures. Payment is usually on a per head/per week basis.

11.4.2 Sporting rights

Sporting rights normally form an integral part of any land sale and usually form only a minor element of capital value within the overall transaction. However, on Scottish sporting estates they are often the main element of value that is usually assessed by past records of the bag or catch. In such cases, ease of access will be a significant factor.

Sporting rights may be divided into three main categories:

(1) fishing – game and coarse;
(2) shooting – driven and rough; and
(3) stalking – red and roe deer.

Sporting rights in England and Wales can be a legal estate and are on occasions reserved out of the sale of agricultural land and woods. In Scotland, only salmon fishing rights can form a separate legal estate.

They may therefore be acquired separately from the land for personal use or letting, and timesharing of stretches of well-known fishing rivers has become quite common. Since 1 April 1989, VAT has been payable on that element of the value of a land sale that relates to the value of the sporting facility. However, a transaction will normally only become taxable where a sporting income or value is separately identifiable. There is a further concession that farm tenants will only be expected to pay VAT on the sporting element of their tenancy agreements if it is greater than 5% of total rent.

Fishing

Salmon fishing

Capital values of salmon fishing vary enormously according to location and reputation of the river and can range up to £6,000 a fish or more. Sea trout are considerably less valuable. Rents can range from £50 to £500 per rod per day. Pollution and salmon disease can have a devastating effect on both rental and capital values and the effect on English and Welsh rivers of the recent restrictions on spring catches remains an open question. Whilst intensive salmon farming is common in Scottish sea lochs, salmon fisheries cannot be created artificially. They are principally associated with rivers in Scotland and parts of Wales and the West Country.

Trout fishing

This can be on freshwater chalk streams in the South (which command the highest rates and prices), on other rivers generally or on artificial or natural lakes or reservoirs. Demand has been high, with rents almost matching salmon river rates on the very best chalk streams. There is evidence of some oversupply of man-made trout lakes in certain areas.

Coarse fishing

Coarse fishing normally occurs in standing or slower-flowing waters in middle England and East Anglia that are usually rented by angling associations or smaller syndicates. Prices and rents vary greatly, but well-stocked old ponds close to large centres of population can provide a surprisingly large income.

Shooting

Shooting rights are, subject to economic conditions, readily lettable to a growing number of field sports enthusiasts. Shoots can vary from a well-organised grouse moor in Scotland or the North with accommodation, through substantial pheasant or partridge shoots in the South or East (perhaps let by the day with beaters and a cordon bleu lunch) down to a rough shoot over a small farm enjoyed informally by friends. Sporting rents vary from significant sums on the very best shoots to a minor additional income to the farm of £1 or £2 per acre. Charges for the best pheasant shoots, mainly in the South, lie in the £17.50–32 per bird range, with the best grouse moors in the North and Scotland ranging up to £110 per brace.

Deer stalking

Red, Fallow, Roe, Sika and Muntjac deer are the quarry, though Red and Roe deer are the principal commercial species. In the UK, Red deer stalking on the open heather hills of the Highlands of Scotland is the most well-known and the most highly valued cost at over £300 per stag. Roe deer stalking is traditionally more highly valued on mainland Europe, but commercial lettings in suitable locations are becoming increasingly popular in the UK at between £200 and £450 per buck.

The build-up of Roe deer numbers throughout the woods of Great Britain has resulted in professional stalkers shooting from high seats for vermin control purposes and for the value of the carcasses. Red deer are also controlled in this way in the Thetford Forest in East Anglia, though in the South West Red deer, and in the New Forest Fallow deer, were traditionally managed by hunting with hounds.

Sporting generally

Sound game, vermin and habitat management practices can enhance the holding capacity and sporting qualities of a property, but they cannot change the nature of it. For instance, grouse will only survive on a well-managed heather moor in the hills of the North or Scotland that benefits from peace, quiet and vermin control. The once famous Langholm Moor in Dumfriesshire was recently closed after a five-year trial period during which the harrier population was allowed to develop. Ultimately they exterminated the grouse population and, having eaten themselves out of house and home, are now reported to be in decline again.

The threat to ban hunting with hounds is already a reality in Scotland and remains likely in England and Wales. If it is banned, the 'follow-on' threat to other fields sports will become more real. The potential political risks associated with investment in sporting estates should therefore be recognised.

Corporate entertaining has increasingly influenced rental values on the best sporting estates over the last 25 years. However it demands large bags and a high level of service. Commercial lettings of shoots by the day are seldom profitable in their own right but more a means of subsidising the owner's hobby.

The purchase of quality sporting rights, as a separate investment, is normally only for the very wealthy investor who can afford an often substantial capital payment with the prospect of significant annual outgoings thereafter. The less wealthy must limit their ambitions to more humble rough shooting, a gun on a syndicate shoot or the purchase of a timeshare on a suitable fishing river. For most investors, sporting rights will be an indirect benefit of the purchase of a farm, wood or estate.

Market trends

With increasing wealth, leisure time and transport facilities, demand for sporting rights has been increasing steadily. Capital performance has generally been very satisfactory, with the market for the very best becoming international. However, they are about enjoying expensive hobbies and are threatened by the combination of the high sterling and the increasingly powerful anti-blood sports lobby. They must therefore be viewed as politically sensitive investments.

11.4.3 Stud farms and training establishments

Stud farms

Subject to planning, agricultural land may be developed for the breeding of thoroughbred bloodstock, riding horses or ponies and demand has been increasing with over 2m people now members of the various horse societies. For stud farms in the most favoured locations, such as Newmarket, Lambourn and Malton, demand is usually relatively strong. Values are lower in locations further from these recognised breeding centres where the best stallions stand. The centre of the national bloodstock industry is Newmarket, where both the National Stud and Tattersalls Sale Paddocks are based. Stud farms in the favoured areas command a substantial premium over vacant farmland.

The environment of a good stud farm is of great importance if the young stock are to grow and develop properly. The type of soil, particularly to facilitate the building of bone, is critical, and the best are to be found on free draining chalk soils. A stud farm typically varies in size from 50 to 250 acres. It will either be a private stud (where the owner maintains his own animals only) or a public stud (where one or more stallions are kept and the mares visit during the covering season and often the foaling season as well). Stables must be of high standard, with special boxes and facilities for covering and foaling purposes. The cost of putting up post and rail fencing is high because of the need for small paddocks and double fences.

To establish a stud farm can take up to 20 years for the hedges and shelter belts to mature. Good quality residential accommodation at the stud will be required for the stud groom and other employees: for a medium-sized stud a minimum of five or six houses might be required.

Stud farms usually change hands by private treaty in a limited and highly specialised market. Purchasers will usually be closely connected with the bloodstock industry. It is exceptional for stud farms to be bought as an investment on a tenanted basis.

Training establishments or yards

At various centres in the country, but particularly at Newmarket, Lambourn and Malton for racing, there are established training facilities with extensive gallops and all-weather tracks. Training yards usually comprise a trainer's house together with a number of cottages and hostels for stable lads; a minimum of 15 boxes with tack, feed and hay stores; and often special open and covered exercising areas. Business rates are payable on both stud farms and training yards.

Market trends

The specialised but volatile markets for both stud farms and training yards expanded throughout most of the 1980s, declined in the early 1990s and then recovered again. They currently remain relatively strong.

11.4.4 Mineral bearing land

All minerals (other than oil, gold, silver and coal) usually belong to the freehold owner of land, but may have been reserved to a predecessor in title. On acquisition, purchasers should always check that the mineral rights are included. The principal minerals are coal, sand, gravel, silica sand (glass), ironstone, clay (brick-making or china), limestone and in certain areas other special deposits (tin, copper, etc). With limited exceptions, all coal belongs to the Coal Authority and oil/gas deposits to the Government.

Strict planning regulation affects mineral excavation and specific areas are designated in most County Mineral Plans. In the past, virtually no excavation was permitted on land classified as Grade I or II. Geological maps indicate the approximate location of minerals, and resistivity surveys and test borings can indicate mineral deposit patterns, depths and volumes. Development is usually carried out through a sale or lease to one of the principal mineral companies.

The sale of mineral-bearing land incurs CGT on chargeable gains. Profits from the commercial operation of mineral workings are liable to income tax (or corporation tax), with capital allowances (including a depletion allowance of 50% of the royalty rate of the minerals) available for certain expenditure. Mineral royalties are taxed, broadly, as one-half as income and the other half as capital.

From April 2002 mineral operators have to pay a new aggregates extraction tax of £1.60 per tonne. The Government claims that this is only a tax on operators designed to encourage the recycling of materials. The idea that it will have no long-term effect on owners through future levels of royalty income seems somewhat naive.

Tipping, fishing, boating and water-skiing rights may be reserved and can provide high levels of income and reversionary asset value on completion of excavation. The 'hole in the ground' was often worth more than the original land. However, with the rate of landfill tax, fixed at £2 per ton for inert material, rising to £15 per tonne of degradable materials in 2004 and then by £3 per ton annually towards £35 per ton in the medium to long term, this situation may be changing. Certainly further increases in illegal fly tipping around the countryside can be confidently forecast.

The end value of restored land is often uncertain and any hint of noxious materials on site could result in a negative value.

Minerals are a speculative investment if the land is purchased with mineral exploitation in view by an investor who is not a mineral operator. While some farmland can produce high yields from unexpected mineral excavation, high prices should not be paid merely to include it in a speculative 'mineral land bank'.

11.4.5 Public leisure/entertainment, retail land uses and commercial uses for redundant farm buildings

Like most subsidiary forms of land use, these categories are all relatively marginal to the whole but potentially significant profit centres on individual properties in the right locations. The managerial skills required are, however, very different from those of a farmer or forester and, if management of the main activity is not to suffer, they are best treated as a separate activity. Their common characteristic is that they are intended to appeal to the general public. They come in three main categories, though they often overlap with each other.

The passive leisure land uses

The obvious examples are leased golf courses, caravan and camping sites and mobile home parks – though the higher the site's standard and more extensive the facilities (eg a shop), the less managerially passive they become.

These properties are usually located at or near seaside areas or in areas of scenic beauty. Mobile home parks may be for permanent (all year round) occupation in certain areas specified by local councils. Planning controls are stringent on all large-scale parks or sites. Special facilities are required under the Caravan Sites and Control of Development Act 1960 including washing and toilet facilities, electricity and roads. The Mobile Homes Act 1975 confers on caravan homeowners a limited security of tenure. Planning permission is almost always required and not easy to get in areas viewed as being of high landscape value.

An investment of this type can be lucrative but is high risk, demanding considerable pre-acquisition investigation. The Caravan Club provides information on sites and the pitfalls associated with them. Fashions change and the weather greatly affects the income from holiday parks, particularly in coastal areas, where serious storms can result in large losses.

The active leisure entertainment land uses

These are typically owner-managed golf courses, wildlife parks, pleasure gardens, theme parks, riding schools/pony trekking centres and grand houses open to the public. Planning permission is required for wildlife parks, pleasure gardens, golf courses and riding schools. Location is of paramount importance since it is essential to be close to urban populations with good road access. Initial development costs can be high. It is probable that future legislation and higher design and maintenance standards will further aggravate the position. For country houses it is especially important to check the building status for planning purposes. 'Listed' buildings are graded under the Town and Country Planning Act 1971 and the Town and Country Planning (Scotland) Act 1972, which impose varying degrees of responsibility on the owner, including the need to obtain listed building consent for demolition, improvements or even minor alterations.

Houses having historic and amenity value are frequently opened to the public as a trading venture, enabling the owner to continue to maintain the family home. The trading venture is intended to support the upkeep of the property and its general environment. Other large houses can be acquired for institutional purposes, such as research centres, out of town offices, training centres and health farms.

Wildlife parks and golf courses can be difficult to sell and demonstrate that an investment of this kind is speculative in all but the prime locations. It is more often seen as a means to an end by existing owners rather than as the reason for a commercial purchase.

Retail land uses

Farm shops and garden centres are the obvious examples. Farm shops are usually ancillary to farm businesses and intended to enable the farmer to obtain better prices than he would get on the wholesale market. However, EU hygiene regulations and the like are becoming ever more restrictive.

Most garden centres were run by individuals or small companies, but there are now an increasing number of larger enterprises with multiple sites. Planning consent is required.

The location of both farm shops and garden centres is important, with the best sites being on main roads and close to large centres of population. The general increase in leisure time and television programmes on gardening and cookery have stimulated the popularity of these enterprises, though the 'pick your own' method of sale in certain seasons has been less successful. Good car parking facilities and a high profile site are essential.

Enterprises of this kind can be a valuable source of additional income and capital if correctly developed out of a farm unit (which is usually owner-occupied), but they are seldom sold as separate investments.

12

COMMERCIAL PROPERTY

Updated by

PAUL WRIGHT

Investment Management Director, Zurich Financial Services

ANDREW BULL

FRICS, European Director, LaSalle Investment Management

12.1 PROPERTY INVESTMENT

Property investments appeal to different types of investor dependent on an investor's requirement for income or capital growth, and the level of risk the investor will accept. Properties can be subdivided according to location, type and size. Small industrial units and multi-million pound office investments are unlikely to be of interest to the same investor. Risk-averse investors such as insurance companies and pension funds will prefer to invest in 'prime' properties in established locations let to blue chip tenants on long, full-repairing and insuring leases. A factor of considerable importance to these investors is the security of rental income and capital gain. Other investors will, however, be prepared to accept a higher level of risk by purchasing 'secondary' properties if the return is considered to be sufficiently attractive. One reason to invest in property, for example by pension funds, is the risk diversification benefit of property when held together with such assets as equities.

The purchase of a commercial property involves the giving up of a capital sum now in exchange for future returns such as the benefits of owner-occupation, income flow and/or capital gain. Underlying any property investment decision will be the option of alternative investments, ie stocks, shares, cash, unit trusts and even works of art. In selecting an investment, the investor will seek the highest real rate of return on capital invested but, depending on the object of the investment, may 'trade off' a reduced rate of return in consideration for increased liquidity or security of income. An investor's tax status will also be an important factor.

12.1.1 Property valuation

In its simplest form, the basis of property valuation is the capitalisation of rental income of a property over a term of years or in perpetuity (depending on whether the property is leasehold or freehold) at an investment rate of return that reflects all the elements of risk associated with that property (security of income, obsolescence of the building, economic factors and the cost/inconvenience of management). The capitalisation rate chosen to value the property will also reflect the expectation of future rental growth and consequently tends to be significantly lower than the yields available from fixed-interest securities. This phenomenon (also illustrated by the dividend yield of equities) is known as the 'reverse yield gap' and since the 1970s has varied between about 1% and 8%. This relationship has ceased to exist during in recent years, as a lower inflation environment has resulted in investors applying reduced growth rate assumptions when comparing property to fixed-interest investments. A 'risk-premium' over long-dated gilts is therefore being required to compensate investors for the perceived additional risks.

12.2 TYPES OF COMMERCIAL PROPERTY

Direct investment in commercial property falls mainly into the following categories:

(1) retail, including supermarkets and retail warehouses;
(2) offices, including town centre, out of town and campus;
(3) industrial, including factories, warehouses, hi-tech and trade centres;

and, to a much lesser degree:

(4) farmland and forestry;
(5) leisure.

Most investors with a significant long-term investment portfolio aim to hold the majority of the investments balanced between the retail, office and industrial categories, where there is a well-defined investment market.

12.2.1 Purchase of commercial property

Because of the large amounts of capital required for the purchase of even the smallest commercial property, the commercial property investment market is, like the equity market, generally confined to UK and foreign insurance companies, and pension fund and property companies, together with a number of wealthy private individuals or family trusts. UK insurance companies and pension funds began investing in commercial property in the mid-1950s, broadening their asset bases beyond the equities and government securities that had hitherto formed their principal media for investment. UK pension fund investment reached a peak as a percentage of their assets in 1979 and significant net new investment was not then seen until the late 1980s.

Institutional exposure to property in recent years has averaged around 5% of total assets by market value. However, because of the performance of the equity market over this period, significant property net investment has been necessary to maintain this weighting.

It is, however, clear from other market evidence that a high degree of polarisation within the property market still exists, highlighting the need for careful stock selection when purchasing commercial property investments.

12.2.2 Lease of commercial property

During the 1980s commercial buildings were generally leased for a term of 25 years with five-yearly rent reviews to the property's current open market rental value. During the early 1990s the supply/demand balance was so radically altered that the market became one in which tenants' desires were paramount. There has been marked owner reluctance to grant shorter leases, but the trend to shorter leases and the granting of tenants' options to determine leases continues. At the same time, increased incentives by way of cash payments and rent-free periods have resulted in reduced returns to landlords. Since this change, tenants have continued to negotiate shorter leases even in the stronger landlords' market experienced in recent years, moving towards European length leases. There is now general consensus that there will be no return to the standard 25-year lease, other than in certain restricted submarkets such as large City of London offices.

The Code of Practice for Commercial Leases was published in March 2002, outlining guidelines that Royal Institution of Chartered Surveyors (RICS) members are encouraged to use in their professional activities. The Code makes recommendations that are considered best practice in conduct and negotiating commercial leases in the duration of a commercial lease. It has been implemented as part of the present Government's commitment to improve flexibility and choice in the commercial property market. Therefore, lease terms may also be impacted by the Code when its recommendations are implemented, with a further impact on property owners' returns.

Under the terms of what is known as a 'full repairing and insuring' (FRI) lease, the occupational tenant is responsible for (or at least for the cost of) carrying out all repairs to and insurance of the property. While the day-to-day management of a commercial property investment is of vital importance in terms of maintaining the performance of the investment, and in particular in achieving the best possible rent on review, in the case of a letting of an entire building (as opposed to one which is in multiple occupation) the process is essentially one of collecting the rent and checking that the repairs and insurance are in place. In multi-occupied buildings the repairs and insurance are carried out by the landlord, or the landlord's managing agents, with the costs being recovered from the tenants. An investment in commercial property has historically been regarded as a passive investment, with the day-to-day and portfolio management responsibilities being undertaken by a firm of managing agents.

12.2.3 Rent reviews

Investments in commercial property provide regular opportunities for increasing the income obtained from the property through rent reviews. Since World War II the time period between rent reviews has altered. Formerly leases were granted with a period of 21 years between rent reviews, but latterly this decreased to 14 years, then to seven years and is currently five years. Generally, rent reviews result in the rent increasing to the property's then open market rental value and most institutional leases provide for the rent review to be on an upwards only basis. As mentioned earlier, oversupply and reduced tenant demand resulted in rents falling, increased incentives and shorter lease terms. However, leases granted with terms long enough to have five-yearly rent review provisions have on the whole continued to include upward only rent reviews. The Code of Practice for Commercial Leases, as mentioned above, may affect rent reviews as one of its recommendations is that downward rent reviews should be considered when granting a lease. Downward rent reviews are not common within modern leases and their implementation is not welcomed by property owners who require a secure income.

12.3 SHOPS

12.3.1 General

Historically, three factors have affected the rental and capital value of shops: location, location and location. Because the quality of the location can readily be ascertained, shops have been regarded as one of the most secure forms of commercial property investment. In the past, principal high street locations were rarely subject to major change, except when a town centre redevelopment scheme or a new shopping centre was planned, when it was usually possible to predict the significant effect that these new centres would have on the existing shopping patterns. The provision of sufficient and accessible car parking and an attractive environment will ensure that retail parks and out-of-town centres continue to prosper, although future out-of-town schemes will be limited by current planning regulations that now support town centre regeneration. The retailing sector is undergoing significant change, with many retailers repositioning in the market, restyling their outlets and merchandise, and taking over competitors. In addition there was dramatic growth in 'speciality' retailing where a number of retailers have been successful in targeting specific markets and responding quickly to changes in consumer demand. Hence the more established chains experienced greater competition for prime pitches in the high street.

A large number of the best shop units in the UK are now owned by the institutions, although a proportion are still owned and occupied by the major retailing organisations. In recent years rental growth has been considerable throughout the retail sector. There has been keen competition to make further investment in this category, while the availability of suitable investments is extremely limited in relation to the amount of investment money available.

In the property investment market, shops are categorised as prime, secondary and tertiary.

12.3.2 Prime

Prime shops are those situated in the best trading locations along the principal high streets in the larger towns where major multiple retailers, such as Boots, WH Smith and Marks & Spencer, are to be found. The rental income obtainable from shop units within these locations varies enormously, depending on the importance of the particular town.

12.3.3 Secondary

Secondary shops are those either on the fringes of the best trading positions within the larger towns or in the best shopping positions in the smaller towns. Because of the shortage of prime shop units now available for commercial investment, the institutional demand for this type of property has grown in recent years. Since the prospects for rental growth in these locations have proved more erratic than those in prime locations, investors expect a higher yield.

12.3.4 Tertiary

Tertiary shops are those on the fringes of the secondary trading positions and shops in neighbourhood shopping parades, including the corner shop. There is a negligible demand from multiple tenants for representation in these locations. Therefore, covenant strength is poorer and the management load heavier. Consequently, demand for these properties derives principally from private investors. This market is usually very active with sales of all sizes taking place by private treaty or auction.

12.3.5 Out-of-town shopping

Out-of-town shopping has evolved through the recognition of the car-borne shopper and may generally be divided into food and non-food retailing. The main DIY specialists (eg Homebase and B&Q) are often found grouped together and require units of 35,000–50,000 square feet. Out-of-town food retailers now include most of the major food chains. Good surface car parking and main road prominence are essential criteria.

Out-of-town shopping often provides a combination of retailing and leisure facilities for the consumer, including cinema, tenpin bowling, restaurants, a night club and sports facilities.

12.4 OFFICES

12.4.1 General

In the early 1970s many provincial towns, as well as central London, became seriously over-supplied with office accommodation and rents either remained level or fell. This started to happen again to a lesser extent in the early 1990s. A factor in the demand/supply imbalance is the lengthy period from planning to completion of a development.

The quality of an office building is of greater importance than that of a shop unit. Occupational tenants are setting ever higher standards, requiring good quality finishes, modern lifts, central heating, adequate car parking facilities, the ability to accommodate a growing range of sophisticated office equipment (notably computers, word processors and communications equipment) and, particularly in central London, double-glazing and air conditioning. The costs of maintaining offices, especially the mechanical services, the unified business rates, and the cost of refurbishing the accommodation, mean that the tenant and investor are subjected to high outgoings. These have increased as a direct result of technological changes having shortened the lifetime of buildings and services.

The most expensive office locations in the UK have historically been the West End and City of London. Since the tenant will be responsible for all outgoings under the terms of his lease, the actual cost of occupation will probably be double the cost of the rent alone. Because of the security and perceived prospects for long-term rental growth offered by buildings within the West End and City of London, there has been a strong institutional demand for investments. Increasingly, foreign as well as UK investors have been active in this market.

The other principal office areas in London follow a similar but less expensive pattern to that of the City and West End, although in the late 1980s an upswing in demand coupled with relatively restricted supply resulted in these locations experiencing dramatic growth in rents. Outside London, rents vary from centre to centre, with the towns immediately to the west of London along the M4 corridor being the highest outside London.

12.4.2 Conclusion

Offices form the backbone of most commercial property investment portfolios because of the amount of money involved and the past performance of rental growth on rent review. They are likely to remain a dominant feature of institutional portfolios and the preferred areas are those in central London and certain selected provincial centres. However, it is becoming necessary to spend large capital sums more frequently to maintain the quality of the investment. Over many years the cost of central London office occupancy and the inconvenience of commuting have encouraged companies to move their operations to suburban and provincial locations.

12.5 INDUSTRIAL

12.5.1 General investment: factories and warehouses

The declining importance in Great Britain of the industrial and manufacturing sectors, the volatility of the economy and the relatively short economic life of industrial buildings have resulted in investors requiring higher yields for factories and warehouse premises than for shops and offices. In this context, institutional investors generally prefer warehouse buildings, as opposed to factories, because these tend to be less specialised and therefore require fewer remedial works when a tenant vacates the premises. Industrial processes also tend to have a more destructive effect on the actual fabric of the property.

12.5.2 Location criteria

Although the uses of factories and warehouses are different, both in practical and in legislative terms, it is convenient to categorise them together, since the locational and investment criteria are similar. The most desirable investments in this category are situated on well-located industrial estates, close to major conurbations and motorway access points or the national airports. It is interesting to note that proximity to rail services is not an important criterion in the UK, being less important than a good supply of labour and good estate services for the factory owner.

12.5.3 Institutional criteria

The insurance companies and pension funds have developed certain criteria that they look for in modern industrial and warehouse buildings. These criteria relate to clear working height, floor loading capacity, the presence of sprinklers, the proportion of office space to warehouse space within the unit, the number of loading doors, the presence of a concreted hard standing in front of the unit and adequate car parking. While these institutional criteria are often in excess of the criteria required by occupiers, investors would be wise to purchase units meeting institutional criteria, since they will find a wider market in which to sell the property in the future.

12.5.4 Yields

Yields available on prime industrial and warehouse investments are higher than those on prime shops and offices. Rental growth experienced over the late 1970s was, generally, very satisfactory but became static in the early and mid-1980s during the economic recession, and improved again in the late 1980s. Investment in modern industrial and warehouse buildings is a more recent trend than investment in offices and shops, and now forms around 18% of a typical portfolio. Opportunities do exist for non-institutional investment where very high yields can be obtained from obsolescent or poorly located properties, but these carry commensurate risk.

12.6 BUSINESS PARKS

While many areas of traditional manufacturing industry were affected by the economic recession, the hi-technology field experienced considerable growth. This resulted in a new direction in the design and use of industrial buildings with tenants becoming increasingly discerning towards their preferences in building design and working environment. The most radical change has been the introduction of the building that comprises a two- or three-storey structure designed to permit the interchangeability of functions such as offices, research and development, laboratories or industrial. An out-of-town location, extensive car parking and landscaping with imaginative and functional finishes both internally and externally create a high quality corporate image. The first and still largest business park in the UK is Stockley Park off the M4 very close to Heathrow airport. Both back office and headquarters type functions are now moving to such business parks. Business parks may also serve research and development purposes, for example the science parks at Oxford and Cambridge that benefit from close associations with the nearby universities.

12.7 AGRICULTURE

Having experienced growth in popularity with institutional investors, at one point forming in excess of 5% of some investment portfolios, farmland and forestry have been increasingly less popular as a result of falling values and the perception of a continued fall in values. In addition, investors have begun to appreciate that in many instances the economic support or tax benefits of these investments have been and are likely to be subject to political tinkering, thus dramatically altering the value of many investments at a stroke.

Smaller, more picturesque farms, especially those with attractive houses, have, however, become increasingly attractive and prices have continued to rise for successful businessmen desirous of changing their place of domicile and lifestyle (see also Chapter 11).

12.8 LEISURE

Investments in the 'leisure industry' include hotels, marinas, golf courses, sports centres and entertainment facilities. The growing demand for leisure facilities, both home-based and from tourists, is resulting in increasing investment in this field. It is, however, regarded as an investment in management expertise rather than in the property that the particular leisure activity occupies, and great caution is therefore necessary. Quite often an investor's return will be geared to the operator's turnover or profitability rather than to the premises' rental value, which can sometimes be very difficult to determine.

While the returns from leisure industry investments, in terms of capital gains, can be substantial for the astute investor, the risks are considerable and such investments are not recommended to small investors.

12.9 CONCLUSION

Commercial property is a unique asset class that appeals to different investors for different investment reasons. It is important for a potential investor to obtain specialist advice in relation to property investment as there are many issues that may affect a property investment.

13

BUSINESS VENTURES (WITHOUT PARTICIPATION IN MANAGEMENT)

MIKE WILKES

PKF, Chartered Accountants

13.1 INTRODUCTION

There are always people with experience and no money looking for people with money and no experience. The former sometimes have the money and the latter have had the experience. That is not to say that, in general terms, such arrangements should always be avoided. There are plenty of good ideas that need financing and the rewards to the investor can be substantial, but such investments call for faith in someone else's judgement, nerves of steel and an instinct for gambling. Many ventures have turned out well after being (sometimes more than once) on the verge of disaster. Those who do not like walking along the edge of a precipice should keep to gentler paths.

Individuals seeking finance will often paint the picture of their prospects in rosy colours, not through dishonesty but through enthusiasm, and such enthusiasm should always be discounted. Unfortunately it is often highly contagious, so that impersonal, dispassionate, professional advice is essential. The pitfalls should be considered every bit as carefully as the opportunities. It is easier to lose money than to make it; but money is seldom to be made without accepting an element of chance.

In some cases money, once put into a venture, is effectively locked in, come what may. At best it may be possible to withdraw it only at considerable cost. On the other hand, by good judgement and good luck (and any successful venture requires both), there are fortunes to be made. The essential feature of the investments considered in this chapter is that the investor relies wholly on the expertise of someone else – company director, active partner, racehorse trainer and so on – and will probably be involved in matters of which he is ignorant or, at least, inexperienced.

It must never be forgotten that taxation will make inroads into both income and capital gains, and, in this respect, professional advice should always be taken. There may be other ways of making investments so that, with this in mind, every scheme requires careful expert consideration.

Equally, if losses are incurred, steps should be taken to see that the maximum tax advantage is obtained. The advice of an accountant or a solicitor or probably both can be invaluable, not only in dealing with legal and financial problems that are puzzling the prospective investor, but often also in pointing out problems of which the layman may be totally unaware. The effects of taxation are touched on in the following sections, but complex problems can arise which it is impossible to deal with briefly. In every case the solution will depend on the individual facts.

The view is sometimes held that professional advice is an expensive luxury that can be dispensed with: nothing could be further from the truth. If it seems expensive it is because the mass of all-pervading legislation of recent years has made it dangerous to take any steps in commerce (or indeed in much else) without considering the application of statute law, statutory instruments and regulations. Professional advice taken at the outset often avoids difficulties and disputes at a later stage that may well prove far more expensive in legal costs.

13.2 THE CURRENT BUSINESS CLIMATE

After remaining at a consistently low level for a fairly long period, interest rates have now started to rise, mainly in an effort to stem the increase in property prices. Latest indicators appear to show that property values may have begun to level out, especially in the South East, where there have been substantial increases over the last 12 months. Unless this levelling continues it seems inevitable that further interest rises will be necessary. The number of individual Lloyd's Names has continued to decrease, and the number of Names participating in the 2004 account continue to fall compared with the number of Names underwriting for the 2003 account. The Lloyd's 'Blue Book', that lists the Names participating in the 2003 account, is a very slim single volume, a far cry from the two thick volumes that were required to list all the Names underwriting for the 1986 account. Many former Names have resigned and either ceased underwriting activities altogether, or transferred to corporate 'Name companies' that can offer some financial protection, but despite the number of resignations, syndicates still in run-off have forced some Names to continue until the accounts in which they have participated can be closed. Lloyd's, like insurance generally, is a cyclical business and after several poor years the tide began to turn in 2002 with Lloyd's producing a profit of just under £835m. In 2003 the profits are estimated to be in excess of £3bn, but although the outlook may appear attractive in the short term, it is difficult to predict if this improvement will continue in the future, and Lloyd's no longer accepts new Names with an unlimited liability.

13.3 MINORITY HOLDINGS IN PRIVATE COMPANIES

13.3.1 Introduction

It was for many years a feature of company law that a private company was one that restricted the transfer of its shares and any company that did not do so was a public company. Under the Companies Act 1980 (a statute enacted largely as a move towards European uniformity) this distinction was swept away and although the words 'public' and 'private' are retained, their meanings are now quite different. A public company is defined in the Companies Act 1985 (a consolidating Act bringing together the provisions of the Companies Acts of 1948, 1967, 1976, 1980 and 1981), and any company not within that definition will be a private company. The principal distinction is that a public company (denoted at the end of its name by the letters 'plc' or by the words 'public limited company') must have an authorised and allotted minimum share capital which is at present £50,000 but which may be altered by Statutory Instrument by the Secretary of State. At least one-quarter of that allotted share capital of a public company must be paid up before it can commence business. No such minimum capital requirements exist in relation to private companies. A company need no longer restrict the transfer of its shares to be a private company under the new Act. References in this part of the chapter to 'private companies' are intended, generally, to refer to the smaller family company where control rests in the hands of a few shareholders who are probably the directors or related to the directors. As regards the transfer of shares see 13.3.4.

A minority holding in a private company may be acquired in a number of ways: it may be inherited; it may be bought from an existing shareholder; it may arise when a company is newly formed to undertake the starting of a business venture; or it may arise on the allotment of shares by a company taking over an existing company or undertaking.

A minority holding is, for the purpose of this chapter, any holding of shares or other securities which does not give the holder control of the company, and thus includes a holding of non-voting shares or debentures. Assuming that a company has shares of one class only, of which each has one vote, a holding of less than 50% is a minority holding. However, in some companies there are different classes of shares and, for example, shares of one class only might carry a vote, the others carrying no vote or giving the right to vote on certain specified matters only. In other companies there may be one class of shares carrying one vote each and another class of which the shares carry a hundred votes each, so that a holding, in nominal value, of more than half the company's issued capital does not necessarily carry control. Careful scrutiny of the company's capital structure is vital before making an investment in a private company.

13.3.2 Powers of the minority

At general meetings of a company, a vote is first taken by a show of hands (subject to anything in the articles of association), giving each member personally present one vote regardless of the size of his holding. Under common law any one member may demand a poll, the votes then being counted, normally on the basis of one for each share held. The articles may include a requirement that a poll must be demanded by more than one member, but such a requirement is limited by s 373 of the Companies Act 1985 so that, except for certain purposes, an article is void if it requires the demand for a poll to be made by more than five members, or the holders of more than one-tenth of the voting rights, or the holders of more than one-tenth of the paid-up capital entitled to vote.

When a poll is held, each member has (in the absence of any contrary provision in the articles) one vote for each share held. Thus on a poll, one member holding 60% of the issued shares will be able to outvote a dozen members holding the other 40% between them.

An ordinary resolution requires a simple majority of members voting, so that a minority shareholder cannot, in the face of determined opposition, prevent its being passed. However, a special or extraordinary resolution, which is necessary for certain fundamental decisions, requires a majority of three-quarters of members voting, so that on a poll, where each share carries a vote, the holder of 40% of the issued shares, although a minority shareholder, could block such a resolution. An extraordinary resolution is required for, among other things, winding up a company that cannot, by reason of its liabilities, continue in business, and the articles of the company may require such a resolution for various other purposes. A special resolution is necessary for, inter alia:

(1) the alteration of a company's objects (although, in that case, the holders of not less than 15% of the issued share capital may apply to the court to have the alteration cancelled);
(2) the alteration of a company's articles;
(3) the change of a company's name (subject to the approval of the Department of Trade and Industry);
(4) a reduction of capital (subject to the approval of the court);
(5) the re-registration of a public company as private or a private company as public under the 1985 Act;
(6) the re-registration of an unlimited company as limited; and
(7) the winding-up of a company voluntarily.

In addition to considering the effective powers of the majority, it must be remembered that the day-to-day running of the company's business is in the hands of the directors. As a last resort, majority shareholders can remove and appoint directors; minority shareholders cannot. In this connection it is important to note that most companies' articles of association preclude the payment of a dividend in excess of that recommended by the directors. If, therefore, the directors feel it is desirable for any reason to retain the profits, or the bulk of the profits, within the company rather than distribute them by way of dividend, minority shareholders may find that they are not receiving a satisfactory return on their investments and, even with the assistance of the majority shareholders, there may be little they can effectively do about it.

Arising out of the matters discussed in the previous paragraph, it will be appreciated that the majority could deal with the affairs of a company in a way which might be to the detriment of the interests of the minority, particularly where the minority controls 25% or less of the voting power. The law, however, provides protection for an oppressed minority in two ways. First, the minority may petition the court to wind up the company on the ground that it is just and equitable to do so. This is, in many cases, an unsatisfactory course to pursue since the assets will be sold at their break-up value, the goodwill will disappear and the minority will not have achieved its object, namely that the company should continue to operate but that its interests should be safeguarded. Secondly, the minority may petition the court for relief under s 459 of the Companies Act 1985.

Protection under the 1948 Act was provided where the court was of the opinion that the company's affairs were being conducted in a manner oppressive to some part of the members (including the petitioner) and that to wind up the company would unfairly prejudice that part of the members although the facts would justify winding-up on the grounds that to wind up would be just and equitable. The court, on being so persuaded, could make any order that it thought fit. There is a considerable body of authority on what constitutes oppression for this purpose.

Under s 459 of the Companies Act 1985, protection is afforded by the court if it is satisfied that the conduct of the company's affairs is 'unfairly prejudicial to the interests' of some part of the members. A petition may also be brought under this provision based on 'any actual or proposed act or omission' of the company. The meaning of 'unfairly prejudicial' is not defined and awaits judicial interpretation.

13.3.3 Liability for uncalled capital

The essential feature of a limited company is that the liability of its shareholders is limited to the capital they put in or agree to put in, and no further demands can be made on them by the company or its creditors except where shares are issued which are not fully paid. The holder of such shares may be called upon by the company to pay the unpaid balance, and failure to pay on a call may result in forfeiture of the shares. Any holder of partly paid shares must therefore always bear in mind that a contingent liability attaches to them. If the additional capital is required for development of the business, it will probably be all to the good. It sometimes happens though, that it is needed because the company is in difficulties and may amount to throwing good money after bad.

13.3.4 Transfer of shares

Difficulties may arise in connection with the disposal of a minority holding of shares in a private company. One of the hallmarks of a private company under the Companies Act 1948 was that it restricted transfers of its shares, and if the articles did not so provide, it was not a private company. The usual form, following reg 3 of Table A in Pt II of Sched 1 to the Companies Act 1948, provided 'the directors may, in their absolute discretion and without assigning any reason therefore, decline to register any transfer of any share, whether or not it is a fully paid share'. It follows that, in such cases, the board must approve the proposed new shareholder and, where the articles are in the form set out above, the court will not inquire into the directors' reasons for refusing to register a transfer if none are given. Thus, whatever the value of the shares might be in terms of the assets and liabilities disclosed in the company's balance sheet, it may well be difficult to find a purchaser at anything approaching that value. The Companies Act 1948, s 28, which made restrictions on transfers essential for a private company, was repealed by the Companies Act 1985. There is nothing to prevent a private company from imposing such a restriction in its articles and in the case of any company whose articles already include it, it will remain in force unless the articles are amended. The articles of any company in which it is proposed to invest should therefore be examined with this point in view. The new Table A (under the Companies Act 1985), which sets out a suggested form 8 for the articles of association of a company, does not include any provisions relating to the refusal of directors to register a transfer of fully paid shares, but it is not unusual to see an express provision to that effect included in the articles of association of private companies.

Dealing with shares in a private company is often also restricted by a provision in the articles that a member wishing to dispose of his shares must first offer them to the other members at their fair value which is frequently determined in the absence of agreement between the intending seller and the directors, by the auditors, or an independent chartered accountant. The articles should therefore be examined with this in mind and also with a view to discovering whether, on death, a member's shares may pass to his personal representatives to be dealt with according to the will. In addition, minority shareholders who are employees might be required under the articles of association to transfer their shares on ceasing to be employed by the company in question.

13.3.5 Loans

An investor may prefer to put money into a company by way of loan rather than by purchasing shares. A loan may be charged on all or any of the company's assets or its uncalled capital, or may be on a debenture, secured or unsecured. The nature of a debenture is difficult to define and Lindley J said in *British India Steam Navigation Co v IRC* [1881] 7 QBD 165, at p 172, '. . . what the correct meaning of "debenture" is I do not know. I do not find anywhere any precise definition of it'.

It is always necessary to proceed with caution when lending to a company. Its memorandum and articles should be inspected to ensure that the borrowing is intra vires, and the terms of any loan or debenture must be clearly set out and agreed. Independent professional advice is essential. In particular, where the lender is the settlor in relation to a settlement of which the trustees or a beneficiary are participators of the company, quite unexpected income tax liabilities may arise under s 677 of the Income and Corporation Taxes Act (TA) 1988 when the loan is repaid.

Money invested in a company by way of loan will normally entitle the lender to interest at a fixed rate. If the company fails investors should not, if adequately secured, be out of pocket: if the company prospers they will receive their interest regularly, and in due course the loan will be repaid, but they will not share in the prosperity of the undertaking.

13.3.6 Taxation

Two applications of taxation must be borne in mind. First, prior to 6 April 1999, when a dividend was received, a 'tax credit' was given equal in amount to the income tax at the rate of 20% which would have been payable on the aggregate of the dividend and the tax credit. The company had to pay advance corporation tax (ACT) on the dividend at a rate of 20% on the aggregate, such ACT ranking as a credit against the company's corporation tax liability. However, with effect from 6 April 1999, ACT was abolished, and the tax credit available to investors was reduced to 10%. Higher rate taxpayers are now given relief for the tax credit, and the total of the net dividend and the notional tax credit is taxed at a special rate of 32.5%. Basic rate taxpayers have no further tax liability.

Secondly, if and when shares are disposed of and a chargeable gain results, capital gains tax (CGT) may become payable. FA 1988 changed the base date from 1965 to 1982, which favoured many long-term investors, but that Act also unified the rates of tax on income and capital gains so that the maximum rate of CGT increased from 30% to 40%.

Incidentally, a notional capital gain may arise where assets are given away or even disposed of for consideration that is less than their full open market value. A person who makes such a gift or sale at an undervalue is treated as if he had received full market value. Although FA 1989 abolished the general right to hold over gains on gifts, it may still be possible for gains arising on such transactions to be deferred or 'held over' if the gifts made are treated as business property (and shares in unquoted trading companies generally fall within this category).

The tax payable on a capital gain arising from the sale of shares on 5 April 2004 will normally be computed as follows:

Sale proceeds	x
Less incidental costs of disposal	x
	x
Less cost/31 March 1982 value	x
Less indexation up to the amount of the gain	x
(adjustment for inflation based on the increase in the	–
RPI from acquisition to 5 April 1998)	
Less capital losses on other transactions in the year	x
Less capital losses brought forward (if any)	?
Less taper relief (if due)	?
	–
Less £7,900 annual exemption – £8,200 from	
6 April 2004 (unless utilised against other gains)	?
Net gains taxed at 10%, 20% or 40%	x

Note that taper relief may be due on gains arising from the disposal of shares deemed to be business assets held for at least one complete year, or other assets held for at least three complete years. In the case of non-business assets, a 'bonus' year is granted if held on 17 March 1998. If available, it is deducted after losses realised during the same tax year, and losses brought forward from earlier years. However, such losses can be set against gains not eligible for taper relief first, in order to minimise any tax charge.

Indexation relief ceased on 6 April 1998, and was replaced with taper relief. For disposals after 5 April 2000, this has the effect of reducing the chargeable gain by a fixed percentage, according to the number of years the investment has been held after 5 April 1998. The maximum relief is 75% for business assets (held for at least four complete years, for disposals made during the tax years 2000–01 to 2001–02), which for a 40% taxpayer gives an effective rate of charge of 10%. This period is reduced to two complete years for disposals made after 5 April 2002. For non-business assets (held for at least ten complete years) the taper relief is 40%, although as mentioned above, a 'bonus' year will be given for non-business assets that were held on 17 March 1998.

The definition of 'business assets' was extended with effect from 6 April 2000, but assets so redefined will not be treated as business assets for periods of ownership prior to 6 April 2000. This may result in the period of ownership being a mixture of business assets and non-business assets, and the overall gain must then be time apportioned before taper relief can be calculated.

For disposals prior to 6 April 2000, business assets included assets used for the purposes of a trade carried on by the owner, and shares in a trading group company where the individual was able to exercise at least 25% of the voting rights. It also included shares in a trading group company where the individual was able to exercise at least 5% of the voting rights, and was a full-time employee of the company. Even if the quoted company is a non-trading company, shares held by employees without a material interest (10% or more) will still be treated as a business asset for taper relief purposes.

For disposals after 5 April 2000, all shareholdings in unquoted trading companies (including Alternative Investment Market (AIM) companies) will be treated as business assets, as well as shares held by full- or part-time employees of quoted trading companies. All individuals who hold shares in a quoted trading company will also qualify if the owner is able to exercise at least 5% of the voting rights.

13.3.7 Losses

Looking on the gloomy side, it is possible that a loss may arise on the sale of shares in a private company, or on its liquidation. Such a loss may arise because investors cannot recoup their original investment, but even where they do get their money back, an allowable loss could still have arisen for disposals made prior to 6 April 1995 because of indexation (ie the adjustment made to reflect inflation and calculated as a percentage of the allowable cost reflecting the increase in the RPI during the period in which the investment has been held).

Unfortunately, following changes implemented in FA 1994, no loss created as a result of indexation will be available after 1994–95.

Reinvestment relief

Reinvestment relief was first introduced in March 1993, and made it possible for individuals and trustees to roll over capital gains by reinvesting in ordinary shares in a qualifying unquoted trading company. It was originally intended as a relief for entrepreneurs on the selling of their own business, but was only given real substance in FA 1994. The relief was then extended for disposals made after 28 November 1993, so that it became available for any capital gain that was reinvested. There were further extensions to the relief in subsequent Finance Acts, but the relief was finally abolished with effect from 6 April 1998. However, a similar deferral relief is still available for reinvestment in EISs and VCTs (up to 5 April 2004), which is incorporated in the original rules for each of these investments.

Capital losses are not normally available to be set against an individual's income, although they do attract CGT relief. However, where individuals have subscribed for ordinary shares in a qualifying trading company and incur an allowable loss on disposing of the shares, they may claim relief from income tax instead of CGT. This provision is to be found in TA 1988, s 574. Note that this relief applies only where taxpayers have subscribed for the shares and not where they had bought them from another shareholder, unless that other is his or her spouse, and acquired the shares by subscription. It applies only to ordinary share capital and stock and the company must be a 'qualifying trading company' in the terms of the definition provided by the section, ie:

(1) it must exist wholly or mainly for the purpose of carrying on a trade (other than dealing in shares, securities, land or commodity futures);
(2) it must be resident in the UK from its incorporation until the date on which the shares or stock are disposed of; and
(3) none of its shares or stock must have been quoted on a recognised stock exchange at any time since 12 months before the date on which the shares or stock were issued. However, following changes in the Finance Act 2001, relief will not be lost for shares issued after 6 March 2001 where a company becomes quoted after the investor has taken up his shares.

Example

Wendy sells her shares in SAL Ltd, an unquoted trading company, on 1 April 2004 for £30,000. She originally purchased the shares in January 1985 for £5,000. In May 2003 Wendy invested £10,000 in ordinary shares in a VCT. Wendy's CGT position for 2003–04 would be as follows:

	£	£
Proceeds		30,000
Less:		
Cost	5,000	
Indexation relief (to 5 April 1998)	3,915	
		8,915

175

Net gain	21,085
Less: reinvestment relief	(10,000)
Gain	11,085

Less: taper relief (from April 1998)

Business asset gain –	3 years	$\frac{3}{5} \times 11,085 = 6.651$
Non-business asset gain –	2 years	$\frac{2}{5} \times 11,085 = 4,434$
Total period of ownership –	5 years	

Business taper relief –	
6.651 × 75% (5 years)	(4,988)
Non-business taper relief –	
4,434 × 20% (6 years incl. bonus year) =	(887)
Net chargeable gain	£5,240

If Wendy was a higher rate taxpayer, and had held the shares for less than a year, her combined income tax and CGT relief could amount to 60% (20% income tax relief for the investment in the VCT, and 40% deferral of CGT).

The relief will be given if the loss results from a sale at arm's length for full consideration, a distribution on a winding-up, or a claim that the value has become negligible giving rise to a deemed disposal. Partial claims are not allowed and if the loss exceeds income for the year of claim, the excess may be either carried forward or set off against capital gains. Information may be obtained from the Small Firms Service of the DTI.

13.3.8 Loans

Until relatively recently, professional advisers normally recommended that a person making a loan to a private company should do so on terms which made the loan a debt on a security. This is because such loans constitute an asset for CGT purposes whereas normal loans are outside the scope of CGT (which is fine until the investor seeks relief for a capital loss). As a general principle, losses are available to offset capital gains only if they arise from assets that are chargeable assets for capital gains purposes.

As already stated, as a general principle, a debt on a security does constitute an asset for CGT purposes. This definition is itself obscure.

There is a further problem that even where a loan constitutes a debt on a security, relief may be withheld on the basis that the security is a qualifying corporate bond (QCB) (in this particular context, a QCB is one where the investor does not qualify for an allowable loss for CGT purposes). It is possible to ensure that a debt on a security does not fall within the definition of a QCB, but it is necessary for the loan to have certain qualities and in particular the loan should normally contain provisions under which it may be converted into ordinary shares or preference shares. Professional advice is essential here.

Loans that are not debts on a security or QCBs

Even where a debt does not fall within the category considered above, it may in certain circumstances entitle the lender to relief as a capital loss if it becomes irrecoverable. The conditions which render the loan a qualifying loan for this purpose are in s 253 of the Taxation of Chargeable Gains Act (TCGA) 1992. These are as follows:

(1) The money lent must be used by the borrower wholly for the purposes of a trade carried on by him or for the setting-up of a trade subsequently carried on by him.
(2) The borrower must be resident in the UK. The Act does not say at what point the borrower must be so resident and neither does it require the business to be carried on here.
(3) The debt must not be a debt on a security. If it is, it will fall within the provisions referred to previously.

13.3.9 Relief for financing costs

Interest paid on a loan to an individual is eligible for tax relief only if the money borrowed is used for certain purposes. These include the acquisition of an interest in a close company or in a partnership. In the case of a close company it must be used for the purchase of ordinary shares in a trading or estate company, or for the making of a loan to such a company to be used wholly and exclusively for the company's business. Individuals will be entitled to the relief if they hold:

(1) not less than 5% of the company's ordinary share capital; or
(2) some part thereof, however small, and have in the period between the application of the loan and the payment of the interest been personally engaged in the conduct of the business in the case of a partnership, and 'worked for the greater part of his time in the actual management or conduct of the company', in the case of a company.

During the same period he must not have recovered any capital from the company or partnership. For details of the complex provisions regarding this tax relief, reference must be made to TA 1988, ss 360 and 362.

13.3.10 Conclusion

It will be appreciated that many problems may arise in connection with company law and tax law. The latter in particular has become a matter of great complexity and specialist advice should always be taken. When all the legal hurdles are overcome, the sky's the limit and, if all goes well, the end result may be that the company 'goes public' or is taken over by a public company, leaving the shareholder with readily realisable shares in a company which may be or become a household name.

13.4 PRIVATE INVESTMENT COMPANIES

The first part of this chapter is concerned primarily with trading companies, but much of what has been said applies equally to private investment companies. These are companies which do not carry on a trade but invest, usually either in real property or in stock, shares and similar securities, and receive rents, dividends and interest. The line between property investment and property dealing companies is a difficult one to draw and presents a problem that the courts have often been called upon to solve. The question is essentially one of intention, but it is not always easy to decide how the available evidence (which may be scanty) should be interpreted. Some of the differences between dealing or trading companies on the one hand and investment companies on the other are dealt with below.

First, when a property is disposed of at a gain, the gain in the hands of a dealing company is part of its trading profit and is taxed at the appropriate rate of corporation tax. Where the disposal is made by an investment company, the gain may be a chargeable gain as defined for CGT purposes and taxed as such. Secondly, an investment company is charged to corporation tax prima facie on the full amount of its income and must make a management expenses claim by virtue of which a deduction is allowed for the cost of management. Management expenses (nowhere defined in the legislation) are usually less than the expenses allowable against trading profits. Thirdly, an investment company, if it is a 'close investment-holding company', is less favourably treated than a trading company as regards distributions.

Because of provisions contained in FA 1989, the company is generally ineligible for the small companies corporation tax rate. This means that it has to pay tax on its profits at the full 30% rate rather than at 20%. Furthermore, restrictions may apply to repayment claims for tax deemed to be withheld from dividends declared by the company.

In general the CGT calculation of gains and losses arising on shares and loans to private trading companies applies equally to shares and loans involving private investment companies. However, there are two important differences. Apart from the availability to claim business assets taper relief, it is not possible to claim income tax relief under TA 1988, s 574 as described in 13.3.7.

A further disadvantage that attaches to an investment company (or indeed to any company that makes chargeable gains) is that a double tax liability may arise on capital gains. On the sale of an asset by the company, tax becomes payable (as explained above) on the chargeable gain. That net gain increases the company's assets and hence the value of the member's shares in it. On a disposal of those shares a further chargeable gain may arise.

A private investment company has larger funds at its disposal than each individual shareholder and may thereby take advantage of opportunities not presented to the smaller investor. Furthermore, the minimum commission charged by a stockbroker may add disproportionately to the cost of investments of the smaller investor. Both of these advantages, however, attach to any method by which small investors join together. So long as the basic agreement governing the project is carefully drawn up and fully understood by all those co-operating, a joint co-operative investment scheme may avoid the drawbacks of a private investment company while at the same time possessing many of the advantages. The taxation of unapproved investment companies (whether private or public) and their shareholders is discussed at 7.8.

13.5 ENTERPRISE INVESTMENT SCHEME (EIS)

13.5.1 Introduction

A new investment incentive scheme was announced in the November 1993 Budget, intended to provide a 'targeted incentive' for new equity investment in unquoted trading companies, and to encourage outside investors to introduce new finance and expertise. The Business Expansion Scheme (BES), introduced by FA 1983, came to an end on 31 December 1993, and was replaced by the EIS with effect from 1 January 1994. There are numerous and complex conditions that must be satisfied in relation to the investor, the trade, and the investment. Although many of the rules included in the provisions were common to both the EIS and its predecessor, the BES, there are some important differences.

For shares issued by a qualified unquoted trading company, relief is given to investors at the lower rate of 20% on the amount subscribed for the shares in the year of assessment in which the shares are issued or the income tax payable, if lower. Tax reliefs, which are expressed in terms of tax, double taxation credits and tax deducted at source from annual payments, are ignored for this purpose.

In addition to income tax relief, an individual may claim CGT deferral relief in respect of any other capital gain that is reinvested in an EIS during the period beginning one year prior and ending three years after the disposal that creates the capital gain. The maximum investment that may attract income tax relief for 2004–05 and future years is £200,000 pa (£150,000 for 1998–99 to 2003–04 and £100,000 for 1997–98 and earlier years). These limits apply to husband and wife separately. It is also possible to carry back up to half of an amount invested by an individual between 6 April and 5 October in any year to the previous tax year, subject to a maximum of £25,000 (£15,000 for 1997–98 and earlier years). However, the relief carried back must not take the individual over the limit for the previous year.

Unlike reinvestment relief, which applied prior to 6 April 1998, the CGT deferral relief contained within the EIS legislation does not require that an EIS income tax claim must also be made. The income tax relief and the CGT relief can be claimed independently, and either can be claimed without the other. Only individuals are able to claim both income tax and CGT deferral relief, as trustees are only able to claim CGT relief.

Provided the shares have been held for at least three years (five years for shares issued before 6 April 2000), the shares are exempt from CGT on disposal. Unlike investments in the BES, however, a loss on the shares disposal both before or after the five-year period has elapsed may still attract income tax or CGT relief.

There is no maximum amount of money that a company can raise in a particular tax year under the EIS, although prior to 6 April 1998 this was limited to £5m. In addition, participation is restricted to companies with gross assets of less than £15m before an investment, and no more than £16m after it.

It must be borne in mind that one of the conditions for the granting of this relief is that the company must, throughout the relevant period (see 13.5.4), be unquoted. This means that the company's shares or securities must not be dealt in on either the Stock Exchange or Unlisted Securities Market (USM). Although a company's shares may be dealt in on the AIM, this will not in itself disqualify it, but it is probable that the £15m gross assets test will rule out many AIM companies.

If, at the end of the three-year (or five-year) period, the company is still unquoted, investors may find themselves effectively locked in. If there is no quotation and investors cannot find a purchaser for their shares they can realise their investment only if the company either disposes of its assets and winds up or sells its undertaking to a quoted company, so that its shareholders finish up with either quoted shares or cash. The directors may, however, be reluctant to accept the loss of directorships that would follow a winding-up and might well follow a takeover.

It must also be remembered that the EIS was introduced to encourage the investment of risk capital and that that is exactly what such an investment is. Tax benefits may follow an investment under the scheme but there is no certainty that the investment will be successful. Companies in commercial enterprises often have difficulty in producing a prospectus that is of much use to the prospective investor. Projections, by directors, of future profits should be read with caution. The cost of such professional reports as are required for a public flotation will often be prohibitive for new, small and possibly speculative enterprises.

13.5.2 Tax relief available

If all the conditions set out in 13.5.3 are complied with, a claim for relief may be made. It must be accompanied by a certificate from the company (authorised by the Inspector of Taxes) to the effect that it has, at all necessary times, complied with the conditions set out in 13.5.4. The claim may be made at any time after the company has carried on the qualifying trade or activity for four months and must be made not later than two years after the end of the year of assessment in which the shares were issued. If the four-month period expires after the end of that year, it must be made within two years after the end of that period.

If a claim is allowed before the end of the qualifying period (see 13.5.4) and any subsequent event results in a contravention of any of the conditions, the relief will be withdrawn. If the company fails to carry on the trade for four months by reason of a winding-up or dissolution for bona fide commercial reasons and not as part of a tax-saving scheme, the claim will not fail for that reason. Provision is made in the legislation requiring that information leading to a loss of relief must be sent to the Revenue.

Example of EIS income tax relief

Malcolm's total gross income for 2003–04 is £40,000. He inherits £50,000 during the year, which he decides to invest in a qualifying EIS company. All his taxable income comes from an employment.

Malcolm's income tax position for 2003–04 is:

	£
Total income	40,000
Less personal allowance	4,615
Taxable income	35,385

Tax thereon:	
£1,960 at 10%	196.00
£28,540 at 22%	6,278.80
£4,885 at 40%	1954.00
	8,428.80
Less EIS relief – lower of	
(a) £50,000 × 20% = £10,000 or	
(b £8,428.80	(8,428.80)
Tax payable	Nil

In practice, a claim would normally be included in the claim to relief page of the self-assessment tax return. A claim is only permissible if you have already received the appropriate certificate, but it is not necessary to submit this with the return. It should, however, be kept safely in case it is necessary to provide it at a future date.

13.5.3 Individuals eligible for relief

For individuals to be entitled to the relief under the BES they had to be resident and ordinarily resident in the UK at the time of issue. This requirement does not apply to investors in the EIS, and relief is available for non-residents if they are liable to UK income tax. There is a further relaxation in that an investor can become a paid director, without forfeiting entitlement to relief under the EIS. This is, however, subject to the proviso that the individual was not connected with the company or its trade prior to the issue of the EIS shares.

The words 'connected with' are given a very wide meaning. An individual is connected with a company if he:

(1) or an associate (defined below) is an employee of the company or of its partner, or is himself its partner or is a paid director of the company or of a company that is in partnership with it;

(2) possesses (directly or indirectly) or is entitled to acquire more than 30% of the company's issued ordinary share capital, loan capital and issued share capital, voting rights or such rights as would entitle him to more than 30% of the assets available to equity holders on a winding-up;

(3) has power to secure that the company's affairs are conducted in accordance with his wishes by means of the holding of shares or the possession of voting power of that or another company or by virtue of any power in the articles or other document regulating that or any other company; or

(4) is a party to a reciprocal arrangement under which some other person subscribes for shares in a company with which the individual (or any other individual who is a party to the arrangement) is connected.

For the purposes of (1) above, 'associate' means:

(a) the individual's husband or wife, parent or remoter forebear, child or remoter issue or any partner;
(b) a trustee of any settlement in relation to which the settlor is or was the individual or any of the persons mentioned in (a) (other than a partner), whether living or dead; or
(c) where the individual is interested in any shares or obligations of the company which are (with certain exceptions) subject to a trust or form part of a deceased's estate, any other person interested therein. It may, in this connection, be difficult to ascertain who is an associate and who is not.

The shares must be held in a qualifying company for at least three years (or five years for shares issued before 6 April 2000) and any income tax relief claimed will be clawed back if shares are disposed of within this period.

However, although income tax relief may not be available, or withdrawn because the investor is treated as connected, CGT deferral relief may still be due.

13.5.4 Qualifying companies

Two expressions used in connection with the qualification of a company require explanation.

(1) The 'relevant period'. In relation to 'qualifying companies' and 'qualifying trades' this means the period of three years beginning with the issue of the shares or, if the company was not at the time of such issue carrying on a qualifying trade, the period of three years from the commencement of such a trade.
(2) A 'qualifying subsidiary'. This means a subsidiary company that is not less than 90% owned and controlled by the parent company, no arrangements being in existence by virtue of which it could cease to be so owned and controlled. That condition must be satisfied until the end of the 'relevant period' unless there is an earlier winding-up or dissolution for bona fide commercial reasons which is not part of a tax-avoidance arrangement and on which the subsidiary's net assets are distributed not more than three years after the commencement of the winding-up. Prior to FA 1997 the subsidiary had to exist wholly or substantially to carry on qualifying activities or be a 'dormant' company, ie one that had no corporation tax profits and did

not include the making of investments as part of its business. Following FA 1997, this rule was relaxed and the business of the group as a whole is now considered. Relief is not now denied unless the non-qualifying activities form a substantial part of the whole group's activities.

The conditions to be complied with by the company are as follows:

(1) It must, throughout the 'relevant period', be an unquoted company which must exist wholly or 'substantially wholly' for the purpose of carrying on wholly or mainly in the UK one or more 'qualifying trades' (see 13.5.5) or must carry on a business which consists wholly of either:
   (a) holding shares or securities of, or making loans to, one or more 'qualifying subsidiaries'; or
   (b) both (a) and the carrying on wholly or mainly in the UK of one or more 'qualifying trades'.
(2) The company's share capital must not, at any time in the 'relevant period', include any issued shares that are not fully paid up.
(3) The company must not, at any time in the relevant period, control (whether alone or with any connected person) another company or have a 51% subsidiary or be controlled by another company (whether alone or with a connected person) or be a 51% subsidiary nor must any arrangements be in existence at any time during the relevant period which could bring the company within any of the prohibited situations. An exception is made, however, for companies having subsidiaries which are themselves qualifying companies under (1) above.
(4) The original rules provided that a company's interest in land could not exceed one-half of its total assets. This condition was, however, removed with effect from 29 November 1994, under the provisions of FA 1995.

Another significant change from the BES rules is that qualifying companies can now include foreign companies. Provided they trade in the UK, they will not be required to be incorporated or resident in the UK.

13.5.5 Qualifying trades

Some guidance was given by the Revenue, in a Statement of Practice dated 12 September 1986, of what, in their view, is meant by carrying on a trade 'wholly or mainly' in the UK referred to in 13.5.4. Each case is determined on its facts including the 'totality of the activities of the trade'. Thus, regard is had to such factors as the location of capital assets, and the places where purchasing, manufacturing, selling and other things are done. The carrying on of some activities outside the UK does not disqualify the company if, in the Revenue's words, 'over one-half of the aggregate of these activities takes place within the country'. The phrase 'over one-half' suggests that some precise measurement must be possible. The Statement of Practice goes on to say that a company would not be excluded from relief solely because its output is exported, or its raw materials imported, or storage or marketing facilities exist overseas.

A 'qualifying trade' is one that does not to any substantial extent comprise:

(1) dealing in commodities, shares, securities, land or futures;
(2) dealing in goods otherwise than in an ordinary trade of wholesale or retail distribution;
(3) banking, insurance, moneylending, debt-factoring, hire-purchase financing or other financial activities;
(4) leasing (except for short term), chartering or ships;
(5) receiving royalties or licence fees;
(6) providing legal or accountancy services;
(7) oil extraction activities; or
(8) providing services of the nature of those set out in (1)–(7) for a trade carried on by any person who controls the trade carried on by the company.

A trade under (5) above is not disqualified if the company carrying on the trade is engaged, throughout the relevant period, in the production of films or in research and development and if all royalties and licence fees received by it in that period are for films produced by it, or of sound recordings or other products arising from such films or from research and development.

In addition to the restrictions listed above, there are further exclusions of the types of activity that will qualify for shares issued after 17 March 1998. These are:

● property development;
● farming or market gardening;
● holding, managing or occupying woodlands or any other forestry activities, or timber production;
● operating or managing, or managing property used as, hotels or comparable establishments;
● operating or managing, or managing property used as, nursing or residential care homes.

The trade must be carried on on a commercial basis and with a view to realising profits. It must have been carried on by the company for four months before the relief will be allowed and, if not carried on at the time of the issue, must be begun within two years thereafter.

13.5.6 Qualifying investments

For the investment to qualify for relief it must itself comply with a number of conditions:

(1) it must be made by the individual on his own behalf;
(2) the shares must be taken by subscription and not by purchase from an existing shareholder;
(3) the shares must be new ordinary shares which, throughout the five years from the date of issue, carry no present or future preferential rights to dividends, assets on a winding-up, or to redemption; and
(4) the shares must be issued for the purpose of raising money for a qualifying trade or activity carried on, or to be carried on, by the company.

FA 1995 contained provisions that relaxed the rules for shares issued after 28 November 1994 to allow relief to individuals, even where they are involved in the control of another company carrying on a similar trade.

Although the investment must be made by an individual, to qualify for relief, it may be made through an approved investment fund. Particulars regarding some of such funds are obtainable from the British Venture Capital Association.

13.5.7 Withdrawal of relief

Relief for investment in an EIS will be clawed back if an investor disposes of the shares within a period of three years (five years for shares issued before 6 April 2000), unless the disposal arises because the company has gone into liquidation. In these circumstances further income tax or CGT relief may be due to the investor. Where the investor receives no payment as a result of the liquidation, the net amount of his investment may qualify as a capital loss. Prior to 7 March 2001, relief was also clawed back if the company became a quoted company during the three-year qualifying period.

The comments set out above should be taken as a guide only. They do not cover every detail of the legislation but should help in identifying most of the difficulties to be faced in crossing this morass of regulations.

13.5.8 Venture capital trusts (VCTs)

Proposals to create a new relief for investment in VCTs were announced in the 1993 Budget. This announcement was followed by a consultative document, and FA 1995 contained provisions introducing the relief with effect from 6 April 1995.

VCTs are companies that are similar to investment trusts and to obtain approval they must meet a number of conditions, in particular:

(1) the ordinary share capital of a VCT must have been quoted on The Stock Exchange;
(2) the VCT must not retain more than 15% of the income that it has derived from shares or securities;
(3) the income received by the VCT must have been derived wholly or mainly from shares or securities;
(4) the value of investments held by the VCT must consist of at least 70% of qualifying shares or securities;
(5) at least 30% of the value of a VCT's qualifying holdings must be made up of ordinary shares;
(6) the value of a VCT's holding in any one company must not exceed 15% of its total investments.

It may be possible for a VCT to be granted provisional approval provided the 70% and 30% conditions mentioned in (4) and (5) above will be met within three years, and the other conditions in the current or next accounting period. This provisional approval will be withdrawn if the VCT fails to meet the conditions within these time periods.

FA 1995 included changes to the rules, which govern the types of company in which VCTs may invest, and these were brought into line with those applicable for EIS relief with effect from 17 March 1998.

Further rules were also introduced for VCTs, for accounting periods ending on or after 2 July 1997, although not in respect of funds raised by the issue of shares before 2 July 1997. These were:

(1) guaranteed loans and securities cannot qualify as part of the fixed proportion of qualifying investments that a VCT must hold; and
(2) VCTs must ensure that ordinary non-preferential shares represent a minimum of 10% of their total investment in a company.

13.5.9 Qualifying holdings

These must consist of holdings in unquoted companies that exist wholly or mainly for the purpose of carrying on a qualifying trade in the UK. For these purposes a qualifying trade is as defined for the EIS, and the gross assets of the unquoted company must not exceed £16m, immediately prior to the VCT's investment.

Income tax relief

Relief can be claimed by resident individuals aged 18+, and is available in two different ways.

First income tax relief at the rate of 20% is given for amounts subscribed for new ordinary shares in the VCT, although the amount subscribed in any one year must not exceed £200,000 for shares acquired on or after 6 April 2004 (£100,000 for earlier years). The relief is withdrawn unless the shares are held for at least three years (five years for shares issued before 6 April 2000).

In addition, dividends from ordinary shares held in VCTs are exempt from income tax, to the extent that the value of the shares acquired each year does not exceed £200,000 (£100,000 for 2003–04 and earlier years).

Income tax relief is available in a similar way to that given for EIS investments, and is limited to the liability for the tax year in which the relief is claimed, but for shares acquired after 5 April 2004, the maximum income tax relief is increased to 40% (20% for earlier years). However with effect from 6 April 2004 no CGT deferral relief will be available. For years prior to 2004–05, the total relief, when coupled with a claim to CGT deferral relief (shown below) could have amounted to 60% for a higher rate taxpayer. Unlike EIS investments, however, dividends paid on VCT investments are free of income tax, and VCT income tax relief must have been available in order to claim VCT CGT deferral relief.

Example

Kate has a total gross income of £150,000 for 2003–04 (all earned income) and during the same year had a chargeable capital gain of £50,000 (after deducting the annual exemption available). Her earnings include a bonus of £50,000, and she decides to invest this in a qualifying VCT. Her total tax liability for 2003–04, before claiming income tax relief or CGT deferral relief, would be as follows:

	£
Total chargeable income	150,000.00
Less personal allowance	(4,615.00)
Taxable income	145,385.00
Income tax thereon:	
£1,960 at 10%	196.00
£28,540 at 22%	6,278.80
£114,885 at 40%	45,954.00
	52,428.80
Add chargeable capital gain	
£50,000 at 40%	20,000.00
Total tax payable	72,428.80

After claiming both the maximum income tax and CGT deferral relief, her liability would be:

Income tax liability (as above)	52,428.80
Less income tax relief on VCT investment	
£50,000 at 20%	(10,000.00)
	42,428.80
Add capital gain	50,000.00
Less CGT deferral relief	(50,000.00)
Chargeable capital gain	Nil
Total tax payable	£42,428.80

Capital gains tax

Where investments in VCTs have qualified for income tax relief, disposals after the three- or five-year period are exempt from CGT.

Prior to 6 April 2004, capital gains deferral relief was also available for investments in VCTs, provided the VCT shares for which the individual subscribes were issued during a period beginning 12 months before, and ending 12 months after, the date of disposal of the asset creating the capital gain which is to be deferred.

In common with investments in the EIS the deferred gain may be reinstated if the investor disposes of the shares, other than to his or her spouse, or ceases to be resident in the UK within three/five years of the issue of the VCT shares.

The relief is also withdrawn if the company ceases to be a qualifying VCT within three years of the issue of the shares, or within three years of the commencement of trading, if later, or the investor ceases to qualify for the 20% income tax relief.

13.6 DORMANT PARTNERSHIPS

13.6.1 Introduction

It is not unusual for a person commencing a trade to find him- or herself short of capital. In such circumstances an investor who is persuaded of the trade's potential viability may be prepared to put up the capital but not want to play any active part in the carrying on of the business. The investor is then a 'dormant' or 'sleeping' partner. Since partners are generally entitled to take part in the running of the business, this arrangement must be the subject of a special agreement.

Unless the business name consists of the names of all the partners, it must comply with the provisions of the Business Names Act 1985. This Act governs names that may and may not be used for business purposes and how and where they must be disclosed. A register of such names was formerly maintained but was closed in February 1982.

13.6.2 Loan creditors

It is important to distinguish dormant partners from loan creditors. If the investors receive a fixed rate of interest on their investment they are probably not partners at all. Under s 2 of the Partnership Act 1890 the receipt of a share of the profits is prima facie evidence of partnership, although the receipt of such a share or of interest at a rate varying with the profits does not of itself make the lender a partner. This apparent contradiction was explained by North J, in *Davis v Davis* [1894] 1 Ch 393, and it appears from his judgment that the Act means that all the relevant facts must be taken together, no special weight being attached to the sharing of profits. It is difficult to see how the Act could be intended to mean that, although, in fairness to North J, it is equally difficult to see that it could be intended to mean anything else either. In the majority of cases there is (and there certainly should be) a written agreement making the position clear. If the agreement so declares, and the name of the dormant partner is included in the firm's name, there is little doubt of the existence of a partnership.

13.6.3 Rights and liabilities

Once it is established that the 'investor' (to use a neutral term) is a dormant partner and not merely a loan creditor, certain rights arise. For example, he is entitled to inspect and take a copy of the firm's accounts and, in the absence of any agreement to the contrary, to investigate their contents.

A dormant partner is, generally, personally liable for the firm's debts even if the creditors were unaware of the partnership at the time when the debts arose. This liability extends to the whole of the partner's personal fortune. Such an arrangement can therefore carry considerable personal risk, although this can be curtailed by the formation of a 'limited partnership'.

Under the Limited Partnerships Act 1907 it is possible for partners to limit their liability to the amount contributed by them to the partnership at its inception, although there must always be at least one partner whose liability is unlimited. Limited partners may not receive back any of their capital so long as the partnership continues, and if any of it is returned to them, their liability up to the amount of their original contribution will remain. They are, of course, entitled to draw out their share of the firm's profits.

Limited partners must always be dormant partners. Should they take any active part in the running of the business, the limitation of their liability is lost, and it will then extend to the whole of the partnership's debts and to the full extent of their personal assets.

The law relating to dormant partnerships is liberally sprinkled with traps for the unwary, and the law relating to limited partnerships is particularly unsatisfactory. No partnership of any sort should be entered into without taking legal advice, and although the law does not require a partnership agreement to be reduced to writing, it is always desirable that it should be. Whatever the relations may have been at the outset, it is only too easy for the partner entering too readily into informal arrangements to find the whole of his personal estate at risk in respect of liabilities that the partner played no part in incurring. It is when things start to go wrong that dissensions occur, and by then it may be too late to correct matters that should have been dealt with at the outset.

13.6.4 Taxation

A trading partnership, like any other trader, is normally assessed to tax on the basis of the profits of the trading year ending during the tax year of assessment. For example, if the accounts are taken to 31 December, the profits for the year ended 31 December 2002 form the basis of the assessment for the tax year 2002–03. This general rule is subject to various complications relating to the opening years, the closing years, changes in partnership treated as a cessation, and losses. Having determined the amount of the assessment for, say, 2002–03, that amount is apportioned among the partners in accordance with their profit-sharing arrangements for that fiscal year.

Earned income is defined in TA 1988, s 833(4)(c) as income which is 'derived by the individual from the carrying on or exercise by him of his trade . . ., in the case of a partnership, as a partner personally acting therein'. Any partnership income not falling within that definition is investment income. Since a dormant partner (whether with limited liability or not) does not, by definition, act personally in the business, it must follow that any income derived from the partnership will be investment income. This will be of significance in relation to retirement pension schemes.

13.7 LIMITED LIABILITY PARTNERSHIPS (LLPs)

FA 2001 created a new business vehicle, with effect from 6 April 2001. An LLP is a hybrid, as it takes the form of a company with its own legal identity, but for tax purposes it is treated as transparent.

The members of an LLP carrying on a lawful trade or business with a view to profit are taxed as if they were partners in a partnership, and assessed on their shares of profits and capital gains in respect of LLP assets. For tax purposes, dealings by an LLP are treated as if they were dealings by the members themselves.

Unlike a normal partnership, there is no joint and several liability between the members, and their liability in most cases will be limited to the capital contributed, together with any further capital they may have agreed to contribute in the event of the winding-up of the LLP.

Despite this obvious advantage, there can be other disadvantages. In particular, since an LLP is technically a company, the provisions of the Insolvency Act 1986 apply and in certain circumstances members may also have to repay sums withdrawn during the two years preceding insolvency. In addition, LLPs must file accounts and disclose certain financial information, which will be available to competitors. There will also be a restriction in the way any losses can be set against general income for members of LLPs that are not carrying on a profession. The distinction between a trade and a profession is not always clear, and this distinction may now take on a new significance.

13.8 MEMBERSHIP OF LLOYD'S

13.8.1 Introduction

Over 300 years ago, Edward Lloyd opened a coffeehouse in the City that proved to be a popular meeting place for men with an interest in shipping. In 1692 he moved to larger premises on the corner of Lombard Street and Abchurch Lane, where the financial quarter had become well-established, which soon became known as a centre where ship-owners could take insurance cover. With the increasing size of ships and value of cargoes, the size of the risks grew and individual underwriters were obliged to join in syndicates, so creating the system that still functions today. Lloyd's itself, as in its coffeehouse days, does no more than provide accommodation and facilities for the underwriters; it is not, and never has been, an insurer. Lloyd's was incorporated by Act of Parliament in 1871, and that and later Acts regulate the fundamental rules and authorise the making of byelaws by the members. An Act of 1911 authorised the underwriting of non-marine risks, regularising what had already become well-established practice.

Lloyd's of London published a business plan on 29 April 1993, which set out proposals intended to improve the profitability of Lloyd's by increasing capacity, cutting costs and capping losses arising prior to the

1986 account. However, the most fundamental proposal was to allow corporate membership of Lloyd's from the 1994 account. This introduced the concept of limited liability for the first time in the history of Lloyd's.

Members of Lloyd's (called 'Names') are grouped into syndicates and share in the syndicates' profits or losses. As regards losses, each member of a syndicate is liable only for his agreed share (unlike a partnership loss where each partner is jointly and separately liable for all losses) but at present that liability extends to the whole of a Name's assets. Generally, Names take no part in managing the affairs of their syndicate. They are thus entirely in the hands of their Underwriting Agent (see 13.8.3).

Income and gains received by Names comprise:

(1) investment income and capital gains on deposits and reserve funds (see 13.8.2);
(2) investment income and capital gains on premiums received and invested by the syndicate; and
(3) underwriting profits (excess of premiums over claims) if any.

It must not be overlooked that both capital and underwriting losses may also arise. Figures are produced three years in arrears.

Following a series of unprecedented disasters, further problems surfaced in 1991 with claims of fraud and mismanagement, and some syndicates remained open until the Reconstruction and Renewal plan was finally agreed, since they were unable to reinsure to close. Names suffered unprecedented losses.

Despite the drop in membership from the late 1980s, many Names increased their premium limits for 1996 and including corporate members the capacity of the market was over £11bn. Many non-corporate members, however, no longer have the readily realisable wealth formerly relied on (see 13.8.2) and rely instead on bank guarantees secured against property.

It is suggested that much of the malaise stemmed from the Lloyd's Act 1982 which ruled that brokers could no longer own agencies managing syndicates. The intention of this was to prevent conflicts of interest but it probably resulted in brokers moving business elsewhere.

Certainly the problems of Lloyd's were considered. As well as many resignations there was much litigation and constant bad news that tended to scare off potential members. During 1996 Lloyd's announced details of a Reconstruction and Renewal plan, which involved the creation of a reinsurance company, Equitas, to reinsure 1992 and prior year liabilities. This gave Names an opportunity to end the uncertainty about past liabilities, and allow those who wished to leave Lloyd's, to do so.

While it may be possible to reduce the element of risk by taking out high level stop loss insurance policies and entering into members' agency pooling arrangements (MAPAs), one cannot avoid the fact that under the present regime an individual Name accepts unlimited personal liability.

13.8.2 Application for individual membership

Lloyd's no longer accepts application from individual Names, so the information given is only relevant to existing individual members.

It is generally recommended that members should spread their risk among a number of syndicates. Membership of one syndicate only may mean a heavy financial loss in the event of a major disaster. MAPAs, which were first introduced on 1 January 1994, allow their members to take a smaller share in a wider range of syndicates, and thus help to reduce the exposure of each Name.

Advice on the choice of syndicates can be obtained from a Members' Underwriting Agent (not the same as a Managing Agent, although they may be so in practice), and the policy for investing syndicate funds and the likely premium income will be explained by the syndicate's Underwriting Agent (see below). In addition, the result of the last seven 'closed years' will be made available. A 'closed year' is one in respect of which the underwriting account has been closed by reinsuring any outstanding liabilities, usually at the end of the third year.

Members must be able to show that they have a minimum of readily realisable assets, which include Stock Exchange securities, life policies at their surrender values, reversionary interests and real property, but not the member's principal residence. Gold (up to 30% of the total), which must be held by an approved bank in the form of bullion or coins, is valued at 70% of market value. Such things as shares in private companies, jewellery and antiques are not included.

Where the member's wealth comprises items not readily realisable but is in other respects satisfactory, Lloyd's will accept, in whole or in part, a guarantee or letter of credit from an approved bank, as collateral for which the principal residence may be included. The object of the means test is to ensure that, as far as possible, funds will be available at short notice to meet a claim, however large it may be.

13.8.3 Conditions of individual membership

The Members' Underwriting Agent controls the underwriting affairs of the underwriting members of his agency. The agent maintains the accounts and records and deals with taxation, reserves, investments and other day-to-day matters as well as watching the statistics that give a guide to current trends. It is also the agent's duty to ensure that the rules laid down by the Committee of Lloyd's are complied with. Every underwriting member enters into an agreement with the agent, which sets out the terms and conditions on which the agent acts, including salary or fee and rate of commission.

Every individual underwriting member is required to deposit with the Corporation of Lloyd's approved investments or cash that the Corporation holds as trustee. The Lloyd's deposit must be maintained at a minimum of £25,000. For further details enquiries should be made to the deposits department at Lloyd's. The investing of the deposit may be delegated to the Underwriting Agent or may, within the Committee's rules, be dealt with by the member. The income arising on investments deposited remains the income of the member.

A member's premium limit is the maximum premium income that may be underwritten by him in any one year. It is allocated to the syndicate and is then divided among the members in proportions agreed in consultation with the agent. The limit may be increased or decreased according to the deposit's market value and may be raised if additional amounts are deposited and evidence of sufficient means is produced. If the limit is exceeded the member is normally required to increase the deposit.

An entrance fee is payable in cash on election and varies according to the category of membership. Entrance fees are not deductible from profits for tax purposes. An annual contribution to Lloyd's Central Fund is also required. The Fund was set up in 1926 for the protection of policyholders in the event of the inability of a member to meet his liabilities out of his syndicate's trust funds, deposit, reserves and personal assets. The reserve is the amount that, under the Rules, must be set aside each year to meet the estimated cost of winding up the Name's underwriting accounts.

13.8.4 Taxation

The special provisions covering the taxation of the income of underwriters are in TA 1988, ss 450–457, as amended by FAs 1993–1995. This changed the way in which Lloyd's Names were taxed from the 1994 underwriting account. The 2001 account profits will not be assessed for 2001–02, but in 2004–05, the year of distribution. Briefly, the effect of the current legislation for underwriting years from the 1994 underwriting account is as follows.

Underwriting profits are assessed on the basis of the profits distributed during the year of assessment. Thus the profits of the underwriting year ending 31 December 2000 are assessed for the fiscal year 2003–04.

Underwriting profits are profits or gains arising from underwriting business or from assets forming part of a premium trust fund, and income arising from personal reserves and the Lloyd's deposit. However, capital gains arising from personal Lloyd's funds and deposits are not treated as part of Lloyd's trading income, and are added to other personal capital gains arising during the tax year.

A premium paid for reinsurance is deductible as an expense. Losses of an underwriting business are allowed against other income of the year of assessment in which they are incurred, or alternatively against that of the previous year if the underwriter was carrying on an underwriting business in that year. They cannot, however, be carried forward against general income of a later year but can be set against future underwriting profits, which includes personal Lloyd's income from the Lloyd's Deposit and Personal Reserves.

For many years it was possible for Names to transfer part of their underwriting profits into a Special Reserve Fund. The object of this fund was to provide a source of money that could be called on in years in which a loss arose. However, the old style Special Reserve Fund was quite limited, in that only a maximum of £7,000 could be transferred each year and tax relief was only available at a rate equal to the difference between the basic rate and the higher rate of tax.

A new type of Special Reserve Fund was introduced with effect from the 1992 account, although any existing old style special reserves could be transferred to the new reserve fund. Transfers to the fund qualify for both basic and higher rate relief, and it is possible to transfer 50% of Lloyd's profits into the reserve each year, provided the value of the funds held in the reserve does not exceed 50% of the Name's overall premium limit. Any income or gains arising from assets held in the reserve are exempt from income tax and CGT.

Withdrawals from the reserve will be made to fund losses, cash calls, or on resignation or death. This will be treated as underwriting income of the Name at the time of withdrawal. The tax calculation will be based on the actual value of the withdrawal rather than the 'book values' of the assets comprising the withdrawal. In effect, the increase in the value of the fund attributable to income and gains will not be taxed as it arises, but on withdrawal.

13.9 INVESTMENT IN ANOTHER'S EXPERTISE

The first difficulty in making an investment of this kind lies in discovering the innovator whose expertise is to be given financial backing. The innovator seeking capital has many avenues open. Investors may consult the National Research Development Corporation, the Council for Small Industries in Rural Areas, Investors in Industry Group plc (formerly known as the Industrial and Commercial Finance Corporation) or the Small Business Capital Fund. Alternatively they may look for capital through their bank or a merchant bank, through local accountants, solicitors or insurance brokers, through the Rotary Club or the Round Table, through the local branch of the British Institute of Management or through the Small Firms Council of the Confederation of British Industry. The prospective investor can approach any of these agencies to inquire whether they know of any worthwhile ideas for which backing is sought.

Once the innovator has been located, the venture's prospects must be examined carefully, not only by the investor's accountant but also by an expert in the technical field where appropriate. Inquiry should be made of how much of the investor's own capital is being put into the venture. If they have little, they cannot be expected to put much in, but their intentions in this respect indicate their real confidence in the venture. Plans should be prepared carefully and the amount required should be calculated meticulously, all contingencies being taken into account. The information required includes particulars of the product or process, with technical explanations and specifications of patents, if any. Its advantages over existing products or processes must be explained and the costs of development detailed, together with reasoned estimates of future sales. Mere hopes based on speculation will not do.

In general terms, an investor may back another's expertise by means of a private company, a partnership or a loan. A loan will probably be the least attractive method for two reasons. First, adequate security is unlikely to be available. Secondly, the income is limited to interest at a fixed rate, thus denying the lender any participation in profits should the venture prove an outstanding success – the greatest attraction of this type of investment. For private companies and partnerships, it is necessary to determine the appropriate proportionate interests of the investor who is putting in capital and the expert who is putting in expertise. Both may be of equal importance: indeed both are essential, but 50:50 holdings can mean deadlock and are better avoided if possible. This immediately gives rise to a problem that needs professional advice and probably tough negotiating.

Some of the legal aspects of the arrangement (including any liability for taxation on profits or gains arising) are dealt with in general terms earlier in this chapter. As already stressed, every case will present individual problems, and both commercial and professional advice should always be sought. Adequate financial and administrative control is essential for investors, and they will usually be wise to insist on their own accountant auditing the books and their representative keeping a close eye on the running of the business.

13.10 RACEHORSES

13.10.1 Introduction

Investing in racehorses is not for the faint-hearted. The rules regulating racing in this country are made by the Jockey Club, from whom detailed information may be obtained. Anyone proposing to invest in a racehorse is presumably already well acquainted with the turf and will know something about horses. Investment may be either in horses in training or in stallions. (Investment in stud farms and training establishments is discussed at 11.4.3.)

The increase in the cost of buying and running a horse led to an expansion of syndicated ownership regulated (for horses in training) by the Jockey Club 'rules of racing'. New syndicates are, however, no longer accepted by the Jockey Club and where a horse is owned jointly it must now be by way of a legally enforceable partnership of which each member is registered as an owner. The number of partners is restricted (as it was for syndicate members) to 12. The partnership agreement (which should be drawn up with legal advice) must be registered with the Jockey Club. All partners are jointly and severally liable for entrance fees, stakes, forfeits and jockey's fees. That is to say that any one of them may be held individually liable for the full amount and will then have to recover the due amounts from the other partners.

It is recommended by the Jockey Club that anyone proposing to become a part owner by way of a partnership should contact them before taking any steps in the matter. The rules governing joint ownership are complex and the Jockey Club would prefer to advise at the outset rather than unscramble an arrangement that contravenes the rules.

An interest in a racehorse may be bought through the medium of a limited company, but it must be realised that the investor is then buying a share in the company and not a share in a horse. There are a number of public limited companies engaged in these activities.

13.10.2 Stallions

As well as investments in horses in training, investments may be made in syndicated stallions. In this case there are no rules of the sort set out for horses in training – ad hoc arrangements are made in each case. A stallion may stand at stud until it is 20 years old, but the value of a nomination falls as it approaches that age. A stallion will give about 150 services each season, covering each mare three or four times. Stud fees at present range generally up to about 4,000 guineas, although that figure may be greatly exceeded in special cases.

In a typical syndicate there will be 40 shares, most of which will be held by shareholders with one share each. The agreement usually provides for a committee, including the major shareholder(s), to be set up. The committee will be empowered to decide all matters relating to the management of the stallion and the affairs of the syndicate as agent for the shareholders, although its powers regarding the stallion's disposal are usually limited. Generally each shareholder is entitled to one nomination per share for the season. The maximum number of nominations for the season is fixed, and insofar as it exceeds the number available to shareholders, the excess may be sold and the proceeds set against expenses borne pro rata by the shareholders. The agreement usually provides that the committee must approve mares to be served by the stallion and that a barren mare must also be approved by a veterinary surgeon. A veterinary surgeon will examine any maiden mare before service. Restrictions are usually placed on the disposal of shares and nominations, but it may happen that during the season in question the shareholder has no mare suitable for nomination and in such a case the nomination will be sold.

13.10.3 Taxation

Income tax

It was held in *Benson* v *Counsell* (1942) 24 TC 178 that receipts from the sale of nominations were receipts of annual income chargeable to income tax under Schedule D Case VI, although they were not trading receipts within Case I. This decision was based on the fact that the taxpayer had not bought the rights to nomination sold: what he had bought was an interest in the horse. The sale of the rights merely realised the horse's reproductive faculties and it thus became an income-producing asset. In 1915 the Earl of Derby unsuccessfully contended that a stallion at stud was 'plant' for the purposes of capital allowances (see *Derby (Earl)* v *Aylmer* [1915] 3 KB 374).

Capital gains tax

The sale of a share in the horse, whether it is in training or a stallion, does not give rise to a taxable gain, since TCGA 1992, s 45(1) takes out of the charge to CGT any gain accruing on the disposal of, or of an interest in, an asset that is tangible, movable property and a wasting asset. There is no doubt that a horse is tangible and movable, and that it is a wasting asset (ie one with a predictable life not exceeding 50 years).

13.11 BACKING PLAYS

It is possible that, somewhere, a playwright has just written a play that will take London by storm and play for years to packed houses. It is, on present showing, most unlikely. It is estimated that only one show in seven put on in the West End will be successful, which suggests that somewhere along the line there is a failure to foresee what the public will and will not like. In past years flops have included Stop the World I Want to Get Off, Exclusive, Metropolis, Sherlock Holmes, Someone Like You, Look Look, Dean, Barnardo, Can-Can, Fire Angel, King, Top People, Y, Ziegfeld, Troubadour, Bus Stop, Bernadette, My Lovely . . . Shayna Madel, Rick's Bar Casablanca and Children of Eden. Together they have lost millions. The last one alone is said to have lost £2.5m.

This is not the place to consider the reasons for this failure rate, but those tempted to put money into a play should realise that their chance of making anything out of it is slim. It is statistically more probable that money put in will be lost without tax relief. This is the ideal investment for those who enjoy losing money.

Those who put up the money for a theatrical production – the 'angels' – normally split the profits with the management: the angels usually take 60% and the management 40%, although the proportions are a matter for agreement. The agreement usually also provides for an 'overcall', ie a liability on the part of the angels to put up additional capital should it prove necessary. Before the profits are divided between angels and management there has to be deducted such of the fees and expenses of management as may be specified in the agreement. The agreement should be scrutinised carefully by an adviser familiar with these matters to ensure that the angel is getting his fair share.

Anyone determined to risk this gamble against heavy odds should first become familiar with the track records of various producers. Eager investors should then attempt to force their money on one who seems successful. If a producer makes the approach, consider why his usual sources of finance are not available. There is no central exchange through which investments can be made, although assistance may be obtained from the Society of West End Theatre. While not arranging investments itself, the Society will give advice and maintains a list of prospective backers. Since backers will normally have no opportunity even to read the play, they are simply betting on the producer's wisdom.

The cost of mounting a play varies enormously. A large-scale musical can cost millions to stage, and with production and running costs at their present levels a show has to run for a considerable time before the production costs are covered and anything is paid out. If the production is successful the investor will receive an agreed share of the net profits that will, first, recoup the costs and, thereafter, constitute income for tax purposes.

As a variant of the traditional method of financing, advantage may be taken of the provisions of TA 1988, s 574, which enables losses on unquoted shares in certain trading companies to be set off against a taxpayer's income. The resulting loss is thus, to some extent, cushioned by income tax relief.

13.12 OPTIONS ON BOOKS

An investor with sufficient faith in a little-known author may back that faith by purchasing an option, exercisable usually for one year, to develop the book into a film or play. A little-known author is suggested as, in the case of a best-seller writer, the option is likely (if it is available at all) to be extremely expensive. It is much less expensive to buy such an option than it would be to buy the copyright outright.

Once the option is purchased it will become necessary to write or procure a script from the book and then to persuade a film company or theatrical producer to take it up. The time involved in these activities may necessitate the purchase of another year's option.

Would-be purchasers should consult a firm of literary agents for further advice. A list of agents is published in the *Writers' and Artists' Yearbook.*

13.13 PREVIEW OF THE YEAR AHEAD

Although world stock markets have recovered slightly after substantial falls following the events of 11 September 2001, the uncertainty of the political situation in Iraq after the Iraqi war has prevented the restoration of the 'feel good' factor.

The Government has increased the tax relief available for EIS and VCT venture capital investments, but many potential investors are still reluctant to invest because of the inherent risks connected with this type of investment. VCTs were often preferred to EISs because they were viewed as being a slightly safer investment, but although the rate of income tax relief on VCTs has been increased in the March 2004 Budget, the CGT deferral will no longer be available. This can mean that the overall tax relief available may be reduced from 60% to 40%.

Membership of Lloyd's is no longer available to new individual Names, although participation through a corporate vehicle is still possible. Although the risk of losses is considerably reduced, unfortunately the opportunity to make exceptional profits is similarly reduced.

Many professional partnerships have converted to limited liability partnerships (LLPs), often in an attempt to reduce the cost of their professional indemnity insurance premiums, which have escalated dramatically following the recent increase in third party claims.

USEFUL ADDRESSES

Registrar of Companies/Registrar
of Limited Partnerships
Companies Registration Office
Companies House
Crown Way
Cardiff CF4 3UZ

Tel: (029) 2038 8588
Web: www.companies-
house.gov.uk

Lloyd's of London
Lime Street
London EC3M 7AH

Tel: (020) 7623 7100
Web: www.lloydsoflondon.co.uk

National Research Development
Corporation
101 Newington Causeway
London SE1 6BU

Tel: (020) 7403 6666

Rural Development Commission
141 Castle Street
Salisbury
Wiltshire SP1 3TP
Tel: (01722) 336255

Investors in Industry Group plc
91 Waterloo Road
London SE1 8XP

Tel: (020) 7928 3131

British Venture Capital
Association
Essex House
12–13 Essex Street
London WC2R 3AA

Tel: (020) 7240 3846
Web: www.bvca.co.uk

Development Capital Group
Limited
21 Moorfield
London EC2P 2HT

Tel: (020) 7588 2721

Department of Trade and Industry
Small Firms Service

To obtain address of nearest centre, dial 100 and ask the operator for Freefone Enterprise

British Institute of Management
3rd Floor
2 Savoy Court
Strand
London WC2R 0EZ

Tel: (020) 7497 0580

Confederation of British Industry
Centrepoint
103 New Oxford Street
London WC1A 1DU

Tel: (020) 7379 7400
Web: www.cbi.org.uk

Jockey Club
42 Portman Square
London W1H 0EN

Tel: (020) 7486 4921
Web: www.thejockeyclub.co.uk

Society of West End Theatre &
    West End Theatre Managers
    Ltd
Bedford Chambers
The Piazza
Covent Garden
London WC2E 8HQ

Tel: (020) 7836 0971

14

LIFE ASSURANCE

Updated for this edition by

PAUL WRIGHT

Zurich Financial Services

VINCE JERRARD LLB, ACII

Legal Director, Zurich Financial Services, UK Life

14.1 INTRODUCTION

Assurance contracts may be divided into three broad types, according to the nature of the primary benefits provided:

(1) life assurance policies (including single premium bonds) pay out a lump sum on death or on the expiration of a specified period;

(2) purchased life annuities pay periodic sums as long as the annuitant is alive;

(3) pension contracts provide pensions and other benefits and are available through one's work or occupation.

Within each of these categories there are further subdivisions. Pension contracts are dealt with in Chapter 15.

14.2 THE MARKET IN RECENT YEARS

14.2.1 Life assurance business

In the 1990s life assurance business benefited from a buoyant stock market, a recovery in the housing market and relatively low building society interest rates. However, more recently, turbulent stock markets have had a negative effect, especially on investment business which had been an important growth area in recent years. The market has now seen a return to life assurance protection to underpin production.

The industry has also had a number of negative effects, including the problems of personal pension mis-selling in the late 1980s, issues surrounding the design, suitability and performance of some sales of endowment policies (which now account for a much lower share of the market) and high profile corporate problems such as those suffered by Equitable Life and Independent Insurance.

The pensions market was further damaged by the uncertainty that had surrounded the run up to the new 'stakeholder' pensions, finally launched in April 2001, which have received mixed reviews having generally failed to encourage pensions provision in their target market. Yet more uncertainty surrounds pensions with new proposals to simplify this complex area of financial services put forward by the Pickering Report in July 2002, but not yet implemented.

The 'restructuring' of the industry looks likely to continue with more mergers, acquisitions and de-mutualisations. A further reduction in the number of active life companies is expected in future years as margins remain under pressure and as solvency requirements prove to be an issue for some companies.

14.2.2 Individual savings accounts (ISAs)

This tax-favoured savings vehicle was introduced in April 1999. The ISA has been a success, although the product's complexity is a disadvantage. In launching the ISA, the Government has created the 'CAT mark', a standard that a product can achieve through being clear and through carrying low charges. In effect, this is a 'control' over product design, a development that continued with stakeholder pensions and has been built on further in the report by Ron Sandler.

The scheme will run for a minimum of ten years, and UK-resident individuals aged 18+ can invest up to £5,000 pa (£7,000 pa from launch until April 2006). There are three investment areas – equities, life assurance and cash deposits – each of which will allow savings to grow free of income tax and capital gains tax (CGT).

While equity and cash investment have enjoyed participation in tax-favoured products in recent years (PEPs and TESSAs respectively), life assurance has been disadvantaged in comparison. The ISA is an important opportunity for the investment industry but the current low limit for life policies has restricted the participation of the life companies. However, this is set to change from April 2005, when the insurance level of the ISA rises to the same as the equity level. The rest of this chapter deals with non-ISA life policies.

14.3 LIFE ASSURANCE POLICIES

14.3.1 Legal nature

Life assurance policies are contracts between the individual policyholders and the life insurance company. The general principle underlying life assurance policies is that the insurance company is the collecting house of pooled risks and investments of policyholders and offers benefits directly to them based on personal contracts.

The life company maintains the underlying investment funds in its own right but, depending on the policy's nature, undertakes to pay the policyholder either a specified sum, a sum which is increased periodically out of the company's profits, or one which varies with the value of part of the underlying fund.

An important characteristic of the life assurance policy as an investment is that it does not produce an income, as such, but is essentially a medium- to long-term accumulator. The income and capital gains of the underlying funds accrue to and are taxed in the hands of the insurance company, but the benefit is passed on, to a greater or lesser extent, in the growth in value of the policy. Many types of policy, however, allow regular or irregular encashment of part of the policy (withdrawal plans or encashment of bonuses) to serve as 'income', if required (but see 'Withdrawal plans and policy loans' at 14.3.4 and also 14.3.6 concerning part surrender of single premium policies).

14.3.2 Preconditions

To take out a life assurance policy an insurable interest in the life to be assured must exist, ie a pecuniary interest that would be adversely affected by the death of the life assured. At the time the policy is taken out, the policyholder must have an insurable interest in the life assured commensurate with the sum assured. Individuals have an unlimited insurable interest in their own and their spouses' lives.

Usually, where life assurance is taken out as an investment, the contract is applied for and held by a person on his or her own or spouse's life, or on their joint lives, for his or her own personal benefit or for their joint benefit. Policies can, however, be the subject of gifts, in which case they are generally written in trust for the benefit of the beneficiaries (see 14.3.7). They can also be assigned, by way of gift, or for value, or as security for a debt (eg as collateral security for a house mortgage or an overdraft).

14.3.3 Divisions and types

Endowment, whole of life and term assurances

All life policies provide life cover – a sum or sums assured payable on death. Most policies, other than temporary assurances, also provide investment benefits – sums payable on surrender or maturity. Life policies may be divided into endowment, whole of life and term policies, depending on the emphasis that is placed on savings or on protection (life cover):

(1) An endowment policy, which has a high savings element, is one under which the benefits are payable at the end of a predetermined period (the endowment period) or on death, if earlier.
(2) A whole of life policy is one under which the benefits are in general payable on death, whenever it occurs.
(3) A term policy is a temporary assurance, the sum assured being payable on death within a specified period only.

Both endowment and whole of life policies may be surrendered (ie cashed in) prematurely for a cash lump sum, the size of which depends on the contract's nature. Term assurances generally do not have an investment element as far as the individual is concerned, and so rarely have any surrender or cash-in value.

With-profit, without-profit and unit-linked policies

Within the endowment and whole of life categories, life policies can be of different types, depending on the way in which the sums payable by the company are determined:

(1) *With-profit* contracts are policies under which a minimum sum is guaranteed to be paid by the life company, augmented from time to time by bonuses declared by the company according to its profits. These bonuses may be reversionary (bonuses added to the sum assured, either yearly or triennially) or terminal (bonuses declared at the end of the policy as an increment to the final payment). Reversionary bonuses may be simple or compound: simple bonuses are based only on the sum assured, while compound bonuses are based on the sum assured plus previous bonuses. Reversionary bonuses are usually expressed as a percentage of the sum assured or of the sum assured as increased by previous bonuses. Under a with-profit endowment policy the individual receives at maturity the minimum sum assured plus the bonuses, reversionary and terminal. The recent poor performance of stockmarkets has seen many with-profits companies making severe cuts in their reversionary and terminal bonuses.

A development in recent years has been the creation of what are called 'unitised with-profits' policies. These are with-profits business but are structured to give the appearance of unit linking, particularly in terms of the policy charging structure. Frequently, unitised with-profits business offers a 'smoothed' growth, often with a guaranteed minimum rate, but the guarantee may only apply to maturity and death values and not to earlier surrenders.

(2) *Without-profit* contracts are policies under which the life company guarantees to pay an absolute sum and invests the premiums in such a way as to produce that sum, bearing any shortfall in the return or retaining any profit in excess of the guaranteed return.

(3) *Under unit-linked* policies the life company maintains a number of underlying funds, which are divided, for accounting purposes only, into 'units'. The company undertakes to pay to the policyholder an amount equal to the greater of the guaranteed sum and the value of the units allocated to the policy. The underlying fund might consist of specific types of investment media often with a choice of geographical spread (such as property, equities, unit trusts, investment trusts, government securities, local authority and bank loans or deposits, or building society deposits) or the fund may consist of a combination of some or all of these ('managed' or 'mixed' funds). Out of every premium a proportion is allocated to the purchase of units that are credited to the policy. The movement in value of the underlying fund is directly reflected in the price of the units allocated to the policy and hence in the value of the policy benefits. Many types of policies give the policyholder the right to transfer his or her policy link from fund to fund at his option, by way of a simple procedure at low cost (eg a policy that is linked to an equity fund may be switched to become linked to fixed interest securities or bank deposits).

A life company generally has full investment freedom of the type of investments it chooses, subject only to the investments being a suitable 'match' for its liabilities. In the case of unit-linked policies the Insurance Company Regulations only permit linkage to certain types of assets, such as those listed in (3) above.

If the contract is one under which a guaranteed minimum or guaranteed absolute amount is provided, investors know that they will get at least that sum. At the same time, in the case of with-profit policies, the investor has the advantage of having the guaranteed minimum augmented from time to time by reversionary and terminal bonuses, or, in unit-linked contracts, augmented by the movement of the value of the underlying fund (capital growth plus reinvested income).

Regular premium and single premium policies

A further broad division of life policies (of all types) depends on how premiums are payable:

(1) regular premium policies (also known as annual premium policies) are those under which premiums are payable annually, half-yearly, quarterly or monthly, either throughout the policy's duration or for a limited premium-paying period of time; and

(2) single premium policies are purchased by way of one single premium or lump sum (although such policies can usually accept further investment at any time).

Qualifying and non-qualifying policies

A brief introduction to qualifying and non-qualifying policies is given at 14.3.6. The distinction between the two types of policy is important because their proceeds are treated differently for tax purposes in the hands of the policyholder.

14.3.4 Characteristics of regular premium policies

Investment and protection

All endowment and whole of life policies have an investment or savings element as well as a life insurance protection element. The extent to which the policy is slanted towards investment depends on the policy's nature and duration and the relationship between the premiums payable, the age of the life assured and the extent of the life cover provided.

In general, policies that have a low sum assured relative to the premiums payable over the policy life have a high savings or investment element, and conversely, high sums assured relative to the premiums payable mean that the policy is tilted more towards life assurance cover than towards investment. In considering life policies as investments, temporary or term assurances will be excluded, as these generally do not have a surrender value and benefits are payable only on death. They are usually taken out purely for life cover protection, to provide for one's family or to cover a prospective liability such as inheritance tax (IHT).

The type of policy that individuals should take out generally depends on their circumstances and objectives, weighing up not only the required degree of investment relative to protection but also the required degree of certainty of result relative to the potential for increased gain.

In general, the incidence of inflation and the conservatism of companies in guaranteeing a long-term return has meant that without-profit policies have tended to provide a relatively poor rate of return compared with with-profit and unit-linked policies although returns on the latter two types have been hit by recent falls in the stock markets.

A with-profit policy gives the prospect of sharing in the company's investment performance where this exceeds that needed to meet the guarantee. The need to satisfy the guarantee may still lead the company to a more conservative investment strategy but the smoothing effect in the declaration of bonuses can provide a useful cushion in falling investment markets.

With no guaranteed investment return a unit-linked policy could be viewed as a little more risky but may also offer the prospect of better fund performance.

Withdrawal plans and policy loans

In the past, a feature of many regular premium policies with a high investment content was the facility, after a period of years, to operate withdrawal plans, under which the premium was reduced to a nominal amount, eg £1 pa, and regular or irregular sums could be taken from the policy by way of partial surrender to serve as an income, leaving the balance to accumulate. This withdrawal facility was challenged by the Revenue and withdrawn from qualifying policies issued on or after 25 February 1988. Policies issued before that date may continue as qualifying policies despite the presence of such an option. Substantially the same result may be achieved by taking out a series of smaller policies and cashing in individual policies from time to time while continuing the remainder and it may be possible to take withdrawals from a policy provided it has not suffered such a large premium reduction as was previously allowed. Many policies also give the policyholder the right to borrow from the insurance company at a beneficial rate of interest on the security of the policy.

14.3.5 Characteristics of single premium policies

In the main, the relevant single premium policies for investment purposes consist of single premium 'bonds' which are whole of life assurance policies. For many years these have been, in the main, unit-linked policies often marketed as property bonds, managed bonds, equity bonds, etc by reference to the initial underlying fund to which the policy was linked. There are also single premium endowment policies, but these are less significant.

In recent years, considerable volumes of business have been written as with-profit bonds. Although these do not generally incorporate the usual guarantees on future values, they may prove to be attractive in a time of recession and stock market uncertainty.

The main investment characteristic of single premium unit-linked bonds is the high allocation of the premium to investment in the underlying fund, with relatively low life cover. Virtually the entire premium is allocated to 'units', save only for the initial management charges, resulting, in effect, in the investment of most of the premium in the chosen fund. Most companies offer a wide choice of unit funds for the bond linkage.

Subsequently, at no cost or for a small administrative charge, policyholders may switch their investment to one or more of the other funds and are thereby entitled to select a fund that reflects their own view of market conditions. Switching does not amount to a realisation for tax purposes, which is an important investment advantage.

The income produced by the underlying fund is reinvested, net of tax and annual charges, in the fund. A bond, therefore, serves as an automatic income accumulator as well as giving the investor the benefit of the capital growth from the fund, less a deduction for the insurance company's tax on capital gains.

At various times in recent years, market conditions have also made guaranteed income bonds very attractive for both life companies and investors. They may be structured as single policies paying annual amounts as a spendable 'income' by way of part surrender; or may be a combination of policies, some providing the annual 'income' and one providing the investment return at the end of the investment period, usually five years. The Revenue has challenged the efficiency of some of these arrangements, contending that the annual payments are actually Schedule D Case III income and not part surrenders of capital but FA 1997 confirmed the position to be that which it was thought to be by the industry.

A case decided (on the hearing of a preliminary matter) in mid-1994 raised the question of how much life assurance protection a single premium bond had to provide for it to qualify as a life assurance policy. At first instance the judge decided that a policy providing a death benefit equal only to the surrender value at the time of death was not a life assurance contract. An appeal against this decision in 1996 reversed it and restored the previous industry understanding.

Withdrawals

Most unit-linked single premium bonds allow the investor the right to make regular or irregular withdrawals by way of partial surrender to serve as an income. The same result can be achieved by splitting the investment into a number of smaller policies and encashing individual policies in full from time to time. As these policies are not qualifying contracts they are not affected by the Revenue's attack on withdrawal plans referred to in 14.3.4, but see the item 'Withdrawals' in 14.3.6.

Ease of encashment

One of the most important characteristics of single premium bonds is the ease of encashment: there are few formalities other than production of the policy, a surrender form and proof of title. In the case of property bonds, some companies reserve the right, in exceptional circumstances, to defer encashment for a period so as to protect the general body of policyholders by avoiding forced sales of property.

14.3.6 Taxation

Taxation of the life company

Taxation of life companies is extremely (and increasingly) complex. Broadly speaking, in respect of their life assurance business, companies are generally taxed on the excess of their investment income and realised capital gains over management expenses (the 'I-E' basis). For proprietary companies there is a formula to determine the proportions of the company's income and gains that should be allocated to policyholders and shareholders, respectively.

To enable UK life companies to compete more equally for the business of residents of other EU states, companies are able to write such business in an 'overseas' life fund, broadly on a gross roll-up basis with no UK tax on the income and gains, but with no relief for expenses.

Registered friendly societies are in a somewhat different position, being exempt from corporation tax in respect of tax-exempt life or endowment business. This is life and endowment business where total premiums under contracts do not exceed £270 pa with effect from 6 April 1995. Policies that can be written on the tax-exempt basis are generally qualifying policies provided they satisfy a minimum sum assured test. Such policies can give tax-free proceeds even to higher rate taxpayers, but non-qualifying friendly society policies are taxable at basic and higher rates.

Taxation of the policyholder

Qualifying and non-qualifying policies

The income tax treatment of a life policy in the hands of the policyholder depends on whether the policy is a qualifying or a non-qualifying policy.

Policy provisions in standard form are usually sent to the Revenue by the life company for confirmation of compliance with the qualifying rules ('pre-certification'). Generally (although the rules do vary for different types of policy) a qualifying policy is one where the premium-paying period is ten years or more and where the premiums payable in any period of 12 months do not exceed more than twice the premiums payable in any other period of 12 months or ⅛ of the premiums payable over ten years. In the case of a whole of life policy, the sum assured payable on death must not be less than 75% of the premiums payable until age 75; and in the case of an endowment policy, the sum assured payable on death must not be less than 75% of the premiums payable during the term of the policy, but for endowments this percentage is reduced by 2% for each year by which the age of the life assured, at commencement, exceeds 55. Taxation of company-owned policies is considered later.

Qualifying policies

Tax relief on the premiums   In the case of a qualifying policy issued before 14 March 1984, policyholders are eligible for tax relief on the premiums if the policy is written on their or their spouse's lives, if either of them pays the premiums, and if the person paying is resident in the UK for tax purposes. The current rate of tax relief on premiums paid is 12½%. If eligible, the premiums may generally be paid to the life company net of the tax relief and the company will obtain the difference from the Revenue. Tax relief is allowed to the policyholder to the extent to which the total gross premiums paid by him in the year do not exceed £1,500 or, if greater, ⅙ of his taxable income after deducting charges on income but before deducting personal reliefs. Tax relief will not be available if a person other than the life assured or his or her spouse (such as an assignee) pays the premiums.

No life assurance premium relief is available for policies issued for contracts made after 13 March 1984. For these purposes a policy issued on or before 13 March 1984 is treated as being issued after that date if the benefits it secures are increased or its term extended (either by variation or by the exercise of an option built into the contract) after that date.

Policies intact   While the policies are held intact there is no tax charge to the policyholder.

Tax-free proceeds if kept up for minimum period   If a qualifying endowment policy has been maintained for at least three-quarters of its term or ten years, whichever is shorter, and has not been made paid-up within that period, the entire proceeds will be free of income tax in the hands of the policyholder. For a whole of life policy the appropriate period is ten years. If, however, a qualifying policy is surrendered or made paid-up within these periods, the profit ultimately made on realising the policy (whether by cashing in, death, maturity or assignment for value) is potentially subject to the higher rate of tax – but not the basic rate – as with non-qualifying policies (see below).

Capital gains tax   No chargeable gain arises on the disposal of either qualifying or non-qualifying policies (note that surrender and payment of the sum assured under the policy are treated as 'disposals' for these purposes) where the disposal is by the original beneficial owner or by an assignee who gave no consideration for the policy (eg received the policy by way of gift).

On the other hand, if an assignee realises a profit on a policy (or an interest under it) that he or she, not being the original beneficial owner, acquired for value, it is liable to CGT in the same way as other chargeable assets.

To deal with the trade in second-hand policies (which were taxed under the then more favourable CGT regime), anti-avoidance legislation was introduced in 1983 so that, broadly speaking, post-26 June 1982 policies remain in the same income tax regime despite being assigned for money or money's worth. Such policies may give a potential liability to both income tax and CGT although TCGA 1992, s 37 prevents a double tax charge arising.

Person liable for the tax charge   See below.

Non-qualifying policies

Tax relief on the premiums   No life assurance premium relief is allowed on premiums paid under non-qualifying policies whether issued before or after 14 March 1984.

Policies intact   As with qualifying policies, while the policies are intact there is no tax charge on the policyholder.

Termination   The basic principle is that, on final termination of a non-qualifying policy, on death, cashing in, maturity, or sale, the only income tax charge, if any, is to higher rate income tax but not basic rate. To determine whether a charge arises, the gain – basically, the excess of the cash surrender value over the premium paid – is divided by the number of years the policy has been held ('top slicing'). Any previous withdrawals are also taken into account. This slice is then added to the taxpayer's other income for the year (after reliefs). If the slice, then treated as the upper part of the individual's income, puts the investor in the higher rate bracket, the average rate of tax on the slice at the higher rate less the basic rate is applied to the whole gain. If the slice does not attract the higher rate of tax, the gain is, similarly, free of tax. Note that the benefit of top slicing does not apply for the purposes of the higher personal allowances given to those aged over 65 years.

With effect from 6 April 2004, to reflect the reduction (from 1 April 2003), of the tax rate on the policyholder's share of life fund income and gains from 22% to 20%, the credit given on chargeable event gains fell from 22% to 20%.

Note also that it is only the income in the year of encashment that is relevant. If no chargeable events occur during other years, the individual's income, no matter how high in those years, is irrelevant. Thus, bonds or other non-qualifying policies can be realised tax-effectively in a year when the policyholder's other income is relatively low (eg after retirement).

Example – no income tax charge

A basic rate taxpayer whose income after personal reliefs is £1,000 below the higher rate threshold cashes in a single premium bond, held for eight years, for a total gain of £5,000. This gain is divided by eight to produce a 'slice' of £625. The slice, when added to other income, still does not take the investor into the higher rate of tax. No tax is payable on the £5,000 gain.

Example – income tax on the gain

Since April 2004, if the slice (£625 in the above example), treated as the upper part of the taxpayer's income, falls wholly in the higher rate band of 40%, then the £5,000 gain will be subject to income tax at the rate of 20% (ie £1,000).

Note that, on death, the gain that may be liable to tax is calculated, broadly speaking, as the cash surrender value immediately before death plus previous relevant capital payments under the policy, less the premiums paid. In this way the 'mortality profit' made under the policy at that time is not taxed as part of the chargeable gain.

Withdrawals   Annual tax-free withdrawals or partial surrenders of up to 5% of the premiums paid are permitted up to a total amount equal to the premium or premiums paid. Unused allowances are carried forward. If more than the 5% annual allowance is taken, a chargeable excess occurs. The excess becomes liable to the higher rate of tax (but is not liable to the basic rate) if, when added to the taxpayer's other income, it falls into the higher rate.

The Sandler Review, mentioned earlier, also recommended the removal of the '5% withdrawal' facility. This recommendation was considered as part of the Budget for 2003 but has been postponed pending a wider review of life assurance taxation.

The 'top-slicing' procedure referred to above applies with some modifications: the first chargeable excess is divided by the number of years since commencement; subsequent excesses are divided by the number of years since the previous excess. The amounts withdrawn are taken into account in computing the gain or loss on final cashing in: the final gain or loss is equal to the cash surrender value, plus previous withdrawals, less the premium or premiums paid, less excesses previously brought into charge.

Example

Original investment is made in a bond of £5,000. The bondholder takes withdrawals of 6% pa for nine years and cashes in the bond after ten years for £8,000. The final gain on cashing in is £8,000 + £2,700 (ie 9 x 6% × £5,000) − £5,000 − £450 (ie 9 × 1% × £5,000) = £5,250. The 'slice' is therefore £5,250/10 = £525. This slice is added to the investor's other income in the year of cashing in to determine if any tax liability exists on the slice and, if so, the rate of charge, after deducting 20% (since 6 April 2004). The net rate of charge, if any, on the slice is then applied to the gain of £5,250.

Personal portfolio bonds are single premium policies, usually written offshore, which enable the investor's benefits to be closely linked to a portfolio of assets personal to the investor. FA 1998 introduced a new tax charge on such policies by deeming a gain of 15% of the total premiums paid to the end of each policy year and previous deemed policy gains. This charge was not imposed in respect of any policy year ending before 6 April 1999. This provision does not apply to 'managed portfolio bonds', which give the investor access only to generally available, pooled assets.

Person liable   The person liable for the tax charge is the policyholder if the policy is held beneficially, or the individual for whose debt the policy is held as security. Thus, if a policy is assigned by a parent to his or her child by way of a gift and the latter encashes it after attaining majority, the liability, if any, is the child's regardless of the donor's income and is determined by the child's income at the time of encashment.

Where a policy that is held in trust is cashed in, any chargeable gain is treated as income of the settlor and the tax is his or her liability, although the settlor can recover from the trustees any tax liable in this way. If a policy, previously held in trust, has been assigned to the beneficiary in execution of that trust and is subsequently encashed, any gain forms part of the beneficiary's income and is taxed accordingly.

FA 1998 contained provisions to counter what were known as 'dead settlor trusts', through which it was possible to avoid tax on life policy gains realised after the settlor's death. The new rules result in tax being charged on the trustees (or perhaps the beneficiaries) where the trust's settlor is dead (or not resident in the UK) at the chargeable event. The new rules do not apply where the settlor had died before 17 March 1998 and the policy was effected before that date.

Timing   Where the taxable event is the death of the life assured or the maturity, total encashment or sale of the policy, the gain is treated as arising at the date of that event. In contrast, however, withdrawals from policies are treated as happening at the end of the policy year in which they take place.

14.3.7 Suitability

Life assurance policies are different from the normal run of investments in that they are capital assets that do not produce income as such. All income and capital gains produced by the underlying fund of investments accrue to the life company, while the policyholder receives the benefit in the form of an increase in value of the policy: the net income and gains after tax are taken into account in the value of the units or bonus additions, as the case may be. For this reason, life assurance policies are a very useful means of obtaining capital growth and accumulating income for medium- to long-term investment if immediate income is not required. This can be particularly important for higher rate taxpayers and various types of trust.

Both regular premium and single premium policies (qualifying or non-qualifying) also have the advantage that while they are held intact, the policyholder has no administrative burdens or tax returns to render, as the income and gains are the company's responsibility.

The medium- and long-term investor

Both single and regular premium policies are ideally suited to the medium- or longer-term investor seeking an institutionally managed investment. Life companies have considerable investment freedom and with-profit policies reflect the results of investment across a wide spread of assets. Unit-linked policies offer a choice of property, equity, fixed interest, managed and many other types of unit funds, as well as the ability to switch investments between funds as market conditions change. Indeed, the keynote of most unit-linked policies these days is choice and flexibility to meet changing circumstances, so as to maximise the potential growth and protect the real value of the investment against inflation, particularly over the longer term; while with-profit policies offer the relative stability of participation in the company's profits. For the individual who wants a direct link to a managed fund of commercial properties there are few investments comparable with a property bond, or a policy linked to a property fund, or a managed fund with a property content.

Qualifying policies issued pre-14 March 1984 may have the added attraction of tax relief on the premiums – something not available to other comparable forms of investment – as well as freedom from tax on the proceeds if maintained for the required period. The ability of companies to defer realisations and thus make deductions for capital gains liabilities at a rate lower than the life company rate on chargeable gains has been a continuing advantage (but see 14.3.6 for more recent changes).

Beneficiaries

Life policies are suitable investments for individuals seeking personal investment benefits for themselves or their spouses, or for making gifts to beneficiaries. Since policies are automatic income accumulators, they represent useful investments as gifts for children or for children's own capital. As gifts of policies do not cause chargeable events, a higher rate taxpaying spouse can give a policy to a basic rate (or non-taxpaying) partner before encashment. In this way, any gain otherwise taxable may avoid being taxed by virtue of the new independent taxation regime introduced in April 1990, which no longer aggregates the investment income of married couples. Policies can also be taken out by trustees as investments of the trust, provided the power is given in the trust instrument to invest in non-income-producing property and provided an insurable interest exists, eg a policy on the life of a beneficiary for the ultimate benefit of that beneficiary.

A donor wishing to take out a policy for the benefit of children or other beneficiaries can do so at the outset by completing a standard trust form produced by the life company at the time of application. Trusts can range from very simple forms for the benefit of named beneficiaries absolutely (under the Married Women's Property Acts or corresponding legislation in Scotland and Northern Ireland, for spouse or children) to more elaborate forms, such as children's accumulation trusts and trusts where the settlor reserves a right to apply the benefits among a class of beneficiaries which may even include the settlor (although to be efficient for IHT purposes the settlor should be excluded from any personal benefit). Similarly, it is relatively simple to make a gift of an existing policy by assigning it to a beneficiary or to trustees for a beneficiary.

The tax considerations described in 14.3.6 should, of course, be taken into account, as well as the taxpayer's potential income and tax position at the time of prospective encashment (as it is that time that is primarily relevant, not any time during the currency of the policy).

Companies

Companies have frequently found it useful to invest surplus funds in life policies, particularly where providing for a future liability or the replacement of an asset in the future. An insurable interest in the life of the assured must exist. In the past, the only tax consequence of such an investment has been that applicable to a close company in the case of a single premium bond or the premature encashment of a qualifying policy, but FA 1989 contained new provisions so that, broadly speaking, all policies owned by companies (and those assigned to secure a company debt or held on trusts created by a company) are treated, in effect, as non-qualifying policies and taxable as Schedule D Case VI income. In this case no credit is given for tax deducted in the life company's funds and no top-slicing is granted.

The new rules apply to policies effected on or after 14 March 1989 and those altered after that date so as to increase the benefits secured or extend the term.

A measure of relief is given in cases where a qualifying endowment policy is used to secure a debt incurred by the company in purchasing land to be occupied by it for the purposes of its trade (or in constructing, extending or improving buildings occupied for that purpose). In such cases, and subject to certain conditions, only the excess policy proceeds over the amount of the debt is taxable as a policy gain.

14.3.8 Charges

In the case of with-profit and without-profit policies, the company's charges are implicit in the premium rate for the sum assured. In the case of unit-linked policies, the company's charges consist of a proportion of each premium and charges inside the unit funds. For example, in the case of unit-linked single premium bonds, typically an initial charge of 5% of the premium is made. This is followed by annual charges in the order of 1.25% of the value of the fund (although this does vary from company to company) deducted from the fund, either monthly or with the same frequency as the fund valuations. These charges cover items such as the company's expenses and profit margins. Such annual charges can become quite significant where the policy has achieved a high value. For this reason some companies have adopted the approach of using a policy charge which is designed to ensure that each policy contributes a fair amount to the company's expenses, irrespective of the policy's size. In such cases any annual management charge deducted from the funds is reallocated to the policy.

The charging structure described above is often referred to as 'front-end loading'. Alternative structures have also been developed in recent years, eg allocating 100% of the investment initially with higher annual management charges over the first five years. Another variant includes an 'exit charge' levied on encashment – often an amount starting at 5% for encashment in the first year and reducing by 1% for each year the policy is maintained in force over the first five years.

Switching a unit-linked policy between funds can usually be done for a small administrative charge that is far lower than the equivalent cost of switching other investments.

14.3.9 Mechanics

Life assurance policies are generally taken out through the intervention of an intermediary such as an insurance broker or adviser tied to the life assurance company, or a solicitor, accountant or estate agent acting as agent, or directly with the life company itself. The intermediary, although often the policyholder's agent, is generally paid a commission by the life company itself, although some insurance brokers charge the client fees (which are offset against their commission) for the work involved in preparing reports and undertaking financial planning for the client entailing the use of life assurance policies. The Financial Services Act 1986 introduced the concept of polarisation to the industry. This seeks to make clear to consumers whether they are dealing with a representative of one company or a broker who will survey the market on the client's behalf.

The Financial Services and Market Act 2000 replaced the Financial Services Act 1986 and replaced the numerous regulators under the old regime with just one, the Financial Services Authority. A consultation paper issued early in 2002 proposes changes to the polarisation regime, introducing the concept of a 'multi-tied' adviser, representing a limited number of product providers. Such 'depolarisation' will become a reality in January 2005. It also proposes changes to the 'independent' sector, requiring independent advisers to offer their customers the right to pay a fee rather than commission taken from the product charges.

14.3.10 Maintenance

Policies can be held in the individual's own name (usually in the case of policies held for the individual's personal benefit) or by trustees. As long as the policy is not cashed in there are no tax returns and no paperwork. It is only where excessive tax relief is taken on qualifying premiums or gains arise on the happening of a chargeable event (eg a single premium policy that is encashed or a qualifying policy encashed prematurely) that tax considerations arise. It is perhaps largely because of the ease of administration that many individuals with personal share portfolios take advantage of share exchange schemes introduced by life companies enabling them to exchange their shares for single premium bonds at reduced dealing costs.

Holders of unit-linked policies may receive annual fund reports, though the level of useful information provided varies between companies. Because the investment performances of unit-linked single premium bonds are directly related to the underlying funds, it is advisable to review the performance of the respective funds regularly with a view to switching between funds. This can be done with relative ease and at a low cost but for the majority of investors a carefully selected managed fund satisfies the requirements for a large proportion of their investment.

14.4 PURCHASED LIFE ANNUITIES

14.4.1 Legal nature

There are two broad types of purchased life annuities:

(1) Immediate annuities are contracts under which, in consideration of a lump sum paid to the life company, the company undertakes to pay an annuity to the annuitant for life, or for some other term, the rate of the annual annuity depending on the age and sex of the annuitant and on the yields prevailing for fixed interest investments at the time.
(2) Deferred annuities are similar to immediate annuities except that the annuity commences at a future date.

Both annuity contracts are direct contracts with the life company. Some annuity contracts provide for a guaranteed minimum number of payments; some allow the contract to be surrendered for a cash sum that takes into account the growth in the purchase consideration and any annuity payments that have already been made. Other types of annuity contract allow for a cash sum, representing the balance of the original purchase consideration, to be paid on death.

14.4.2 Preconditions

There are generally no preconditions to investment in purchased life annuities. The purchaser of the annuity is generally the annuitant him- or herself or someone else who wishes to provide for annual payments to the annuitant.

14.4.3 Characteristics

An annuity contract represents a fixed interest investment providing either regular annual payments for the life of the annuitant (lifetime annuities) or for a fixed period (temporary annuities). These payments represent a partial return of capital plus a rate of interest on the investment. In the case of deferred annuity contracts the initial purchase consideration is accumulated at a fixed rate of interest before the annuity commences. Frequently, deferred annuity contracts are purchased with the object of taking advantage of income accumulation before the annuity commencement date and of cashing in the contract before that time (these are commonly known as 'growth bonds'). In general the life company fixes the rate of the annuity in advance, although cash surrender values may be related to yields on government securities at the time of cashing in. The actual investment yield earned by the life company is irrelevant to annuitants, as they enjoy a guaranteed benefit.

In the past, two separate purchased annuity contracts were sometimes combined. For example, a temporary immediate annuity for a limited period was combined with a deferred lifetime annuity. This combination, known as a 'guaranteed income bond' (more frequently now written as a cluster of endowment policies), had as its object the provision of a short-term 'income' in the form of the temporary annuity, with the cashing in of the deferred annuity before the annuity commencement date to provide the return of 'capital'. The contracts were so structured that the cash-in value of the deferred annuity generally equals the total purchase price of the two contracts. The tax consequences of this combination have to be closely watched, especially for higher rate taxpayers (see 14.4.4). Another combination is that of an immediate lifetime annuity, to provide an income for life, and a deferred annuity that can be commenced at a later stage to augment the income or, if the additional income is not taken, to pay a lump sum on death.

Investment and interest rates are such that, at present, annuities do not appear to offer very good value for money, a particular concern in the pensions market where part of the pension benefit is, generally, required to be taken in the form of an annuity.

Some insurers have introduced unit-linked and with-profit annuities with the aim of providing higher levels of income over the longer term. With unit-linked annuities, units in the fund are cancelled to provide each annuity payment. This means that the level of income can vary up or down according to the units' value and may fall sharply in the event of a stock market crash. With-profit annuities are linked to the with-profit fund and usually provide a guaranteed minimum annuity. Generally, with-profit annuities are more stable than unit-linked annuities, but still provide the prospect of a higher income than traditional guaranteed annuities.

14.4.4 Taxation

The life company

In the past, annuities paid represented charges on the income from investments held by the life company for its general annuity business. To the extent, therefore, that the annuities paid equalled or exceeded the interest earned by the company, the interest did not bear tax, and could be passed on to the annuitants gross (although then subject to taxation in the hands of the annuitant).

FA 1991, however, made the taxation of general annuity business much the same as ordinary life assurance for accounting periods beginning after 31 December 1991 with a generally detrimental effect on purchased life annuities.

The annuitant

Annuities paid are divided into capital content and income content, according to actuarial tables prescribed by the Inland Revenue. For example, if a man aged 70 purchased an annuity of £1,800 pa payable half-yearly in arrear for a consideration of £10,000, £900 of the annuity might be regarded as capital with the balance of £900 being treated as income for tax purposes. In other words, every annuity is deemed to be partly a return of the original capital invested plus a yield or interest element. The interest element of each annuity payment received by the annuitant is treated as unearned income, although since the abolition of the investment income surcharge for individuals by FA 1984 this is not currently a significant disadvantage.

Despite this treatment of payments as part capital and part income, the Revenue appears to regard annuities as substantially a right to income so that they cannot be transferred between spouses to take advantage of independent taxation.

In the past, if an annuity contract was encashed or assigned for value, or any capital sum paid on death, any profit made by the annuitant over and above the purchase price of the annuity, unlike single premium bonds, was subject to basic rate tax (as the company would not have paid tax on the income of its general annuity business) and higher rates if applicable. However, as part of the change to the company's tax position, FA 1991 also brought the chargeable event regime for annuities into line with that for life policies, eg by not charging gains to basic rate income tax.

Higher rate tax is charged in much the same manner as on single premium policies. In other words, the gain element is 'top-sliced' by the number of years the annuity contract has been in existence, and the

223

resulting slice is added to the taxpayer's other income in the year of encashment to determine whether the higher rate of tax is applicable. The rate on the slice (less 20%) then applies to the entire gain. In calculating the amount of the gain the capital element of any annuities paid prior to encashment (but not the interest element) is included as part of the gain.

14.4.5 Suitability

Immediate life annuities are suitable for investors who wish to purchase a continuing income for the rest of their lives by way of a lump sum. Deferred annuities are a means of providing an income to start at a future date, or of accumulating a lump sum with a view to encashment at a future time when other income may be sufficiently low to offset the tax disadvantages of encashment.

14.4.6 Mechanics

Like other life contracts, annuities may be purchased through an inter-mediary or from a life company direct.

14.4.7 Maintenance

As far as immediate annuities are concerned, annual tax returns and tax payments are necessary in respect of the interest element of the annuities. In the case of deferred contracts, no maintenance is required while the annuity contract is intact and not paying an annuity, since the income is income of the life company and not the annuitant. On cashing-in, tax returns are necessary and tax may be payable.

14.5 CONCLUSION

Life policies remain a very simple way of making lump sum or regular investment, although they are best used for medium- to long-term savings.

They act as 'income accumulators' and the life company deals with all tax liabilities while the plan is maintained in force. Withdrawals can often be taken to provide the policyholder with a spendable 'income' and these too can often be taken very simply and with little paperwork. This makes policies easy to administer from the policyholder's viewpoint and they are attractive to many people as a result. Complication in this with-drawal process (ironically partly in the name, according to the Sandler review, of simplicity) would be most unwelcome.

As a pooled investment, they offer a spread of risk normally unobtainable by individual investors, including exposure to the commercial property market. Inexpensive switching between the company's funds, the built-in life cover and the prospect of tax-free proceeds are also attractive benefits of investment through life policies.

Regulation continues to focus on selling practices, but is beginning to turn its attention to product design and after-sales service. It remains essential that quality professional advice is available to the public to help them make appropriate choices in this rather complex but important area of an individual's financial planning.

USEFUL ADDRESSES

Association of British Insurers
51 Gresham Street
London EC2V 7HQ

Tel: (020) 7600 3333
Web: www.abi.org.uk

National Association of Pension Funds
NIOC House
4 Victoria Street
London SW1H 0NX

Tel: (020) 7808 1300
Web: www.napf.co.uk

Inland Revenue Public Enquiry Room
West Wing
Somerset House
Strand
London WC2R 1LB

Tel: (020) 7438 6420

Society of Pension Consultants
St Bartholomews House
92 Fleet Street
London EC4Y 1DG

Tel: (020) 7353 1688
Web: www.spc.uk.com

FSA (Financial Services Authority)
25 The North Colonnade
Canary Wharf
London E14 5HS

Tel: (020) 7676 1000
Web: www.fsa.gov.uk

IFA Association
12–13 Henrietta Street
Covent Garden
London WC2E 8LH

Tel: (020) 7240 7878

Life Insurance Association
LIA House
Chorleywood
Rickmansworth
Herts WD3 5PF

Tel: (01923) 285333
Web: www.lia.co.uk

Pensions Management Institute
PMI House
4–10 Artillery Lane
London E1 7LS

Tel: (020) 7247 1452
Web: www.pensions-pmi.org.uk

15

PENSION CONTRACTS

Updated for this edition by

PAUL WRIGHT

Zurich Financial Services

STUART REYNOLDS LLB,

Strategic Alliances Director, Zurich Financial Services

15.1 INTRODUCTION

Pension schemes in the UK can be divided, broadly, into three classifications: the State scheme; personal pension arrangements; and occupational schemes.

Approved pensions schemes have many of the constituents of the perfect investment: tax relief on contributions, largely tax-free growth, the prospect of a tax-free lump sum and a wide choice of underlying investments in large pooled funds to spread the risk. The major disadvantage is the need to purchase an annuity (taxed) at retirement. Recent changes have removed some of the problems that this can cause.

Not surprisingly, these benefits are carefully guarded by the appropriate authorities through a considerable number of rules and restrictions. This chapter summarises the main benefits and the conditions for their enjoyment.

15.2 HIGHLIGHTS OF THE PREVIOUS YEAR

Last year we discussed how '...the Revenue and the Department of Work and Pensions (DWP) had, to slightly different degrees, taken up the challenge of radically simplifying the legislative framework for pensions.'

Although there have been some amendments, the changes have largely progressed as envisaged, leading to the Finance Act 2004 covering tax simplification of pensions, and the Pensions Bill which is expected to receive Royal Assent in November 2004. With the exception of one or two aspects of the Pensions Bill which are due to be implemented in April 2005, the changes are due to be introduced in April 2006.

In place of the current eight sets of tax regimes there will be one, with one set of rules applying to all types of pension schemes, whether new or old, final salary or defined contribution, occupational or personal. Previous changes to the tax treatment of pensions have normally resulted in each successive change providing lower tax relief than the previous regime. Those entitled to benefits under the previous regime have had their benefits protected by a process known as 'grandfathering', with only new entrants to existing schemes and new schemes being subject to the new rules. Grandfathering was at the heart of the complexity of the current system. Complex transitional and tax avoidance rules became necessary and whole armies of advisers were needed to understand the implications of transferring between different generations of scheme.

The new lifetime limit, starting at £1.5m of pension saving (2006–07) and increasing to £1.8m (2010–11), will apply equally to new and old pensions, with the limited exception of those with pension funds in excess of that figure at the date when the reforms are introduced. Savings above the limit will be subject to a tax 'recovery' charge (subject to some protection for pre 'A-Day members') designed to claw back the tax reliefs previously given. In practice, this will mean that there will be little incentive to make savings above this amount using pensions.

The only limit on contributions will be an annual limit of £215,000 for tax year 2006–07, increasing by £10,000 each year so that by 2010–11 it will be £255,000. This applies to the total increase in value of an individual's pension fund, which will be largely academic for most people.

Tax relief will be allowed on personal contributions up to the higher of 100% of UK relevant earnings or £3,600 per annum.

All schemes will be able to allow members to take up to 25% of the fund as tax-free cash (subject to some protection for pre A-Day members).

The Revenue changes are welcome. Considerable work will be needed by scheme administrators to implement the new rules when they come into force on 6 April 2006 but there is little doubt that the proposed changes will achieve a radical simplification of a system that was creaking under its own weight.

As well as simplification, two further themes continue to emerge. First, we can all expect to have to work longer in future. With an ageing population and a declining workforce able to pay for the pensions of future pensioners, future governments face a pensions timebomb which resolutely refuses to be defused. Lacking the political will to increase the state pension beyond age 65, the Government has embarked on a strategy to make it 'easier' for all of us to continue working longer. Age discrimination will, in due course, become illegal. More flexible retirement pensions will allow, to use a Revenue euphemism, 'scope for a more sensitive and considerate passage from work into retirement'. More obviously, those wishing to retire at age 50 must do so before 2010 (when the minimum age, in general, moves to 55)!

Second, over the last couple of years we have seen the normally obscure subject of pension scheme funding move quickly from the pages of actuarial journals, through the business and personal finance pages, and on to the front pages of the popular press. Funding deficits on final salary schemes (driven by three poor years of equity performance) rose dramatically. Initially this led to fears within the City that the higher contributions from employers needed to make up the deficits would affect corporate earnings. Fear soon became panic, with a number of high-profile cases where scheme members faced losses as both their scheme and their employer became insolvent. Of course, pensions from final salary schemes have never been 'guaranteed'. The 'pensions promise' has always depended on the employer being solvent and the scheme having adequate funds to meet its liabilities. This revelation that the confidence in final salary schemes may have been misplaced made resolving the issue front-page news and a potential vote winner. The Government responded with a package of reforms designed to improve the security of pension schemes. New plans have been announced to introduce a Pensions Protection Fund, guaranteeing at least part of an employee's pension if their employer becomes insolvent, as well as new rules to prevent solvent employers winding up pension schemes that are in deficit.

Behind all the political talk of a 'pensions crisis' and the complexities of final salary funding requirements, lies the truism that a pension is simply a pot of money put away to provide an income in retirement. If the amounts paid into the fund and the investment returns achieved are not big enough neither will the pension. The blunt alternative for those wanting that elusive 'scope for a more sensitive and considerate passage from work into retirement', is to save more or work longer.

15.3 THE STATE PENSION SCHEME

The benefit the State provides to those in retirement falls into two main parts: the basic retirement pension and an additional earnings-related component. Everyone is entitled to the basic retirement pension payable at State retirement age, subject to payment of the necessary NICs.

The State retirement age currently is 65 for males and 60 for females. It will be equalised in the future at 65 for both males and females. This will apply to women retiring after 6 April 2010 with a sliding scale for women retiring over the previous ten years. For women whose dates of birth are on or after 6 April 1955, the common State retirement age of 65 will apply. Women born before 6 April 1950 will benefit from the current age of 60. For those women with dates of birth between those dates, the sliding scale applies. For each month (or part of a month) that a woman's date of birth is after 6 April 1950, her retirement date will be deferred by one month.

The additional earnings-related component is currently provided by the new State Second Pension (S2P). This replaced the State earnings-related pension scheme (SERPS) from April 2002.

Table 15.1 New State retirement ages for women

Date of birth	Pension age
6 April to 5 May 1950	60 years 1 month
6 October to 5 November 1950	60 years 7 months
6 April to 5 May 1951	61 years 1 month
6 October to 5 November 1951	61 years 7 months
6 April to 5 May 1952	62 years 1 month
6 October to 5 November 1952	62 years 7 months
6 April to 5 May 1953	63 years 1 month
6 October to 5 November 1953	63 years 7 months
6 April to 5 May 1954	64 years 1 month
6 October to 5 November 1954	64 years 7 months

For dates of birth between those shown the retirement age will be on a corresponding basis. Thus, a woman born on 9 July 1953 would have a retirement date of 9 November 2016 (ie 63 years 4 months)

SERPS

SERPS was introduced in April 1978 to provide an additional State pension based on earnings (within certain limits) rather than the flat benefit provided by the retirement pension. SERPS also provides a widow's benefit if a husband dies after retirement and also, in certain circumstances, if he dies before retirement. SERPS is funded by the higher rate NICs payable by both employers and employees. The self-employed do not contribute towards, or benefit from, SERPS.

In recent years the State pension scheme has come under pressure by increases in life expectancy and larger numbers of retired people in the population. These concerns led the Government to reduce the benefits under SERPS so that only those reaching State pension age in the years 1998 and 1999 will receive the original maximum benefits. Those reaching State retirement age in or after the year 2010 will receive a pension of only 20% of their earnings (within certain limits) instead of the 25%

originally intended, and the relevant earnings to be taken into account will be the average of lifetime earnings and not the best 20 years' of earnings, as was the original rule for SERPS. A sliding scale will operate for those retiring in the years 2000 to 2009.

No further SERPS entitlement accrued after 5 April 2002 but existing entitlements remain unaffected.

State second pension (S2P)

The State second pension (S2P) replaced SERPS from 6 April 2002. It is designed to provide a better pension than SERPS for those on modest incomes (below £26,600 for 2004–05). The rate at which S2P accrues for someone earning between £4,108 per annum and £11,600 per annum (in 2004–05) is at least double the rate of SERPS that would have accrued to a person on a similar level of income. In addition, carers and the long-term disabled are able to receive S2P credits and accrue additional pension even thought they are not working.

In other respects, the S2P is very similar to SERPS with the exception that the S2P is based on three earnings bands rather than one. Accrual rates are also higher for those on lower earnings than for those with higher earnings, achieving the Government's objective or providing a better pension for those on modest earnings.

15.4 CONTRACTING-IN AND CONTRACTING-OUT

Those who are participating in S2P, or its predecessor SERPS, (ie those employees earning more than the lower earnings limit) are said to be 'contracted-in'. Since SERPS was introduced it was possible to opt-out of the scheme (referred to as 'contracting-out'). It is also possible to contract out of the S2P.

Until 6 April 1988, this 'contracting-out' was only possible through an employer-sponsored occupational pension scheme, which guaranteed to provide a broadly equivalent level of benefits to the SERPS benefits being lost. Since 6 April 1988, employers have been able to offer contracting-out on a 'money purchase' basis without having to provide the guarantee previously required. In both cases NICs are reduced for both the employer and employee but with the loss of SERPS benefits.

However, this change still left the decision whether to offer contracted-out status firmly in the employer's hands. Further changes that took effect on 1 July 1988 gave the individual employee the right to contract out of SERPS on an individual basis, without his employer's consent.

The personal pension plans that enable this are also money-purchase arrangements.

Contracting-out through personal pension plans involves the payment of 'protected rights contributions' to the relevant pension contract. The contributions are identified separately from any other contributions paid and create a 'protected rights fund'; it is the 'protected rights benefits' paid out of this fund at retirement which replace the S2P or SERPS benefits lost through the decision to contract out. The Pensions Act 1995 introduces a system of age-related contracting-out rebates which applies for 1997–98 and onwards.

Contracting-out via a personal pension plan is an annual decision and the individual can contract back in for the purposes of future benefits.

In general, contracting-out will be of benefit to younger employees but may not match the likely S2P or SERPS entitlement for some older people and for those on lower earnings.

15.5 TYPES OF PENSION SCHEME

With the introduction of stakeholder pension schemes, the traditional distinctions between personal (individual) pensions and occupational (employer-sponsored) pensions have become blurred. From 6 April 2005, when the simplification reforms proposed by the Revenue take effect, the distinctions will almost completely disappear. However, in the context of life assurance investments, the following are the main types of pension:

(1) *Personal pensions*   These are contracts between the individual and the life company, which often take the form of deferred annuity contracts. Traditionally they have been intended for the self-employed and individuals not in pensionable employment. With the advent of the stakeholder pension reforms it is now possible for individuals without earnings to have a personal pension. In addition, within strict limits, some members of occupational pension schemes may also contribute to a personal pension.

(2) *Group personal pensions*   Like personal pensions, these are contracts between the individual and the life company but, in addition, the employer agrees to make contributions to his employees' policies. These payments are usually in addition to the employees' own contributions which are deducted from their salaries.

(3) *Occupational pension schemes*   These take the form of contracts between the trustees of the scheme (set up by the employer) and the insurance company (in the case of an insured scheme) and provide benefits for employees as a group or on an individual basis.

Controlling directors of director-controlled companies other than investment companies are also eligible for occupational pension schemes.

(4) *Additional voluntary contribution (AVC) plans* These allow employees who are members of occupational pension schemes to make additional contributions to top up the pension provided by the scheme.

(5) *Free-standing AVC (FSAVC) schemes* These are similar to additional voluntary contribution plans, but employees make contributions to a separate scheme established by the insurance company rather than their employer.

(6) *Stakeholder pensions schemes* These were introduced from 6 April 2001. They may be established by insurance companies and affinity groups, eg trade unions, as well as by employers. They share the same tax rules as personal pension schemes but must adhere to additional criteria, including a restriction on the maximum charges that can be levied.

Since April 1988, individuals can opt out of their occupational pension scheme and provide for their own benefit via a personal pension plan. It is often not advisable to do this if the occupational pension scheme is a good one.

15.6 CHARACTERISTICS OF PENSION CONTRACTS

As with life assurance policies there is a wide variety of types of investment. Companies offer with profit contracts with a level of guaranteed benefits but the right to participate in profits and unit-linked contracts with a wide choice of unit funds and the ability to switch between funds to provide growth on top of any guaranteed benefits. A further development has been a series of guaranteed equity funds, where investors can benefit from the performance of an index, usually the FT-SE 100 Index, but are protected from stock market falls.

An attractive option for some employers is to split their pension investment between an insurance company and other investment media by what is known as a 'self-administered scheme'. One of the attractions of such an arrangement has been the facility of investing part of the pension fund in the employing company itself either by loans or equity investment (see 15.7.6).

An attraction of all pension contracts is that the income and capital growth produced by the investment of the premiums accumulate on a gross basis, because pension funds are not generally subject to UK income tax or CGT, although from 2 July 1997 approved pension schemes are no longer able to reclaim the tax credits against the dividends from UK equities.

As the contracts provide essentially for retirement annuities and pensions, they cannot generally be surrendered for cash and benefits must take the form of pensions (part of which can be commuted on retirement). An important feature of many of these contracts is the 'open market option' at retirement, enabling the annuitant to use the accumulated fund to purchase an annuity or pension from any other company offering a higher rate. It is also possible to defer the purchase of an annuity to no later than age 75. Before then it may be possible to take income withdrawals from the fund, although these are subject to income tax and there are strict limits on the level of income that can be taken.

Although funds invested in these contracts generally remain 'locked in' until retirement, the availability of loans, on commercial terms, to companies taking out pension schemes or to individual members of these schemes can overcome this limitation (see 15.7.6).

15.7 ELIGIBILITY, TAXATION, CONTRIBUTION LIMITS AND BENEFITS

15.7.1 The life company

The income and gains attributable to the life company's pension liabilities are effectively free of UK tax, and it is thus able to pass on to its policyholders the entire gross increase in value of the assets and income, after deduction of its charges, without any deduction for UK tax. However, from 2 July 1997 the life company is unable to reclaim the tax credits against the dividends from UK equities.

15.7.2 Personal and stakeholder pension plans

Eligibility

Broadly, any UK resident can contribute up to £3,600 per annum to a personal or stakeholder pension scheme.

You will be eligible to make further contributions only if you are in receipt of 'relevant earnings'. This means either earnings from non-pensionable employments or from businesses, professions, partnerships, etc. Generally, you are not eligible if you belong to a pension scheme operated by your employer, but you are eligible if it provides only a sum assured payable on your death while in the employer's service.

Controlling directors of investment companies are not eligible for any form of personal or stakeholder pension in respect of earnings from such a company, nor are certain other controlling directors who are in receipt of benefits from their employer's occupational scheme (although they can contribute up to £3,600 per annum without evidence of any earnings).

Tax relief on premiums and limits

If you pay either single or annual premiums to a personal or stakeholder pension within the limits mentioned below, you enjoy full tax relief on those premiums in the relevant years. However, an 'earnings cap' applies so that contributions to a personal or stakeholder pension will only be possible in respect of earnings up to £102,000 for 2004–05 (previously £99,000 for 2003–04). The legislation provides that this figure will be increased in future years in line with the RPI (although this did not apply for 1993–94).

Contributions are paid net of basic rate income tax. The 10% lower rate band does not affect the rate at which tax is deducted from contributions. Higher rate relief is claimed either through the PAYE coding in the case of employees or, for the self-employed, through the annual tax return, by a separate claim or, in some cases, by a reduction in subsequent payments on account under the self-assessment system.

Contributions up to £3,600 per annum do not require the individual to have any relevant earnings, but contributions above this limit (up to the earnings cap) are restricted to a maximum of 17.5% of your net relevant earnings. This means relevant earnings from your non-pensionable employment or business, etc less certain deductions such as expenses, trading losses and capital allowances. There are higher limits for older taxpayers, which are currently as shown below.

Prior to 6 April 2001, it was possible to pay an amount not exceeding 5% of your net relevant earnings to a separate term (life) insurance contract to provide a lump sum payable from a personal pension plan in the event of your death before age 75. Premiums that were used to provide this life cover had to be included as part of the contributions you were permitted to pay to your personal pension plan. It is still possible to maintain existing contracts on the same basis and to increase them if their terms permit. From 6 April 2001, new life assurance arrangements must have their contributions limited to 10% of relevant pension contributions.

An amount not exceeding 5% of your net relevant earnings can be used to provide a lump sum payable from the personal or stakeholder pension in the event of your death before age 75. Premiums used to provide this life cover must be included as part of the contributions you are permitted to pay to your personal or stakeholder pension.

Age at beginning of year of assessment	%
36–45	20.0
46–50	25.0
51–55	30.0
56–60	35.0
61 and over	40.0

Contributions may be paid to a personal or stakeholder pension and their forerunner, a s 226 contract (see 15.7.4), at the same time, but the contribution limits apply to the 'aggregate' of contributions to the two plans (although the 'aggregation' is not always straightforward and paying contributions to both a personal/stakeholder pension and a s 226 contract can restrict the overall contribution possible in some cases, particularly where contributions are above the earnings cap).

If your employer pays contributions to your personal or stakeholder pension, these too must be taken as part of the maximum contribution that can be made to your plan. Employer's contributions are not treated as the employee's income. Protected rights contributions paid to your personal or stakeholder pension to enable you to contract out of S2P or SERPS can be paid in addition to the maximum permissible contribution calculated as the appropriate percentage of your net relevant earnings.

Concurrency

In some cases it is possible to contribute both to a personal (or stakeholder) pension and an occupational pension scheme at the same time. This is called 'concurrency'. You are eligible to make concurrent contributions if your earnings were £30,000 or less in at least one of the last five tax years and you were not a controlling director in the current tax year or the last five tax years. Only years from 2000–01 onwards count when determining whether you are eligible to pay concurrent contributions. If you are eligible you may contribute up to £3,600 to a personal or stakeholder pension as well as a maximum of 15% of your earnings to an occupational pension scheme (see 15.7.5).

'Basis years' and carry-forward

You do not have to use your current earnings to calculate the maximum contributions you can pay to a personal or stakeholder pension. The earnings limits are calculated using a 'basis year', which can be the current tax year or any one of the previous five years. Once established, this basis year can be used for up to five further years, even if earnings drop in any of the intervening years.

The system of basis years replaced the earlier system of carry forward from 5 April 2001. Prior to 6 April 2000, to the extent that contributions paid in any year fell short of the maximum contribution limits, it was possible to 'carry forward' the shortfall of unused relief for up to six years. The shortfall could be used (on a first-in, first-out basis) to obtain relief against a contribution paid in a subsequent tax year, to the extent that the subsequent contribution exceeded the maximum contribution limits for the year in which it was paid. This was subject to the overriding limit that the maximum relief was restricted to the amount of net relevant earnings for that year.

Year for which relief is granted and carry-back

Generally, tax relief is given in the year in which the contributions are paid. However, you can elect to have any contribution you pay treated for tax relief purposes as if it has been paid during the previous tax year. To do this you must make a formal election either before or at the time the contribution is paid and, in any event, no later than by 31 January in the year following the end of the tax year to which the contribution is to be carried back. Prior to 6 April 2001, the carry-back system was more extensive and it was eg possible to carry back contributions for up to two years if you had no relevant earnings in that year. It was also possible to combine the use of the carry-back and carry-forward facilities.

Benefits payable and age at which they may be taken

The personal pension scheme established by the pension provider can allow the individual to make more than one contract (or arrangement) under it. The advantages of this were that, as benefits from an arrangement could, prior to April 2001, generally, be taken only once if they are to include a cash lump sum, multiple arrangements gave the opportunity to take benefits in stages. From 6 April 2001, it is possible to take benefits at different times from the same arrangement.

Your pension may start being paid at any age between 50 and 75. It is not necessary for you actually to retire before the annuity can commence. In certain occupations the Revenue allows an annuity to start earlier than age 50 (eg jockeys, motor racing drivers, cricketers, etc).

It is no longer necessary to purchase an annuity when benefits are taken. The annuity purchase can be deferred until age 75. Until then, or the date when the annuity is purchased if earlier, income withdrawals are taken up to a limit broadly equal to the amount of the single life annuity that could have been taken. The amount of income withdrawals must be reviewed every three years and the withdrawals are taxable in the same way as annuity payments.

Where your personal or stakeholder pension incorporates a sum assured, the lump sum would be paid and this can be arranged to be free of IHT by writing it in trust where the scheme itself is not set up under trust. The whole of any annuity payable either to you, your spouse or your dependants will be treated and taxed as income (and not, as is the case with purchased life annuities, partly as income and partly as a return of capital: see 14.4). The annuity is taxed as employment income and subject to the PAYE system.

A lump sum may be taken from the fund, between ages 50 and 75, up to a maximum of 25% of the fund then being used to provide you with retirement benefits.

You are permitted, instead of taking the annuity from the life company with whom you hold the contract, to utilise the fund built up for your annuity to purchase an annuity from any other company, thus obtaining the best terms then available ('open market option'). If your pension is provided by an organisation that is not a life assurance company, your pension annuity (and life assurance) must be provided by a life company.

15.7.3 Contracting-out via a personal or stakeholder pension

Scheme certificates

If a personal or stakeholder pension has an 'appropriate scheme certificate' from the Occupational Pensions Board, it will be able to receive protected rights contributions (and may be funded by them entirely) and so enable the individual employee to contract out of S2P or SERPS. A plan that receives only protected rights contributions (a 'rebate only' pension) can be effected by an employee who is a member of a contracted-in occupational scheme but wishes to contract out on an individual basis.

Contributions

Protected rights contributions consist of a national insurance rebate. For 2003–04, the rebates are age related and vary between 4.2% and 10.5% of the individual employee's band earnings (the earnings between the upper and lower earnings limits). Both employer and employee continue to pay full national insurance but the rebate is paid by the DSS to the individual's plan after the end of the relevant tax year.

(From April 1993 to April 1997 a system of flat-rate rebates operated with an incentive of 1% of band earnings payable for those over 30.)

The protected rights pension must commence between State pension age and the age of 75. From 6 April 1996 males will be able to take their protected rights pensions at age 60 in the same way as females. It must increase at 3% per annum or the rate of the RPI, whichever is lower, and must not discriminate between males and females, married or single people in terms of the annuity rates offered. No lump sum benefit can be taken from the protected rights fund.

A protected rights pension must continue for the benefit of a widow/ widower or dependant on the individual's death, at a rate not less than one-half of the individual's pension. On death before retirement age the protected rights fund can be paid to the deceased's estate or nominees but no life assurance sum assured can be included in the protected rights benefits.

15.7.4 Retirement annuity contracts (s 226 contracts)

In many ways, s 226 contracts were similar to personal pensions, but there are some key differences, eg no employer's contributions; contributions paid gross and the tax reclaimed; no facility for an employee to contract out through a s 226 contract; and no general entitlement to take benefits before age 60. One important way in which a s 226 contract could be more favourable than a personal pension was in providing a cash commutation equal to three times the annual annuity payable after the cash had been taken. This figure was often more than the 25% of the fund available as a lump sum under a personal pension. (Contracts entered into on or after 21 March 1987 are subject to a maximum cash lump sum of £150,000 per contract.) The earnings cap does not apply to s 226 contracts and the contribution limits are also different from those applying to personal pensions.

No new s 226 contracts could be entered into after 30 June 1988, but contracts in existence by that date can continue much as before. Contributions can continue to be paid to such contracts and regular contributions can be increased in the future.

Note that, although many s 226 contracts contain an open market option to allow the annuity to be purchased from a life company other than the one with whom the pension plan has been effected, exercising such an option after 30 June 1988 has the effect of transferring the policy proceeds to a new personal pension (unless the policyholder has a second s 226 contract already in existence with that other life company). Thus, in the absence of another s 226 contract, the benefits will be paid out of a personal pension with the resulting less favourable calculation of the maximum cash lump sum compared to the s 226 contract.

15.7.5 Occupational schemes

These are schemes provided by an employer for the benefit of some or all of his employees but they are not available to directors of investment companies. To be effective, the scheme should be approved by the Pension Scheme Office (PSO), which is a branch of the Revenue.

'Approval' will prevent contributions paid by the employer being taxed in the employees' hands as a benefit in kind. 'Exempt approval' gives the additional benefits of the gross roll-up in the fund and tax relief for the employee in respect of regular contributions he makes to the scheme. Exempt approval also means that the employer's contributions are deductible business expenses without relying on the normal rules for deductibility applying to Schedule D income. In most cases approval is given under the PSO's discretionary powers, which are extremely wide-ranging.

It is not possible for an employer to make membership of an occupational scheme (other than one providing death in service benefits only) compulsory. Employees are able to opt out of their employer's scheme and so become eligible to effect their own personal pension, independent of the employer. In general, leaving an occupational scheme is unlikely to be wise except where its benefits are extremely poor; expert advice should be sought if this is contemplated.

Contributions

The employer must make some contribution to the scheme although the employee may indirectly provide the necessary funds by agreeing to a reduction in salary – 'a salary sacrifice'. Contributions by the employer to an exempt approved scheme are deductible business expenses, although relief on non-regular contributions may be deferred by being spread over a maximum of five years. The employee may make personal contributions of up to 15% of his remuneration. Personal contributions attract tax relief at the highest rate paid by the individual.

Old and new style occupational schemes

From 6 April 2001 a new type of occupational pension scheme can be set up. These 'new-style' schemes have contribution and benefit limits identical to those that apply to personal and stakeholder pensions (see 15.7.2). It is also possible for schemes to be partly one type or another and for an 'old style scheme' to convert to the 'new style' arrangements.

There are no specific limits on the amount of contributions that may be made to an occupational scheme; instead (subject to the various 'income-capping old style' rules referred to below) the controls operate on the level of benefits that is allowed. If a scheme becomes 'over-funded' (ie where the scheme has more capital than is necessary to meet its prospective liabilities), payment of further contributions may be restricted or capital may have to be returned to the employer. If a refund is made to the employer, it is taxable at a special rate of 40%.

Benefits and limits: old style schemes

The benefits that can be provided by an approved occupational scheme are regulated by a series of Revenue limits. These limits have been restricted over the years including important changes announced in the 1987 and 1989 budgets. Each generation of limits has in general been preserved or 'grandfathered' for those who were members of existing schemes at the time of the budget when the changes were announced. Other changes, the majority of them relatively minor, have also been made at other times. Details of the earlier limits can be found in previous editions of this work and in the *Zurich Pensions Handbook*. The limits that apply to members joining new 'old style' schemes are summarised below.

The Revenue limits are based on a percentage of the individual's 'final remuneration'. This must be calculated in one of the two ways permitted by the PSO, namely:

(1) the remuneration in any of the five years preceding retirement, leaving service or death (as applicable) together with the average of any bonuses, commissions, etc averaged over at least three consecutive years ending with the year in question; or

(2) the highest average of the total earnings over any period of three consecutive years during the last ten years of service.

Certain items are excluded from the calculation, eg share option and share incentive gains and golden handshakes, and some controlling directors have to use the second definition of final remuneration. There is also a maximum amount of earnings that can be taken into account (£102,000 for 2004–05; previously £99,000 for 2003–04). This figure should increase in future years in line with the RPI (although indexation did not apply for 1993–94).

Within this framework, an individual can accrue a pension at the rate of one-thirtieth of final remuneration for each year of service with his employer up to a maximum of two-thirds final remuneration. To achieve this it is necessary to achieve 20 years of service.

The benefits can be taken on retirement between age 50 and 75. The benefits must be in the form of a pension but part of the pension can be commuted for a tax-free lump sum. The maximum lump sum is three-eightieths of final remuneration for each year of service or 2.25 times the pension available before commutation, if greater. The maximum lump sum, again available after 20 years of service, is one and a half times final salary.

It is also possible to incorporate widows' and dependants' benefits, including a lump sum of up to four times salary, together with a refund of personal contributions, which can be paid free of tax.

Company directors

In general, the same rules apply to 'controlling' directors as to any individual in an occupational pension scheme. However, because a director of a family company is in a rather different position from an ordinary employee, the Revenue have imposed some limitations on directors with at least 20% control, eg the measurement of final salary is more stringent than for non-controlling directors. Directors with 20% control and members of families controlling more than 50% of the company are not eligible to join a company's approved pension scheme if it is an investment company.

15.7.6 Loans and self-investment

One of the disadvantages of pension schemes is that the capital invested in the fund is 'locked-in' until retirement. Previously, the use of loans made to the pension planholder or occupational scheme member has helped to reduce this disadvantage. However, lower expected returns from equities have over recent years reduced the attractiveness of interest only loans designed to be repaid from equity based investments, including many pensions.

Typically, a lender who makes an interest-only loan might expect the individual to repay the capital out of any lump sum entitlement from the pension. Such lump sums will not be assigned to the lender as security for the loan but, for example, where the loan is for house purchase, the mortgage over the property, assigned life assurance protection and the existence of the pension cash entitlement will usually satisfy the lender's requirements.

It is important that the pension contracts remain independent of the loan arrangements and that effecting the pension does not guarantee the availability of the loan. The pension must not be taken out to obtain the loan as the pensions legislation requires the pension scheme to be solely for the purpose of obtaining retirement benefits.

Another approach to 'unlocking' some of the pension fund is for the fund to be invested, in part, in shares of the employer company, in making loans to the company or in purchasing premises from which the company trades.

There are restrictions on the availability and amount of loans that can be made to the employer company (so-called 'loanbacks') under the Social Security Act 1990. In addition, Revenue rules have also restricted this type of 'self-investment'. Loans are limited, for the first two years of a scheme's existence, to 25% of the fund's value excluding transfer values, followed by a limit of 50% of the fund. In practice, these restrictions have over time all but removed the attractiveness of such loans.

The other approaches, which are also subject to restrictions, are usually only available to self-administered schemes in which the trustees have wide powers of investment compared to 'insured schemes' where the investment is usually confined to a policy issued by the insurance company concerned.

15.7.7 Contracting-out via an occupational scheme

As already mentioned, it is possible to use money-purchase schemes to contract out of S2P, or its predecessor SERPS.

A contracted-out money purchase (COMP) scheme will receive protected rights contributions as is the case with a personal or stakeholder pension. However, from April 1997 a COMP will receive the payments partly in the form of monthly direct flat-rate payments from the employer and partly in the form of age-related payments from the DSS as with a personal or stakeholder pension. The total rebates from all sources range between 2.6% and 10.5% for 2003–04.

With a COMP, the Revenue's limits on maximum benefits apply to the aggregate of the protected rights and non-protected rights benefits; a contracted-in occupational scheme member may obtain the maximum benefits from the occupational scheme, in addition to the protected rights benefits, from a rebate only personal pension effected to contract out of S2P or SERPS. The age-related incentive payable from April 1993 did not apply to a COMP.

Protected rights benefits from a COMP can be taken at age 60 by both males and females.

15.7.8 Unapproved occupational schemes

These may be established by employers to provide benefits greater than those otherwise allowable. In this way, for example, benefits in excess of two-thirds of final salary can be provided and top-up pensions can be given to employees with short service or those who are subject to 'income capping'.

There are none of the special tax benefits normally received by approved pension schemes and employer contributions will only obtain relief under the normal business expenditure rules, but lump sums can be paid free of tax from funded schemes. However, such schemes do retain certain tax benefits including, in some cases, the ability to roll up income at the basic rate of tax rather than at the special rate of tax applicable to some trusts. In appropriate cases this can result in a saving of tax where the employee is a higher rate taxpayer, as is likely to be the case. In 6 April 1998, realised capital gains were taxed at the basic rate (23% for 1997–98) but are now taxed at the rate of 34% applicable to all trusts. Until 30 November 1994 it was also possible to set up offshore schemes with enhanced taxation benefits. Although the employee is subject to tax on payments into the scheme (whether set up offshore or not), it was also possible to arrange for a degree of tax-free growth and freedom from tax on lump sum benefits. This is no longer possible as FA 1994 imposed a new tax charge on schemes set up to avoid tax in this way. The new rules apply to all schemes set up after the November 1994 Budget and existing schemes that are varied after that date.

15.7.9 FSAVC schemes

Since October 1987, all occupational scheme members are entitled to top-up their pensions by making contributions to a separate pension scheme of their own. Such a 'free-standing' additional voluntary contribution (FSAVC) scheme may not be commuted for a cash lump sum and must be aggregated with the occupational scheme to determine the maximum permitted benefits. The overriding limit on personal contributions, 15% of salary (capped where appropriate), remains.

Although regulated by the occupational pension scheme tax legislation, FSAVC schemes also have similarities to personal pensions in that they are individual arrangements independent of the individual's employer. The maximum limits on benefits and contributions are, however, those applicable to occupational schemes (see above). An employee's contributions to such schemes must be paid net of tax relief at the basic rate.

As long as contributions to the FSAVC do not exceed £2,400 per annum, the employer need have no involvement in an employee joining an FSAVC scheme. Even where the contributions exceed £2,400, the employer's involvement at the outset is restricted to providing sufficient information to allow the maximum contribution that can be paid to be calculated by the FSAVC provider. In some cases the funds built up in the FSAVC together with the benefits from the employer's scheme may exceed the Revenue limits. Where a scheme is overfunded in this way any over-provision is returned to the scheme member subject to a tax charge. This charge also applies to AVC schemes established in-house by employers.

From 6 April 2001, it is also possible to have a stakeholder pension, and indeed a personal pension, alongside an occupational pension scheme if earnings are less than £30,000 per annum. This will restrict the market for FSAVCs to those with higher earnings.

15.8 SUITABILITY

Personal, stakeholder and occupational pension schemes provide highly tax-efficient benefits. In consequence they are suitable for and extremely attractive as investments for those with earned income who wish to provide for personal cash and income during retirement and protection for their wives and families during their working lives. Because the premiums are deductible for tax purposes from earned income, the effective cost is relatively low, while the tax-free growth inside the pension fund enables substantial accumulation of funds for pension benefits. The emerging benefits, in the form of tax-free cash commutation and pensions, receive beneficial tax treatment. However, the fact that pension benefits can only be taken after certain ages tends to make such schemes suitable only for those prepared to take a long-term view.

15.9 CONCLUSION

The tax-deductibility of premiums, largely tax-free growth and prospects of a tax-free lump sum make pensions an extremely attractive investment.

There are, of course, some restrictions (lack of access to the fund until a minimum age, ability to take only a proportion as a lump sum, limits on the investment permitted, etc) but these do not detract from the investment benefit of pensions where the pension is effected for the right reasons, ie as long-term planning for retirement.

USEFUL ADDRESSES

See end of Chapter 14.

16

COMMODITIES

WILLIAM ADAMS

Updated by

LENNY JORDAN

This chapter is intended as an introduction to the commodity markets and a brief review and forecast of markets themselves. The sections are:

(1) introduction to commodities;
(2) types of commodities – physical and futures markets;
(3) characteristics of commodities;
(4) methods of participation in commodity markets; and
(5) review and outlook for commodities in 2003–04.

16.1 INTRODUCTION TO COMMODITIES: WHAT THEY ARE

The commodity markets had their origins in the industrial expansion of the 19th century. Industrialisation led to a rapid growth in demand for basic commodities, which created increased price volatility as supplies became more dependent on the arrival of shipments from abroad. This price volatility meant more efficient means were needed to price and allocate commodities. The early commodity markets therefore enabled traders to buy and sell contracts for physical commodities, on the basis of today's prices for delivery in the future.

Today's commodities exchanges still provide this service, although they have generally evolved to provide more of a pricing mechanism, where traders buy and sell the right to a commodity (a future), rather than trading the physical commodity itself. That said, the commodity exchanges are still backed by physical delivery and if a futures contract becomes prompt, then it is the physical commodity that has to be delivered or taken up.

The prime reason for the markets is still to provide a means whereby trade users can fix the price at which they sell or buy their raw materials in the future. For fabricators using commodities, this means that the price of their finished goods can be determined before being produced, by locking-in (hedging) the cost of the commodities needed to produce the finished goods. Likewise a producer can plan in advance whether it is profitable to continue producing the commodity in the period ahead. If the future price is above the full cost of production, the producer can sell futures against forward production and guarantee a profit for the period ahead.

Today's commodity markets are very sophisticated and form an integral part of the world financial markets where banks, producers, consumers, merchants and investors are all participants.

This chapter deals largely with the concepts of the commodity markets with insight into those commodities that can be bought and sold through, or are regulated by, the London Clearing House, The London Metal Exchange and the London International Financial Futures Exchange.

16.2 TYPES OF COMMODITIES

16.2.1 Softs and metals

The raw material commodities can be subdivided into two categories: soft commodities and metals.

The term 'soft commodities' loosely describes all non-metallic commodities: cocoa, coffee, sugar, rubber, grain, potatoes, wool, edible oil, nuts, etc. The London Commodity Exchange was merged with LIFFE and is Europe's primary soft commodity exchange, operating markets in coffee, cocoa, sugar, the BIFFEX Freight Index and UK domestic agriculture markets.

The London Metal Exchange (LME) is the centre for trade in the main non-ferrous base metal futures, eg aluminium, copper, zinc, lead, nickel, tin and aluminium alloy. The London Bullion Market Association (LBMA) looks after the interests of London's bullion markets. The bullion markets are physical, and not futures, markets.

The London Clearing House (LCH) deals with the clearing and settlement of the futures markets. Membership of LCH guarantees the fulfilment of the contract to both buyer and seller, thus avoiding the need for both buyer and seller to be concerned with each other's financial health. In effect, the LCH becomes the counterparty to each trade that its members carry out with other members.

16.2.2 Physical and futures

The commodity markets can be broken down into 'physical' and 'futures'. The physical markets deal with trading of the actual commodity and would normally result in the physical exchange of a commodity. A futures contract deals with commodities that are traded for delivery at a predefined future date and in the majority of cases the commodity is not expected to be delivered. As a futures contract is a tradable contract, it is generally liquidated before the contract becomes prompt. This means that the contract is cancelled by a corresponding and opposite contract, which means the trader's net position is square and that any difference in buying and selling prices is settled in cash.

By buying or selling in the futures market against a physical position, hedgers are able to safeguard themselves against the risk that the value of their unsold goods will depreciate through a fall in price or, alternatively, against the risk that pre-booked forward sales will show a loss if the commodity price rises.

Example

A merchant, who has taken delivery of 25 tonnes of copper, but has not secured a buyer for the metal, is exposed to the risk of copper prices falling. To offset this risk (exposure), he can sell one futures contract, the basis being the price at which he bought the physical metal. Upon finding a buyer for the physical metal, he then buys back his futures contract on the basis of the price at which he sells his physical metal. This means that while he holds the copper in stock, he is not vulnerable to a fall in the copper price, as any fall is offset by a profit on his futures contract (hedge), and vice versa.

This mechanism for hedging risk works when the futures markets are liquid, ie when there are sufficient buyers and sellers to make a two-way market.

Market liquidity is increased by the existence of speculators. The speculator buys or sells a commodity on the expectation of making a profit. By taking the opposite view in the market to the hedger, the speculator takes on the unwanted risk that the hedger wants to avoid.

Investment in physical markets is complicated by having to pay the full cash cost of the commodity, the warehouse and insurance costs, etc. Metals have the advantage over soft commodities in that they are generally less bulky and are not perishable.

Investing in futures avoids many of the disadvantages of physical commodity investing. The speculator can avoid taking physical delivery of the commodity as long as the future contract is closed before the contract becomes prompt. By dealing in futures, the speculator is able to trade soft commodities as easily as metals, without the worry of the commodity perishing, or the more expensive storage costs.

16.2.3 Financial futures

The third category of futures is financial futures, which regards money as another commodity. Financial futures grew rapidly in the 1980s and have enabled traders to use their money more flexibly by trading and hedging interest rates, bonds and stock market indices in the same way they would trade other raw material commodities.

These financial futures contracts are structured, regulated and cleared just like the raw material commodities and provide opportunities for investment managers, financial treasurers and traders seeking profit opportunities.

Interest rate market contracts are the most important of the financial futures. These range from short-dated three-month papers to long maturity government bonds and are denominated in most of the world's major trading currencies. The major contracts are traded in three time zones, providing around-the-clock access.

Stock index contracts are also well established and becoming increasingly popular, as are the option derivatives on the stocks. In addition to speculation, these products enable investors and fund managers to hedge their portfolio rapidly or to gain immediate access to the market (see 16.3–16.5).

16.3 CHARACTERISTICS OF COMMODITIES

Commodity markets are sophisticated and internationally traded; their price movements are often volatile. It is these characteristics that provide many attractive trading opportunities.

16.3.1 International markets

The word 'commodity' is defined in an economic sense as 'an exchangeable unit of economic wealth'. In most cases these units of economic wealth are recognised internationally and therefore have a real value, which is recognised and traded internationally. This widespread need for the commodities also means the markets are liquid and have high turnover as each commodity often passes through many traders'/industrialists' hands before being consumed. The liquidity, high volume and interest in these commodities means that in most cases it is possible to trade large volumes fairly quickly without disrupting the balance in the market.

16.3.2 Frequent opportunities

The prices of commodities fluctuate continuously as buying and selling pressure shifts. The driving forces for prices in the long term are the supply and demand fundamentals. In the short term, the markets may move in the opposite direction to that suggested by the fundamental factors. This divergence provides further opportunities for trading. In the futures markets, because the prompt date is a date in the future, the contract can be sold short. This means that the trader can sell the contract before buying it back at a later date. Therefore, even if traders expect prices to fall, they can still trade and profit from a falling market. This second dimension to the futures market is not available to most private investors in equities. However, the futures market at times can be very volatile, and the investor directly involved in a commodity will need to follow the market closely and is best advised to seek the guidance of an established broker and investment adviser.

16.3.3 Real assets

Raw material commodities are real assets with intrinsic values. This means that they could always be sold for cash and in the long term are a good potential hedge against inflation or currency depreciation.

16.4 METHODS OF PARTICIPATION IN COMMODITY MARKETS

There are many opportunities for investors to participate in the commodity markets and a host of investment vehicles that can be used to do so. The following deals with the more direct approaches of investing in commodities and commodity futures.

16.4.1 Physical (cash) metals

Possibly the least speculative means of becoming involved in the metals is to buy physical metal. Once bought, investors pay insurance and warehousing costs, but because payment has been made in full and there is no gearing involved on the initial capital investment, they do not have to pay additional margin payments.

One method is to buy cash metals when prices have fallen considerably below the costs of metal production, which in theory should eventually lead to production cutbacks at plants that are no longer economically viable. This brings about a change in the supply and demand balance of the metal.

It should be made clear that an oversupply situation in the metal markets can last for a number of years, so this should be seen as a long-term investment strategy. In addition, it should be realised that world production costs also fluctuate; in times of falling metal prices, producers attempt to cut production costs in an effort to remain economically profitable.

The long-term cyclical nature of commodity prices is inherent in the markets, as high prices encourage additional production and less consumption, eg through the emergence of substitutes. Consequently, a market where supply and demand is balanced could become one with oversupply. This leads to lower prices. Conversely, in a period of low prices, production decreases and when the economy recovers, consumption increases, which eventually leads to a drawdown in stocks and higher prices as demand for metal outstrips supply. These cycles mean that the further prices diverge from the world production costs, the more likely there is a change in the direction of the price trend. These factors influence the market over the long term and may take a few years to change the direction of a commodities price.

16.4.2 Cash and carry

The cash and carry is a risk-free way of trading in commodities for a known return on funds employed. In addition, a cash and carry sometimes provides opportunities for a capital gain.

This method of trading takes advantage of markets where forward prices are at a premium to cash (spot) prices. This premium is known as a 'contango'. In normal (contango) market conditions, the futures price is above the cash price. The exception to this occurs when there is a physical shortage of the commodity for nearby delivery; when this occurs, forward prices trade at a discount to the cash price. The discount is known as a backwardation. Normally the contango reflects the cost of storage, insurance and the opportunity cost of tying up money while holding the physical commodity. In other words, the contango reflects the interest payments lost by not having the money in the bank, plus the cost of insurance, plus the cost of storage.

A cash and carry is a trade involving the purchase of a commodity for immediate delivery and simultaneously selling an equal amount of the commodity for a future delivery date. In a contango market, this means you are buying at a lower price and selling at a higher price. The difference is the gross profit. Occasionally, while the investor is holding a cash and carry, a shortage in the commodity occurs and the market's contango narrows or even turns into a backwardation. In this case holders of the cash and carry can sell their cash commodity and simultaneously buy back their future position, thereby making a capital gain. Contangos are limited to the cost of capital, storage costs and insurance, while backwardations have no natural limits. In recent years, market regulators, in particular the LME, have imposed backwardation limits to ensure orderly markets are maintained, unless there is a fundamental reason for the tightness. Intervention by the regulators prevents market aberrations/manipulations.

16.4.3 Futures

The basic commodity traded on the exchanges is the outright futures contract. This provides the investor with a high-risk vehicle to trade commodities and requires the services of a futures broker. The buying or selling of a futures contract by an investor/speculator involves them taking a view on whether prices are set to rise or fall during the period of the futures contract. At any time during the life of the futures contract, the contract can be closed-out by making a corresponding and opposite trade.

For example, an investor buys one March 2001 Cocoa. To close out his position he needs to sell one March 2001 Cocoa before the March 2000 Cocoa contract becomes due. If on 4 January he sells one LME three months copper, with a prompt date of 4 April, when he closes the contract he needs to buy one lot of LME copper on the basis of the three months' price and then adjust the contract to the (prompt) date of his original short position – in this case 4 April.

Because dealing in futures is for forward delivery, only a proportion of the contract value is required initially as payment. This initial payment, known as 'initial margin', is normally around 10% of the full contract value. Therefore, an investment in £100,000 worth of copper will only require an initial outlay of some £10,000. This means that the funds the investor initially commits are geared at 10%.

Your risk, however, is on the full £100,000 value of the commodity; therefore a 10% move in the price of the commodity against you would mean a 100% loss on your initial funds. Should the value of the commodity move against you, then you would be required immediately to provide funds equal to the open position loss of your futures contract. This difference is called 'variation margin' and is paid in addition to the initial margin. Both initial and variation margins are used by the broker as collateral against any difference in the contract's current market value and its starting value when the trade was initiated.

It is this gearing and the need for variation margin payments that gives commodity markets their high-risk reputation. Of course, it is the ability to make 100% on the investor's initial payment with only a 10% movement in price that makes the market attractive to speculators.

The LME introduced a new Index contract on 10 April 2000 aimed at asset managers, fund managers and investors wishing to trade the metal as an asset class, without having to be experts in individual metals. Monthly futures contracts out to 12 months forward, and options contracts out to three months, are available.

16.4.4 Options

A less risky way to invest in the commodities is to buy options. An option is a traded contract that gives the buyer the right, but not the obligation, to buy a futures commodity at a specific price (strike price) at a predetermined date in the future. The risk is limited to the initial payment that the buyer has to pay for the option, which is known as the 'premium'. The advantage of trading options is that for a predetermined cost there is the potential for a significant gain. This premium can be traded, as it is calculated on the basis of the underlying future's current market price, volatility and the time until the option is declared. Therefore, should the option become profitable, the option-holder can, at any time prior to the declaration of the option, lock in a profit by one of the following means:

(1) trading a futures contract against the option position;
(2) selling the option and making a profit out of the difference between the premium paid to buy the option and the premium collected when sold; or
(3) waiting until option declaration and notifying the broker that the holder intends to declare the option, in which case the option position is converted into a futures position at the option's strike price. The investor then has to close the futures contract to take the profit, by establishing an equal and opposite futures position.

If the futures price moves in the opposite direction to the option, the option-holder allows the option to expire and the loss is limited to the initial premium paid.

There are numerous types of options and, by combining various types, the investor can produce option strategies that provide different opportunities.

The basic options are call and put options. A call option gives the buyer the right to buy a futures contract; a put option gives the buyer the right, but not the obligation, to sell a futures contract (see also **6.6**).

A grantor (uncovered seller) of an option takes on unlimited risk, as by selling the option he or she gives the option buyer the right, but not the obligation, to take up a futures contract at a predetermined price on a predetermined date in the future. Option grantors are traditionally the trade (consumers and producers), who use options as a means of raising cash. Investment fund managers and risk seekers also grant options, but option granting is a high-risk activity, whereas option buying will provide an investor with a highly leveraged position with a limited liability.

16.4.5 Managed funds

Investing in commodities through managed funds provides the ideal vehicle for investors to gain exposure to the risk/rewards that the futures markets offer, but do not have the time, inclination or expertise to follow and trade the markets. The types of funds on offer vary on the level of risk/reward. Some offer a guarantee that at least the initial sum will be returned after a preset period, but this guarantee means that the fund is relatively low geared and therefore less risky than a highly geared fund where all the initial investment is at risk.

Funds generally operate on the basis that the fund manages the money it raises by investing the money with a number of commodity trading advisers (CTAs). This enables the fund managers to select the best performing CTAs and as market conditions change, the allocation of money with each CTA can be optimised. The fund manager monitors the returns from the CTAs and handles the fund's administration and risk management.

Normally the only cost to the investor will be standard brokerage charges plus a management fee of between 1% and 3% and an incentive fee, which is assessed on the fund's performance. This fee generally averages around 15%–20% of the increase in value of the fund in an agreed accounting period.

Commodity funds generally have full jurisdiction over the money invested with them, although some funds specialise in certain market segments and have preset risk management principles.

The performance of all funds relies heavily on fund managers' judgement and how accurately they anticipate the markets. In selecting a fund manager, the investor needs to see how the manager has performed in the past. Although this by no means guarantees future performance, it does give some insight into how skilled the manager and the operation are.

The traditional funds are registered overseas to provide tax incentives for investors. Generally, the minimum investment into traditional type funds is around £10,000. The advantage of managed funds is that they provide individual investors and institutions with access to a market that is growing rapidly in volume and provides numerous opportunities for investors to diversify their investment portfolio.

16.5 REVIEW AND OUTLOOK FOR 2004–05

16.5.1 Introduction

Prices for base metals will be supported by the global economic recovery during 2004–05, but because producers will increase output in order to meet demand, the spectacular gains of 2003–04 are unlikely to be revisited. Soft commodities will be supported as well, but there a distinction must be drawn between those with demand-based fundamentals and those whose price levels are event-driven.

16.5.2 Economic outlook

The recovery that had been struggling to get under way since the beginning of 2002 finally materialised in 2003. Shares began their bull markets in March and proved once again to be leading indicators. Year-end world GDP reached a respectable 2.5%, led by the US at 3.2% and the UK at 2.2%

The Eurozone economies struggled to turn in positive performances, with overall 2003 GDP growth registering a meagre 0.4% increase. Germany, the traditional engine of Continental growth, has been unable to implement structural reforms, and the consensus is that any significant adjustments are at least five years ahead. The situation in France is similar.

One notable contributor to the global recovery was Japan, whose 2003 GDP increased by an unexpected 2.6%. Much of this improvement was due to increased exports to China, whose robust activity currently helps provide demand for exports from many Asian economies.

A lurking problem is the yen–dollar exchange rate. The Bank of Japan spent a reported $60bn during 2003 trying to suppress the yen, on top of foreign currency reserves of near $500bn. If the yen appreciates as the Japanese recovery continues, then the Bank may be forced to consider devaluation as an alternative to expending revenues to purchase US treasuries. Needless to say the US will not look favourably on yen devaluation at the time when it is promoting revaluation of the Chinese renminbi.

With the recovery officially under way, the interest rate cycle has turned, and the Bank of England has lead the way by hiking rates. The US Federal Reserve is following suit, although at a more cautious pace. Here, Alan Greenspan has followed the course that he prescribed last year, to allow the US recovery to become firmly established before engineering restraint.

There was no sign of 'irrational exuberance' however, as stock markets entered a trading range during Q2 of 2004. Two causes of this were the bogging-down of military operations in Iraq and the forthcoming US presidential election.

Just as US investors sat on the sidelines during the war in Afghanistan and during the run-up to the Iraqi invasion, so many put their plans on hold during Q2 and Q3 of 2004. The run-up to a presidential election has often been a time of caution for investors, but if the campaign reveals a leader early on, then plans will be put into action. The end of 2004 should see the veils of uncertainty lifted and 2005 will see renewed activity.

Perhaps the most significant change in economists' view of global conditions has been the shift from concerns over deflation to concerns over renewed inflation. While the consensus is that a deflationary cycle has been avoided, it is worth noting that the UK consumer prices index (CPI) lingers at just above 1%, almost a percentage point below the Bank of England target of 2%.

Eventually rising commodity prices will contribute to inflationary pressure, and with employment growing and wages increasing there will be less constraint on manufacturers' pricing power. Also, during this cycle the elements to the inflation-deflation analysis will be revised in light of globalisation. For example, China, like many Asian economies, has been an exporter of wage deflation, but is now exporting commodity inflation.

The soft dollar has so far checked commodity inflation, but should the US economy gather momentum, and should US rates rise, then the dollar will attract investment and will begin to appreciate.

Event risk is again a concern. A strategic terrorist attack would upset stock markets and would unsettle consumers. US GDP fell 1.3% during Q3 of 2001, and during September of that year, retail sales and durable goods orders fell sharply as unemployment claims rose dramatically. While the biggest economies are gaining sufficient momentum to absorb negative sentiment, sectors such as travel and tourism may suffer setbacks that would bring many companies to the brink of insolvency.

Forecasts for world GDP growth in 2004 lie in the vicinity of 3.6%, with the 2005 figure being slightly lower, at 3.2%, due to increased interest rates.

16.5.3 Metal market review and outlook

2003–04 witnessed spectacular gains in all LME commodities, as a classic bull market unfolded, the result of: a) supply shortage due to several years of output curtailment; b) renewed demand caused by a turn in the economic cycle; plus c) speculative buying. For the veterans, it was just like the good old days.

One contributing factor to the metals rally has been dollar weakness, which is expected to continue in 2004–05, despite GDP forecasts above 4%. Contributing to dollar weakness is the US's large balance of payments deficit, and an annual trade deficit of $500bn.

In most cases, prices surpassed their previous bull market highs by a wide margin. The added boost was provided by China, which is now the world's largest consumer of copper and zinc, and which is a net importer of nickel. Only in March 2004 did the central Government order the banks to curb lending, which had the effect of stabilising commodities prices.

Going forward, the question of China's potential reserves is bound to affect the global supply-demand balance. For most of its recent history, exploration was limited by the Government, and it is only recently that Western companies have been allowed to participate. Because it takes at least five years to explore and develop a mine, assessment of China's supply should only become clear towards 2008.

With prices generating improved margin, companies will eventually bring more production online, which will lead to price stability throughout this cyclical recovery, but, if the recent past is any guide, the next cyclical downturn will see an industry burdened by excess capacity. This may become more of an issue if China's hoped-for reserves are developed.

Still, the near future should see prices well supported, and in the case of nickel, supply bottlenecks are still in the equation. Prices, as in the case of nickel and lead (see below) can see extreme trading ranges. Traders looking for alternatives to outright long and short futures positions can substitute options strategies such as buying call spreads or put spreads at levels of support or resistance.

Indicators to watch in order to gauge market strength or weakness are the Primary Metals Leading and Coincident Indices, published by the US Geological Survey at http://minerals.usgs.gov/minerals Also notable are the monthly figures for Industrial Production, with components for Manufacturing Output and Mining Production, published by the US Federal Reserve at www.federalreserve.gov/releases

Aluminium

Global consumption increased by approximately 8.0% in 2003, far exceeding expectations, and the LME 3-months buyer price reached $1836/tonne on 19 April 2004. Those contrarians who heeded last year's advice in this chapter have been amply rewarded.

Last year's condition of oversupply due to excess capacity was checked due to shortage of alumina, the cost of which has exceeded $400 per tonne. The fundamental issue of producer infighting is on the back burner until the next cyclical downturn. While demand is robust, stocks have not been run down, as with other base metals.

Conservative estimates call for global consumption to increase by more than 5% in 2004, moderating to an increase of 3–4% in 2005. Production is expected to increase by nearly 7% in 2004, but to increase by 4% in 2005. Aluminium is expected to be well bid at $1500–1600 per tonne through 2005.

Copper

Closely tied to the economic cycle, the price of copper has increased due to a shortage of concentrate, and LME stocks have been run down. China now accounts for nearly 20% of world consumption, and while capacity is increasing, imports are still necessary to fulfil demand.

Although the dramatic price increase to $3029/tonne on 2 April 2004 is seen as having been due to fund speculation, consumer demand is expected to hold prices firm through 2005. Global production is expected to increase by about 3% in 2004, followed by more than 4% in 2005. Global consumption is forecast to increase by more than 5% in 2004, moderating to 4% in 2005.

Lead

Much of the price rise in 2003 was due to a Western metal deficit of 90,000 tonnes because of reduced production. Backwardation (cash prices above futures prices), a feature almost inconceivable in 2002 and early 2003, occurred at the LME during the end of 2003 and through mid-2004. LME stocks are currently at their lowest level since 1991 and secondary sources now comprise more than 50% of refineries' input.

The remainder of 2004 will see a shortage of metal because Western mine and refinery output is not expected to increase significantly, although firm prices will enable some European producers to increase production.

The balance of production increases will come from China, however, where many Western battery manufacturers are shifting operations. With demand increasing at 10% annually, China continues to increase imports of concentrate and it will struggle to increase output until into 2005.

Meanwhile, the Western metal deficit is expected to persist until into 2005. Production is expected to be only marginally greater during 2004, but perhaps increasing by 4% in 2005. Consumption is expected to increase by 3% in 2004, followed by 2% in 2005. The outlook is for prices to be supported at $600/tonne.

Nickel

Demand is strong and no major new mines are in development for the near future. The current supply deficit is thus expected to continue. With global annual demand growing at approximately 7% per year and supply only growing at 5% per year, there lies the possibility of producer rationing.

Out of concern for public hygiene, there will be continued demand from use of stainless steel in hospitals, laboratories and homes. Meanwhile, shortage of supply, together with dollar weakness, has enabled strengthening of demand for US scrap.

Despite increased production, China will remain a net importer in 2005. Demand is expected to be met by former Soviet Union countries and from increased production in Australia.

With supply being a problem for the foreseeable future, producers are looking far and near for new sources. One of these lies in Spain near Seville, where Rio Narcea is expected to open a mine towards the end of 2004.

Because the deficit is expected to persist into Q3 of 2005, prices in 2004 will be supported at $13,000/tonne, subsiding to $11,000/tonne in 2005.

Tin

LME stocks have declined from approximately $25,000/tonne at the end of 2002, to just under $7,000/tonne during March of 2004. In 2003 China's output continued to increase, but so did its demand, and the net result was that exports fell by approximately 8%.

While there has been stock building in Indonesia, and increased production there and in Peru, global production will struggle to meet demand through 2004, and so the market will remain in deficit through most of the year and into late 2005.

Contributing to demand is the global shift in the electronics industry to lead-free solders, rising shipments of semi-conductors, and Japan's recovery. Accordingly, prices will be well supported at $7000/tonne through 2004–05.

Zinc

Oversupply limited the rally in zinc during 2003–04, with the peak three-month LME contract of $1155 during February 2004 failing to breach the December 1999 level of $1245/tonne. Prices will continue to be supported, however, because Western production is currently being hampered by shortage of concentrate.

In an environment characterised by increasing demand, the problem of excess capacity, which has dogged zinc during the past several years, is temporarily being shelved. As with aluminium, the fundamental issue of producer infighting is on the back burner until the next cyclical downturn.

During 2004–05, the price of zinc will play out between reduced stocks, Western demand exceeding supply, and increased exports of refined zinc from China. Global zinc consumption is forecast to increase approximately 5% in 2004, followed by 4% in 2005.

Price levels for base metals

Now that the markets have entered the middle period of the current bull market, range trading has become a feature. The recent three-month LME levels shown in Table 16.1 may be referred to.

Table 16.1 Recent LME three-month contracts' peak levels

Commodity	Dates	Three-month official prices $/tonne
Aluminium	19 Apr 04	1836.50
	10 May 04	1588.00
Copper	02 Apr 04	3029.00
	30 Jun 04	2617.00
Nickel	06 Jan 04	17,660.00
	10 May 04	10,575.00
Lead	18 Feb 04	933.00
	21 Apr 04	698.50
Tin	26 May 04	9490.00
	8 Jul 04	8515.00
Zinc	18 Feb 04	1155.00
	30 Jun 04	988.00

16.5.4 Soft commodities review and outlook

Cocoa

The stratospheric rise in cocoa prices from below US $0.40/lb during 2000 to almost $1.00/lb during 2003 has levelled off in the region of $0.70 to $0.80/lb, and the current price range is similar to that of the late 1990s. With the improvement of the global economy, and consumption growing in the Far East and Eastern Europe, prices are expected to remain firm for the next year.

Cessation of civil war in the Ivory Coast has led to restored confidence in local markets, although the country still remains divided between a rebel-sympathetic north, and a government-controlled south. The French and neighbouring countries have managed to engineer a peace accord, but the situation is still tense.

Government agencies, rebel groups, and smuggling intermediaries have a mutual interest in maintaining supply and revenue, and have in the past managed to allow shipments to be exported. Until a lasting peace is confirmed by years of stability, however, volatility will remain just beneath the surface.

Because of the price improvement during the past few years, traditional producers such as Ghana are increasing capacity. In addition to the majors, investment is increasing in Nigeria, Malaysia, Colombia, and Vietnam. Perhaps the threat of competition is forcing all parties in the Ivory Coast to co-operate.

Current favourable weather conditions in Indonesian and African growing areas should lead to a global crop comparable to 2003–04, at approximately 3 million tonnes. Consumption is forecast to be greater than last year, and only marginally greater than production. With world stocks at roughly 30% of annual consumption, the market is in balance for the time being.

Coffee

After a record crop of nearly 50 million bags in 2002–03, Brazil's current forecast is for lower production, at approximately 30 million bags, due to the biennial tree cycle. Difficult weather conditions during the fruit-setting period, however, will see the 2004–05 harvest reach only 40 million bags.

The International Coffee Organization indicates that wholesale prices, which could hardly have fallen, have begun to improve. The composite price for Robusta has risen this year to near $0.40/lb from a dismal low of near $0.20/lb in 2001–02. During the same period, Arabica has risen from below $0.60/lb to nearly $0.70/lb.

Because Brazil accounts for 30% of global production, any reduction in supply will be welcome for its competitors in Central America, who have been struggling in recent years. Unfortunately, the dollar's depreciation is limiting profits for many producers.

The coffee bar phenomenon in the US and lately in the UK has continued to support demand. Still, traditional markets are nearly saturated, and the industry is pinning its hopes on new markets in the Far East.

The current market is in balance, but global stocks are expected to be in deficit during 2000–04 for the first time in several years. Should adverse weather conditions develop in Brazil during the next two years, coffee may become the speculative play. Robusta could then be seen at $0.80/lb, and Arabica could reach $1.60/lb, taking levels from 1998–1999.

Sugar

Last year's price improvement, due in part to speculative buying on the back of the Iraq War, ended in dismal failure. The rally which saw prices north of 8 cents/lb collapsed to the region of 6 cents/lb. The market continues to be weighed down by global stocks pushing towards 70 million tonnes.

Contributing to supply is the former Soviet Union, the world's largest importer, which is increasing beet production, and whose long-term goal is that of self-sufficiency. Brazil's cane crop is again expected to be plentiful, at 25 million tonnes, although more and more production is being converted into ethanol.

A substantial increase in demand is coming from China, however, whose 2003–04 crop has suffered drought, and the supply deficit is expected to be met by Thailand and other Asian producers. Still, global production during 2004–05 is expected to approach 150 million tonnes, while consumption is seen at 5 million tonnes less.

16.5.5 Summary

Base metals have entered phase two of a classic bull market, and so the easy money has been made. Prices are well supported, however, so a bear market is not in the offing. Traders comfortable with range trading should look for oversold and overbought conditions.

With the global economy in a cyclical recovery, shortages of concentrate and event risk lurking beneath the surface, new highs can't be ruled out despite increased production levels. Because of a foreseeable supply deficit with little or no new production coming online, Nickel affords the best opportunity for speculation.

With the situation in the Ivory Coast stable for the time being, contrarians may look for a pullback in prices in order to establish new long positions. Sugar seems destined to struggle for another year. Coffee, on the other hand, may have awoken from its slumber.

17

GOLD AND OTHER VALUABLES

JOHN MYERS

Solon Consultants

17.1 INTRODUCTION

17.1.1 A long-term hedge in precious metals

Traditionally, investors have looked upon precious metals and other valuables as a long-term hedge against political or economic chaos. When inflation has soared, when currencies have weakened, when stock markets have plummeted, precious metals have gained in attraction; historically, the greater the fear, the higher the price rise. Gold, the archetypal precious metal, once sought for its allure and its rarity, reasserts its worth when ephemeral standards of value fail.

Many people, perhaps still entranced by Nebuchadnezzar's Babylon and the touch of Midas, regard gold as intrinsically valuable, internationally acceptable and negotiable. For these reasons, it maintains an image as the ultimate form of money, as a store of wealth unaffected by wars and political turmoil. However, events have tarnished that image. At times, hedging – with the help of futures, options, gold mining shares, physical holdings and indices – has damped oscillations. In addition, exchange controls have weakened. That has made it easier for wealthy people who dread war, terrorism and local hyperinflation, to shift into dollars, euros or Swiss francs, instead of gold. Of late, therefore, political crises across the world have had little effect on the bullion market. The Gulf War, the break-up of the former Soviet Union and the successive Balkan conflicts have only marginally affected the price. Even the crisis of 11 September 2001 did not generate extensive panic buying although demand and prices have since risen significantly in many parts of the world. Prospectively, a succession of such crises might well lead to a sharper and sustained response in the bullion markets.

Meanwhile, critics of those who try to control our affairs may fear that inflationary actions and devaluations by politicians and monetary authorities will degrade currencies. Those in power would find gold more difficult to debase. The Irish dramatist George Bernard Shaw once suggested that, 'you have to choose (as a voter) between trusting the natural stability of gold and the honesty and intelligence of members of government. And with due respect to those gentlemen, I advise you, as long as the capitalist system lasts, to vote for gold.'

Yet the British economist John Maynard Keynes dismissed the metal as 'a barbarous relic'. He doubted the truth of the view that 'something that has been a store of value for 5,000 years will not go out of fashion'. Nor did he give intellectual weight to the physical characteristics of bullion bars, wafers or coins. Gold has unique properties: superior electrical conductivity, ductility and malleability. The metal is largely immune to the effects of weather, moisture, oxidation or seawater, and to the corrosive effects of most acids and alkalis. For their part, gold hoarders persist in the belief that their holdings will endure, and offset any severe downturn in portfolios of stocks and shares during a monetary or political crisis. Furthermore, gold, silver and platinum prices are usually denominated in US dollars. The 'bugs' therefore see these metals as a hedge against steep falls in currency markets.

A few financial advisers echo the hoarders' beliefs, and recommend wealthy investors to keep perhaps 5–10% of their assets in precious metals. Some intrepid souls, with cash to spare, continue to hold 10–15% of their wealth in gold. The truly enchanted are even bolder. In 1997, Robert F Hague disclosed his fiscal recalcitrance to the *New York Times*. This retired US investment banker kept 90% of his portfolio in gold bullion, coins, unit funds and individual equities. Hague told the journalist: 'I've felt for many, many years that we're going to have to use gold to straighten out our financial system. The reason the economy and the market look so good is the excess of credit and debt. All is false. There will come a time when we recognise gold as the ultimate money.'

Keynesians forcefully disagree; they point to the negative annual returns that buyers of gold bullion or coins can experience. Most investors should stay away from gold, says John Markese, executive director of the American Association of Individual Investors in Chicago. If a person 'just has to buy some gold', then owning shares in a broadly based natural resources mutual fund is probably the safest route.

Investment specialists have also been critical of the gold bugs, especially in the US. Putting money into commodities such as gold and silver 'is not for most average investors', says Thomas O'Hara, chairman of the US National Association of Investors Corporation. 'Gold is very risky; it provides no regular income, such as occurs from investing in common stocks.' Metal prices are 'volatile and subject to manipulation from speculators'. Investing in gold or silver is 'primarily for very wealthy individuals'. Others should perhaps be careful not to become gold's fool.

At times, silver, platinum and palladium have become respectable vehicles for investment. Admittedly, they are riskier than gold. The prime use of silver is as an industrial material, with at least a chance that its price will fall during a recession. Platinum and palladium are alternatives, but prices can be highly volatile. Their recent popularity has depended primarily on their use in automotive catalytic converters that, with technical developments, now require decreasing amounts of the metal. Nevertheless, worldwide demand for these rare metals has tended to rise, boosted at the margin by, for example, platinum jewellery sales in China and Japan, and by the US Mint's introduction of a platinum bullion coin.

17.1.2 Development of the gold market

In the past century, gold has recorded occasional major price rises in world markets. Its longer history, of course, is as a coinage metal and a measurement of national wealth. In 1934, as part of the 'New Deal', US authorities raised the bullion price and fixed it in the US at $35 per oz. This fix lasted for 40 years, until President Nixon severed gold's links with the dollar. On the open market, bullion then reached $200 per oz, mainly because of petrodollar inflation and weak central banking strategies.

In the inflationary 1970s, investors rushed to convert paper money into gold. The price of a troy ounce of gold went up to $825, the last big surge in the bullion price. It then dropped to $300 per oz in mid-1982, only to rally again, reaching $500 per oz in June 1983. After 1987, gold fell back. In 1991, the dollar price per oz averaged $362.26, down 6% on 1990, and declined further to $280 in 1999. Global events often trigger such fluctuations, as happened at the end of the century.

At that time, a threat to the gold market had originated with the International Monetary Fund (IMF), which first proposed the sale of approximately $30bn of gold to help pay off developing countries' debts. Then, following pressure from the US Congress, the IMF officially confirmed its plan to revalue 14m oz of gold to help pay for its share of a debt relief initiative. The revaluation allowed a borrowing country to buy gold at the market rate, and immediately return it to the IMF as loan repayment. The IMF's ultimate decision not to sell brought the fund into line with Australia and Japan: in 1999, both countries confirmed they had no plans to sell.

None the less, banks' willingness to dispose of gold holdings gained credibility through a US Federal Reserve Bank study, which concluded that central banks should sell their gold, as it offered a cheaper source of supply than mining for new gold. This study led to speculation that the US, one of the world's largest gold owners, could change its gold policy, and start to sell.

On the European scene, the UK Treasury shocked the gold market when, in May 1999, it announced the intended sale of half of the UK gold reserves. Surprise at the unexpected sale and its timing shook the market more than the sale itself. Gold lost 10% of its value following the announcement, falling to a 20-year low in June 1999. The announcement also affected gold mining shares. The FTSE Gold Mines Index fell by more than a quarter, and the North American gold mines index by 29%. The currencies of the big gold producers were hit, particularly the South African rand. Hedging activity also increased considerably in 1999 after the UK Treasury advertised its gold sales. In response, the World Gold Council (WGC) launched a 'Hold on to our gold' campaign and registered several thousand supporters.

Subsequently, a group of central banks announced that they had put a five-year cap on sales from their gold holdings and lending. Under this Central Bank Gold Agreement, known as the 'Washington Agreement', the banks decided to restrain their sales, at least until the agreement's expiry in September 2004. The participants in the agreement control a large proportion of the world's official global gold reserves. They tend to operate in different ways. While some have added to their stocks, others have disposed of a proportion of their bullion holdings but, because of the agreement, without prompting wild oscillations in the price.

In the UK, the Treasury held further auctions in March 2000, and announced plans to continue sales every two months throughout 2000 and 2001. However, sales methods contrasted unfavourably with similar sales in the Netherlands, which did not cause any noticeable disruption to the gold market. Commentators attributed this to the Dutch central bank's rejection of the auction system.

A National Audit Office (NAO) review of UK practice, published in January 2001, applied three criteria for the gold sales programme: transparency, fairness and value for money. On the third point the NAO made recommendations on 'the advantages and disadvantages of adapting the existing sales methodology, for example by changes to the auction design or even by using the London gold fix as an alternative or additional means of selling gold'. The NAO held the view that selling smaller amounts of gold more regularly through the London fix would be less destructive than the auction method. Following this review, the Bank of England cut auction sales from 25 tonnes to 20 tonnes.

Elsewhere in Europe, the Swiss voted in a referendum to end the link between gold and Swiss franc note issues. The law no longer requires a link between the Swiss franc and the price of gold, opening the prospect of gold sales. The Swiss National Bank commissioned the Bank for International Settlements (BIS) to conduct gold sales in 2000, and announced that it would sell 1,300 tonnes (41.8m oz) over the coming years, representing almost half the country's reserves.

In the first years of this century, a significant development occurred in the industry's trading practices, affecting supply and demand. The

Canadian gold company Placer Dome announced it would stop its hedging practice. Subsequently, producer hedging declined sharply, as did the production growth rate. The output of gold from world mines declined, mainly because of temporary production problems at several mines.

Meanwhile, the Russian economy suffered successive crises. The country's central bank has generally run contrary to the trend of other central banks by increasing its gold reserves. However, changes in export legislation allowed Russian commercial banks to export gold directly, so that Russian political and economic events can potentially affect the market sentiment on gold.

Asian markets have also become more significant. China and India are among the gold jewellery industry's primary targets. Chinese investment and demand for gold jewellery has increased substantially in the past few years. Recent moves by the People's Bank of China have changed the pricing structure for gold, bringing it into line with international markets. In India, the country that, of late, has consumed more gold than have most others, villagers buy gold in good harvest years, because they can easily sell it later for cash. In addition, the Indian Government has set up a framework that permits banks to offer gold deposit schemes. The aim was to reduce gold imports into the country by using some of the country's existing stock. Participants in the scheme could deposit gold bars, coins or jewellery and receive transferable three- to seven-year certificates with an earning potential of 3–4%. Under the schemes, the banks melt down the gold deposited, and lend it to manufacturers on advantageous terms.

In parallel, gold producers have been taking an optimistic view of new applications for the metal. It has been finding uses as a cold engine catalyst in the motor industry and in pollution control, air conditioning and odour abatement systems. Researchers anticipate that gold catalysts could offer advantages in 'clean-energy' fuel cells, in combating cancer and in drug delivery microchips. Analysts also predict further growth in the demand for gold in dental care.

17.1.3 Developments in the silver market

Most of the world's silver comes from Mexico, Peru, Canada and the US. Experts estimate that total world silver production since 4000 BC is perhaps 40bn oz. Silver tends to be the most volatile in price of all the precious metals, partly because, since the early 1990s, the market has often been in deficit and vulnerable to fluctuations in supply and demand. For example, in 1980, the price reached a record high of $52.50 per oz, but dropped to a record low of $3.51 in the early 1990s.

The pattern persisted throughout that decade. By 1998, demand for silver had fallen by 2%, because of the then high price, the strength of the US dollar and an Asian financial crisis. Total supply to the market also fell, despite official sector sales of the metal increasing sevenfold to over 50m oz. According to Gold Field Mineral Services (GFMS), the silver market in 1999 had a structural deficit for the tenth consecutive year. Fabrication demand outstripped supply from mine production, depleting the above-ground stocks of silver by 105m oz.

The actions of the US investor Warren Buffet have had a significant effect on the market – at one time he held about 130m oz, or 16% of the world silver supply. He bought the metal in 1998, and at the start of 1999 the silver price rose and borrowing rates increased, following Mr Buffet's annual statement on his silver holdings. Subsequently, he has liquidated at least some of his holdings.

Worldwide silver consumption for industrial applications grew by a quarter between 1990 and 1999. The electrical and electronics sector spearheaded this rise, using silver in products such as CD-ROMs, semi-conductors and cell-phones. By the end of the century, usage had increased by 12.2% to 166.6m oz. In 2000, for the eleventh consecutive year, there was a large silver shortage, with fabrication demand outstripping supply by 151.2m troy oz, further reducing above-ground stocks to meet silver demand.

This demand may well continue as new and diverse applications emerge. According to a report by Dr Jeffrey R Ellis, a professor of chemistry at Florida International University, the use of silver in biocide applications could increase, with growth expected to surpass 11m troy oz by 2006. Another factor pointing to growth in silver consumption is concern over environmental and health-related issues – prompting a trend, especially among Japanese manufacturers, to replace lead in soldering materials.

Despite these record levels of fabrication demand, private disinvestment and official sector sales kept the price under pressure and silver prices averaged $4.95 per troy oz. The silver price softened, largely because of continued Chinese selling and ongoing disinvestment, including liquidation of fund holdings. Silver fabrication demand fell by 4.9% in 2001 according to industry sources, mainly due to a global recession, the collapse of the electronics industry and the bursting of the 'tech bubble'. Eastman Kodak, which uses silver in the production of film, reported lower sales. However, jewellery and silverware fabrication demand increased by 2.2%, with the Asian market making most of the gains. Global silver supply fell by 6%, despite a 1.5% increase in mine production. The deficit between conventional supply and demand was 89.4m oz, although official sector sales almost entirely filled this gap. The Chinese Government accounted for three-quarters of the 9.7% rise in these official sales.

17.1.4 Other precious metals

Platinum, palladium, rhodium, osmium and iridium have industrial uses in manufacturing and jewellery fabrication, which make them vulnerable to marginal shifts in supply. For example, during 1999, Russia reduced exports of palladium, the most important of this group of metals. This reduction, combined with a rise in demand, meant a significant shortfall had to be met from stocks. Hedge funds and releases from the US stockpile made up the shortage. About a third of platinum output goes into catalytic converters for the automobile industry, but this demand is susceptible to the development of better technologies. In early 1992, the market faltered when a US company announced a breakthrough that eliminated the need for platinum. Prices recovered when later reports showed that the device was merely an add-on to existing converters. The miniaturisation of electronics is also detracting from physical demand for these precious metals. Conversely, higher sales of devices such as digital pagers and cellular phones have partially offset the decline. Increasingly, an important use for platinum is in jewellery manufacture, accounting for about half the total. Demand for platinum jewellery has been mainly from Japan, but sales in China have been growing at a significant pace.

In the 1990s, the 'wild card' in the market for platinum and palladium was the uncertainty of supplies from its main producers. Labour unrest in South Africa affected this sensitive market, and political and economic problems continued to beset the other major producer, Russia. Ten years ago, South Africa produced 75% of the total world output of platinum, and the former Soviet Union, 20%. Demand reached record levels in 1991, but so did supplies. Russia increased exports by a third, causing a fall in prices to a six-year low. In 2002, Russia restricted its sales of palladium, resulting in a net drop in sales of 56%. Continuing the trend, South African mines increased their output by 7.5%, and North America's production leapt by 16% through the expansion of the mining process in several areas.

Palladium prices peaked at over $1,000 in early 2001, which prompted the substitution of silver, and an overall reduction in palladium content. Demand fell accordingly. Electronics were in decline and manufacturers of auto-catalysts decreased their demand by 9%, mainly by the use of other metals in catalysts. Prices then began to spiral down. Increased Russian and South African production exacerbated the decline.

Sectoral increases in demand were attributable partly to the production of more diesel-powered cars, which took a third of the car market in 2000, and partly to a requirement for heavier catalyst loadings to meet Euro III emission standards. A slight fall in jewellery demand offset these factors. The fall was attributable to the weakness of the Japanese market, where fabrication fell by 20%. For the first time in 20 years, net investment in platinum was negative, with sales of coins and investment bars halved to 40,000 oz and a net sellback of 100,000 large bars in Japan. Investors sold back bullion coins and bars to profit from the high prices.

In recent years, palladium's prime role has continued to be as a catalyst in the electronics and motor industries. For the moment, the automobile industry remains the biggest user of palladium, accounting for two-thirds of the demand. With the implementation of green legislation, demand may continue to rise. However, the instability of supplies and rising costs have prompted car companies to reassess their needs for alternatives. After some years of rapid growth, the industry's purchases of palladium declined, as car makers responded to higher prices by using metal from stocks. However, actual consumption of palladium, in catalysts fitted to cars and trucks, went up to meet emissions legislation throughout the world. A large auto-catalyst manufacturer, Degussa-Huels, reportedly developed a platinum-based catalyst as an alternative to those made mainly from palladium. This new auto-catalyst meets the EU's 2005 requirements for low emissions, and even lower targets in the US.

Burgeoning demand for capacitors saw uses in electronics rise 8%, even though palladium lost a share of the market to base metals. The rise is ascribable to the manufacturing of multi-layer ceramic capacitors (MLCCs). Manufacturers of these capacitors increased their output to meet demand for mobile phones and the WAP (wireless application protocol) models used for internet communications. However, the high price of palladium has made its future in this sector less secure.

In dentistry and other applications, demand has tended to fall, and the use of palladium alloys has decreased worldwide. For example, in North America and Germany, palladium consumption plunged in 2000, as a weak euro compounded the impact of high dollar prices. Dental laboratories are switching from palladium to gold and, especially in Europe, to base metal alloys; furthermore, technical improvements are encouraging the greater use of metal-free materials, for example porcelain.

Rhodium plays an important role in the motor industry, which accounts for 90% of the metal's sales. Admittedly, the use of rhodium in catalytic converters is in decline, and demand fell in the 1990s. However, catalyst manufacturer Johnson-Matthey believes that emerging uses could cause demand to pick up in the coming years.

In 2001, supplies of rhodium declined sharply, by 21%; Russian and South African exports fell, and automobile makers decreased their intake, having built up stockpiles in previous years. Thus, the market moved into a surplus after two years of deficit. The electronics industry, which saw a large fall in demand in 2001, was also responsible for a 22% drop in the consumption of ruthenium.

Increased consumer demand for rhodium and limited availability of the metal combined to force the price per oz up from $1,000 at the beginning of 2000 to just over $2,000 at the end of December, having touched $2,600 in August. As with other precious metals, the need to comply with stricter regulation on emissions increased demand for rhodium from the automotive industry. Gross auto-catalyst demand rose from 509,000 oz in 1999 to 793,000 oz in 2000. Demand for rhodium in other applications went up by almost 10% to 92,000 oz in 2000.

The glass industry has increased rhodium demand, largely because of investment in plants to manufacture the high quality, thin glass used in liquid crystal displays (LCDs), which make use of rhodium-platinum alloys in the production process. This industry's demand for rhodium is set to continue as the wider application of LCDs in computer screens and in other consumer electronic devices – for example, in mobile phones – is expected to double demand for LCD glass.

At the turn of the century, the London Metals Exchange converted from mutual ownership to a shareholder organisation. The aim is to maintain the exchange's position as the leading non-ferrous metals market. The exchange is also making use of a screen-based trading system.

17.1.5 Gold investment media

Investors who wish to secure an interest in precious metals, for example gold, silver, platinum or palladium, have a choice of media. Most have little appeal to ordinary investors. For example, gold jewellery makes a memorable gift, but does the buyer really want to ask his or her spouse to sell the Patek Phillippe watch to pay a child's tuition bill? Other options include:

(1) Buying bullion in the form of assayed ingots or bars which, to avoid costly insurance premiums, are usually kept in a bank vault, although that can give rise to expensive storage charges.
(2) Avoiding the cost and risk of keeping gold bars in a vault or under the bed by using the services of commercial banks to hold the metal in a customer's 'gold statement account'. When a customer wants to draw on his account, the bank advances the cash equivalent of the gold's value at the prevailing price, less commission.
(3) Speculating in gold futures contracts, or options, or indexes, through a broker. This approach is for gamblers who, undaunted by the wild swings in gold prices in the past, believe they can predict future values, or gain a turn by hedging.
(4) Investing in mining stocks through equities of companies that mine gold and other precious metals, or diversified funds that specialise in mining companies. Mining stocks have not been stellar performers

of late, and few funds have recorded significant growth. In recent times, mining companies have driven down costs in an attempt to improve share prices and achieve an operating profit at a low gold price. At times, the strategy can fail: for example, in 1997 gold shares fell by about 45%. In practice, performance of funds often varies widely, as do annual charges and management fees.

(5) Buying government-minted bullion coins, for example, sovereigns from the Royal Mint, or American eagles produced by the US Treasury. (Rare coins are another matter – they are 'collectables': see Chapter 19.)

Other approaches are attracting publicity. As a case in point, e-gold is an electronic currency, issued by e-gold Ltd (www.e-gold.com), a company incorporated in the Island of Nevis. The currency is said to be 100% backed at all times by gold bullion in allocated storage. Other e-metals are issued: e-silver is reportedly 100% backed by silver; e-platinum, 100% backed by platinum, and e-palladium, 100% backed by palladium. However, the most popular e-metal is e-gold. In practice, e-gold is the basis of an account-based payment system, which enables participants to use gold as money. Specifically, this e-gold payment system enables people to transfer specified weights of gold to others' e-gold accounts. Only the ownership changes – the gold in the grade vault stays put.

A further innovation takes the form of a stock market-listed trust, which enables savers to invest directly in gold. Gold Bullion Securities (GBS), a trust quoted on the London Stock Exchange, allows investors to take a direct wager on the price of gold. As with any other stock, traders can buy and sell interests in GBS through stockbrokers. Four of the City's largest banks have pledged to make a market in the shares. The stock has the backing of gold held in the vaults of HSBC, one of Britain's largest banks. Until now, private investors have had to use mining stocks as a proxy for the precious metal. Mining stocks tend to be an imperfect sub-stitute for bullion itself.

In practice, this form of trust is an exchange-traded fund. GBS deducts an annual charge of 0.3 per cent to cover storage and insurance costs, as well as its own fees. Each share represents a tenth of a troy ounce of gold, valued in dollars in line with the prevailing bullion price. The company is negotiating with the authorities over the shares' eligibility for inclusion in tax-efficient packages, including ISAs and pensions. The GBS website (www.goldbullion.com) provides further information.

Comparable schemes operate in Russia, Australia and other countries. Their popularity may at times give rise to uncertainties. Investors who opt for a gold account bear the risk of leaving the actual metal in the bank's possession. Alan McGregor, a partner with AVC Advisory, an investment and financial planning agency, has repeatedly urged investors to verify that the 'creditworthiness of the institution where the asset is held is of sufficient quality'.

17.1.6 Gold coins

Of these diverse possibilities, gold coins have been popular as bullion investments. The majority of individual investors who physically own gold hold only coins, according to the WGC. Enthusiasts believe that 'when the price of gold moves, the price of coins containing gold can move faster and further'. In reality, bullion coins generally track the gold price within a few percentage points below the metal's spot price. Thus, when gold prices fall, bullion coins can be worth even less.

Yet many countries still mint bullion coins. Past examples have included the Russian Chervonetz, the Mexican Peso, the Austrian Corona and Philharmonic (it has a fiddle on the obverse), the Luxembourg Lion, the Australian Nugget, the South African Krugerrand, and others enjoying culturally redolent names. So, Mauritius has had its Dodo; France, its Napoleon; China, its Panda; Canada, its Maple Leaf; Japan, its Hirohito and Akihito. Some coins are 24-carat gold; others are 22 carat, with an alloy added for strength. However, many nations' bullion coins contain a single ounce of high-carat gold. The 2003 $50 Canadian Maple Leaf gold coin, for example, contains no alloys, and trades at about $440. Other new style coins in 2003 included Australian Kangaroos and American Eagles.

The Royal Mint's Britannia has depended on an aesthetic appeal (as a Coin of the Year) to justify a premium over its bullion value. Although the Britannia competes with the American Eagle, it has a significant difference: the US Mint produces many tens of thousands of Eagles, while the Royal Mint usually limits production of the 1-, ½- and ¼-oz sizes. An issue from the Royal Mint of the Diana, Princess of Wales Victorian Anniversary gold proof memorial coin, had a mintage of 73,500, and then the Mint released significant quantities of a Queen Mother Centenary Crown in gold. The Royal Mint also produced a Golden Jubilee Gold Proof Crown. More than 5,500 went on the market and sold out within weeks. The obverse of the coin features an equestrian portrait of the Queen, in keeping with crowns struck in Coronation year and for the Silver Jubilee in 1977.

The success of the commemorative 2001 D-mark coin prompted Germany's Finance Ministry to attempt a repeat effort. In May 2002, it produced half a million 100-euro gold coins weighing half an ounce, and a hundred thousand 200-euro gold coins weighing one ounce. The issue was massively over-subscribed; as a result, these gold euros traded well above issue prices in the grey market. In June 2004, The People's Bank of China reissued a series of palladium coins, a total of 8,000 of the proof half-ounce pure palladium Panda 100 Yuan coins characterised by the 'Kissing Pandas' motif, depicting a mother and its cub in an embrace. The coins come in a presentation package with a lower mintage than their gold and silver equivalents; the Bank has authorised 75,000 gold and 600,000 silver versions.

Among other issues attracting interest are three South Korean bullion coins. These comprise:

(1) The Seoul Olympics Folk Dancers proof gold coin, denominated as 25,000 Won; its precious metal content is 16.81 gm of 925 fine gold, and its mintage, 111,000.
(2) The Olympics Turtle Ship 1 oz proof gold coin, denominated as 50,000 Won; its precious metal content is 33.62 gm of 925 fine gold, and its mintage, 30,000.
(1) The Olympics Horse & Rider 1 oz proof gold coin, denominated as a 50,000 Won; its precious metal content is 33.62 gm of 925 fine gold, its mintage, 30,000.

Until recently, a general deterrent for the UK private investor wishing to invest in gold coins, or for that matter in wafers and bars, was a liability to pay VAT. Although investors could avoid the tax by buying and holding gold offshore, UK demand for this form of investment collapsed after the Chancellor imposed the tax in 1982. However, in March 1999, the Government announced a VAT exemption for investment in gold, introduced on 1 January 2000. From that date, investors throughout the EU have been able to buy gold bars, wafers and coins exempt from VAT, in line with an EU Directive. In the UK, the threshold for which customers have to provide personal details has been raised to £5,000 per individual transaction, and £10,000 spent cumulatively over one year. As with all purchases of precious metals, experts advise buyers to deal only with reputable sources.

A further word of warning – do not take delayed delivery. According to Craig R Smith, chief executive of Swiss-America, a gold coin brokerage, delayed delivery is the 'number one scam'. Smith recommended shopping for the lowest price that has immediate delivery. 'Dealers that keep you waiting for 30 days', he said, 'are using your money to make money.'

In July 2002, the US Mint put into auction a 1933 $20 coin, a Double Eagle, at an estimated value of $4–6m. Minted after President Roosevelt began to wean America off the Gold Standard, the Double Eagle never became legal tender. Instead, the coins stayed in a bank vault, until the Mint destroyed them in 1937, but thieves stole a few. The one in auction is the only extant example.

The International Mint Market Development Council, a consortium of government mints, has launched a website designed to promote interest in coins and collecting (www.worldmints.com). It features links to credible numismatic organisations, a dealer locator and a discussion forum. Participants include the official mints of Austria, Japan, Australia, Canada, Singapore, Spain, the US and the UK.

In the aftermath of 11 September 2001, private investment demand for coins, particularly in the US and in Europe, has increased noticeably. According to the WGC, US 'online' organisations reported a notable increase in business, especially while currencies were fluctuating. In the ten days following the attack, the US mint sold 45,000 oz of Eagles, twice the amount of its most successful period the previous year.

17.1.7 Silver, platinum and palladium coins

Silver coins have become popular with mints. Dealers and traders sold more than 5.3m silver dollar American eagles between December 1990 and March 1991, a record volume for a silver bullion coin. Investors favour silver coins and bars to hedge positions in silver futures and shares of companies that mine silver. Sales of the American silver eagle in 2001 were the highest since the programme began. To continue to produce these coins, the US had to purchase silver on the open market, and the US Mint became a significant buyer of silver, accounting for about 1% of global demand each year.

Both the silver Kookaburra (released April 1990) and the platinum Koala feature in Australia's bullion coin programme. The Koala is one of only a few platinum bullion coins on the market. One of the earliest was the platinum Noble from the Isle of Man, minted originally in 1983. Following that example, the Australian Gold Corporation selected platinum because of the metal's rarity. Worldwide, platinum output totals 5m oz a year, compared with 40m oz of gold. Japanese buyers have accounted for about half of world demand for platinum, and the designers chose the Koala image on the coins partly to develop sales in Japan. According to the Gold Corporation, the day after the coins appeared there, dealers sold 4,093 oz of the platinum Koalas at prices averaging $515 per oz. The coin was made available in 1-, $\frac{1}{2}$-, $\frac{1}{4}$- and $\frac{1}{10}$-oz coins, with nominal values in Australian dollars of $100, $50, $25 and $15. Australia has also issued the Emu, a legal tender coin minted in palladium.

In 1997, the US Mint introduced the platinum Eagle bullion coin. Sales benefited directly from high investor interest in platinum at the time. A further boost in demand arose from a US rule change in January 1998. For the first time, US investors could include platinum in their Individual Retirement Accounts. In total, the US silver and platinum Eagles hold almost 80% of their markets. A 2003 version of the Eagle bullion coin is now available, costing about $800 for a 1oz coin.

Russia issued a giant 1-kilo (32-oz) silver coin in 1995, minted to commemorate the 50th anniversary of the end of World War II. The coin bears the first depiction of Stalin on a Soviet or Russian coin, and the denomination is 100 roubles. Members of the Russian Parliament reserved the first 1,000 of the 1,500 coins issued. According to the Russian Mint's website, fewer than eight coins from the original mintage remain in the vaults.

A set of four historical commemorative coins, two made of silver, one of platinum and another of palladium, also come from Russia. The full set sold for about £500. As the Russians urgently need hard currency, the Mint there has been selling palladium coins aggressively to collectors and metal speculators. The content is 99% palladium, and the price has been 20% above the metal's daily spot market price. Carrying the image of a ballerina, the coins bear a face value of 25 roubles. The coin contributes to what the Russians hope will be a long-lasting series of 'palladium ballerina' coins. Of 30,000 minted, 3,000 were of proof quality.

Knowledgeable dealers believe that the palladium coin serves as an important long-term precedent, and that palladium could be the investment metal of the 21st century. Only three countries (Russia, South Africa and the US) have enough palladium reserves to mine the mineral commercially, but other countries (for example, Bermuda, France, the Isle of Man and Tonga) have made special-issue commemorative coins from imported metal. The Russian coins are just one case of the increasing competitiveness with which mints are seeking customers. Mexico, for example, has been offering the Mexican Rainbow Proof Coin collection consisting of a set of gold, silver and platinum coins. When the Mexicans launched them, they priced the first year's coins bearing the date 1989 at £440.

17.1.8 Hedging

In the 1990s, the WGC attributed the declining gold price to the growth in hedging. Graham Birch, head of gold and mining at Mercury Asset Management, agrees. He argued in a *Financial Times* article in May 1998 that hedging had been a significant factor in weakening the gold market, affecting the stock value of many gold companies. In North America, 50 publicly traded and closely watched companies mine gold as their exclusive or primary line of business. These companies have the same exposure to oscillations in the price of bullion; their output is a globally traded, volatile commodity. They have, at times, managed this exposure using a diverse set of instruments, including forward and futures contracts, gold swaps, gold or bullion loans, rolling forward commitments called spot deferred contracts, and options. Significantly, companies in the gold mining industry now reveal details of their risk management methods. Quarterly reporting gives investors extensive information on companies' use of forward sales, swaps, gold loans, options and other explicit or embedded risk management activities. The data enable analysts to measure the risk, and dampen volatility in prices.

A spot-deferred contract is a long-term forward sale of gold, which allows mines to choose annually whether to deliver against the contract or wait to deliver the gold. Ultimately, they must deliver the gold committed under this contract, but the mine has the option of deciding whether to defer delivery, perhaps because spot prices exceed the contract price. The mine would agree a new delivery price that covers the market forward price plus the loss that the mine would have borne had it met its forward commitment. Thus, spot deferred contracts are similar to rolling one-year forward contracts, except that the former ensures that a creditworthy mine has long-term access to forward contracting (at market rates). A mine reduces the risk of being unable to roll over an existing forward position. If a mine were to roll over a forward contract in which it had a loss, it would have to record the accounting loss on the contract at the rollover. With a spot deferred contract, mine owners roll forward these losses until the ultimate delivery of the gold, and defer accounting losses.

Mines that apply insurance strategies can use either exchange-traded or over-the-counter, gold 'put' options. Alternatively, they can dynamically replicate 'puts' by trading forwards and futures. Thus, mining companies can choose from a rich menu of risk management instruments, which permit them to customise their gold price exposure. Equities and funds specialising in mining stocks offer the investor an alternative route. Shares in technologically proficient mining companies with large reserves and low production costs may, on occasion, be more attractive than investing directly in their physical output.

The growth of speculation in the futures and options market has been an area of some controversy. To cover future price rises when they open mines, owners may sell gold forward; they raise gold loans that they will repay later at a fixed rate. The more traders cap prices, the greater the incentive for producers to hedge to protect their profitability. Other analysts disagree, pointing to a reduction in hedging by mining companies, as noted above (cf 17.1.2). GFMS take the view that the trend of producer buyback programmes, or 'de-hedging', will surpass 2003 in terms of total ounces of de-hedged gold. None the less, the options and futures market can provide flexible instruments for well-informed speculators to exploit any short-term volatility in the gold price.

17.2 HIGHLIGHTS OF THE PREVIOUS YEAR

17.2.1 Trends in demand

Various factors explain the resurgence of the gold price over the past two years. Many investors sought the relative safety of tangible, physical assets following the 11 September 2001 atrocity, the subsequent worries over a global economic recession, and fears of protracted struggles in Iraq and the Middle East. Investing in bullion was also a refuge from the falls on the world's stock markets after the dot-com bubble burst in late 2000. Gold prices can correlate negatively to prices for bonds and equities, and can thus offer an effective portfolio diversification when other financial assets perform badly. For example, the FTSE 100 index, which is based on the share prices of Britain's blue-chip companies, lost about 40% of its value between 2000 and 2003. On average, the gold price rose 30% over the same period. In 2002 and 2003, GFMS estimates that gold attracted some $10bn from dedicated investors and speculators such as hedge funds.

Recent trends in foreign exchange markets and relatively low returns on money-market deposits also served to support precious metal prices. The gold price and the US dollar have an inverse relationship – the bullion price tends to rise when the dollar is weak, and vice-versa. A soft dollar, in fact, makes gold cheaper for holders of appreciating currencies (notably the euro, the yen, the British pound and the Swiss franc).

In January 2003, gold hit a 15-year high of $430.50 per troy oz – primarily because of an ailing US dollar and renewed strong fund buying. Twelve months before it had been priced at $356 per oz. Commentators suggested that as currencies, particularly the euro and the dollar, are still influencing the market, gold is likely to trade at about $420-$425, but indicators still show the price has growth potential, so another assault on $430 per oz is a possibility. Analysts also concluded that, if the dollar were further undermined by the US's ballooning trade and fiscal deficits, and dipped to the $1.30 level against the euro, gold could challenge the $450 per oz barrier.

In 2003, other precious metals followed in the footsteps of gold and rose sharply. Platinum peaked at $866 per oz, its highest price since 1980, although dealers related this movement to a half million-ounce supply deficit in 2003. Silver also rose, to a six-year high of $6.40 per oz. Only palladium fell out of line with the trend; its price of $233 per oz was well below its 2001 peak of $1,090 per oz.

However, the higher prices had a negative effect on jewellery markets, especially in India and the Middle East. In 2003, jewellery demand, which accounts for three-quarters of gold's end-use, fell by 7.1%, according to GFMS, which projected a further 9% drop during the first-half of 2004.

Silver prices ended 2003 on a buoyant note, recording a 26% gain over 2002. The market's increase in 2002 also means that, over the two years, the price had risen by almost half from the November 2002 low point of $4.05 per oz. Three main factors account for these price movements – a rise in fabrication; higher government sales, mainly from China; and a surging growth in investment. Mine production also fell, especially in Australia. However, investor interest has mainly been short-term and speculative, with little evidence of strategic purchases for silver holdings.

For the five years ending in 2003, platinum supply has generally been in deficit. However, in 2004, Johnson-Matthey expects the supply and demand of the metal to be more or less in balance. Fund buying has been strongly influencing the price, which reached a 24-year high of $936 per oz in April 2004. Subsequently, funds closed out some of their long positions, leading to a sharp price correction.

In 2003, the palladium market surplus rose to 1.19 million oz, with Russia increasing its output by more than 1 million oz and Norilsk Nickel selling all its production. Demand rose slightly in 2003 and the early part of 2004, but further expansion in supply from mines and recovery of the metal from scrapped auto-catalysts has offset growth in demand. Meanwhile, hedge funds and speculators have taken large positions, making the market vulnerable to large corrections.

17.2.2 The Washington Agreement

On 8 March 2004, European central banks announced reaching a 'collegial commitment' to renew the Washington Agreement of 1999, which was to expire in September 2004. Under the terms of the commitment, the banks have agreed to raise their limit on gold sales from 400 tonnes per annum to a maximum of 500 tonnes per annum for the next five years. The commitment removes some uncertainty regarding the future supply of gold. Collectively, the agreement signatories hold 14,395 tonnes of gold, representing 45% of official gold holdings. Countries and agencies, including the US, which are unlikely to sell, hold another 13,437 tonnes. This positive development counters rumours of unexpected mass sales by the official sector.

While European countries hold nearly 40% of their reserves in gold, Canada has sold its entire holding of 1,023 tonnes, making it the only one of the seven leading industrialised nations that has no gold backing for its currency. The Canadian sales have left the impression that all central banks have significantly reduced their gold holdings, and that gold has lost its monetary value. However, statistics show that official global reserve holdings have only declined by 4,611 tonnes in the past 33 years from 36,575 tonnes in 1971 to 31,964 tonnes at the end of 2003. The US has maintained its holdings at about 8,000 tonnes, and French, German, Chinese and Taiwanese purchases have largely offset gold sales by Canada, Australia, Britain and Switzerland, among others. In practice, China and Japan, which hold less than 2% of their reserves in gold, may well increase their holdings to reduce their dependence on US dollar and foreign debt instruments. The movement to re-establish the Islamic dinar, which is 100% backed by gold and silver, may also have a dramatic effect on overall demand. Given an increase in global investment demand for gold, because of uncertainties about the US dollar, the market should absorb planned central bank sales.

17.2.3 China and India

Industrialisation in China is likely to lead to increased demand for gold, as is the ability of Chinese citizens to purchase gold and silver bullion for the first time in 50 years. In addition, China ranks third in the world for gold jewellery consumption, according to new figures. The Chinese edition of the gold yearbook reveals that China's gold consumption for jewellery ranked after India and the US in 2003, at 201.1 tonnes. In that year, China's gold output reached 213 tonnes, ranking the country fourth in the world, after South Africa, the US and Australia.

India consumes annually about a third of the world's mined supply, with 80% of demand coming from jewellery makers. In addition, the country has private hoards amounting to 13,000 tonnes of gold. The country's gold consumption has been steadily rising since late 2003, following a rise in disposable income among India's large middle class; many of them depend heavily on agriculture for their livelihood. India recorded a bumper harvest in 2003, and forecasters expect a similar crop in 2004. Thus, the strong growth in farm incomes after a second straight year of good monsoon rains has been boosting demand for gold in 2004, leading to higher imports. Rural demand is likely to remain high. In addition, a number of people who invested in the stock markets have been ploughing back their capital gains into gold.

Furthermore, the WGC's promotional activities are helping to keep consumer interest in gold high, especially among Indian women. Although diamond and silver jewellery are becoming more popular, gold remains the overwhelming choice of most women, accounting for 80% of the Indian market. Increasingly, women professionals are wearing lighter gold jewellery to work instead of traditional heavy gold ornaments, which they reserve for social occasions, such as weddings. Consequently, women consumers have a wider array of choices, including lighter gold pieces, heavy ornaments, and items that have either traditional or modern designs. Choice increases interest in gold and gold sales.

Speculation is also adding to interest in gold among Indian traders and investors. In 1962, after the Indo-China war the Indian Government had banned futures in gold in the world. Recently, it has allowed futures trading in both gold and silver. The National Multi Commodity Exchange of India, based in Ahmedabad, will give bullion traders the option of hedging the risks arising from price fluctuations.

17.2.4 Supply

In reality, production costs vary widely, according to the nature of the mine (open pit or below ground), its depth, the nature and distribution of the ore-body, and the grade. Around the world, grades vary a great deal. Generally, the largest South African underground operations run at 8–10 gm per tonne (approximately eight to ten parts per million), with more marginal South African operations grading at 4–6 gm per tonne. At a grade of 10 gm/tonne, it takes more than three tonnes of ore to produce one ounce of gold. Many of the world's operations are open pits, which tend (generally) to be of lower grade than the underground mines, running from as low as 1 gm to 3 or 4 gm per tonne. This low grade shows how rare gold is in the ground and gives an idea of how much rock miners have to shift to produce the metal. In practice, production costs (a mix of both grade and operating costs) are important in determining the quality of a gold mining venture.

The world's deepest gold mine is currently the Savuka mine in Witwatersrand, South Africa. This operation mines to a depth of 3,777m. Some of Savuka's miners are working at a depth of almost 2.4 miles, mining an ore grade which contains almost 20 cubic centimetres of gold in every cubic metre of rock – almost 20 parts per million by volume. At the other end of the scale, there is a myriad of one-man bands, panning for alluvial gold or working shallow outcrops in many parts of Africa, Latin America and Asia, and finding perhaps only a few ounces in any one year. Increasingly, developing countries (other than South Africa), including some of the poorest, are mining gold. Many of the World Bank's Heavily Indebted Poor Countries are gold producers. In some cases, gold represents a high proportion of the country's exports; for example, it accounts for over a third of exported goods of Ghana and around half for Mali.

GFMS estimates average quoted cash costs for 2003 at US$222 per oz. Estimated cash costs (including depreciation, amortisation, reclamation and mine closure costs) are US$278 per oz. However, these figures do not allow for green field exploration and other ancillary costs, so most mining analysts add a further US$30–40 per oz, depending on the mining company concerned, to estimate true total costs. Thin margins made by the mining companies in the second half of the 1990s meant that exploration expenditure did tend to suffer, and this lies behind market expectations that the trend in output will be broadly flat in the next few years.

The high cost of mining is prompting interest in other approaches. For example, a group of enthusiasts in New Zealand is pioneering an unusual attempt to add to the supply of gold; they intend to reclaim gold from the mudflats of Coromandel Harbour. The plan involves sucking silt from the harbour and piling rocks from flood works into a 5–10 ha reclamation area, where the enterprise will establish a ferry wharf and yacht berths, sending the sludge to Waihi to extract gold estimated to be worth up to US$30m. Supporters say it would solve several problems at once by removing toxic tailings waste from the harbour, creating an all-tide wharf, and providing a place to dump hundreds of tonnes of silt and fill from planned flood protection works.

17.2.5 Recent applications

Gold performs critical functions in computers, communications equipment, spacecraft, jet aircraft engines and a host of other continually changing applications. Recently, BP, in collaboration with Johnson-Matthey, has developed new alloys. The patented gold-palladium catalyst formulation is the first reported use of this gold catalyst in a fully developed large-scale chemical process for making emulsion-based paints, wallpaper paste and wood glue.

Another application takes the form of drug delivery microchips, which contain reservoirs covered by thin gold membranes. Pharmaceutical manufacturers fill each reservoir with drugs or other chemicals and then seal it. Doctors implant the microchips, or integrate them into an intravenous delivery system, or the patient swallows the chip. To administer a dose of the drug, a small electric voltage causes the gold cap to dissolve, and allows the drug to release from the reservoir. The physician or the patient can control the timing of each dose with microprocessors, remote controls, or biosensors.

Researchers at the National University of Singapore have patented novel gold complexes for use in pharmaceuticals for the treatment of cancer. Currently, the most widely used treatments for many types of cancers are platinum-based drugs, with the drawback of serious side effects. The scientists in Singapore discovered that phosphine-supported gold complexes have promising anti-tumour activity, and plan clinical trials.

17.3 COUNTERFEITS AND FRAUDS

17.3.1 Counterfeit coins

One problem of purchasing coins made from gold bullion or other precious metals is the risk of forgeries. In the 1970s, when inflation was soaring, interest in UK sovereigns was so high that the Mint found itself unable to produce enough. As a result, dealers increased the premium (the difference between the face value and the metal value). The coins began to sell at almost one and a half times their face value. The opportunity attracted Middle Eastern forgers, although, in practice, informed vendors and buyers could easily detect the counterfeit coins.

Controversy over the long-running 'Hirohito' coin scandal still affects market sentiment in Japan. Originally issued in 1986 to commemorate the 60th anniversary of the late emperor's accession to the throne, Japanese police alleged in 1990 that 100,000 were Middle Eastern fakes. The scandal caused a delay in the issue of the Akihito coins (called Heisei after the new emperor's era). In the event, the authorities decided to release only 2m coins; the initial plan had been to issue 3.8m Heiseis. To discourage forgers, the coins contained 30 (not 20) grams of gold. This amount represented about 50,000 yen worth of gold in a coin that the Japanese sold for 100,000 yen. However, despite the Hirohito scandal and the delayed issue, the Japanese bought most of the 2m coins.

17.3.2 Gold mine frauds

Fraud has also beset precious metal investing. Typically, promoters sell interests in gold mines that are nearly worthless or non-existent. Telephone sellers may call offering gold not yet mined. They say they will sell it for $100 below the going price.

Such frauds are an international problem. One commentator believes there are 'probably 30 to 40 gold mining scams going on now'. He cautions investors to be distrustful of salespeople who offer interests in gold mines. Typically, they promise gold at far less than the market price; the explanation is usually that the mine owner has some special process or patented techniques for extracting the metal.

Fingerprinting techniques developed by scientists, led by Watling and Herben at the Western Australian Department of Minerals and Energy Centre, might make salting of gold mines – a technique used since the mining industry began – a problem of the past. 'Salting' is the addition of precious metals from one mine to another, to give the illusion of great discoveries of gold.

The new process will give every mine a unique identity, which should make life more difficult for salters of mines and gold thieves, and for fraudsters who claim that gold ingots come from a specific mine. Watling hopes that experts will fingerprint much of the world's gold so they can pinpoint its origins; gold will no longer be an untraceable international currency. Watling is applying the same technique to diamonds from De Beers.

However, fraudsters may still be able to rely on naïvety, as investors in the Busang mine on the island of Borneo, Indonesia, found to their cost. In February 1997, a small but then reputable Canadian mining company, Bre-X, hailed it as the biggest gold discovery of this century, with 71m oz in prospect, worth £15.5bn. In May 1997, it turned out to be one of the biggest illusions since the days of Houdini. The company collapsed, and $6bn in share value was wiped out. In May 1999, the defrauded investors were outraged when the Canadian police announced they would not be pursuing the case owing to lack of evidence. However, the Ontario Securities Commission did file civil charges against Bre-X's chief geologist. The company's chief executive and the geologist at the Indonesian site have since died.

Fraudsters had tampered with samples from the site to boost their gold content. Mining consultants Strathcona Mineral Services Ltd showed that the find was not economically worthwhile. The short-term effect was to reduce investment interest in unit trusts that hold shares in gold mining and exploration companies. Mining companies also made temporary cuts in their expenditure on exploration, partly because investors lost their enthusiasm for gold, but mainly because of a drop in commodity prices. *A propos* the 1849 gold rush, Mark Twain remarked: 'A mine is a hole in the ground with a liar standing next to it!'

Nevertheless, the lure of gold as a route to quick riches is as enduring as ever. Even the Prime Minister of Thailand, Thaksin Shinawatra, fell victim to gold fever not long ago, when he allowed the excavation of a cave said to contain vast quantities of gold bonds left by the Japanese army at the end of World War II. To his great embarrassment the Prime Minister had to concede that the bonds found in the cave were fake; like many before him he had succumbed to a confidence trick.

Another problem for gold-producing countries is the siphoning off of legitimate production by criminal cartels. According to GoldFields, South Africa's second largest gold miner, up to 10% of all gold produced in the country is being stolen by crime syndicates; that represents about 40 tonnes of gold, with a potential value of $380m. Companies in South Africa have been working with the country's police to set up an emergency task force to combat the thefts. The gangs are also targeting platinum. *The Financial Times* reported that about a fifth of gold production in Guyana was lost to crime. Extensive smuggling there moves gold across borders into Brazil, Venezuela and Surinam, where it is used to launder money.

17.4 OPPORTUNITIES AND COSTS

17.4.1 Investment potential

Who should buy gold, in what form should investors purchase it, and how much should they invest in the metal? 'It depends on the investor,' says one dealer. 'Many large portfolios might have at least a small percentage in gold. A person who has little money to invest and is conservative should concentrate on gilts. If you are more aggressive, you could have a larger holding in gold.' These recommendations seem optimistic, given gold's resistance in recent years to the anxiety factor.

For many investors who still wish to hold gold, coins make sense, because they are easier to sell than bullion. Alternatively, investors can buy precious metals in bars or wafers that may, for an extra price, have decorative stampings. A 100-oz gold bar is about the size of a house brick. Dealers sell wafers in various weights, down to a few ounces, although premiums are higher on smaller unit weights. Hoarders could store gold coins, bars or wafers in a safe-deposit box or home safe. Anxiety over the millennium temporarily fuelled a surge in consumer demand for gold and silver bullion, as a hedge in the event of Y2K computer problems with banks and the economy. Coin dealers reported a huge increase in the volume of their sales during 1999.

The safest haven for gold coins or bars is a high street bank, which will reduce the risk of theft. Investment gold transactions since 1 January 2000 have been exempt from VAT. Some banks offer gold purchase programmes, and (given adequate security) may be willing to finance these purchases. If an investor buys on credit, the bank will want to keep the gold in its vault and charge for storage. Some clearing banks in Jersey will deal in Krugerrands and Maple Leaf coins for mainland customers.

17.4.2 Costs of ownership

Among other factors, transaction costs put off some investors. Other deterrents have been the imposition of VAT (no longer levied in the UK since 2000), holding expenses, and the lack of dividends or interest from precious metals investments. Unlike bank deposits and securities, gold's value depends on changes in the market for bullion. Storage, dealing and insurance costs erode any profits from investments in gold bars or coins.

17.4.3 Advisers

Even to investors who have good reasons for buying precious metals, financial advisers offer words of caution. Anyone who buys gold or another precious metal, or gemstones, should use a bank, a specialist trading house, or a reputable dealer, making sure that, in any event, he can obtain possession of the asset when he needs it. In times of great financial crisis, banks may be closed.

In Britain, investors can buy gold coins through dealers, precious metal brokers, investment consultants, some banks and jewellers. These traders sell and buy gold sovereigns and half sovereigns in quantity, and the products of other countries' mints. Advantages can flow from choosing coins in popular demand. The premiums charged (that is, the difference between the price of the coin and the value of the bullion it contains) are higher for coins that sell in low quantities.

Financial advisers suggest that individual investors eager to buy gold would be wise to choose shares of gold mining companies, or gold unit trusts. In contrast to coins, ingots, futures or options, gold stocks represent a productive asset (that is, a company) and may pay dividends. Gold-mining companies' shares might rise two or three times over the percentage increase in gold prices.

17.5 TAXATION

17.5.1 Tax planning

The income, capital gains, capital transfer and inheritance tax considerations, reviewed in Chapter 18 on art and antiques, are generally relevant to valuables. The advice in Chapter 18 also applies to careful tax planning for investments in valuables.

17.5.2 VAT

Since 1 January 2000, when a new EU Directive came into force, transactions in investment gold throughout the EU have been exempt from VAT. Investment gold refers to gold bars weighing more than one gram and with a fineness of at least 995, to non-numismatic coins of a purity greater than 900, to gold-related securities and to forward and future transactions. In the UK, the limit at which buyers must provide personal details has been set at £5,000 per individual transaction, or £10,000 purchased cumulatively over one year.

VAT leaflet Notice 701/21 (March 2002), Gold, replaces the previous edition of February 2000. The new leaflet became effective from 1 March 2002. The significant changes in this notice relate to the exempt VAT regime for investment gold. It also makes clearer the scope of the Special Accounting Scheme in relation to goods sold for the value of the fine gold that they contain. This notice should be read in conjunction with Notice 701/21A (March 2003), Investment Gold Coins, effective from 1 March 2003. This replaces the previous edition of January 2002 and incorporates the list of gold coins published by the European Commission in the *Official Journal of the European Communities* (C342/13) on 30 November 1999. For the purposes of EU and UK law, the coins listed are 'investment gold'. The Notice also lists many gold coins, deemed 'investment gold' for UK purposes.

Additionally, in 2002, Russia abolished its tax on gold exports. However, this is not of great significance, because Russia could already export gold to CIS tax-free countries, and thence to the rest of the world. Of passing interest is the pressure applied in Mongolia by the country's gold miners. They argued that, since the authorities had built up the value of the country's reserves, the 15% value added tax imposed on them was redundant.

VAT regulations still apply to silver and to platinum. As in the gold and silver markets, zero-rating for VAT applies only to transactions between wholesale traders. In the past, zero-rating was not necessary as transfers of metal among traders in London were insignificant. The rapid rise in demand for platinum has increased the need for speedy inter-trader movements of metal.

17.6 PREVIEW OF THE YEAR AHEAD

17.6.1 Trends

Gold has rallied strongly since hitting a 20-year low of $250 four years ago. Nervous investors flocked to the bullion market in the aftermath of the terrorist attacks on 11 September, believing that the precious metal offered a refuge from falling stock markets. Other factors have also conspired to drive up the price. When the price of gold was less than $300, exploration became increasingly unprofitable; the consequence has been a cyclical imbalance in supply and demand. Eventually, this will correct itself as more mines join the production line. Meanwhile, demand from institutional investors has also risen as they have begun to favour gold as a hedge against other investments. The metal often has a negative correlation with the prices of bonds and shares, and particularly of UK equities – the gold price moves in the opposite direction.

The recent strength of gold, however, owes much to a weakening dollar. Although few analysts anticipate a collapse in the US currency, its weakness is unnerving investors who prefer real, rather than financial, assets. Gold, as an asset priced in dollars, also becomes more attractive to non-US investors when the dollar declines. They secure more of the metal for their euro or pound. However, currency movements need careful consideration. Gold prices may well continue to rise. Some prime investment banks remain bullish with regard to gold, reflecting the continuing terrorism fears, volatile stock markets, the faltering dollar and robust investment demand; they are forecasting a peak of $435 for 2004-2005. HSBC comments: 'Upward pressure on the gold price [$435] is likely to continue through 2004.' UBS expects an average price per oz of $420, with highs of $475 and lows of $370, while Barclays Capital suggests that gold could even test the $500 barrier by late 2004, although its analysts view this as unlikely. JP Morgan Chase's price forecasts are less upbeat, at between $376 and $368 per oz for the next year. By 2005, Canadian gold analyst Martin Murenbeeld anticipates a gold price per oz of $460, while UBS Securities sees gold averaging $470 per oz.

Some analysts hold a bullish longer-term view. For example, John Embry of Sprott Asset Management predicts that gold could hit $1,000 per oz by 2010. Alan McGregor of AVC Advisory evidently holds a comparable view, reportedly saying that: 'There appears to be a new growth cycle in place in many commodities, including gold, particularly as the dollar is not as infallible as once thought. Investors are looking for alternatives – the historical standard being gold.' For such bulls, the health of the US economy and the US dollar, more than the physical supply of the metal, influences the price of gold. In that sense, gold is unlike almost any other commodity, in that its price movements are often almost completely psychological. Suppose that the US economy fails to recover strongly, or that the falling value of the dollar sparks rate increases that hold back the recovery. Then, there is a chance that foreign investors may lose interest in many US dollar assets or government bonds, which some economists believe are weak and likely to get even weaker as a result of spiralling deficits and a slowing economy. That, in turn, may push up the dollar price of gold, just as it has the price of crude. Conversely, the World Bank envisages medium-term prices at below $300 per oz as supplies begin to exceed demand, and other commentators are also pessimistic; they expect the average price for the year to hover at about $375 per oz – somewhat below prevailing levels.

Nevertheless, the costs of holding gold may mean that it appreciates less than equities, prompting other commentators to advise caution. Losses from gold investments can be high and gold's role in rapidly developing countries, which face political and economic uncertainties, could decline. In such countries, when financial markets become more sophisticated, bonds, mortgages, property, long-term insurance and similar instruments will provide investment options.

In appraising future prospects, consumer tastes are also relevant. In China, Wang Lixin, the local manager of the World Gold Association, reportedly said that China's newly opened gold market still had a huge potential to accommodate more gold products. He claimed that the developing market should pay more attention to attracting young people and the elderly with gold fashion products, by highlighting their value.

Overall, the key to understanding the bullion market lies with macro-economic factors and investor sentiment. If traders believe that the dollar and major stock markets will plunge, and that oil prices will continue to rise to sky-high levels, they are likely to turn to gold. Yet, in reality, even the most enthusiastic gold bugs are likely to agree that – barring world-wide conflicts, or a return to the soaring inflation and interest rates – gold will probably not regain its historical 1980 peak of $850 per oz. In the near future, above-ground stocks are ample to satisfy gold demand.

17.6.2 New applications

Experts are drawing attention to the importance of nano-technology in replacing or economising in the use of precious metals. This technology creates functional materials, devices and systems through control of matter on an atomic scale, and exploits novel physical, chemical, biological, mechanical, electrical phenomena and other properties at that scale. For comparison, 10 nanometers are 1,000 times smaller than the diameter of a human hair. A scientific and technical revolution has just begun based upon the ability to systematically organise and manipulate matter at a nano-scale. Such advances are likely to have a considerable impact on the cost and performance of catalytic converters, which remove most pollutants from vehicle exhaust. Nano-engineered catalysts can replace platinum and palladium, two precious metals most commonly used in catalytic converters. Platinum and palladium are expensive and in short supply worldwide. Because catalysis only occurs on the surface of the metals, most of the weight – which drives up the price – is essentially just filler. Nano-technology can create catalysts that comprise the entire surface area.

In a practical advance, which promises to economise the use of gold, scientists have created a material with gold nano-particles on a silica-covered silicon surface using a molecular template. Developed at North Carolina State University, the advance provides the first evidence that nano-particles can form a gradient of decreasing concentration along a surface, and promises many applications in electronics, chemistry, and the life sciences. The main advantage of the gradient approach is that it combines large numbers of structures on a single substrate for high-throughput processing. The invention may also save time for chemists when they test clusters of nano-particles for use as catalysts to create new, less polluting sources of energy.

Researchers at the University of Delaware have developed self-assembling and repairing gold micro-wires, which could find application in the development of nano-electronics. The scientists suspend tiny particles of gold in an aqueous solution. To form gold wires more than 5mm in length and about 1 micron in diameter, the scientists insert electrodes into the solution. The wires have uses as microscopic sensors and in the manufacture of circuits.

17.7 CONCLUSION

Gold Field Mineral Services argues that supplies depend more on the use made of gold already above ground than the annual output of gold mines. However, GFMS acknowledges the possibility that the market could become accustomed to central bank sales. If further sales were no longer a perceived threat, a more positive view of gold could develop. Improved sentiment would also prevent producers from hedge selling at every rally. The WGC, for its part, believes the gold market is at a crossroads. Bryan Parker, of the council, suggests the reasons for this are fivefold. First, the renewed Washington Agreement capping gold disposals by 15 European central banks and the IMF's decision to abandon the selling of gold to fund debt relief have helped to reaffirm the metal as a monetary asset. Second, the slowdown in the supply of newly minted gold is likely to continue, with gold jewellery demand already exceeding new mine production. Third, the council spots a new and emerging interest in gold among investors, both private and institutional. Fourth, there is continuing deregulation, for example in China, of the gold consuming markets. Finally, the council reports a return to fashion in gold jewellery.

However, other analysts are not so positive about the European central banks' agreement on gold sales. Some suggest that the banks are likely to remain sellers rather than buyers of gold. The *Financial Times* Annual Global Conference in June 2000 proposed that the limits set by the Washington Agreement implied an increase in official sales. Jonathon Spall of Deutsche Bank suggested that in the future, 'gold will once more be forced to justify its place as an important element of global monetary reserves'.

Developments in e-gold over the next few years may also have a significant effect on the gold market, and merit attention, particularly in conjunction with the opening of gold markets. For example, the Beijing

Gold Economic Development Research Centre is soon to establish a website, with Trasys Gold Ex Ltd. Initially, this site will provide information on the international gold market, but will lead to the development of an electronic trading platform, paving the way for access to the market in China.

The risk of further 11 September-type crises could also affect sentiment and prices in gold, and other markets for precious metals.

Silver, platinum, palladium and rhodium are likely to remain fascinating, if risky, investments. These metals will probably sustain their market as coins, and in the jewellery, automobile and electronics industries, with rhodium remaining resilient to the development of substitutes. Even with technical developments reducing the platinum content of catalytic converters, continuing environmental concern over greenhouse gas emissions is likely to increase the number fitted to cars. Platinum, with its dual market of jewellery and auto-catalysts, seems a better prospect. Johnson-Matthey forecasts a narrower range of price fluctuation for this metal over the coming year. On the supply side, whether the Russian supply of these metals is sustained or not, a long period of stable supply is necessary before the market loses its fear of another stoppage. The decision by Anglo-American Platinums to increase its output seems likely to stabilise supplies.

17.8 OTHER VALUABLES

17.8.1 Precious gems

Apart from precious metals, investors can also consider precious gems. The value of a gemstone depends upon its qualities – among them, its rarity, durability, portability and popularity.

Diamonds are the hardest and most brilliant of gems. The diamond industry has defined four value factors: colour (pure, colourless), clarity (less noticeable marks and blemishes), cutting (the extent to which the cut catches all of a stone's features) and carat (in principle, the larger the stone, the greater the value).

Pearls occur naturally in finished form, and no two are ever alike. There are two types of pearls – natural (produced by types of molluscs found in both salt and fresh water sources, and extremely rare); and cultured (production is scientifically controlled, usually in Japan).

Emeralds – the finest are transparent and have a velvety, grass-green colour. However, emeralds can fracture easily, and therefore require special care when handling. Rubies are red with only limited traces of other tints or hues. Sapphires come in colours ranging range from blue, yellow and green to orange, purple and pink.

17.8.2 Diamonds and De Beers

Of all the precious gems, diamonds are the most significant. The Central Selling Organisation (CSO), now known as the Diamond Trading Organisation, dominates the market. This is the London-based marketing organisation of De Beers, which controls perhaps 60% of the world's diamond trade.

Only about one in six of diamonds mined finds a use in rings or other jewellery. Diamonds worth almost £4.5bn are an important component of the £37bn jewellery market each year. Buyers put the remainder of the £7bn diamond output to industrial use. The market's performance largely depends on the success of its promoters in stimulating demand. To this end, De Beers spends large sums on advertising and sales campaigns, in a concerted effort to persuade more women and men to buy and wear diamonds as jewellery. In an effort to extend their brand image, the De Beers group and LVMH Moët Hennessy Louis Vuitton, a leading luxury products group, have launched Rapid Worlds Ltd. This company has opened shops, De Beers LV, that will promote and develop De Beers as a brand name. One result has been to stimulate demand through retail jewellers, but the mark-ups make it difficult for the investor to achieve gains. The addition of VAT to manufactured jewellery accentuates the problem.

De Beers has kept firm control over the supply and price of the world's diamonds for over a century. With a large share of the uncut diamond market, the company has succeeded in mass-marketing what was once an aristocratic luxury without greatly diminishing its value. Diamonds remain 'the gem of gems', though millions own them. De Beers' aim historically has been long-term price stability and prosperity for the industry, achieved by buying up rough diamonds across the world. In its view, price fluctuations would undermine confidence in the value of diamonds.

17.8.3 Developments in the market

The year 2001 saw the De Beers group privatised, after 113 years as a publicly owned company. Shareholders voted overwhelmingly to turn De Beers into a private company. Under the terms of the deal, De Beers delisted from the Johannesburg Stock Exchange, and ownership transferred to DB Investments, a consortium owned 45% by the Oppenheimer family, 45% by Anglo-American and 10% by Debswana, a joint venture between De Beers and the Government of Botswana.

The deal turned De Beers into an unlisted subsidiary of Anglo-American, narrowing Oppenheimer family influence on that company to a 4.8% stake. The effect was to untie a cross-holding between the companies, ensuring that Anglo-American conforms to new London Stock Exchange rules, which penalise such cross-holdings.

Thus, De Beers has been transformed from a public company with over $11bn in assets to a private company $3.6bn in debt. Overall, the Oppenheimers have reinforced their control on De Beers and its two-thirds share of the world's trade in rough diamonds. Taken in conjunction with other recent moves by De Beers, the new structure will mean that the main investors directly control not only diamond mines in southern Africa and contractual diamond purchases from Russia and Canada, but also the wholesaling trade in London, through which two-thirds of the world's rough diamonds are sold.

In 2002, the European Commission cleared De Beers' 'Supplier of Choice' strategy, which came into effect during 2003. In practice, the impact of SOC on the diamond trade is extensive. SOC requires 'sightholders' to sell their diamonds through well-defined distribution channels that avoid placing polished diamonds in the open marketplace. The SOC programme also reflected a restructuring of its sightholders in mid-2001. De Beers applied new criteria to reduce the list of sightholders, removing about 20 names, and adding a few new ones. Under these arrangements, De Beers' uncut diamond clientele also contribute towards the costs of marketing diamonds.

Expanding demand for diamond jewellery and creating a multi-brand environment is a focal point of the SOC strategy. De Beers and LVMH Moët Hennessy Louis Vuitton agreed to establish an independently managed and operated company, Rapid Worlds Ltd, to develop the global consumer brand potential of the De Beers name. The partnership saw the first exclusive De Beers stores open in 2002. The initiative is a 50:50 partnership, twinning LVMH's marketing and retailing experience with De Beers' industry know-how.

In the aftermath of 11 September 2001, De Beers' chairman, Nicky Oppenheimer, suggested that, although the industry was not immune to the effects of economic slowdown and slackening consumer demand for luxury goods, diamonds were not a perceived luxury. He remarked: 'As people turn to each other in difficult times, so do they continue to turn to diamonds to symbolise their partnership.' However, just two months later, the managing director of De Beers, addressing the French Gemological Society, put a contrary view, stating: 'We are in, and competing within, the luxury goods industry.' In his chairman's review of 2002, Oppenheimer concluded that jewellery outperformed a number of luxury goods in the sector during the year. This saw De Beers reducing its diamond stocks by nearly $1bn, making a voluntary payment of its pre-payment privatisation loan and an increase in sales of nearly 16%.

17.8.4 Developments in the industry's structure

During the first half of 2002, consumer demand was strong in the US. This demand tailed off in the second half as stock markets declined, and fears of economic slowdown and war in the Middle East took a hold. Overall, demand went up by 3%. De Beers attributes this largely to high quality, sustained marketing, and the development of multiple brands. The UK, China, India and the Middle East also reported growth, although the Japanese market continued to decline. Production of natural diamonds was down by about 1m carats in 2001, mostly due to a decrease in Australian production.

South African mining companies are re-considering their position, as new rules and taxes pushed through by the government increase the cost and complexity of investing in the country, *The Financial Times* has reported. The Mineral and Petroleum Royalty Bill introduced in March 2003 demands that companies pay royalties of up to 8% on gross revenue. The legislation envisages a sliding scale, set at 3% for gold, 4% for platinum, with diamonds bearing the full brunt. Unsurprisingly, investors are concerned about this development. Analysts predict that the legislation will discourage new ventures and force smaller players out of the market, contrary to established policy.

Angola is the world's third-largest producer of high quality diamonds. United Nations embargoes placed on the sale of diamonds from Angola and Sierra Leone caused the trade to slow, but violations continued. 'Conflict' diamonds, so-called because they fund civil war in various African countries, caused the industry much concern. Anxiety over the adverse publicity from media images of children maimed by the rebels who control the diamonds, together with pressure from the US and UK governments, led to the industry setting up a body to track diamonds and to stamp out conflict diamonds. The International Diamond Manufacturers Association and the World Federation of Diamond Bourses set up the World Diamond Council in July 2000, with support from De Beers. This body, made up of manufacturers, producers, governments and other relevant organisations, aims to ensure that importing countries will only accept parcels of rough diamonds sealed in a particular way and registered in an international database. Export authorities will only earn credits if they adopt measures ensuring that conflict diamonds are kept out of the market. Sanctions on those breaking these rules will include expulsion from the trade and prosecution.

The council has worked with the UN, government bodies, commercial interests and civil society to introduce a workable system for certifying the source of uncut diamonds. The council formally adopted this system, known as the Kimberley Process, in November 2002 and it came into operation on 1 January 2003. EU regulations enforcing the Kimberley Process came fully into force on 13 February 2003.

Following the adoption of the Kimberley Process, Signet Group plc, the world's largest speciality retail jeweller, has sent a letter to all its trade diamond and diamond jewellery suppliers. The text, based on guidance from the Jewelers of America, requires them to supply the group with merchandise that complies with the Kimberley Process.

Diamond merchants will now warrant that, 'For any product fabricated from rough diamonds mined from 1 January 2003 onward, that the diamonds have been purchased from legitimate sources not involved in funding conflict and are in compliance with United Nations Resolutions. The seller thus guarantees that the diamonds are conflict free, based on personal knowledge or written guarantees provided by the supplier of these diamonds.'

17.8.5 Prospects

Diamonds are not necessarily a good investment. Although some larger diamonds hold their value and may even appreciate, smaller stones of a carat or less are generally money losers, especially if bought at marked-up retail prices. Although De Beers sells three-fifths of all rough diamonds, some wholesalers, manufacturers and mining companies are beginning to sell directly to the public and many US and Canadian companies now sell over the internet, and online diamond sales have continued to rise. Buying loose uncut stones directly can save between 20% and 50% on the price, but the practice does bring risks.

Experts can easily examine large loose stones, free of jewellery settings, for flaws, colour, 'fire' and brilliance, and comparing stones is easier. Diamonds have an internationally recognised evaluation process that allows independent verification. The Gemological Institute of America, the European Gem Laboratory and the American Gemological Society operate strict grading standards. Every diamond purchased of 0.75 carats or larger should have a GIA, EGL or AGS certificate. These certificates can add to the liquidity of investment diamonds.

De Beers has recently raised its prices, in line with market sentiment, giving hope to the market, but its attempt to 'brand' diamonds has led to fresh competition between suppliers. This new feature of diamond sales has provided jewellers with an additional opportunity to advise buyers on the quality of the brand, with less emphasis on price. The opening of De Beer's first 'chain' store in London in November 2002 provided many with the opportunity of investing in a commodity that was previously only available to a select few, through membership or invitation. However, a few analysts believe that this approach is not the way to revive the fortunes of a flagging industry. They believe that there is not enough perceived difference between stones for customers to pay for a brand.

Diamond supply is likely to continue increasing in the coming year, with Israel in particular expected to sustain its exports. The quotas placed on Southern African exporters, in particular Botswana, are also likely to be lower in future, as gems become stockpiled following restrictions over recent years. In 2002 De Beers limited exports from Botswana to 88% of their capacity. A combination of global economic recovery and the stock-piling of stones should have led to reduced quotas towards the end of 2003–04.

De Beers has created a joint venture with TNK Resources Inc, a small company based in Toronto, to ensure its participation in any future diamond windfalls. This step is an apparent recognition of a miscalculation of the potential value of future mining output in both Canada and other sites in Australia. This initiative is one of a series of moves by De Beers, acknowledging the proliferation of small companies prospecting for diamonds in Canada. De Beers is showing interest in joint ventures and other types of partner agreements.

SOURCES OF FURTHER INFORMATION

See end of Chapter 19.

18

ART AND ANTIQUES

JOHN MYERS

Solon Consultants

18.1 INTRODUCTION

18.1.1 A form of alternative investment

Bring and buy works of art and antiques! Why? Ultimately, as any auctioneer, dealer or lover of art and antiques will say, it is not their investment or exchange worth but their civilising and aesthetic values that are important. Nonetheless, promoters of these 'alternative investments' confidently advocate these tangible assets as sound purchases for 'financially secure and intelligent buyers'. The assets they have in mind are, ideally, works of artistic, cultural or historical significance, ie items that are 'museum-worthy by any standards', which will appeal to collectors. Advocates of these purchases generally recommend clients with money to spare to allocate to 'traded artefacts' up to 10% of their capital (excluding their main home's equity value). These advisers declare that possessions such as works of art and antiques can protect their clients against inflation and currency fluctuations.

On occasion, larger institutional investors and corporate bodies also buy paintings, sculptures and antiques to diversify their holdings of securities and real estate. The apologists argue that these investors can afford to ride out slumps lasting up to a quarter of a century, if beneficiaries can wait and the eventual return is adequate. Pension funds and similar bodies are generally free from tax on their gains in art and antique markets. On the other hand, these assets cost money to insure, conserve and store. Capital appreciation has to be substantial to make up for these costs and the interest foregone. On balance, it seems that average returns on art are no better than the stock market. The Mei/Moses index, calculated by two economists from New York University, reveals a long-term annual return of 8.2%, compared with 8.9% for the Dow Jones share index.

Recently, a study by Worthington and Higgs at the School of Economics and Finance at Queensland University of Technology in Brisbane (*Accounting and Finance*, July 2004) examined risk, returns and the prospects for portfolio diversification among major painting and financial markets. The art markets examined were Contemporary Masters, French Impressionists, Modern European, 19th-Century European, Old Masters, Surrealists, 20th-Century English and Modern US paintings. The financial markets comprise gilt-edged securities, corporate and government bonds, and small and large company stocks. The research showed that the returns on paintings were much lower and the risks much higher than conventional investment markets. The analyses indicated that art in financial asset portfolios generated no diversification gains. However, diversification benefits in portfolios comprising solely of art works are possible, particularly with Contemporary Masters, 19th Century European, Old Masters and 20th Century English paintings. A parallel to the Australian study is research by William Goetzmann, a finance professor at Yale. He has investigated the art market's relationship to other investment markets. Goetzmann concluded that the art market has a high 'beta' when correlated with stock markets. In other words, art goes up by more than shares – and down by more, when shares fall.

More or less encouraged by such findings, collectors at times see art and antique objects as investments, the values of which can rise and fall as critics and curators appraise anew the aesthetic, historic or functional worth of a school, genre or work. Other factors that prompt the eager are television and press features, active marketing by auction houses and dealers, and ingenious ways to improve the liquidity of alternative investments. Specialist sales, fairs and exhibitions, magazines for collectors, the track-record of works sold in each field, and the findings of art historians, all sway decisions to buy. However, to allow values to 'mature', prudent advisers counsel buyers to keep items for years, even for decades. Speculative trading in works of art and antiques is, they say, too risky, and the rewards too volatile to justify gambling on perfectly timing a purchase and a sale. Even experts make mistakes in picking the undervalued piece that is sure to re-enter fashion next month or next year.

18.1.2 The dividends

Advocates of alternative investment argue for including fine art and antiques in private or funds' portfolios as long-term investments on grounds that are, essentially, those of the economist: while the number of buyers in the markets goes up, the supply stays static or declines. On the one hand, the flow of 'discoveries' or 'retrievals of lost works' is restricted; on the other, valued items disappear through fires, thefts and other calamities; and, perhaps more significantly, museums and galleries steadily drain from the market the works they obtain and keep. Of course, 'coffin chasers' (ie house clearers and others who deal with collections left after death) generate a regular supply and 'receiver chasers' have other sources, respectably illustrated a few years ago by Phillips' sale of Asil Nadir's office furnishings for £4.5m. In theory, the problems of Lloyd's Names should also have ensured a steady flow of art onto the market. However, Christie's offered a way through Coutts & Co for Names to use works of art as collateral, so that they could obtain bank guarantees for 'funds at Lloyd's' purposes.

The proponents of these art and antiques markets believe that they appeal to individuals and institutions looking for assets that are in growing demand and diminishing supply, so promising a long-term upward movement in prices. This argument seems to have gained wide acceptance among the cosmopolitan buyers who attend important sales and create an international demand for authentic items of quality. Evidently, these buyers are confident that works of art and rare antiques are safe homes for spare capital, or revenue otherwise subject to tax, though the works bring their owners no income and involve some costs and risks. Many deny an investment motivation. Such motives degrade the purity of endeavour among aesthetes, who seek a cultural dividend: the delights of living with satisfying works that give pleasure. Equally, boards of directors and partnerships buy works of art to improve their standing in society and among clients and customers, or to enhance their own and their employees' working environments. The prime movers in these companies will claim that investment is no more than a secondary motive.

Experts concur with the analysis. They point out that works of art and antiques, unlike shares, have no clearly defined market, no bourse to provide verifiable price indices. One ordinary share in a company will be identical to another of the same category in the same company, but individual works of art and antiques will vary in many respects. These variations in authenticity, provenance, condition, rarity and quality, and in the divergent circumstances and terms of sale, mean that similar objects will differ in price. As John Andrew remarked six years ago in *The Independent*: 'Add the effects of restoration, repairs, alterations, copies and fakes to the pricing formula and a minefield appears.' He went on to suggest that 'the biggest trap to snare the unwary in the field of antiques is a lack of knowledge. The prudent individual who researches before buying a consumer durable, or seeks professional advice when investing money, generally throws caution to the wind when buying antiques'.

Andrew gave examples of costs and rewards. Four Charles II silver lockets, genuine antiques, bought for £905 in about 1982, sold at auction for a net sum of £1,764 in 1995 – an equivalent annual return of 5.25% compound interest, well below the 10% per annum compound increase in the Financial Times Share Index over the same span. He also mentioned a silver salver made in Sheffield in 1895, bought in January 1983 for £185, and sold in early 1997 for £350. This equated to a 4.5% compound annual return. However, between 1983 and 1997, the stock market rose at a compound annual rate of 12%. Of course, these figures do not allow for the pleasure dividend that an owner of fine antiques gains from possessing them.

18.2 PREVAILING TRENDS

18.2.1 The market's performance

The Crown Estate owns a substantial portfolio of antiques and paintings. Recognised experts value them every five years on a rolling basis. In the financial year ending 5 April 2004, an independent appraiser valued these assets for the estate. However, the exercise remains incomplete, as the appraisal identified a potential material fall in value that would have eliminated the revaluation reserve and transferred a book loss to the estate's revenue account. A limited review of the valuation indicated enough uncertainty to warrant further investigation. The trustees therefore decided to hold the assets in the balance sheet at their carrying value, pending completion of the review in 2004–2005. The outcome should be interesting.

Other signs have been more optimistic. Over the first six months of 2004, Artprice, which tracks market values, recorded 3,920 new record prices for artists. More than a quarter of these records were set in US and UK auction houses. Examples of record prices from London auctions include £2.2m for a work by Lyonel Charles Feininger, on 2 February 2004; £1.15m for a Nicolas de Stael, on 5 February 2004; and £1.7m, for a Jean-Léon Gérôme on 15 June 2004. Of 400 records broken in New York, 28 exceeded the $1m mark, with $93m paid for a Picasso, $23.5m for a Manet and $10.4m for a Jackson Pollock. On continental Europe, auction houses set records between 1 January and 30 June 2004 in Paris (375), Amsterdam (149), Munich (85), Milan (82) and Stockholm (67). In Switzerland, the highest record was set when Lorenzo Monaco's *Die Verkundigung* sold for €641,000. In Denmark, a work by Christoffer Wilhelm Eckersberg set a record for the artist when it sold for €858,000. Apart from records set during the first half of 2004, 3,430 artists sold their works at auction for the first time.

Along with the UK, Italy is one of the most dynamic European art markets in terms of growth in fine art auction turnover: up 25.8% in the first half of 2004, compared with the same period a year earlier. According to Artprice figures, Italian auction houses generated close to €50m ($61m) from 85 fine art sales in early 2004. Usually, Old Masters produce the highest prices on the Italian art market. During the first six months of

2004, the best price paid was €800,000 for *Venere benda amore* by Lambert Sustris. However, in 2004, in terms of total turnover, modern works occupied the top positions in the artists' turnover rankings. In first place was Lucio Fontana: 42 lots of his works generated €3.2m over the first six months of 2004. In second place was Giorgio de Chirico (€3m), with Giorgio Morandi coming third (€2.2m). Overall, Italy's share of the global fine art market rose to 3.5% in the first half of 2004, which places Italy in fourth place in the Artprice ranking of countries by turnover, just ahead of Germany, which is down to fifth position. The top two countries in this segment remain the US (43.7%) and the UK (33.1%).

Christie's and Sotheby's held prestigious Old Masters sales in London during July 2004. At Sotheby's, Vermeer's *Young woman seated at the virginals* sold for £16.2m. Four other works sold for more than £1m – a portrait by Jan Lievens, for £853,600; an interior scene by Peter de Hooch, for £1,237,600; a rare night scene by Rubens, for £2,469,600; and *The coronation of the Virgin* by Bernardo Daddi, for £1,573,600. In the sale, 41 out of 63 lots changed hands (35% unsold), generating a turnover of almost £30m, including commission. Christie's fared less well, generating about £10m, including commission, instead of an expected £14–20m. In total, 45 out of 106 lots failed to find a buyer, taking the bought-in rate to 42%.

18.2.2 Fundamentals and opportunities

Markets for art and antiques have developed considerably in recent years, especially over the past three decades. According to the Art Sales Index, the turnover of the art sales industry was more than $2.34bn for 2002. This was slightly down on the 2001 figure. The US retains the largest portion of the turnover sales, while the UK sold the highest number of lots over the period. Negative and positive factors have affected growth over time. On occasion, investors have chosen to buy tangible assets because of failures of stock markets and interest-bearing securities to protect their capital against inflation. In the wake of the attacks on the US on 11 September 2001, however, it appears there was a drop in the demand for art; in some cases, sales were down by half. As sales recovered, so changes have occurred in the type of art being purchased. Ostentation seems to be out and contemporary markets have flourished.

Although falls in the stock markets have reduced the disposable incomes of many people, generally there has been a wider spread of higher disposable incomes and an increase in leisure expenditure. Thus, a demand has emerged for assets that have a worth and an interest beyond their monetary cost. Social changes have also had an effect, for example, dealers and auctioneers report that young, wealthy buyers have been entering the market for contemporary works of fine art, such as paintings, prints, ceramics, engravings and sculptures.

Popular television programmes and features in newspapers, magazines and books have stimulated interest in the hunt for works with hidden value. Admittedly, fewer antique shops can afford today's retail rents and overheads, but antique centres and antique fairs have burgeoned, placing many sellers in one location.

At times, antique markets attract large crowds, as anyone who has visited London's Portobello Road on Saturday morning can testify. Dealers come from all parts of the country and start trading between themselves almost at the crack of dawn. Before long, the crowds begin to arrive. Other London street markets are at Camden Passage (on Wednesdays) and Bermondsey (on Fridays). Paris has its flea markets and, in the US, antique fairs in Atlanta and other centres of wealth are popular. Enthusiasts in Georgia start at about 5am and stand in line for the early-risers' pick of art and antiques.

Choice pieces can pass through several hands on their route up-market, via dealers outside the main centres and street markets to a big auction or a listed antique shop. The more reliable dealers belong to the London and Provincial Antiques Dealers' Association or the British Antiques Dealers' Association. Their members usually offer a receipt with a full description; if it proves incorrect, the buyer has a basis on which to claim a refund.

Analysts of alternative investments have studied the ways the markets work. One place to chase bargains is the car boot sale, another a house clearance, where the discerning might find 1960s designer objects. The trash from such sources may end up in the local tip, and ordinary bric-à-brac in a second-hand fair. The inlaid metal matchbox case that is left seems unusual. It might really be a jewelled gold piece from the Fabergé workshop; it could be worth thousands to a connoisseur at the top of the pyramid, who can trace its history from the St Petersburg archive. Of course, it might be a mass-produced design, or sometimes a stolen piece.

Also gaining in popularity are international antique fairs. Some, like Maastricht, are well known and fashionable. In 2004, there was a notice-able increase in US visitors, and collectors who had been absent for a number of years returned. Many dealers commented on the number of museum buyers at the fair. The overall visitor number of 75,000 was up 15% over 2003. However, few dealers conclude sales at the fair, to avoid the complexities of Dutch VAT regulations. Another popular event is Art Cologne, which features modern arts. In Britain, the Royal Academy, Chelsea Town Hall and Olympia shows draw discerning buyers, as does the British Antique Dealers' Association fair and the Grosvenor House Art and Antiques Fair, which marks the start of the London season.

18.2.3 Market weaknesses and strengths

More people are entering the art and antiques market. To what extent can they rely on the assets they buy proving a worthwhile investment, given the repugnance of monetary motives to the aesthetes? In truth, auctioneers and dealers who profess horror at the idea of buying a painting as an investment were, on occasion, the same auctioneers and dealers who persuaded buyers to invest large sums of money in the late 1980s, sometimes in second- and third-rate works, only to see them plunge in price. Values for first-class objects stayed reasonably solid, and bidders still pay high prices for exceptional works. Handsome short-term profits have been claimed and recent sales have demonstrated that high quality works of art with a sound provenance can still perform well as long-term investments.

Observers in recent years have noted a flight to calibre and bijou quality, and away from large-scale but second-rate works by famous names. As a result, investing in art is no longer limited to the moneyed rich with conservative tastes. Impressionist and Modern paintings by leading artists can still command a premium, but auctioneers and dealers are also reporting strong sales to buyers with eclectic tastes; they have been fuelling reviving prices in the contemporary art market. Auctions of postwar and contemporary art have a growing appeal to collectors, and many lots have fetched far more than their presale estimates.

At times, both Sotheby's and Christie's face shortages of objects for sale. The resulting price rises attract speculators, who buy works of art and antiques and then quickly resell them to new collectors – a practice sometimes known as 'flipping'. Gallery owners in New York have also observed 'people with an incredible amount of money, who don't seem to be doing their homework – art neophytes rushing to buy material to cover their walls'. Commentators in London also feel that the newly rich 'have little time for the past, and want to surround themselves with clever exhibitionist ideas which reinforce their personal dynamism' (Antony Thorncroft, *Financial Times*, 17 November 1999).

In a 'flip' market, authenticity, reliable provenance, quality and freshness to the market ought to remain crucial factors, but in practice may not. It is worth noting that the areas that have withstood slumps in recent times have been those that appeal to the connoisseur rather than speculative traders, who tend to focus on short-term fashions in contemporary art.

Another factor affecting art markets is the absence of high-priced paintings suspected to be languishing in Tokyo, Osaka and Kyoto bank vaults, as their owners wait for markets to reach new peaks. Trade sources suggest that some works have been sold secretly at a loss, but the stored paintings may still include works by Chagall, Picasso, Renoir, Andrew Wyeth and Japanese artists. Estimates of the value of this art vary between £5bn and £20bn, although some commentators believe that the collections include fakes and stolen works. Reportedly, the Art Loss Register once contacted Japanese banks, enquiring about works by Picasso and Sisley, which had been stolen or looted. Moreover, the Japanese art market has been preoccupied in recent years with a series of scandals. Reports of debts, bribes, tax evasion, and fraud and jail sentences have done little to build confidence.

18.2.4 Protecting alternative investors

Questions can arise about a work of art's true value when buyers seem to be paying telephone number prices at auction. The amounts paid reflect partly an increasing number of exceptionally wealthy individuals who can afford to spend large sums to buy a work of art. Merrill Lynch and Gemini Consulting have estimated that 7m people with net assets of more than $1m increased their collective worth to $33.2 trillion in 2004, rising at a rate of 9% a year. These rich individuals own more wealth than the gross domestic product of the US, or even the combined GDP of the next highest eight countries. On present trends, these people will be worth $40 trillion within two or three years. *Forbes* estimates that the collective wealth of the top 200 'working rich' substantially exceeds $1 trillion, more than three times the figure in 1989. The analysis suggests that perhaps a few hundred people might today pay more than £10m for a work of art. For them, the main attractions can include the market's performance and the opportunities to 'collateralise' art, a development that, until a few years ago, seemed to have a bright future.

Experience of the last slump in prices is still instructive. After several years of rapid escalation, demand for works sold at auction declined amid controversy over Sotheby's leveraged sale of van Gogh's *Irises* to the Australian entrepreneur Alan Bond. The arrangement led to accusations that auction houses were inflating prices artificially. The J Paul Getty Museum later bought the painting for an undisclosed sum, after Bond failed to pay off his £16m loan from Sotheby's. The interest rate on such loans was as much as 4% above prime.

The once-popular loan system inflated prices, whether the borrower secured the painting or not: like a roulette player with chips on house credit, he found it tempting to raise the stakes. Pre-financing by the auction house created a synthetic floor, while a dealer who stated a price set a ceiling. If the borrower then defaulted, the lender recovered the painting, wrote off the unpaid part of the loan against tax, and chose a better time to offer the work for resale at its new inflated price.

Apart from lending money to foster buying, some auction houses gave guarantees to sellers. The practice added to critics' concerns about the trade's ethics. If a collector has a work of art that an auctioneer wants to sell, the latter can issue a 'guarantee' that the collector will obtain, say, £3m from the sale. If the work does not make £3m, the collector still receives the payment, but the work remains with the auction house for later sale. Guarantees are a strong inducement to sellers, but clearly risky for the auction house.

Leading dealers dislike the system of guarantees and loans. They argue that it creates a conflict of interest. One dealer is on record with the comment: 'if the auction house has a financial stake with both seller and buyer, its status as an agent is compromised. Lending to the buyer is like margin trading on the stock market. It creates inflation. It causes instability.' Advocates defend the policy as 'right, proper and indeed inevitable'. They claim that guarantees are given 'very sparingly'.

Persistent criticism can lead to government controls and levies, which test the industry's stability. These factors and growth in alternative investments have encouraged auction houses to examine their own practices and develop the range of services they offer, sometimes leading to controversy. Conflicts of interest and claims of sharp practice have focused the attention of regulators, as has the incidence of outright fraud and theft. Unethical behaviour has come under the scrutiny of the media and authorities in several centres of the art trade. For example, reports have focused on 'puffing the bid' – fictitious bidders inflating the price by displaying false interest.

18.2.5 Causes infâmes

The UK is not immune from the problems of illicit trading. Estimates put the value of art and antiques stolen each week in Britain at £40m or more. When a burglar steals from a collection, speed of response is vital. Stolen art and antiques can pass rapidly through the trade and vanish abroad. Of course, publicity can help. The 'stolen' section of the *Antiques Trade Gazette* alerts dealers to pilfered items that may come their way. *Trace* magazine notifies the police and the trade of stolen pieces, and the Art Loss Register runs a large international database that auctioneers and dealers can check for burglars' booty. The Thesaurus group's active crime tracking system (ACTS) electronically records, and can match, stolen art and antiques against auction catalogues and dealers' stock. Interpol also maintains a database, and the Metropolitan Police's Bumblebee databank gives members of the public access to property recovered. The National Automated Fingerprint Identification System (NAFIS) can also prove useful. Six years after a gang stole part of the Luton Hoo Fabergé collection, NAFIS succeeded in trapping one of the thieves, who was sentenced in 2003. Outside the UK, police forces in

France, Germany, Italy and Spain record stolen art and antiques on databases, as do authorities in the US, including the Los Angeles police and the Federal Bureau of Investigation. The US Customs Service introduced its Art Fraud Investigation Center in 2001. This unit concentrates on investigating stolen pieces, having previously had to rely on information from other countries' customs.

An interesting innovation that helps to track stolen art and antiques is Asset Guardian's marking system; it takes the form of a discreet identifier on a work, using coded fluids, microdots or microchips (similar to those implanted in domestic pets). The company or its client can hold computerised descriptions of the piece, usually with photographs, which they can also record on *Trace*'s deposit registry.

18.2.6 'Off the chandelier'...

The English poet Shelley, writing on the death of Keats in his *Adonais*, wrote of 'Month following month with woe, and year wake year to sorrow.' London auction houses a century and three-quarters later would recognise the sentiment. Over the past decade, they have suffered a surge of hostile media reports accusing them of dealing in looted works of art, of 'chandelier bidding' and smuggling. Auctioneers have also been under fire for accepting items that are 'not quite genuine'.

A few years ago, in the US, consumer affairs bodies challenged auctioneers. The experience is worth keeping in mind. Teams of officials pored over leading auctioneers' records, identifying such exotic-sounding practices as 'bidding off the chandelier' (puffing by fictitious bidders to drive up the price) and the more normal 'buying in' (leaving a work unsold because it does not reach the seller's undisclosed reserve price). The authorities then applied stiffer controls, including some that governed loans. The New York State legislature also took a close interest in the art market. It shared with the city's Consumer Affairs Department concerns about chandelier bidding, the undisclosed reserve, and auction houses' lending practices. The consumer affairs code now requires that 'if an auctioneer makes loans or advances money to consignors or prospective purchasers, this fact must be conspicuously disclosed in the auctioneer's catalogue'.

According to a US official, in the past there were 'gross irregularities' in some art auction houses. At the time, chandelier bidding amounted to 'an industry practice, both above and below the reserve'. Critics have also been concerned about the practices of not announcing buy-ins and keeping reserves secret. The auction houses contended that, if bidders knew the reserve, it would chill the market. Art dealers, lobbying the authorities, maintained that auctioneers should disclose the reserve, and that bidding should start at it.

Following a three-year investigation into a price-fixing conspiracy between Sotheby's and Christie's, the US Justice Department accepted the criminal guilt of both auctioneers at a federal court in Manhattan in March 2001. As part of the settlement, the two auction houses were ordered to split a $512m fine. In addition, Sotheby's was charged $45m for admitting it had conspired to violate anti-trust laws. Christie's was able to escape this because its senior executives had decided to co-operate with the authorities in return for immunity from prosecution. The judge presiding over the case stated: 'It is important to bear in mind a strong public interest to see Sotheby's and Christie's survive. These two firms dominate the auction market. Should one fail, the other would be in a position to lift market prices.'

In a twist to the affair, Alfred Taubman, chairman of Sotheby's from 1993–2000, was found guilty of plotting to fix auction house prices with his counterpart at Christie's, Sir Anthony Tennant. Although Sir Anthony was indicted with Taubman, he refused to go to New York for the trial and has so far remained free. Taubman was sentenced to a year and a day in prison. His co-conspirator, Dede Brooks, was also sentenced but avoided jail because of her co-operation in the investigation. She served six months' home detention, and had to wear an electronic tag when she went out, at pre-arranged times.

The media *causes célèbres* have reinforced press criticisms that auction houses sell art under conditions that are less than fair. Godfrey Barker put the point forcefully in a *Daily Telegraph* article in 2001. Barker claimed that auctioneers typically say to all 50,000 buyers who pass each year through their gilded doors, 'All goods are sold with all faults and imperfections and errors of description. Buyers should satisfy themselves prior to the sale as to the condition of each lot and should exercise and rely on their own judgement as to whether the lot accords with its description.'

He argued that the conditions of sale were unfair and compared poorly with measures to protect buyers of consumer goods. Barker suggested that auction houses tried to keep their conditions of sale under wraps, and that, when a disaffected bidder has a complaint, he may settle out of court. His article claimed that '100 to 150 cases a year in London are muffled in this way'. In contrast, art dealers comply with a code that requires refund without question.

The top auction houses were the targets of fresh criticism, according to a report in the *Wall Street Journal* in 2002. It alleged that buyers and sellers negotiated secret financial deals before auctioning certain paintings. New York Old Master paintings dealer Robert Simon said the backroom deals undermined the auction house and had led to a great deal of suspicion: 'There's a sense that the sales are manipulated.'

Not surprisingly, the air of mistrust has led British antique dealers to demand reform in the way auctioneers sell works of art and antiques. They believe that a code of conduct should include clauses on:

(1) legal responsibility for the authenticity of goods sold;
(2) a ban on chandelier bids;
(3) auctioneers declaring an interest when they have given guarantees;
(4) preventing auctioneers charging commissions to both buyers and sellers;
(5) withholding from auction staff details of bids received in advance ('commission bids').

For their part, auction houses have sought to demystify the auction process to reassure the new breed of collectors and investors. They have employed capable people to explain the significance of terminology and practices, and the business of reserves. Representative bodies try to set standards and control their members' practices with professional codes. Yet dealing in art from a gallery or an auction house is perhaps not a profession; instead, it is like a trade or a financial service. Its critics argue for regulation, for setting up an independent regulator, an art industry equivalent to the UK's Financial Services Authority. The auction houses and dealers have doubts about these ideas; some outsiders think they have merit.

18.2.7 Money laundering

In the early 1990s, the Swiss Government voiced concern at the country's role as a transit centre for objects of questionable origin – perhaps not a novel feature of the Swiss financial scene – and about money-laundering operations. Legislatures and law enforcement bodies are now attacking these operations with vigour.

Recently, both the EU and the US have strengthened their laws against money laundering, and its policing. *Operation dinero*, directed by North American and European agencies against the Colombian Cali cartel, seized more than $50m in cash and property. The assets included a Reynolds, a Rubens and a Picasso being sold for the Cali group by an offshore bank in Anguilla.

Art and antiques appeal to money launderers partly because they can insert such assets into elaborate and extensive series of transactions, which make it problematic to trace the money beyond its initial movement. Experts say that collectors with large sums of 'dirty' money can pay cash for valuable antiquities from unscrupulous dealers in archaeological treasures. The system benefits middlemen far more than those who did the actual looting. For example, a looter might sell Mayan ceramics stolen from a remote jungle site for $200 to $500. The final buyer might pay $100,000 for the same items. To combat this system, legislators are including art and antique traders within the scope of anti-money laundering statutes and regulations. The laws will apply controls to individuals and firms in the chains, who deal in high value items. The EU member states are taking a close interest in activities in and outside the financial sector that might aid money launderers.

18.2.8 Continued internationalisation

Despite these uncertainties, buyers have been persuaded by plausible arguments that alternative investments might protect them against calamity. As a result, many of the markets for art and antiques have become more international; since the 1970s, North American, continental European, and Middle and Far Eastern investors have begun to frequent sales rooms in great numbers.

A few years ago, rich art buyers revived Russia's market. Prime among them in Moscow and St Petersburg were banks, which had made immense profits in 1992 and 1993 from trading currencies. The most notable were Inkombank, Stolichay, Alpha-Bank, Voznozdenie, Menatep and Moscovia. Eight years ago, none of them owned significant paintings; today they hold Old Masters and contemporary art. Self-promotion is one reason why the banks bought. Another was their anxiety to store value in what appears, for now, to be a stable international currency – art. What mattered most were special tax provisions that favoured investors in 'outstanding art collections' (a heritage measure to keep great art in Russia).

18.2.9 Taxes in the US

Gilbert S Edelson, administrative vice-president and counsel for the Art Dealers Association of America, has warned that 'every US state that has a sales tax has a use tax'. Therefore, a collector who buys a painting in Paris and has it shipped to his home state, for example, must contact the state to find out the amount owed for both sales and use taxes. Failure to comply could bring serious consequences.

Recent prosecutions of high-profile collectors and dealers have thrown a spotlight on the issue. In the US, prosecutors are pursuing zealous campaigns to recover lost taxes and punish evaders. In July 2003, for example, an investigation in Manhattan District Attorney Robert M Morgenthau's office revealed that Bob P Haboldt and Company, a prominent art gallery, had failed to collect taxes on sales of more than 11 artworks between 1 March 1998 and 30 November 2002. The gallery, which specialises in Dutch and Flemish masters, sold works to residents of New York and on occasion, to evade collecting and remitting sales tax, the firm reportedly shipped containers out of the state that did not contain the purchased paintings. The company pleaded guilty and paid $400,000 in fines. To date, through a series of investigations into tax-evasion schemes, Morgenthau's prosecutions have yielded about $17.5m in recovered sales taxes, as well as fines paid to the city and state.

18.3 NATIONAL HERITAGE ISSUES

18.3.1 Export controls

The establishment of the EU has caused concern over the possible repatriation of art works to their countries of origin. However, this concern is not a recent phenomenon and governments have tried in various ways to prevent objects of long-standing cultural value and national heritage works, whatever their origin, from leaving the country permanently.

How does the export licence system work in practice? Owners of heritage works of art and antiques have to allow for the imbroglio of export review when planning a sale in world markets. Consider typical cases. In March 1999, the Export Review Committee delayed the sale of a late Rembrandt painting, *Portrait of an elderly man*, to a Dutch buyer. To keep the work in the UK meant British galleries and institutions raising £9.3m in just three months. A month earlier, the Tate Gallery of Modern Art on Bankside, London, and the Scottish Gallery of Modern Art in Edinburgh, with the help of the National Art Collections Fund, had raised £1.2m to buy Joan Miró's *Head of a Catalan peasant*. In March 2000, the former Arts Minister Alan Howarth placed a temporary bar on the export of *The conquest of Mexico*, a series of eight 17th-century paintings. The Department for Culture, Media and Sport's Arts and Libraries' Reviewing Committee on the Export of Works of Art drew attention to the paintings' significance for the study of colonial conquest, the history of colonial painting and ethnological factors. The deferral was to enable British museums and galleries to raise more than £2.1m.

Late in 1999, the packers were preparing to box and ship the Botticelli masterpiece *The Virgin adoring the sleeping Christ child* to the Kimball art museum in Fort Worth, Texas. However, with the help of lottery money, the National Galleries of Scotland managed to raise the £10.25m needed to keep the painting in the UK. The National Lottery Heritage fund contributed £7.6m, and the balance came from the Scottish Executive, the National Arts Collection fund, banks and private individuals.

This export licensing system is designed to strike a balance between the various interests concerned in any application for an export licence – for example the protection of the national heritage; the rights of owners selling goods; the interests of the exporter or overseas purchaser; and the UK's position and reputation as a centre of international art. However, the licensing system's main purpose is to keep in the UK cultural goods considered to be of outstanding national importance.

Under the extant system, the Waverley rules, the reviewing committee advising the Culture Secretary can recommend a moratorium on the granting of an export licence for up to six months; the delay allows British institutions the chance to purchase. The success of this system depends, however, on these bodies having or raising adequate funds to meet the high prices of works deemed of national interest. In 1991, the Secretary of State resorted to placing long-term export bans on several items, limiting their potential market value.

The criteria defined in the *Waverley Report on the Export of Works of Art* (1952) depend on the answers to three questions:

(1) Is the object so closely connected with British history and national life that its loss would be a misfortune?
(2) Is it of exceptional aesthetic importance?
(3) Is it of exceptional significance for the study of some particular branch of art, learning or history?

The Waverley Committee recommended a minimum age limit of 100 years in 1952. Committee members did not want to discourage 'the vigorous two-way traffic that we should like to see, bringing important works into the country to fill the many notable gaps in our collections'.

Subsequently, the Government adopted a lower age limit, of 50 years. Under the present export licensing controls, works produced and held in the UK for more than 50 years, and valued at or above £39,600, fall within the control. In practice, an expert adviser will judge an application for the required UK licence in the context of the Waverley criteria. However, objects imported from another EU country within 50 years of the date of export automatically receive an EU licence, provided the applicant can supply appropriate documentary proof of legal dispatch from the country of origin. Specific exceptions to the rules are an artist or a producer's own works that he plans to export. The artist or producer's spouse or widow(er) has similar rights. Advocates of the 50-year rule believe that it properly allows the authorities to decide if a work meets the Waverley criteria, whether or not its artist or producer still lives.

The export control can apply to all works of cultural significance, including archives, manuscripts, sculpture, machinery and so on. In practice, the effect of the export control can differ according to the nature of the object. Many national treasures are valued out of the reach of all but the wealthiest investor, but government heritage policy is likely to affect the art and antiques market as a whole, and EU policies, reviewed below, even more so.

18.3.2 Export controls – revisions

Under the arrangements announced in the spring 1998 Budget, no acceptances in lieu require expenditure by the Department. Instead, the Inland Revenue accepts items in lieu of taxes without seeking reimbursement from the Secretary of State. In practice, the Revenue's Capital Taxes Office refers offers of apparently 'pre-eminent' or 'historically associated' objects to the Museums and Galleries Commission, which takes opinions from independent experts. The commission then advises the Secretary of State whether an item is suitable for acceptance in lieu of taxes. The advice covers the item's pre-eminence, condition and value, and any conditions that apply to the offer. In addition, the commission makes recommendations on lodging the item, both temporary and permanent.

A few years ago, the then Department of National Heritage consulted the museums and art trade worlds on several important issues:

(1) Estimates of a fair market price for export-deferred works of art. In particular, the department has sought opinions on a proposal to exclude a dealer's commission from the fair market price, where the commission is on a sale to a connected third party.
(2) Whether any extra conditions attach to a private offer from a UK buyer to purchase an object under export deferral.
(3) Whether the National Heritage Secretary should encourage an owner to prefer a public offer to a simultaneous offer from a private source.
(4) The application of the Waverley rules to works by living artists.

Controversy over the fair market price arose when the Reviewing Committee considered Jean-François de Troy's painting *La lecture de Molière*. The members expressed reservations about the inclusion in the fair market price of the dealer's commission charged by the applicant to its related US company. The committee also urged the Secretary of State for National Heritage only to take account of private offers, if the UK buyer has given satisfactory undertakings. These should include assurances on public access, proper maintenance, a minimum retention period and, for a collection or set of objects, the collection's integrity. Consultation led to changes in the private offers policy, which imposes strict conditions on a private offer to purchase an object under export deferral.

In another case, the Reviewing Committee considered an application to export *The painter's room* by Lucian Freud (1943). This was the first occasion on which a work by a living artist had come before the Committee. Sotheby's had applied for a licence to export the painting to a purchaser in the US. The value shown on the export licence application was £515,812.50.

The department's expert adviser came from the Tate Gallery. He stated why he felt the work should stay in Britain, asserting that *The painter's room* was a vital *oeuvre* from Freud's first phase, and the largest picture that he had painted to that date. The painting: '... declared arrestingly the preoccupation with concentrated realisation of motifs from observation that would be a central feature of his art over the succeeding half century. Memorable in its clarity and strangeness, it was Freud's first key work.'

Against that, Sotheby's argued that the painting stood as an early work within the scope of Freud's output, and was stylistically atypical. 'The depiction of such an estranged world and the absence of human beings, were not characteristic. Later works do not bear any resemblance, and Freud's style quickly evolved into a more realistic and dramatic one.' The painting did not identify with the style upon which Freud built his reputation. It stood more as a curiosity than as an established and characteristic work.

For tactical reasons, the Reviewing Committee submitted no recommendation. In due course, the Secretary of State for National Heritage decided to defer a decision for two months, hoping to see an offer at the recommended price of £515,812.50 or higher. The Tate Gallery announced a serious intention to raise funds for the purchase, extending the deferred period to four months. Later, the owner refused separate offers to purchase from the Tate and the Chatsworth House Trust at the stated price. The National Heritage Secretary therefore refused the export licence.

This case prompted the Reviewing Committee to express reservations about deferring a decision on a licence for any living artist's work, whatever its merit. The members felt that Freud's painting raised an important point of principle: whether the export of works by living artists should stay under control. However, they noted that removing such works from UK export control would not prevent action under EU regulations that govern trade in cultural goods.

The committee felt that the system could act to a living artist's detriment. Suppose a painter or a sculptor is important enough for heritage conservationists to oppose its export. Probably the artist already enjoys an international reputation, and the value of his work might rise if buyers learn that his work is 'of national importance'. A licence deferral could allow national galleries to fill gaps where public collections do not already cover the early part of an artist's *oeuvre*.

In practice, the market for the artist's work is unlikely to fall merely because the Secretary of State might not issue an export licence. It also seems unlikely that many works will come before the committee. The

Freud painting was the first by a living artist to come before it in 42 years. If more do come forward, it is doubtful if matching offers would be forthcoming for all living artists' works subject to licence deferral.

Yet the Waverley Committee's original arguments in favour of the higher limit support the exclusion of works by living artists from the regime. Any restriction on the export of work by living artists could limit the spread of their international reputation. Nor would the export controls apply to artists who export their own work. Many of these artists are under contract to sell their output through dealers, who would be subject to export licence controls. Anomalies could then arise. A dealer, or an overseas buyer, could evade the controls by selling the work back to the artist. He could export it legally under his own name and then resell it to the new owner, bringing the control into disrepute.

Export controls apply not only to the work of artists, but also to the archives of authors, musicians and other public figures. They might prefer to sell their papers through an agent. The latter would be subject to controls and might reduce the price offered because the department might withhold a licence for the early part of the archive. Agents might also see advantages in breaking up a collection of papers. The Government now seems likely to update the Waverley rules in the light of such problems.

Despite these constraints, there is a constant flow abroad of works of art. According to the Reviewing Committee's latest report, only about half of items stay in this country after the committee has recommended deferring an export licence. An important factor is a paucity of public resources to help fund purchases.

The Heritage Lottery Fund's grants for items of over £100,000 in value are awarded at up to 75%, leaving a museum to raise at least a quarter of the cost. That can be substantial. For example, on a £5m painting, which is not unusual, the museum would have to raise £1.25m from its own resources, which may be difficult. In the case of the National Art Collections Funds (NACF), its financial resources, which come from its members and through legacies, are limited. Nevertheless, the NACF contributed nearly £263,000 – half the price – to the purchase of Hugh Douglas Hamilton's 18th century pastel *Studio of Canova*. It met all the Waverley criteria and is now in the Victoria and Albert Museum, having originally been destined for the Getty Museum in California. Since 1995, the Heritage Lottery Fund and the National Heritage Memorial Fund have allocated more than £80m to public collections. The Government has recently increased its grant to the latter to £5m for the financial year 2001–02, and the former has increased its proposed support for museum acquisitions, including export-stopped works, from £5m to £10m.

These arrangements can underpin the market for high quality works. However, non-charging museums, when making an offer for a deferred item, must include 17.5% to cover VAT. That puts them at a disadvantage against overseas buyers. Those rules are governed by EU Directives.

Owners can defer IHT if they promise to let the public view their works and undertake to conserve and protect the assets. About 56,000 works of art now fall within this exemption. Of these, owners who benefit from IHT relief keep 20,900 in small private houses. The concession for conditionally exempt items allows these owners to give public access by prior appointment. In addition, the Government intends to organise exhibitions across Britain so that the public has a better chance to see these pieces. Under this plan, the Government will meet the insurance costs of protecting the art against theft or fire. The new scheme effectively closes the loophole by which some private owners failed to honour promises to put their collections on show in return for exemption from tax.

See also 18.10.1.

18.3.3 Art and the EU

The EU has affected the movement of works of art both out of the EU and between member states. Since January 1993, imports and exports have been subject to spot checks only at member states' frontiers, making illegal trade much harder to detect. Some countries, notably Spain, Greece and Italy, fear the loss of many important works. The UK Government's prime concern is that restrictions will harm the country's art trade, while auction houses anticipate endless bureaucratic wrangles.

An EU export licence is now necessary to export a cultural object out of the Union, if its value exceeds a stated threshold. These thresholds are . defined by age and value, much as they have been under UK export rules. In some cases, the thresholds are comparable with those set for a UK licence; in others, the threshold is set at a higher level, as Table 18.1 below shows. For details contact the Department for Culture, Media and Sport, tel: 020 7211 6200.

Auction houses also face 'an unprecedented threat' from three areas of legislation:

(1) *Droit de suite* – a levy on the resale of contemporary art. In spite of the UK Government's vigorous opposition, the EU finally ratified the measure in Brussels in July 2001. The British art trade claims that *droit de suite* will seriously damage the market and cost thousands of jobs.
(2) *Unidroit* – a treaty that returns 'stolen' goods. The unidroit agreement, which has been signed by a number of governments, covers stolen or illegally exported cultural objects. A Culture Select Committee report submitted in 2001 to the Art Minister recom-

Table 18.1 UK export thresholds

Category by type and age	Threshold (£)

1 Archaelogical objects more than 100 years old which are the products of:
  Excavations and finds on land or under water
  Archaeological sites
  Archaeological collections
	0

2 Elements forming an integral part of artistic, historic or religious monuments which have been dismembered, of an age exceeding 100 years	0
3 Pictures and paintings, other than those in category 3A or 4, executed entirely by hand, on any medium and in any material (1)	91,200
3A Water colours, gouaches and pastels executed entirely by hand in any material (1)	18,200
4 Mosaics in any material executed entirely by hand, other than those falling into categories 1 or 2, and drawings in any medium executed entirely by hand on any material (1)	9,100
5 Original engravings, prints, serigraphs and lithographs with their respective plates and original posters (1)	9,100
6 Original sculptures or statuary and copies produced by the same process as the original other than those in category 1 (1)	30,400
7 Photographs, film and negatives thereof (1)	9,100
8 Incunabula and manuscripts, including maps and musical stores, singly or in collections (1)	0
9 Books more than 100 years old, singly or in collections	30,400
10 Printed maps more than 200 years old	0
11 Archives, and any elements thereof, of any kind or any medium which are more than 50 years old	30,400
12 (a) Collections and specimens from zoological, botanical, mineralogical or anatomical collections (b) Collections of historical, palaeontological, ethnographic or numismatic interest	30,400
13 Means of transport more than 75 years old	30,400
14 Any other categories of antique item not included in categories 1–13, more than 50 years old	30,400

Note (1): Which are more than 50 years old and do not belong to their originators.

mended that the British Government sign up to the treaty, allowing original owners to reclaim artefacts on proof of origin.

(3) The doubling of VAT on art imports into the EU to 5% in July 1999 has adversely affected sentiment in the London market. Until 1994, there was no import VAT in the UK and dealers in London could persuade sellers from across the world to send their works of art there. New York and Geneva now seem somewhat more attractive.

According to a survey by the European Fine Art Foundation, the average price of a work sold at auction in the EU declined by 39% to $7,662 between 1998 and 2001. The average price of a painting sold in the UK, in the same period increased 54% to $24,968; in the US, the average price rose 75% to $79,003. Overall, the EU has lost 7.2% of it market share since 1998. This is due, in no small part, to the cost-effectiveness of holding high value auctions in, for example, New York City. To this end, European auction houses are a relatively low-price marketplace, and the UK a mid-priced market, whilst the US is the leader in fine art prices.

Droits de suite

Payment of artists' royalties, known as *droits de suite*, varies across Europe. Eleven EU member states already pay *droits de suite* royalties (at rates of between 3% and 5% of the selling price) to artists or their families up to 70 years after the artist's death. These sums are payable by the seller, direct to the artist or his estate, provided the sale is over a threshold figure and the work is still in copyright (ie produced by a living artist, or one who has died within 70 years).

In March 1996, the European Commission proposed harmonising national systems that cover 'resale rights' for artists. The purpose is to allow artists to share profits when dealers trade at high prices in a work by an artist who had originally sold it at a far lower price. The proposal applies to pictures, collages, paintings, drawings, engravings, prints, lithographs, sculptures, ceramics and photographic works. In 1997, the European Parliament and Council drafted a new directive on the resale rights that would benefit originators of works of art.

The Commission wanted to extend the measure by introducing a scale of royalties, with beneficiaries securing 4% of the first €50,000 (£32,500), falling to 1% for works selling for €200,000 (£130,000) or more. In March 2000, the EU agreed to compromise. After a five-year incorporation period, ten years' derogation will delay the tax's implementation. It was also decided that the maximum levy that could be paid on any single work of art would be €12,500 (£8,120), to reduce the risk that owners will choose to sell them outside the EU. The royalty would be levied at 4% on sales up to €50,000 (£32,500), dropping to 0.25% above €500,000 (£325,000). The original agreement also guaranteed that London would stay tax-free for five years. However, the minimum value of works of art affected by the tax rose from €1,000 (£650) to €4,000 (£2,600).

The deal struck in March, seen by many as damage limitation, came to an abrupt end, when the European Parliament suspended the original agreement in December 2000, clawing back all concessions made with the UK Government. According to *The Times*, 'its amendments ... restored to one of the most pointlessly destructive bits of regulation ever concocted in Brussels in all its most egregious faults'.

During this time, opposition to the *droit de suite* levy has been fierce. The UK Government campaigned for more than three years on behalf of dealers and auctioneers, arguing that the measure was a disincentive to trade. London dealers fear that its introduction would shift trade to the US and Switzerland, devastating the thriving international market in 20th-century painting. A survey by the Department of Trade and Industry has estimated that *droit de suite* alone could rob the UK of an annual £68m in art sales and 5,000 jobs in the art trade.

Anthony Browne, chairman of the British Art Market Federation, described the imposition of *droit de suite* as the biggest threat to the UK art market. The federation concluded in a recent report that sellers would opt for New York and other EU centres if the UK implemented it. The pressure group, Artists against *Droit de Suite*, including numerous leading contemporary artists such as David Hockney and Emma Sargeant, supported a poster campaign against it, claiming that the directive would deprive them of their right to freedom of choice.

In contrast, the Design and Artists Copyright Society, a non-profit national collecting society for the visual arts, supported the levy, which proposed to address the injustice of 'the starving artist'. They argued that *droit de suite* was not a tax, but a royalty to help artists. France and Germany claimed the tax provided income to impoverished 'starving in the garret' painters, whereas Britain alleged that it benefited mostly a handful of wealthy artists who did not need the money. However, Browne stated that in practice many artists did not bother trying to collect a percentage each time a work was sold, because it was an expensive process. Moreover, there was only significant trade in an artist's work once he became established. In France, Picasso and Matisse gained the most because lawyers, capable of dealing with the bureaucracy involved, administered their estates.

Despite the pressure levied against the EU, the legislation was ratified in July 2001. The regulations come into force on 1 January 2006 for works by living artists and six years later for works by artists who have died in the last 70 years. In addition, the tax will be payable on a sliding scale, falling to 0.25% for sale prices over €500,000 (about £325,000) and capped at €12,500. Artists will receive royalties of 4% of the sale price up to €50,000 and on a declining scale above that figure. Britain and other EU countries, which do not already have royalty systems for artists, will have until 2012 to comply.

The British art trade and the Government, while hardly overjoyed, recognise that they have been able to head off some of the most damaging aspects of the original agreement. In fact, the implementation period is the longest for any EU directive, seen by some as a measure of the Government's tough negotiating stance. According to Arlene McCarthy, the legal affairs spokeswoman for Labour MEPs: 'We have stopped an extremely damaging proposal for the British arts market. It is a good deal.'

In 2002, the European Parliament passed a further series of amendments relating to *droit de suite*. These modify the common position, which had been negotiated after a three-year battle to preserve London's position. Under the amendments, the lower threshold for payment of the tax would be reduced to €1,000, the period of introduction cut from five years to two, and the derogation period from ten years to two. These amendments will now go into conciliation at the Parliament and the Council of Ministers.

Some sections of the art trade remain disappointed, stating that it will make Europe a less attractive place in which to resell important 20th century art. However, a curious outcome means that it will be cheaper to sell the work of a US artist in London than that of a European.

Unidroit

A recently introduced EU directive on the return of 'cultural objects' has been a focus of controversy in some member states. This directive entails forming central authorities or 'art tribunals' in each country. They would have the power to demand the return of an item illegally exported, with compensation if the buyer had exercised due care in the purchase.

This right of return expires after 75 years for public collections and 30 years for private collections. Because the legislation is not retroactive, the British Museum will not be compelled to relinquish the Elgin Marbles; however, the Greek Government is tactfully exerting renewed pressure on the British authorities to repatriate them. In parallel, the Chinese are becoming sensitive and assertive over cultural relics that they suspect were exported illegally. For example, they blocked plans by Sotheby's and Christie's in Hong Kong to auction antiques originally from the mainland. An 18th-century Qianlong emperor commissioned a hexagonal vase and three bronze animal heads for his summer palace in Beijing. Troops led by the Earl of Elgin looted these items in 1860, at the end of the second Opium War. The Chinese describe these antiquities, and other catalogued items, as 'national treasures'.

Earlier this year, Culture, Media and Sport Select Committee of the House of Commons, investigating the illicit trade of cultural goods, advised the Government to sign up to the Unidroit Convention on stolen items. Unidroit would, in effect, make it easier for rightful owners to reclaim items stolen in the UK and shipped abroad. The recommendation has been met with strong opposition, because it may expose dealers unwittingly holding stolen items. Anthony Browne of the British Art Market Federation said that the convention would not work in practice because it did not include 'a clear definition of cultural property'. He stated that because some countries extend their statute of limitations to 75 years, while others have no limit, auctioneers and dealers would have to keep permanent records on everything they sold, to defend themselves against claims.

Antique dealers in France are also opposed to *unidroit*. The Syndicat National des Antiquaires (SNA) launched a press campaign in April 2001, placing quarter-page advertisements in *Le Monde* and *Libération*, among others, warning 'ALARM! – The Unidroit convention, Art in serious danger.' As in the UK, the main concern is the inadequate definition of theft in the convention. The copy warns that 'each state will be able to demand the return of works of art, for reasons that may be ideological, religious, or even electoral'.

VAT

In December 1993, the member states reached agreement on the harmonisation of VAT payable on the sale of works of art imported into the EU. The Seventh VAT Directive took effect on 1 January 1995. Its effect is to tax works of art imported into and sold within the UK, which has the largest art and antiques market within the EU. Britain's negotiators had sought to maintain the country's status as an international centre. The basis for taxing these works, which had applied in the UK (ie VAT on the auctioneers' commission and premium, but not on the whole price), now applies throughout the EU.

For items imported from non-EU countries into the UK, the VAT rate was 2.5% from 1 January 1995 until July 1999. Britain then came into line with the rest of the EU and now charges a rate of 5%, in spite of criticisms in a 1998 review for the EU on the increase. London market auctioneers and dealers feel that the effects will be harmful. Confirmation of their fears came in a sale of institutional assets. The British Rail Pension Fund decided not to sell in London a pair of Canalettos and 22 other paintings. Sotheby's auctioned them in New York in January 1997. The fund had begun investing in art in the 1970s, and spent £40m on about 2,400 pieces. It has now disposed of more than 2,200 for £150m, showing a positive annual return of 5.5% above the RPI. Selling the Old

Masters in New York represented a departure; earlier sales by the fund had mainly been at Sotheby's, London. As a result of the decision the pensioners are more than £6m richer, while London auction houses and dealers are worrying more about VAT.

The British Art Market Federation contends that artwork imports from outside the EU have fallen in value by 40% since the imposition by the EU of 2.5% VAT. If the Government has to implement all the measures in full, auctioneers contend that Britain will lose a lucrative source of revenue and employment. The industry's annual turnover is £2.2bn, and it employs 40,000 people. A limited exodus from Bond Street in central London has already begun. Pace Wildenstein, a large firm of art dealers, sold its Bond Street premises. Phillips opened premises in both New York and Geneva in 1996 'so that we are covered whatever the outcome'.

John Hobbs, a London dealer based in Pimlico Road, set up an office in Park Avenue, New York City, working there with an Italian, Laura Steinberg. A European Fine Art Association study lends support to this practice: the Association estimates that the US market is increasing in value at 10% per annum more than the European market. At that differential rate of growth, the American market overtook Europe in scale in 2002.

Art Sales Index figures on auction sales, quoted in a report by Market Tracking International (MTI) to the European Commission, indicate the scale of art sales at the time by auction houses in Europe and North America. MTI estimates for the Commission put the total level of sales of art and antiques between €21.2bn and €24.8bn (£14bn–16bn), The large range of the estimated total sales arises because few reliable data are available on dealer sales. Auction houses generate about a quarter of the total turnover. However, MTI calculates that a quarter of all art market sales are 'inter-trade', ie between auctioneers and dealers and between dealers and other dealers. This would mean that the net global expenditure on art and antiques lay between €16bn and €18.5bn. Almost half the sales were in the US, and a further 28.5% in the UK.

London dealers estimate that 40% or more of artworks sold (by value) come from Switzerland, America, Japan and outside the EU. Thus, it will make sense for many to buy and sell in the US. New York now accounts for 40% of world art sales, and is growing, while London accounts for 30% and is falling.

The art trade elsewhere in the EU, apart from Paris, is mainly domestic, so that London dealers have seen envy of the city's status as a world centre since the 18th century. Published estimates show that the London market turned over about £2.1bn a year, compared to £3.5bn–4bn for the EU as a whole, Britain included. Britain's art market accounted for between 60% and 70% of the entire European art market. The British

Table 18.2 Analysis of total value, lots sold and average price

Country	Lots sold	Turnover £m (€m)	Average value per lot (£m) (€m)
UK	33,352	550	16,500
		856	25,600
USA	19,194	915	47,800
		1,430	74,400
France	20,745	120	5,668
		183	8,800
Germany	12,339	52	4,241
		81	6,600
The Netherlands	4,598	21	4,660
		33	7,300
Italy	8,386	54	6,490
		85	10,000
Austria	2,815	11	3,896
		17	6,000

Note: € amounts in italics.

themselves may not be large-scale buyers of art, but the London art market is like the City: an *entrepôt*.

Take a Japanese collector selling a modern painting. If he chooses to make the sale in New York, and attracts a bid of $4m, the buyer will pay the auctioneer 15% on the first $50,000 and 10% on the rest, or $402,500 on top of the hammer price. The seller pays 2%, plus expenses – probably a figure in excess of $100,000. The same transaction in London would attract the same costs, but the buyer would have to pay an additional 5% import tax on $4,502,000, or $225,100 extra. The seller meanwhile would have to pay an additional 2% *droit de suite*.

So, to carry out the transaction in London would cost over 60% more than it would in New York. This position has applied since 1999, when the previous preferential treatment of London ceased. Auctioneers and dealers believe that import tax is causing measurable damage to the London trade.

18.3.4 Illicit trading

A recently released report by the McDonald Institute for Archaeological Research at the University of Cambridge, *Stealing history: the illicit trade in cultural material*, states that thieves steal up to $3bn in art and artefacts each year around the world. According to this study, up to 90% of the antiquities auctioned in London – one of the world's leading markets – contained no details of origin. Leading art dealers, however, have vigorously denied knowingly handling smuggled or stolen works. Stolen art cited in the report included:

Mayan ceramics from Mexico and Central America
Mosaics from Cyprus
Lydian statues from Turkey
Icons from Christian churches
Fossils from Nebraska and the Gobi Desert
Beheaded Buddhist statues from Cambodia.

A Unesco 1970 convention prohibits the illicit import and export of cultural property, and unauthorised transfers of its ownership. The 1995 Unidroit Convention, on stolen and illegally exported cultural objects, also seeks to control the illicit trade in antiques and antiquities. UK governments had consistently refused to ratify either.

However, at the end of 2000, the then Arts Minister, Alan Howarth, announced the setting up of a panel of experts chaired by Professor Norman Palmer. The remit of the panel was to examine the scale of illicit trade in art and antiquities in the UK, and to advise on steps to combat it. The panel reported in December 2000, recommending principally UK accession to the 1970 UNESCO Convention and a new criminal offence of importing, dealing in, or possessing stolen or illegally excavated cultural objects. In March 2001, Mr Howarth announced at the Institute of the Field Archaeologists Conference that the Government had signed up to the UNESCO Convention. 'The signing of the convention is undoubtedly an important step, but there is more to come', said Mr Howarth. 'We will be monitoring the export licensing system more closely, and working with the Home Office to establish a database of stolen and illegally removed cultural property. These actions will make life much more difficult for the minority of dealers who choose to besmirch their profession and trade illicitly.' In 2003, Culture Minister Kim Howells backed a Private Members' bill to outlaw the illicit trade in art and antiques. This is of particular relevance as the war in Iraq reportedly led to widespread looting of Iraqi treasures and artefacts, many believed destined for Western shores.

See also 18.7.5 and 18.10.1.

18.4 HIGHLIGHTS OF THE PREVIOUS YEAR

18.4.1 Market trends

In 2003, the number of art works and antiques sold at auction declined by 7%. The average price per-work-sold rose by 6.5% in dollar terms, but declined by 3.2% in sterling terms, according to Art Sales Index. In France, the average price per-work-sold fell by 30%. In the upper echelons of the market, membership of the 'million pound club' declined, with only 149 works fetching over £1m compared with 186 in 2002. The plunge was dramatic according to Artprice: its report on art markets in 2003 encapsulated the trends in apocalyptic terms, 'New York gripped by euphoria, Europe by a rising sense of panic.' Artprice estimates art market turnover for 2003 at €2.2 billion (£1.53 billion), a drop of 17.3% compared to its 2002 figures.

Artprice noted that the number of lots sold in London had dropped significantly in the past three years, but anticipated a revival. The service noted that, since the last quarter of 2003, the art market had begun to rise, and this trend continued in the first quarter of 2004. The analysts suggest that their figures clearly confirm that a sizeable recovery is underway, as indicated by higher trading volumes and a fall in the number of bought-ins.

Particular art and antiques markets can perform at variance with general trends. For example, watercolours, once less attractive to collectors than oil paintings, have become more popular with clients of galleries, dealers and auction houses. The Zurich Art and Antiques Index, which measures the movements of choice art works and antiques in the UK, has seen English watercolours rise in value by a third during the past year. In comparison, values of contemporary art went up by a fifth. One of the main reasons for the rush of interest has been a series of exhibitions and auctions in London and the provinces featuring important watercolour painters. Another factor pushing up prices is that European buyers have entered the market for watercolours created by Turner, and other English artists, during their Continental tours.

An attraction of watercolours and drawings is that they can bring the work of eminent artists within the scope of relatively modest budgets. At auction, a pencil drawing by Sir Stanley Spencer might fetch less than £5,000, whereas his oils could attract six or even seven-figure bids. Henry Wemyss, director of British drawings and watercolours at Sotheby's, is on record with the view: 'At auction you are more likely to get pictures straight out of private collections and this means they are not going to be over-restored, which occasionally happens with watercolours. But, in my opinion, the main reason for buying at auction is neither this nor the probability of achieving a better price. It is simply the thrill of the live bidding process. The auction route, however, does require more time than buying through a dealer because you must do your own preliminary research and this involves putting aside time to attend viewings. Dealers, on the other hand, have already conducted their own refinement processes and this is largely what you are paying them for.'

The 2003–2004 season also saw an important legal decision, in which the High Court decided that leading auctioneers do not owe a general duty of care to bidders, but do owe a duty to anyone who buys a lot relying on the description in an auction catalogue. That duty seemingly requires the auctioneer to give complete and not partial information, not to overplay a case, to outline known difficulties in making the attribution, and to make known uncertainties and qualifications. In the case, which involved Christie's and a Ms Thomson, the auctioneer had a client relationship with her through its services department. This relationship meant that Christie's had to take cognizance of her particular needs and skills and, with these considerations in mind, avoid misrepresentation of lots that she might buy at auction.

18.4.2 Internet sales

Among a widening range of enthusiasts, cyber-galleries have begun to feature significantly as sources of art and antiques. E-galleries and e-auctions on the Web are becoming immensely popular. Buyers find that purchases of art and antiques from websites can be cheaper than purchases of comparable items from conventional galleries. The latter might add between 20% and 55% to the basic price to cover their costs and risks. The virtual competitor might only mark up a price by between 10% and 30%. The saving on a painting that cost, say, £15,000 might be between £1,500 and £3,750.

Websites also auction art and antiques electronically, and many sources provide opportunities to identify what is on offer and to place a bid. Useful sites include www.artuk.co.uk; www.antiques.co.uk; www.bbc. co.uk/antiques; www.icom.org/vlmp; www.icollector.co.uk; and www.invaluable.com. Another interesting source is QXL, a European internet auction house at www.qxl.co.uk. Hugh Scully of the BBC's *Antiques Roadshow* has assembled a team of experts to answer queries and provide valuations.

A pioneer in this market is eBay, an important player in the computer-based online auction market in the US; eBay's total number of registered users now stands at over 50m. However, not all is what it seems. Cautious collectors entering the cyber world should be aware of frauds. For example, for good reasons eBay keeps a watchful eye on transactions and acts against sellers who try to manipulate deals. A typical problem is 'shill' bidding, ie the practice of an unprincipled seller to enter a bid on a piece that he has offered for sale at an online auction, in the hope of triggering a price rise. The Web-based auction world is also worried about the risks that a ring of shill bidders will operate in the online market. A study conducted by the Internet Fraud Complaint Center indicated that from May to November 2000, auction fraud accounted for 64.1% of internet fraud complaints filed. More recently, eBay has suffered a set-back relating to the security of its online transactions, leading many bidders to re-consider. A further setback came when a US court ruled against eBay. Litigants claimed that the auctioneer was using a bidding process devised and patented by another party, for which it did not have the rights. This may affect the way in which eBay operates, and might have long-term consequences.

18.4.3 Museum financing

The balance is shifting in top art and antique markets towards museums and galleries. They are mounting massive exhibitions and launching 'museum stores' that profit from art and antique merchandise. Art museums have become big business around the world, and especially in the US, where reduced revenue from the public purse and corporate parsimony have prompted cultural institutions to seek other sources of funds.

Many US museums and galleries have large endowments and collections of almost immeasurable value. Yet they suffer from seesaw support – and from up and down attendances, membership and other sources of income. So these institutions are shifting their forms of financing, for example to large bond issues; and to underpin these issues, they are seeking credit ratings. The first to try the approach was New York's Metropolitan Museum, which in the 1980s suffered substantial cuts in New York City funding. In 1987, with support from a state educational authority, the museum floated a $40m issue. By 1993, it was able to refinance the debt, and secure another $22m at preferential rates. The issues were successful: by early 1996, the museum had won a higher rating from credit agencies, as did the Art Institute of Chicago.

Reports are becoming more common of innovative financing by museums and galleries, and raised credit standing. As an example, Moody's Investors Service rated New York's Museum of Modern Art as A1 for an issue of $34.7m (£21m) of debt. Cultural institutions in other parts of the world have learnt how to operate in debt markets, without the cushion of government backing or costly bond insurance programmes. New York's Natural History Museum and Boston's Museum of Fine Arts are among other cultural institutions that have used publicly traded debt to finance capital projects. One benefit is a lower interest rate than banks charge for loans. The bonds are tax-exempt, offering investors savings advantages; they do not have to pay federal taxes on the income. US investment bankers have been struck with 'museums' and galleries' strong balance sheets, low debt, and efficient financial management of large-scale events'.

These institutions apply their borrowing mainly to capital projects. However, they do not offer their collections as collateral. Nor do the agencies treat these assets as formally available for debt servicing; but the credit checkers nevertheless feel that, in straitened circumstances, the institutions could sell some works of art from their inventories.

Some other public museums are experiencing organic growth. Perhaps the most spectacular expansion rate has been in Seattle. To house new donations of art, three art museums there have added 200,000 ft^2 of floor space over the past seven years. The largest, the Seattle Art Museum, a showcase for contemporary art, has tripled in size, added 2,556 pieces of art and put an additional 8,000 members on its rolls since 1991. The Photographer's Gallery in London has received £3.5m from the National Lottery to move to a site five times larger than its current residence. This expansion in contemporary art space and the greater purchasing power of art museums could have a substantial effect on world markets.

18.5 PURCHASING ART AND ANTIQUES

18.5.1 Authenticity and condition

Is a painting or a sculpture exactly what it purports to be? Scholars have spent decades identifying works of art and their creators. An examination of the paints that an artist evidently employed may be instructive; for example where Prussian blue appears, it will mean a date after the first quarter of the 18th century. Studies of canvases, workshop practices and historical documents can reveal whether a piece is as described.

The professionals also evaluate the condition of a painting, using diverse technologies and techniques. For example, X-ray photos can expose over-painting that may hide loss or damage, or an artist's first sketches, or his changes of mind. Infrared tests may bring out the original drawing lines, and ultraviolet, later retouching. A careful inspection of the canvas can uncover evidence of damage or relining or, if a painting is on wood, tree-ring counting (dendrochronology) can help to date the work. Reflected or raking light is often a useful means of laying bare any holes, flakes, bumps or dents; and microscopic sectioning can detect different paint layers or pigments. An example of the deference paid to the condition of the canvas is seen in the price of £13m paid for Monet's *Nympheas*. The price reflected in part the quality of the canvas, as much as the painting itself.

18.5.2 Importance, rarity, familiarity

Works of art and antiques in demand are likely to reflect the buyers' consensus on their importance as influential, innovative and stylistically illustrative pieces. A purchaser usually values an assurance, perhaps documented in an art or antiques journal, or given on the authority of a dealer or an auctioneer, that curators, exhibitors and other collectors will endorse an item's historical and aesthetic significance.

Often, market demand also responds to the rarity of art and antiques. The only-one-of-its-kind, or not-seen-at-auction-for-many-years appeal can be strong among buyers who value the unique, or who see an item as a rare example in a collection of works with complementary characteristics. Conversely, they may prefer the familiar to the esoteric, perhaps taking into consideration the 'fungibility' of a piece across borders, ie its attraction to bidders from different cultures. An item that attracts international collectors is more resistant to fluctuations in national economies, and could provide opportunities for arbitrage – trading on variations in prices that arise because of geographical shifts of currencies, taxes, duties and conditions of sale.

18.5.3 Quality and provenance

The consensus of expert opinion is that the buyer should be concerned with the features that establish a work's quality. Another important factor is its provenance, ie its origins and history. An investor who acquires a work (which he plans to hold for some years before disposing of it, possibly in an overseas market) will want to make sure in advance that its history is established beyond reasonable dispute, and that it is marketable.

When negotiating to buy an asset, the purchaser therefore needs to go further in his investigations than would be necessary merely to check that the vendor has a good title to the piece. The research into the history and previous ownership of the work should also indicate clearly the probability that it is a genuine item. A bill of sale which includes a full and authentic dossier of the purchase will be helpful, both for the purposes of an inventory of assets and an eventual disposal. Preferably, valuers of repute, who will be in a position at some time in the future to verify the statements made, will authenticate the dossier.

These precautions are advisable for several reasons. Basically, they provide the buyer with evidence that the vendor has a good title to the piece. Equally, the research is important because there are frauds and forgeries in the alternative investment market, as well as reproductions and 'restorations' that can be difficult to distinguish from the genuine article. Occasionally, the forgery may turn out to have a high value in its own right, but on the whole the investor needs to take due care that the work's authenticity has been verified. It is also important to bear in mind that certificates may be counterfeited.

An ancillary point worth noting is that specialist advisers to the Department for Culture, Media and Sport vet auction catalogues in the UK. They check to see which objects fall within the limited interest category, and which will require an export licence. The department also expects its officials to raise the alert over items that may have been looted.

(See also 18.3.1–18.3.3.)

18.5.4 Fakes and forgeries

Dealers and auction houses take steps to reduce the risk of forgery and mistaken identity. Some offer the buyer a five-year guarantee against forgery. Because the largest houses trade in volume and compete intensively for material, they can sometimes be unwitting conduits for fakes, particularly in ill-documented but now increasingly expensive areas of art. In sectors of the market where fakes are relatively common, some will inevitably turn up at auction; and, where the rewards can be measured in millions of pounds, fakes will proliferate.

Successful fakers may discredit sections of the market and even distort history, but it is sometimes the 'experts' more than the artists who are to blame. When anyone dares to pry into their secret world, they close ranks. Many did so when Tom Keating, Britain's most celebrated forger, faced criminal charges over a handful of his 2,000 or more fakes. The same pattern of events occurred when another trickster, Eric Hebborn, was accused of faking many drawings by Old Masters. Nothing is guaranteed; even the *Mona Lisa* may not be the original. Leonardo's masterpiece went missing from the Louvre for 11 months in 1911 after an audacious theft, and some people still claim that a copy was substituted for the real work. In 1985, the Getty Museum in California reputedly paid $7m (£4m) for a 6th century BC Greek statue, known as a Kouros, only to find that experts could not substantiate its provenance, and it was very likely a fake, possibly made by one of Rodin's assistants in Paris in about 1900. The handiwork of some well-known forgers has itself become sought after. A case in point is that of Keating, whose works have fetched up to £27,500 at auction. One buyer, however, paid £1,500 for an 'original' Keating only to find that it, and its certificate, were themselves fakes.

Nobody can say for sure how much of the art on the market has dubious origins or how many 'wrong' artworks find their way into salesrooms.

Some experts believe that half the items sold on the market may not be 'right'. Dealers, auctioneers and gallery curators admit privately that faking is on the increase. In the case of most paintings by Cézanne and Seurat, provenance is impeccable and there is no reason to believe they are fakes. Then again, hundreds of fake post-Impressionist works have been turned out over the years and an uncertain percentage of them are on the walls of leading galleries all over the world.

As Keating demonstrated, fakes are frequently first rate; several of his 'Samuel Palmers' are still regarded by some people as 'among Palmer's finest works'. In the Netherlands, the Rembrandt Research Project, set up 15 years ago to distinguish true Rembrandts from works produced by pupils and followers, had by 1994 reduced the Dutchman's *oeuvre* to less than half the previous total. Elmyr de Hory, an exuberant Hungarian, fooled the market for years with a profusion of faked Picassos, Matisses and Modiglianis and, at the time of his death, had no idea what had happened to a batch of skilfully forged Old Masters.

In recent years, money launderers have discovered that buying and selling fakes can double their profits. Colombian drug barons were the first, but now the Russian mafia has cornered the market in fake icons. This led to the murder of 30 icon dealers in 1999. Dealers have to cope with innumerable forgeries. Of course, the art world dislikes discussion of widespread fakery. A book on the subject (*Fakes, Forgers and the Art World*, published by Richard Cohen Books in 1995) met with the studied hostility of members of the art establishment. At the last moment, the publisher, on the advice of lawyers, halted publication, and a second company agreed to publish only after the author modified or omitted some specific allegations about people still in the business.

Who are the fakers? They are sometimes talented artists, consumed by the belief that their genius has gone unrecognised and are bent on revenge. Hebborn was born in Romford, Essex, in 1934. While a student in the 1950s he undertook work as a part-time restorer and discovered a gift for filling in missing bits of pictures in the style of the original artists. Later, after he studied works by the Dutch painter Willem van de Velde, he attempted a van de Velde of his own and signed it with the artist's name. He redrew his preparatory drawing on to an old canvas and prevented paint seeping into the age cracks by filling these with a jelly-like substance that resisted his paintbrush and would later dissolve in water. He took care not to use colours such as zinc white and Prussian blue that were not available in van de Velde's day, and the paints he did use were ground in a clearer oil than linseed and had a mixture of artificial resin added. He copied a signature from a photograph.

Hebborn remained unexposed until 1978, when a curator visiting the Pierpont Morgan Library in New York noticed something odd about a drawing of a boy, supposedly by Francesco del Cossa, the 15th century Italian artist. The ink lines had been scratched over with what appeared to have been a 20th century razor blade. A long investigation ensued and Hebborn's career as a forger was at an end, or so the establishment claimed. He had the satisfaction, however, of knowing that three sets of 'experts' had pronounced his del Cossa an original.

The way a scam unfolds is revealed in the example of de Hory, who worked closely with an unscrupulous couple, Fernand Legros and Réal Lessard, in the 1960s, passing off bogus Dufys, Dérains, Modiglianis, Vlamincks and Matisses. Their tactics, de Hory once revealed, were to secure expert opinions, if possible, from the artists' surviving relatives, for example Jeanne Modigliani and Alice Dérain, or to forge them. The fraudsters also paid impoverished collectors to certify that they had previously owned the pictures. Alternatively, they would put a painting in an auction and, if nobody bought it, they had only to pay the handling fee to reclaim it – a small price for the picture's appearance in a reputable catalogue as genuine.

One of the century's greatest forgers was Hans van Meegeren, a Dutchman who, throughout the 1930s and early 1940s, specialised in superbly crafted fakes of the 17th-century master Johannes Vermeer. He was generally successful (though less so than the dealers who profited from his activities), and stumbled only after it was suggested in 1945 that he had handed over a Vermeer, *The woman taken in adultery*, to Hermann Goering, an act of criminal collaboration. Van Meegeren retorted that he had knocked off the Vermeer himself and then sold it to Goering, thus hoodwinking the Nazi, and to prove this he produced *Jesus preaching in the temple*, without models and in the presence of six witnesses, to a standard that astounded the experts.

Fakers provide the artefacts, but dealers and valuers provide the market. Keating, who died in 1984 after a spectacular career, insisted that he had always been quite open about his forgeries. 'It was other people that weren't,' he said. After he was exposed in 1976 and under investigation by Scotland Yard's art fraud division, dealers and auctioneers became singularly reluctant to talk. The art market is built upon confidence: when trade is going well, business prospers, but a scandal can easily start a downward spiral. Keating's 'crude daubs', as he called them, made it more difficult for dealers to convince buyers of the value of a unique, original production of a famous mind. A few scribbles by a master are worth far more than a fine painting by an unknown artist or a forger. Faked art continues to find buyers, alongside and often indistinguishable from, the real thing. In 1977, Christie's sold a Fabergé egg in good faith for $250,000 as an imperial egg (one of only 57 in the world). Eight years later, the same auction house repudiated the attribution. Reportedly, Christie's paid about $5m to the buyer's estate in compensation and costs.

The recent rise in interest in children's art has also produced an increase in the number of forgeries on the market. This type of art is particularly vulnerable because many are simple line drawings (such as Winnie-the-Pooh originals for example) that are easy to copy. Additionally, it is not too difficult to acquire the paper that was commonly used at the time. By comparison, it would be nearly impossible to find the type of material on which the Old Masters were painted.

Most cases against fakers or their associates hinge on the intention to deceive, which has to be proved. Auctioneers will normally offer recompense for fakes only if the buyer can provide proof, usually within five years, and even then only if it can be demonstrated that the saleroom was not reflecting general opinion at the time, or that they could only have uncovered the truth by unreasonably expensive scientific means.

In 2000, the Vatican was at the centre of a suspected art fraud scandal. It was hazarded that works of art were being sold, using mock Vatican certificates of authenticity. These works of art included paintings said to be by Michelangelo, Guercino and Giambologna. They were found in the study of Michele Basso, the former head of Vatican Archives. It was suspected that this was part of a money laundering activity, in which the fakes were smuggled onto Vatican territory, authenticated and then resold.

Recently, *The Times* characterised a swindle that loss-adjusters might encounter two or three times a year. Briefly, the fraudster acquires a work, which closely resembles the style and artistic characteristics of a renowned painter. The next step is to secure an authentication of the painting as a true work by the named artist, and then to insure it for a large sum. The fraudster will then market the work as from a private collector, who urgently needs cash for personal reasons, so that an unwitting collector, who can see the painting in a bank vault, and its authentication and insurance details, might purchase a share of it for a substantial sum. The fraudster then decamps with the money.

18.5.5 Crime and punishing losses

The editor of the magazine *Trace* estimates that, every year, thefts of antiques and works of art amount to at least £500m. Apparently, thieves familiarise themselves with the antiques and arts market while serving sentences; police sources report that the *Antiques Roadshow* is the most popular television programme among prisoners. The value of recovered items put on show by the police goes up to more than £1m for a necklace, and large sums for pieces taken from stately homes. A membership survey carried out by the Association of Art and Antiques Dealers (LAPADA) in the UK revealed that '29 per cent of dealers had been burgled or stolen from'.

The thieves may become skilled at their nefarious trade. On 1 January 2000, a burglar broke into Oxford's Ashmolean museum and removed a £2m Cézanne oil, *Auvers-sur-Oise*. To avoid appearing on security cameras, he laid down a smoke screen, using a grenade and a hand-held fan. Such thefts may remove a work from public view or legitimate ownership for decades. In November 1999 a lost Cézanne, *Bouilloire et fruits*, resurfaced 21 years after a burglar stole it in 1978.

Some of the Metropolitan Police art and antique unit's cases are unusual and instructive. At the trial of John Drewe, details emerged of his ingenious scheme to sell forged paintings as genuine works. A forger, John Myatt, faked paintings by Roger Bissière, Marc Chagall, Nicolas de Stael, Jean Dubuffet, Alberto Giacometti, Henri Matisse, Ben Nicholson and Graham Sutherland. Drewe then falsified the archives in galleries and museums, on which dealers rely to verify the provenance of a work they intend buying. Drewe found private galleries that had gone out of business, doctored their records and meticulously forged old catalogues, using ink and paper of the period. He inserted the spurious records, with detailed references to faked paintings, into the gallery and museum archives, and substituted photographs of the forgeries for pictures of obscure, little-known pieces by famous artists. He used an old typewriter to create slips, identifying photographs of the forgeries as originals, which he pasted into the archives. He also forged a gallery stamp and used it on the back of documents.

The case prompted detailed scrutiny of documents that buttress claims. For example, appraisers focus on labels affixed to frames, which purport to chronicle a painting's itinerary from museum to gallery, to owner, to dealer, to saleroom. Letters, extracts from critics' reviews and curators' reports, invoices, receipts, insurances, bills of lading, customs declarations, all lend support to assertions that the work is genuine and is worth a large sum. Doubts can arise when the sources are critics and curators who are no longer alive, or auction houses and galleries that have gone out of business. Prudent dealers now carry out the type of investigation that merchant bankers, accountants and research specialists conduct when a client buys a company; today, many art experts launch a 'due diligence' enquiry.

Clearly, it is unwise to accept without checking that any provenance is *bona fide*. Of course, an error in the provenance does not prove that a painting is a forgery, but it is advisable to take care. The due diligence process usually means verifying original documents, contacting the experts and critics cited in the support materials and studying catalogues of an artist's work. To reduce the risk, collectors can also take advice from an art foundation that specialises in a named artist. For a fee of £250 or more, depending on the costs incurred in checking the work, an expert will supply a 'photo certificate', which includes a signed opinion and a photograph.

Fears about paintings with false provenance have affected sales. In some sectors, evidence of large-scale fraud and forgery has brought a market to a virtual stop, as happened, for example, with some Russian avant-garde art. Art historians disputed the origins of paintings sold at auction and, in December 1996, Sotheby's withdrew six Russian avant-garde paintings at short notice. A gulf between the opinions of Russian and Western experts is making it difficult to authenticate pictures that are in demand. The buyers affected are mainly rich Western collectors of works by such artists as Malevich, Rodchenko, Popova and Exter. Their works belong to experimental schools that sprang up during the turbulent years between 1905 and Lenin's death in the early 1920s. Fakes create a factious and fractious market. Given a lack of consensus on the authenticity of works, few large auction houses will now sell these controversial paintings.

The forgers and fraudsters of these Russian works rely on the muddled paper trails left by the artists, who lived through the dark days of the century's history. Stalin denounced experimentation in art as in music and literature, and artists died, or went to labour camps. Their works festered in musty storerooms, or vanished altogether.

Generally, the cognoscenti worry that fakes are widespread. In certain categories, some claim forgeries are almost as numerous as genuine articles. Many doubtful paintings, these experts believe, remain undetected in private collections and great museums. A recent book tells of a Yugoslav forger who allegedly 'sold a museumful of fakes to the Tito government'. Out of almost 4,000 items, the author believes, all but a few dozen are of disputable origins. Yet the collection is still open to the public in Zagreb. Even more spectacularly, according to this book, a Mexican fabricator has faked an entire phase of ancient Inca art, many of the artefacts being on show in American galleries.

In 2002, the stolen half of a painting by the expressionist artist Pechstein was recovered. The painting was part of a £2m haul taken from the Bruecke Museum. Other paintings were recovered but Pechstein's *Junges Mädchen (Young girl)* was found cut in two. A passer-by saw it by the side of the road outside Berlin. The painting is now being reconstructed. Stolen art works were also found in the boot of a car parked at a Spanish hotel. The works, including Goya's 1787 work *The swing*, thought to be worth £8m alone, were part of a haul of ten paintings estimated to be worth around £30m. Initially, thieves contacted the owner of the art and demanded a ransom of £1m, but were forced to admit defeat when police taped conversations pertaining to the disposal of the haul. *The fallen donkey*, another Goya stolen in the raid, also estimated to be worth £8m, is still missing.

18.5.6 Exporting art

An intending buyer of art or antiques should keep other precautions in mind. For the UK, the open general export licence (OGEL) covers all items more than 50 years old, if the value per article (or per set) is over £65,000. However, the threshold for some categories vary between nil and £180,000. Items with a value above the OGEL threshold will require a licence. Items exported from the EU are subject to European Community law. The threshold from the UK is £30,400 or €50,000.

Licence applications have to be accompanied by a black-and-white photographic copy of the item; and the decision whether to permit export will be influenced by independent advice. Where the item is regarded as part of the national heritage, the issue of a licence may be delayed or refused on the advice of experts in the field. The procedures may include reference to the DCMS's Arts and Libraries' Reviewing Committee on the Export of Works of Art, described at 18.3.1 and 18.3.2.

It is prudent to bear the requirement in mind when deciding to buy a work of art or an antique of exceptional interest. When these items come onto the open market, some foreign buyers may be deterred by the inconvenience and delays of up to seven months in the review procedure, and by the inherent risk that their offer will merely represent the buying-in price for a domestic museum. The absence of such foreign buyers could mean lower bids and less attractive gains when the time comes to dispose of the item.

18.5.7 National heritage bodies

The National Gallery
The National Museums of Scotland
The Ulster Museum
The National Trust for Places of Historic Interest or Natural Beauty
English Heritage (The Historic Buildings and Monuments Commission for England)
The Trustees of the National Heritage Memorial Fund
The Historic Churches Preservation Trust
Any local authority (including National Park authorities)
Any university or university college in the UK
Any museum or art gallery in the UK that exists wholly or mainly for the purpose of preserving for the public benefit a collection of scientific, historic or artistic interest and is maintained by a local authority or university in the UK
The British Museum

The National Museum of Wales

The National Art Collections Fund

The National Trust for Scotland for Places of Historic Interest or Natural Beauty

The Friends of the National Libraries

English Nature

Any government department (including the National Debt Commissioners)

Any library the main function of which is to serve the needs of teaching and research at a university in the UK

Any other similar national institution that exists wholly or mainly for that purpose and is approved for the purpose by the Commissioners of the Inland Revenue.

18.6 CHARACTERISTICS

18.6.1 Prospects of capital appreciation

Can private investors or trustees and fund managers with powers to buy fine art or antiques justify their purchase? Essentially the question is whether the capital appreciation over a period of, say, 10 years, 25 years or even longer will warrant the diversion of funds and the expenditure incurred in holding the asset.

Frequent reports in the press of record-breaking prices paid for pieces at auction may seem to support the case for alternative investment. In 1989, as the market approached a peak, some 10- and 20-year investments paid handsome dividends. The increasing number of investments that have provided significant capital appreciation short-term also represents an interesting trend that helps to endorse the advocates' case for buying arts and antiques.

The reports advise both private and institutional investors to buy the best examples that can be afforded, and to take expert advice from a reputable dealer or appraiser. They suggest that an artist's early work will in general be less valuable than later, more mature examples. Reasonably enough, they also point out that prices can fall, as happened with Georgian silver after a boom in the 1960s, with 19th century fine art in the mid-1970s, and with many categories of art and antiques in the early 1980s and the recent 1990s. However, even expert advice is fallible, particularly where attribution is concerned. A case in point is the work of Rembrandt, which has suffered the attentions of a Dutch government committee (see 18.5.4). The majority of works once attributed to him are now thought to be by his pupils. Works have lost up to 90% of their value, and the controversy has spawned a 'Save Rembrandt Society'.

18.6.2 Art as investment

One sector of the alternative investment market comprises investors who are nervous about the future. Some works are low in weight, small in size and high in value: they are portable, easily concealed and readily negotiable in markets around the world. Those who fear political, economic, social or tax repression in their own countries tend to regard alternative investments as a means of safeguarding their wealth.

Some market sectors, on occasion, seem to meet demanding investment criteria. Conversely, anecdotal evidence could make enthusiastic bidders at auctions pause. According to one press report, a battle tableau by Ernest Meissonier, a much-favoured painter of a century ago, sold in London in 1892 for £20,700; again in 1913 for £6,300; and again in 1964 for £4,340. Lazare reports that John Singer Sargent's oil sketch *San Virgilio* sold for £7,350 in 1925 and just £105 in 1952. A scholarly study of London auction transactions between 1952 and 1961 found that the average work appreciated just 0.5% a year, a poor return in anyone's passbook. More recently, a painting by Henry Fuseli, an 18th-century Swiss/British artist, bought by Rudolf Nureyev in 1988 for $1.16m, was sold in January 1995 for $761,500. In May 2003, Christie's put into auction a Degas bronze, *Petit danseuse de quatorze ans*. Just four years ago it was sold at Sotheby's for $12.4m. Despite the short interval, Christie's was confident that its rarity was sufficient to reach the estimate on resale of $8m–12m. It sold for $9.2m.

To set against these warning illustrations, there are some promising examples of the gains to be made. Paintings by the Scottish Colourists, S J Peploe, J D Fergusson, Frances Cadell and Leslie Hunter, have shown an average annual appreciation rate of 19% from 1975. Similarly, Renoir's *Tête de Femme* was sold for £1.35m in 1987 and exchanged hands again in 1988 for £1.98m (an appreciation of 35% in one year).

In the contemporary market, a photographic print by Roger Fenton, *The billiard room at Mentmore Towers* sold for £278,500 against a top estimate of just £20,000. It was acquired in 1979 for £1,760. That represents a 24.6% annual compound interest rate. In the same auction, Sotheby's sold an album of photographs of the 1936 Berlin Olympics by Leni Riefensthal for £51,100. The same album had been sold by Sotheby's in 1977 for £170, equivalent to a 28% per annum compound interest rate.

18.6.3 Costs of ownership

Typically, rates of return are only attractive if the owner is prepared to put a value on the pleasure of holding such artworks in his home or at his place of work. The investment may also be justified if the money used for the acquisitions would have been taxed at a high rate. Nevertheless, some items could have been a poor investment for the buyer, after taking into account payments to meet insurance premiums, dealers' or auctioneers' commissions, any liability to capital taxation or VAT, the interest foregone, and security and maintenance costs. The lack of income flows means that buyers of alternative investments are dependent on capital appreciation; yet they have to deduct the following costs from any gains they may achieve:

(1) costs of acquisition and disposal, including premiums and dealers' commissions;
(2) holding costs (insurance, storage, etc);
(3) valuation and provenance research fees incurred;
(4) revenue and possible tax benefits foregone by tying up capital in the asset;
(5) the value of time spent dreaming about the market and, increasingly, the advice of market experts or consultants;
(6) CGT payable on realisation of the asset, or IHT payable on its transfer.

Substantial gains are necessary to justify such an investment in financial terms; or, alternatively, the investor has to be convinced that the assets acquired can be relied upon to sustain their worth in times when traditional investments fail. Figure 18.1 shows how much an investment of £1,000 must grow to produce the equivalent of 8% compound between 1997 and 2007. The interest rate represents an inflation rate of 3%, and a target annual return of 5%. In other words, the painting bought at auction for £1,000 net in 1997 should fetch a net sum of £2,159 in 2007 to match these targets.

Many great works of art were lost in the 11 September tragedy, including sculptures and drawings by August Rodin and a tapestry by Joan Miró. Some experts have predicted that the losses will amount to $100m. Many owners are unlikely to recover the full value of their losses, as a collection would often be insured at approximately half its value. The risk of losing the entire collection in one fell swoop would be deemed as minimal. In the context of the tragedy, the insurance industry is re-assessing the way it rates its exposure to such risks. The outcome is likely to be higher premiums.

18.6.4 The Chester Beatty collection: a precedent

In 1991, 13 paintings from the collection of the late Sir Alfred Chester Beatty were offered at auction. They included works by Toulouse-Lautrec, Degas, Renoir and Chagall. The trustees had previously considered donating van Gogh's *Sunflowers* to the nation: instead they sold at auction for

Figure 18.1 Increase in values required equivalent to 8% compound per annum

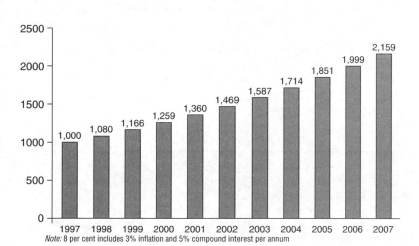

Note: 8 per cent includes 3% inflation and 5% compound interest per annum

£24.75m. Had they donated it, the family would have received £5.5m under the Government's acceptance in lieu scheme. That returns a quarter of the tax deducted as an incentive to donate works of art to the nation.

The sale at auction was subject to combined IHT and CGT. The CGT of £3.07m was calculated as 30% of the difference between the valuation and the sale price at auction. The IHT was levied at a variable rate (between 65% and 80%) because the painting had been exempted at the time of an earlier death in the family. Otherwise the rate would have been 60%. At the 80% rate, the balance left for the family would be £3m–3.5m, probably not enough to settle the full tax on the estate.

18.6.5 Buying at auction

Sales to meet tax bills provide auction houses with a flow of works to offer. Many people who like the idea of buying at a sale worry that they will find it difficult to conform to usual practice, that a sudden twitch will leave them with an unexpected heirloom and an unwelcome bill. The pace can be fast, the enthusiasm contagious, and bidding strategy complex. The amount paid is also likely to include extras, for example a buyer's premium and VAT on the auction house's services.

In reality, the buying process often begins a month or more before the sale date. Catalogues appear and can be bought on subscription, by order

Table 18.3 Increase in values to match compound rates of 5% (inflation); 10% (rise in art markets)

Year	Inflation 5% €	Art 10% €
2000	10,000	10,000
2005	12,763	16,105
2010	16,289	25,937
2015	20,789	41,772
2020	26,533	67,275
2025	33,864	108,347

or at the auctioneer's offices. The descriptions of items have various nuances; for example only information printed in bold type may be guaranteed. There will be an estimated price range, but no disclosure of the secret minimum bid acceptable to the vendor, the 'reserve'. Critics ask, 'Is this secrecy necessary?' Should the buyer be told whether he is bidding against an actual rival or the consignor's reserve? Auctioneers argue that the confidential reserve is a defence against the collusion of 'auction rings'. It is only worth organising a ring when the participants know that the reserve is low enough to ensure a good profit.

Before the sale, lots are commonly catalogued and exhibited. In catalogues, it is common to use famous names to denote works by unidentified painters as 'in the style' of the particular artist(s). Therefore, not all the paintings shown in an auction catalogue under the name 'Manet' will be by that painter. Lots are generally sold 'as seen', so it is as important to know the subtle distinctions employed by the specialists in auction houses to indicate the provenance of a work as it is to study the condition of paintings in advance.

Before bidding at many auctions, it is necessary to register – ie to give name, address and bank reference. A 'client card' for previous registrants can speed the process. At the auction, the registrant may take a pre-reserved seat and a bidding number. It is, in practice, virtually impossible to bid by accident. Just when to start bidding is a matter of strategy. Some buyers come in early and raise quickly to deter competitors; others wait to avoid inciting other bidders with their keenness. Care is advisable when the bidding pace seems unusually fast, or the auctioneer does not indicate the source of the bid. Often he will say 'on the left' or 'the bid is with me' or some similar words that convey the origin and authenticity of the bid. Payment may be cash, approved cheque or, in some cases, by credit card.

18.6.6 Independent sources of information

Research pays off before buying at auction or through a dealer. An independent source of information on the prices of paintings sold at auction is the Art Sales Index. This lists the results of auctions for about 60,000 items each year that were sold for £500 or more. Using this source, an analysis has been made of transactions for a representative selection of 20th-century Modern masters. The analysis showed a compound rate of appreciation in excess of 14% per annum between 1971 and 1991. Such rates of growth have made it easier to argue the case for the allocation of funds to alternative investments.

The growth of interest that has already taken place has prompted the development of improved sources of information on available media, prices and the advantages and limitations of particular types of investment. There are already computerised databases providing information to help determine sound investments. 'Artquest', provided by the Art Sales Index, holds details on paintings, drawings and sculptures that have been sold at public auction around the world. Another database is the 'Thesaurus of Fine Art Information'. This allows dealers, collectors and museums who subscribe to it to search through details of forthcoming auction sales, for any category of antique or collectable of interest. The gradual evolution of a more or less formal infrastructure of information sources in the alternative sector of the investment market will add to the understanding of the opportunities and prospects.

These sources and others show when the average annual appreciation over the past 40 years has outstripped the rate of inflation, although there has been considerable volatility from artist to artist and from sale to sale.

18.7 TAXATION

18.7.1 Tax planning

To attain positive returns, investors should plan to avoid unnecessary tax liabilities. For example, if an investor in the UK eventually wishes to contend that isolated purchases are for the purpose of building up assets as long-term investments, then it is mandatory to record the acquisition of chargeable assets in his tax returns. This step would help to support a claim that capital gains tax (CGT), not income tax, should be the basis for calculating any future liabilities when, despite the parity of the rates of tax, there are advantages in doing so for the individual taxpayer.

The private investor may also face claims by the Inland Revenue that purchases and sales of alternative investments are 'adventures in the nature of a trade'. This would lead to an income tax liability if the investor has been carrying on the trade on his own account, or to a corporation tax liability if he has set up a company for the purpose.

An individual who contributes to a cultural institution can claim the expense as a charitable donation. The Chancellor, in his Spring 2000 Budget, announced changes that allow individual taxpayers to offset such donations against taxable income.

Subsequently, in his Budget of Spring 2004, the Chancellor clarified the income tax charge applied to those who have given away an asset but make use of it free of charge. Intended to be a device to stop people giving away their homes to save inheritance tax, the early indications are that the tax charge could have a wider effect on gifts of other assets including works of art and antiques. As well as gifts, sales of assets to connected parties are to be caught and gifts of cash will be traced so it seems that many gifts could be caught. Without amelioration, the proposals are potentially retrospective in their effect. There will be a little time in which to sort out family arrangements, as the new tax charge is not planned to start until 6 April 2005.

18.7.2 Capital gains

Alternative investments are subject to the general law on CGT, although there are special exemptions. In broad terms, the amount of the chargeable gain is the difference between the asset's cost and the sale proceeds, less an adjustment for the inflationary element of the gain accruing since March 1982. For any asset held on 31 March 1982, it is possible to base the cost of acquisition at its market value on that date. There is, however, no charge on unrealised gains from assets held by an individual at his death.

Special considerations apply in the case of works of art and other alternative investments. Thus, a gain accruing on the disposal of an asset that does not exceed £6,000 (from 6 April 1995) is generally exempt from CGT with marginal relief (see Capital Gains Tax Act 1979, s 128). In this connection the exemption on articles that provide a gain of not more than £6,000 (eg individual pieces of antique silver) would become relevant.

Exemptions also arise for individual objects of artistic, historic or scientific interest (and collections of such objects) that are accepted by the tax authorities as forming 'an integral and major part of the cultural life of this country'. These are often referred to as 'national heritage property'. Under the douceur arrangements (see 18.7.4), gifts of such alternative investments to national heritage bodies (and gifts of these alternative investments to charities) are not charged to CGT. In the case of sales, the notional CGT liability is one of the factors relevant in calculating the sale price that can be negotiated. There is a similar exemption applying to gifts of qualifying heritage property made for the public benefit.

Where national heritage property (accepted as such by the Revenue Commissioners) is transferred by way of gift from one individual to another, or where such property is transferred into or out of settlement, the transfer will be treated for CGT purposes as giving rise to neither a gain nor a loss, provided that appropriate undertakings are given with regard to location, preservation and access. This means that any gain is carried forward, and will be chargeable when the donee disposes of the property in a manner that does not qualify for conditional exemption.

18.7.3 IHT and estate duty

Under the Finance Act 1986, inheritance tax (IHT) replaced capital transfer tax with effect from 18 March 1986. It applies to gratuitous transfers by individuals. The main difference between capital transfer tax and IHT is the treatment of lifetime transfers. Outright transfers between individuals are exempt if the transferor lives on for seven years. Gifts made within seven years of death are charged at death rates, but the charge is tapered where the gift occurs more than three years before death.

The Inland Revenue estimates that it dealt with about 23,500 taxpaying death estates in 2000–01 (about 4% of all deaths), compared with 21,000 in 1999–2000. The contribution to public finances from IHT in 2000–01 was about £2.25bn. The charge on death is retained within IHT, as are most of the exemptions and relief available under capital transfer tax, including transfers between spouses domiciled in the UK. Trust-related transfers remain subject to the full range of charges at the time the transfers are made. The cumulation period for all chargeable transfers has been reduced to seven years, and the threshold below which tax is not chargeable is £223,000 (from 6 April 1998). A flat rate of 40% replaced the former four-rate system.

Estate duty applies to property inherited before 13 March 1975. This may still be relevant to the sale of objects that have been previously exempted from estate duty. Estate duty will not be charged if exempted objects are sold by private treaty to a national heritage body or have again been transferred on a death and have been conditionally exempt on that occasion. Special rules apply when property that has previously been exempted is sold after 6 April 1976. The way in which this property is taxed depends on what had happened since the original exemption was granted – either capital transfer tax, IHT or estate duty only may be payable. This is a complex issue and is dealt with fully in Appendix III (p 46) of *Capital Taxation* and the *National Heritage* (see bibliography at the end of Chapter 19).

18.7.4 Tax liabilities in practice

The Treasury has become more flexible about the art it will accept in the form of heritage sales to museums as a means of saving tax. When IHT is due on an estate, the acceptance in lieu (AIL) procedure may allow owners who are liable to pay the tax instead to offer objects to the Commissioners to satisfy the tax owed, in whole or in part.

On receiving a suitable offer, the Revenue's Capital Taxes Office (CTO) refers it to the Acceptance in Lieu panel at Re:source, the Council for Museums, Archives and Libraries. After the panel has taken opinions from independent experts, it advises the Secretary of State whether the property offered is suitable for acceptance in lieu. Qualifying property under these procedures includes pictures, books, prints, archives, manuscripts, works of art, furniture, craft objects, historic objects and scientific objects. A case in point arose in March 1999, when the Treasury accepted Van Dyck's masterpiece *Portrait of Cesare Allesandro Scaglia* in lieu of IHT, thus ensuring that it stayed in the UK.

Once an item is deemed suitable for the scheme, the Revenue calculates the tax by a reduction of 25% of this charge (known as the "douceur" or sweetener) of the normal IHT liability. This arrangement allows the vendor to offer an item to the nation, and to satisfy all tax liabilities on the estate. For example, if an artwork's market value is estimated at £1m, the normal IHT liability would be £400,000. The net market value would therefore be £600,000. The douceur, at 25% of the normal tax liability, would be £100,000, and the tax settlement value would be £700,000. Accordingly, the vendor can make more savings on his tax bill than if he sold it on the open market.

However, a recent AIL review recommended that the Revenue increase the rate of the douceur to 50% in those cases where a 40% tax rate is applicable. In this way, museums can often buy chattels for perhaps 70% of their full value. The problem is that museum purchasing grants have been more or less frozen for some years, and the National Heritage Fund and the National Art Collections Fund have limited resources.

The Revenue Commissioners exercise their powers under the National Heritage Act 1980, the Inheritance Tax Act 1984 and supplementary Finance Acts. As indicated above, they may accept certain property, in whole or part, in lieu of IHT (and its predecessors, estate duty and capital transfer tax), and of liability to pay interest on these taxes. Objects can only be set against IHT, and not against CGT. The Secretary of State for Culture, Media and Sport has first to agree that the property is 'preeminently of national, artistic, historic or scientific interest, or has important historical associations, taking account of its valuation and condition and the benefits of adding it to a national, local authority, or university collection'. However, the standard that has to be applied has changed. Since 1998, the same criteria now apply to chattels – they must be of museum quality and must be 'pre-eminent for their national, scientific, historic or artistic interest'.

The Culture Secretary also has the power to direct the placing of this property, and can permit accepted items to remain in situ if they are so closely connected with a building or context. The Royal Commission on Historical Manuscripts advises on the location of records, archives and manuscripts. Chattels accepted in lieu therefore belong to local museums, galleries or public libraries, and are effectively lent back to the original owner. In situ offers must provide for public access, and the public has a right to see these items. In March 1998, the Secretary of State announced measures to strengthen and extend public access to these assets. All objects should be made available to the public, without the prior appointment previously required. Owners are also obliged to 'publicise their undertakings, and disclose any other information relevant to the public access'.

In 2002 a pair of antique armchairs valued at almost £1m went on display at a Scottish Museum after being accepted by the Government in lieu of IHT. *The Dundas chairs*, made in giltwood in 1765, are from the most expensive set of furniture commissioned from Thomas Chippendale. The Acceptance in Lieu of Tax scheme helps to keep items of national importance within the country. *The birth of Venus*, an important surrealist painting by the Scottish artist Edward Baird, also went on display at the Scottish National Gallery of Modern Art after it was accepted to cover a liability to pay IHT. In the financial year ending April 2004, owners offering items instead of paying inheritance tax saved for the nation artistic and cultural works worth £12.7m.

Under the old arrangements, the Secretary of State would reimburse the Commissioners for the tax forgone. In its accounting, the Revenue would treat this payment as tax due. From July 1985, the DCMS and the Revenue could draw sums from the reserves to cover the cost of large, important items. However, in the spring 1998 Budget, the Chancellor announced new arrangements whereby the Revenue now accepts property in lieu of taxes without seeking reimbursement from the Secretary of State. The Secretary of State does have to report to the Chief Secretary to the Treasury when offers are expected to be in excess of £10m in any single year, or if one offer is likely to exceed £1m. (See also 18.7.3.)

18.7.5 VAT

Works of art and antiques bought second-hand come within the framework of the EU and the UK's VAT regime. Briefly, most lots at auction do not carry a liability to pay VAT on the hammer price, although auctioneers have to charge VAT at the prevailing rate (17.5%) on the 15% buyer's premium that they generally levy.

Since July 1999, special arrangements have applied to imports of older works of art, of works created after April 1973, and to limited editions of certain items. The VAT rate on these imports is 5%. As defined for VAT purposes, a 'work of art' typically means:

(1) a picture, collage or similar decorative plaque, painting or drawing (mounted or unmounted), executed entirely by the artist's hand;
(2) an original engraving, print or lithograph produced in limited numbers from a plate executed entirely by the artist's hand;
(3) an original sculpture or statuary in any material, executed entirely by the artist;
(4) a tapestry or wall textile made by hand from original designs in limited numbers (not more than eight copies);
(5) a ceramic executed entirely by the artist and signed by him, as single items or in limited editions (not forming part of an article of jewellery);
(6) an enamel on copper, executed entirely by hand, limited to eight numbered copies, bearing the signature of the artist or studio;
(7) a photograph taken by the artist, printed by him, or under his supervision, signed and numbered, and limited to 30 copies.

By definition, antiques are as objects, other than works of art or collectors' items that are more than 100 years old.

When works of art or antiques are imported, or are either imported or acquired within the EU from the creators or their heirs, several options are available. These include the use of 'margin' schemes, the 'auctioneers' scheme', or the import or reselling of the item under the normal VAT rules. Table 18.4 illustrates the practical implications of sales within and outside the margin scheme.

Customs & Excise gives extensive details of margin schemes and the auctioneers' scheme and their implementation in Notice 718, including an update issued in March 2000. Notice 701 explains the VAT arrangements that apply when a stately home owner sells a work of art or an antique. The Revenue Commissions' Notice 1844 covers the arrangements for the temporary import of works of art and antiques without payment of import charges (customs duties and VAT). VAT leaflet 701/36 offers guidance on the treatment of insurances paid on works of art and antiques.

(See also 18.3.2.)

Stamp duty is normally payable only when the transfer is of an interest in an alternative investment, and not when it is the work itself that is being

Table 18.4

Step	Within margin scheme £	Outside margin scheme £
Value for VAT at import	3,000	3,000
Import VAT @ 5%	150	150
Purchase price for margin scheme	3,150	
Selling price	4,000	4,000
Output tax due		700
Total selling price		4,700
Margin	850	
Output tax due/net VAT liability	127	550

transferred, since chattels are transferable by delivery and no document is required to effect a transfer of the interest.

18.7.6 PAYE and national insurance

Regulations are in force to prevent employers avoiding PAYE and national insurance payments by remunerating their staff in kind. These regulations cover gifts of precious metals, fine wines, diamonds and other assets for which 'trading arrangements' exist that enable employees to swap assets, often for cash.

18.8 MECHANICS

18.8.1 Suitability

Research on individuals' investment preferences indicates that works of fine art and antiques, perhaps not unexpectedly, only begin to figure to a significant extent in the portfolios of the wealthy. Initially, investors concentrate on property, building society investments, insurances, unit trusts or investment bonds, and possibly equity investments or gilts or National Savings certificates. The more esoteric investments tend to be bought when extra capital is available. Neither individuals nor pension funds have so far engaged in the purchase of alternative investments as a routine policy, although the British Rail Pension Fund was, at one time, an exception; it invested approximately £40m in 2,400 works of art, but the trustees and managers subsequently decided not to make any more purchases in this market.

In November 1988 the BR Pension Fund disposed of 31 museum-worthy pieces of silver for £2m, having paid £400,000 for them ten years previously. In 1989, it sold paintings and sculptures, including works by Manet, Renoir, Monet, Picasso, van Gogh and Cézanne. Altogether, the items put on sale realised £38.5m, leaving the pensioners with more than £30m after paying all expenses and commissions. In 1990, the fund sold its collection of 19th century continental 'European art' and Victorian paintings for £6m compared with its mid-1970s purchase price of £1.2m. One of a batch of 16 Old Masters, which were sold at Sotheby's in December 1994, went for £3.4m, compared with a purchase price of about £150,000. The fund has seen a 14.3% annual cash rate return and a 6.7% real rate of return, but later sales have generated lower returns. (See also 18.3.2.)

In 2003, Vivendi Universal instructed Christie's to sell the art collection owned by Seagram. The first disposal is a canvas by Miró, estimated at $400,000–600,000. This disposal is a further indication that corporate art buying continues to decline. Among other corporate sales was a sculpture by Claes Oldenburg from the collapsed energy group Enron. It fetched $405,000, $170,000 less than its cost two years earlier.

In general, pension fund investment managers see a problem in the marketability of such assets. It is not easy to convert alternative investments into cash at short notice without sustaining losses. In addition, pension fund trustees and investment advisers are cautious about committing themselves to a line of action that might be criticised in the future. They say that it is difficult to obtain accurate valuations regularly and, even when valuers can supply a dependable service, there are few reliable and independent indices against which to compare a portfolio's performance, as fund managers can with equities.

Yet the infrastructure for making alternative investments is being established, and in the course of the next few years there may be improvements in the information sources and indices available to investors and trustees. A well-publicised example is the service provided by London-based art investment managers Poensgen Sokolow. It produces the quarterly Art Market Analysis, and offers portfolios of important works with starting prices of about £10m. The improvement of the information facilities and the build-up of reputable sources of impartial market intelligence might eventually help to make such alternative investments attractive, both for individuals and for investment managers with responsibilities for closed funds, for example small self-administered pension schemes.

18.8.2 Sources of information

Sources of information and intelligence are diverse and scattered. There are, in each of the areas of alternative investment, several specialist journals. In addition, various societies or clubs give the collector access to specialist knowledge. Auctioneers produce useful catalogues that highlight pieces coming on to the market, and those interested can find out about the prices paid at these sales.

The specialist journals and some of the directories produced by associations of dealers and auctioneers identify the areas in which particular firms are knowledgeable. The dealers will usually charge high commissions to cover their costs of holding expensive assets for periods, which can sometimes be extensive, before a buyer emerges. On the whole, auction sales are a source of more competitively priced items, although many of the leading London firms now charge a commission to both vendors and buyers.

It is, however, becoming more difficult for the private collector to keep pace with developments in his chosen fields of alternative investment. Although London remains an important centre of trading activity in art and antiques, nowadays many important sales take place outside the UK, which has become a net exporter of such pieces. In earlier times, collectors could rely on a steady flow of fine works.

One development that is undoubtedly helping in the dissemination of information is the World-Wide Web, which gives access to art, artists and museums worldwide. Art and the internet might seem strange companions: while art is traditionally considered material culture – paintings, sculpture, etc – the Web is the realm of the immaterial, the virtual, and the unreal. But recently there have been exciting artistic developments. Websites featuring gallery tours, excellent computer art reproductions and links to artists are appearing daily. However, this new approach is unlikely to signal the end of art, as everyone knows it. Museums will not permanently shut down, and real art will not go out of style. With the invention of photography around 160 years ago, some visionaries insisted it was the end of painting. Events proved them wrong. Similarly, the World-Wide Web is unlikely to bring 'real' art to its knees. Most of the websites emphasise that they do not replace art, but rather enhance the enjoyment and understanding of it. Frequent 'surfers' of the internet will be aware of art-related websites. For the uninitiated, the internet can be a threatening place, and it may seem easier to pick up a book than to fight a path through the Web. But many of the really interesting websites have material not available in books.

For anyone online who wants to find out what art resources are available, the easiest approach is a keyword search tailored to a specific medium, artist or museum. However, such searches often produce lists of possibilities too copious to follow at one sitting. Does one want to visit the Louvre or the Metropolitan Museum of Art or the Smithsonian? It is all possible, that is in a virtual sense. At www.metmuseum.org, the surfer can take a tour of the Metropolitan's collection, with computer reproductions of its famous artworks. The Web user can also discover the museum's plans, sign up for membership and shop in the museum shop. Most museums with rich endowments have websites like this.

Websites are advantageous to museums for a number of reasons. First, they are useful advertisements. Viewers can see many of the works in the museum's collection, even if the works are in storage. Also, more sensitive objects such as drawings and textiles are often hidden away for years for preservation purposes. Through the Web, visitors can see them without risking damage to the works. Not all websites correspond to actual museums. Some online services maintain only virtual collections of art.

There is a plethora of online resources on the arts. To avoid the intimidation of the sheer abundance available one should start slowly, perhaps by taking a leisurely tour of a favourite museum or completing a keyword search of a popular artist. Then an enquirer can roam around. Another approach is to use CD-ROMs of art directories, featuring artworks and artist information. These services are regularly updated, and available on subscription.

18.8.3 Advisers

Collectors in the British art market have the services of many thousands of dealers and several hundred auctioneers who in total have about 35,000 employees. Their transactions account for more than half of Europe's trade in works of art, which the European Fine Art Foundation estimates is growing in value at about 6% a year. Lately, the established London firms have experienced competition in specialised fields from provincial dealers and auctioneers. To keep abreast of news and intelligence on alternative investments today requires many contacts and information sources. In this context, it is important to locate one or two specialists among the dealers and in the auction houses who can be relied upon to assist the dedicated and wealthy enthusiast.

To a degree, investors seeking advice on specific pieces can depend on appropriate museums or art galleries, where curators are normally willing to give an opinion on the quality and authenticity of a work. Museum experts are also likely to be familiar with the market and with dealers who specialise in a sector, although they are usually reluctant to recommend a particular firm. However, curators do not normally give opinions on market values.

Leading auctioneers are more willing to express a view on the price a piece might command if offered for sale, and specialist dealers will have opinions on the value of an item in their field of expertise. Such valuations are important if the investor plans to make a sale; they will help him to arrive at a sensible reserve figure.

Dealers and auctioneers are generally keen to offer help, in particular to itemise and appraise assets. At the outset, their valuers advise on insurance cover and the security of precious items, pending sale. They then prepare a full inventory of the chattels, identify those that are of value, and make arrangements for the disposal of the residue. Any gifts or bequests will also be valued for IHT purposes, and recommendations will be made on the handling of any works that have national or historic interest. The experienced auctioneer or dealer will advise on how best to sell items for disposal.

Given that the market for art and antiques has become international, it is important to choose with care a time and a place when specialist collectors are likely to be at a sale. The valuer will charge a fee, and the auctioneer or dealer will be thinking of a commission on sales.

Before confirming instructions for an inventory and appraisal, it is advisable to discuss the eventual consignment contract for an estate, which may include important pieces. Some firms in the art and antiques market refund part of their valuation fee if any of the items they appraise are sold through their auction or dealing rooms within a year or so of the appraisal. There may also be opportunities to negotiate lower commission rates on sales. Within the trade, auctioneers and dealers are often prepared to cut their selling commission from 10% to 6%, with scope for reductions in standard rates when the estate is large and valuable.

A further point to bear in mind when negotiating commission rates is the possibility that an item at auction may not reach the reserve price suggested by the valuer. In some instances, the auctioneer may be willing to make no charge to the vendor, or levy a reduced commission, if a lot fails to sell at the reserve that the firm has recommended. Auctioneering and dealing in art and antiques are highly competitive businesses, and many firms are willing to consider special terms when an estate contains worthwhile items.

For buyers who use dealers' services, there are often the attractions of 'buy-back' offers. These usually have many caveats attached to them. Dealers may undertake to buy back at a price geared to their valuation at the time of the repurchase; or they may only be willing to commit themselves to buy back at the original price paid by the investor. Almost no dealer is willing to purchase at the original price plus inflation since the date of the transaction; if any do make such an offer, the buyer might well consider it prudent to make such checks as he can that the firm is likely to be still in business at a future date when a resale might be contemplated.

Professionals who advise on alternative investment can also help when it comes to reviewing a portfolio. To offer sound advice, they should be in close touch with the market trends so that they can recommend optimum times for the disposal of pieces that have reached a current peak in value. Equally, they should be well placed to identify pieces coming onto the market that would make a collection more representative and therefore more valuable in terms of the chosen theme.

Other relevant skills relate to the installation, placement and maintenance of a purchase. The well-qualified adviser should perhaps have a background in art history, maybe curatorial know-how, an intimate knowledge of the art market and up-to-date familiarity with trends in prices and values. A good understanding of handling, shipping, conservation, restoration, insurance and security matters can also be of practical benefit.

18.8.4 Commercial galleries

New collectors may not necessarily understand the more recondite points of aesthetics when collecting art, but they are often keenly aware of the financial implications. They are also conscious of the social benefits of being a part of the collecting 'realm' and the prestige of owning museum-calibre works. In this context, one US dealer offers a useful checklist for those entering the art market for the first time:

(1) Use the expertise of dealer-owned galleries, which represent the artists they exhibit. Ask for biographical materials on the artists. Seek advice from individuals in the art industry.

(2) Let the dealer know which artists are of interest, so that he can send details of exhibits and new works. Probably, the collector will then have early and first-hand information, and a place on a special list for private previews.

(3) Galleries do not always display their entire inventory. It is worth asking to see the 'back rooms', and putting questions to knowledgeable staff.

(4) Dealers seldom give a 'collector's discount' to occasional buyers. However, in big centres it is not uncommon for dealers to offer perhaps 10% discounts. Most works are marked up substantially to allow for price negotiations.

(5) Whenever possible, view a one-person exhibition to see several pieces of an artist's work. This should reveal the depth of an artist's vision and quality of his work.

(6) Take time and advice when making a purchase. Most dealers will hold an item for 24 hours or longer, or offer first refusal.

Commercial galleries normally put on three kinds of exhibition: one-person shows, theme shows and exhibitions from stock. Galleries tend to show from stock at the quieter times of year. From the exhibitor's standpoint, the one-person or theme show is the best way to achieve the preferred effect: they allow the gallery to suggest the cultural significance of an artist's work. A few galleries can put on first-class exhibitions from stock because their backroom holdings are strong. They are able to mount exhibitions of acknowledged masters, or works that can reasonably be described as 'museum quality'.

Some of the galleries and dealers are promoting art and antiques as alternative investments, because they believe there are worthwhile opportunities to create and manage portfolios. They contend that the investor can specialise in one or two categories of investment but still spread the risks by diversifying the selection within these categories. In addition, they suggest that it is possible to use market intelligence and research to time purchases and sales to maximum advantage and to build up interest among potential bidders.

18.9 MAINTENANCE

18.9.1 Safeguarding the investment

A prime consideration ought to be security. Robbery, accidental damage, fires, floods and other catastrophes remove many works from the market each year, usually forever. Computer systems are being introduced to log details of missing works, for example the Art Loss Register and the New York-based International Foundation for Art Research. Their aim is to deter robbers by making details of stolen works quickly available to auction houses, dealers and collectors.

The immediate conclusion is that a purchase needs secure storage. For economic reasons, a bank vault may be appropriate when items are not continuously on display. Even when the items are bulky, the cost of hiring vault space will be far lower than the valuation and subsequent insurance premiums for pieces held in less secure places. In other cases, the collector should insured their assets against all risks, and the items in a collection should be revalued at five-yearly intervals, or more frequently, to ensure that the insurance cover is adequate.

18.9.2 Insurance

Brokers and insurers who carry out these valuations with the aid of expert dealers or auctioneers will at the same time advise on cost-effective outlays on security measures, ie expenditures that will bring more than just compensating savings in premiums. The valuers will, in particular cases, photograph pieces in a collection to provide a record in case of damage or loss.

Note that the London head offices of insurers charge travelling and subsistence expenses, so it is usually sensible to contact the nearest regional office. However, if the item is a specialised work of art, a prudent course is to consult fine art brokers. They may advise that it is unnecessary to insure well-known items against theft, giving substantial savings in premiums, arguing that any subsequent disposal by the thief in the art market would lead to his capture. For example, in 1994, the gang that removed, in 50 seconds, one of Norway's greatest icons, Edvard Munch's painting, *The scream*, from Oslo's National Gallery, were captured when they tried to sell it to members of the Metropolitan Police's art and antiques unit, who masqueraded as unscrupulous dealers.

By and large, burglars usually avoid stealing such items unless they already have a buyer or can realise the value of precious metal or gemstones from which an antique is made. Most thefts of antiques are opportunistic and involve works of art valued at less than £1,000. Some involve careful planning, especially when the thieves believe they can assuredly convert antiques into cash. A collector may also wish to put his art or antiques on show. This can present problems: as values rise, it can be difficult to insure valuable exhibits. When the Metropolitan Museum of Art set up its exhibition, *Van Gogh at Arles*, in the early 1980s, the paintings had a global value for insurance of about £1bn; today it would be £5bn, and the show could never be considered. In the wake of the May 1990 sales, every van Gogh owner wants to believe his painting is worth £50m and will not let it off the wall if insured for less. Even then, the problem is compounded by enthusiastic dealers or auctioneers: when consulted on insurance values, they may be tempted to set the maximum imaginable price on a painting to maintain the image of its market value and tempt the owner to sell.

18.9.3 Security

One security measure often overlooked is to preserve confidentiality when buying an alternative investment. News of purchases attracts those inclined to steal, a problem also faced by owners who have to allow access to the public to gain tax exemptions. (See generally 18.7.)

In addition to tighter security, it is important with some works of art and antiques to consider the 'ambient' conditions in which a piece is to be displayed. Adverse lighting, for example, can cause a valuable watercolour to fade, and many items of antique furniture and musical instruments need a suitably humidified atmosphere to survive without deterioration.

Normally, specialists in the field will advise on the best methods of preserving the qualities of a piece. They are also a useful source of information on firms that carry out restoration and repair work to appropriate standards, and on removal firms that have a good record of handling delicate and valuable pieces with due care.

Recovery of stolen works is being helped by improved information sources. The Art Loss Register (www.artloss.com) and *Trace* magazine (www.trace.co.uk) are reinforcing the authorities' efforts to track down lost and purloined items. The Invaluable group (www.invaluable.com) also offers computerised screening for items registered as stolen against pre-sale catalogues. The registry is useful for dealers. Artscope International and police intelligence hotlines improve the chances of tracing the loot from theft and burglary. (See also 18.5.5.)

18.10 PREVIEW OF THE YEAR AHEAD

Artprice, one of the leaders in art market information, lists 21m auction prices and indices covering more than 306,000 artists collected from 2,900 international auction houses. According to the service's figures, the beginning of the 21st century failed to bring a new dawn for the art market. Dealers and auctioneers admitted that business was not good, but a survey of company accounts showed just how difficult times have been for many of these enterprises. The Business Ratio *Report on antiques and fine art dealers and auctioneers* (Prospect Swetenhams) analyses accounts filed by 102 leading British auctioneers and art and antiques dealers between 2000 and 2003. The tables make gloomy reading. Average sales dropped by a fifth and pre-tax profits plummeted by almost half. Even Richard Green, Britain's biggest art dealer by some distance, was not immune to the market's difficulties. Sales by his two companies dropped from £91m in the year ending July 2002 to £53.5m in the following 12 months. A few companies defied the downward trend, notably Mallett, which increased sales from £17.1m to £25.3m in the last two years covered by the report, and Daniel Katz, whose business rose to £12m.

Galleries and auction houses are suffering, mainly because of reluctant buyers and increasing competition from the internet. In the market's lower price echelons, eBay, the auction website, offers a vast variety of goods pulled from cellars, attics and garages, and effectively reduces their selling prices; which can in turn drastically change competitive realities in the world of art and antiques.

The harsh economic climate has forced Christie's and Sotheby's to try harder to attract both vendors and buyers. Thus, Christie's has offered guarantees (promises to pay sellers a certain sum, regardless of the price reached in the saleroom), and both houses have built 'skyboxes' in their New York salerooms so that wealthy bidders can watch the action without having to appear on the saleroom floor. Through such ploys, the art market has so far defied doomsayers who predicted its collapse at the top end. Perhaps it is true that art, because of the emotional attachment, is the last asset the financially discomfited rich will sell.

18.10.1 EU rules

The art market in Europe has suffered because of the EU's imposition of increased VAT. The fine arts industry has issued a report suggesting that the Europe-wide tax on imported artworks has driven as much as 7% of the art market to the US. America has now taken over from the EU as the biggest player in the international art market, with a share of 47%. Particularly damaging is the *droit de suite* levy that the seller pays to the artist or his heirs each time a painting is sold. Europe's auction houses lost out when Christie's in New York sold one of the world's finest private art collections. Had Christie's held the sale in Paris, Unicef, the beneficiary, would have had to pay large amounts in tax. Completing the sale in New York meant that net gains were higher.

It is estimated that the potential sales loss, had the levy had been applied fully in Britain, could total £300m. Despite this, the levy will operate throughout the EU by 2006. Furthermore, dealers now pay £40 a time when EU art tax paperwork has to be completed. This slows transactions and ultimately leads to the transfer of deals where the bureaucracy is less restrictive. The effect will be to reduce further the size of the European market, and its value to buyers.

18.10.2 Prudence

Fears of a fresh slump in the art market are raised on occasion. One factor has been the recent surge in prices, especially in the market for contemporary art and antiques, which brings to mind the conditions of the previous recession. However, most auction houses and dealers seem to sustain their confidence in the strength of demand in traditional markets for art and antiques. In that market segment, 'times have changed', said a Christie's spokesperson. 'The players have become more educated, they know what they are looking at and, if they don't, they come to these sales armed with professional advice.'

Recently, it has been the private buyer, with a sound knowledge of quality and provenance in a specialised niche, who has sustained the market in art and antiques. Collectors can take pleasure and gain financially from a work of art, the two forms of appreciation. It also seems possible that art management specialists who take on responsibility for high-value portfolios are likely to increase in number. In the UK and Europe, governments will continue to regulate the market, inhibiting it in some cases, but ensuring wider access in others, not least through better protection for the consumer. The possibility of international agreements between the US and Europe to harmonise taxes is likely to attract attention in the next few years.

The 1990s illustrated that, if art is a market, it is a highly knowledge-intensive one. To make informed judgements, the prospective investor needs expertise or access to it. A connoisseur's intuition, and familiarity with the patois of the auction house and dealer, are as vital as knowing what is on sale, where and when. As the French art expert, Jacques Attali, pointed out, 'nobody is in a position to establish laws for a market as unstable and as irrational as this. Each work of art is singular; each motivation is unique; each transaction has its own requirements.' In the coming years, he says, buyers will become increasingly discriminating. The supply of recognised works of art will diminish, but new types will appear. The art market will become 'a kind of avant-garde of museums, a selection process of what may subsequently become part of our collective memory'. It is in keeping with his remarks to add the footnote 'investments can damage one's financial health'.

The art market, dealers and collectors alike, have responded nervously to reports of an economic slowdown in the US: the extent to which their concerns are founded will be revealed over the coming year. Already, speculation over the knock-on effects of a US recession has led to a more cautious approach from potential buyers. Dealers at the BADA and Olympia antique and fine art fairs in London last spring found that, while enthusiasm and interest was strong, there was a definite hesitation over the purchase of items.

Top auction houses are more confident. Philippe Ségalot, international head of contemporary art at Christie's, told the *Art Newspaper* that 'there will be no dramatic change, but we are probably going to experience a slow-down and stabilisation of the market'. Furthermore, Marc Glimcher, president, Pace Wildenstein, commented on how the art market is essentially different from the world economy: 'The funny thing about the art world is that, in the beginning of a recession, the art business is almost always very good ... people are considering putting money into art from a financial standpoint.'

Some observers believe that a recession actually encourages the emerging artist market, as investors will look toward lower priced contemporary works that provide value for money.

SOURCES OF FURTHER INFORMATION

See end of Chapter 19.

19

COLLECTABLES

JOHN MYERS

Solon Consultants

19.1 INTRODUCTION

19.1.1 Collectables as alternative investments

Investors in alternatives look for havens for their hard-earned funds, but with an eye to pecuniary and gratifying rewards. Collectables, so many now believe, can satisfy these objectives. The number of desirable items is small, and values increase whenever the demand for them exceeds the supply. Prices can be low enough for individuals of modest means to choose a field in which they can build collections and become experts, and it is these individuals, not investors, who generally drive this market.

In practice, collectables offer scope for applying ingenuity and imagination; an existing set can be thematic, but then split and combined with new examples to form a fresh topic. Thus, insight is the key to success in this market, as David Hirsch, an expert in stamps, once pointed out. He believes that, if a collector develops the confidence to spot a good buy and act on this judgement, he should fare well. Hirsch advises against following the flock and merely buying what is popular today; a good collectable should hold its value regardless of how buyers may view it at one moment.

Hirsch also feels that investment should not be the prime motive. In his view, buyers should heed advice from experts, but act only if the case is convincing. The biggest worry for investors *qua* investors is the trap of viewing holdings as assets. A collector 'needs' items to complete a collection. In contrast, an investor 'needs' nothing and acquires items solely on their merits as investments. However, if the purchases perform double duty as enjoyable possessions, that is a plus, and a reward in kind if the market collapses and the financial element fails.

In the high reaches of the collectables market are books, manuscripts and scientific collections of national, scientific, historic or artistic interest – that is, items of pre-eminent heritage quality, which can qualify for conditional exemption from inheritance tax (IHT). The main condition for exemption is that the owner agrees to keep the object in the UK, preserve it, and allow reasonable public access. The Inland Revenue will charge IHT if the owner persistently fails to keep this agreement.

To comply with the public access provisions, introduced in 1998, an owner must allow viewing of the object without appointment, and make it available on request to public collections on short-term loans. Information about the heritage scheme is available from the Revenue's website; it aims to improve public awareness of the rights to see exempt works.

At www.inlandrevenue.gov.uk/heritage, the Revenue publishes a register of exempt works. Each entry describes an exempt object, and gives the name and address of a contact. It also shows the broad location, usually the county, in which the object is normally available for viewing. The register includes more than 20,000 objects of national, scientific, historic or artistic interest. Among them are works by Leonardo da Vinci, Dürer, Titian, Rubens, Van Dyck, Manet, Monet and Picasso. British artists represented include Hogarth, Reynolds, Gainsborough, Stubbs, Constable, Turner, Moore and Hepworth. Other entries refer to Chippendale and Adam furniture, silver by de Lamerie, and clocks by Tompion.

Payments for exempt collectables form the upper echelons of a framework for prices in alternative investment markets. Another high strut in this framework is the movement in the costs of living extremely well. The Forbes index has recorded the outlays of a luxury lifestyle since 1976, illustrated in Figure 19.1. Between then and now, the prices of luxury goods have increased on average by more than 500%. In parallel, the income of the top 5% of families in the US increased by 72% between 1973 and 2002. According to Robert Frank, professor of economics at Cornell University in New York and author of *Luxury Fever*, this concentration of wealth is the reason for the continued boom in upmarket spending.

Many authors writing on alternative investment, such as Frank, have reiterated that investors can be collectors, but a collector should not think of himself as an investor. It may happen that way, but the outcome is accidental. Nevertheless, some advisers feel that a significant portion of almost any rich client's savings for the future should be put into collectables. The argument is that these investments can complement other forms of investment, but not replace them.

19.1.2 The urge to collect

The fashionable urge to collect seems to extend to an ever-widening range of items with memorable, nostalgic or merely eccentric qualities – classic postage stamps, old cars, numismatic coins, oriental carpets, banknotes, scripts, medals, vintage wines and spirits, musical instruments, playing cards, *objets de vertu*, bric-à-brac, scientific instruments and printed items, to name but a few. The enthusiasm for collecting these items has stimulated the formation of many bodies, including the Ephemera Society, set up in 1975; its growing membership, running into thousands worldwide, comes from as far afield as Alaska and Latvia. The society benefits from a lively range of activities and publications, and it holds fairs each year.

Despite this evidence of enthusiasm, many investors remain wary of collectables. Caution is sensible when considering esoteric investment media, but several factors have recently made them more appealing. Players on the stock markets are constantly aware that equities can be volatile. Every threat of a crash can send shareholders scurrying to spread their risks. In times of uncertainty, collectables may offer a hedge against escalating prices; for many people with catholic tastes and a disposable income, they may well warrant a small proportion of an investment portfolio.

Thus, collectables, in common with art, antiques and valuables, can attract wealthy buyers from all quarters of the world. They can use their cash or borrowing power to diversify their assets in the manner of new renaissance merchant princes. Quality of life is one aim; another is to spread risks. The buyer of an alternative investment compares an opportunity to buy a collectable with the uncertainties involved with stocks and shares. When equity markets teeter on the edge or fall, an art deco ornament or a rare musical instrument might just hold its value, or even record spectacular gains.

A case in point was a vase by Venini, an important name in the glass collector's world. A lawyer from Milan, Paolo Venini (1895–1959) started the company that made the vase in 1925. He understood the value of design and, in the early years, he hired Carlo Scarpa (1906–1978), the Frank Lloyd Wright of Italian architecture. Scarpa's designs show beauty in their use of shape, curves, and proportion, rather than in their decoration or attachments. Later, Venini hired a young illustrator, Fulvio Bianconi (1915–1996), whose designs include the Fazzoleti or handkerchief vase. Venini made thousands of these vases in dozens of sizes, patterns and colour combinations for the tourist trade. This vast production keeps the price reasonable, as the supply is plentiful. However, Venini *Pezzato*, or patchwork, vases are beautiful, rare, and collectable.

In the 1960s, a Venini vase sold through a department store at £20. Nine years ago, at a Geneva sale, a bidder paid 176,000 Swiss francs (£70,000) for it. Valuers thought the transaction anomalous; successive appraisals of other Veninis offered for sale had been lower. The appraisers recalled that a bidder, who had paid £500 for a Venini glass vase in 1978, could not find a buyer to take it off his hands at a higher price. He chose not to sell at the time, and was wise to wait. At an auction in 1984, the same

Figure 19.1 Cost of living extremely well

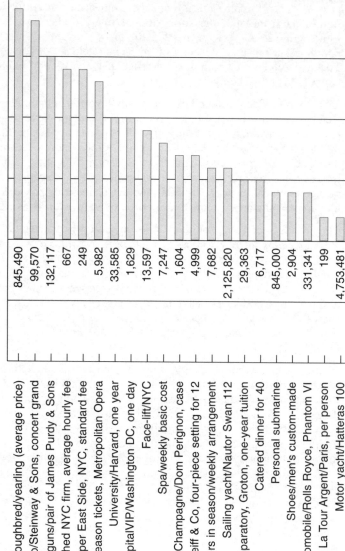

Annual % change in prices 03/04, current costs in $

Thoroughbred/yearling (average price)	845,490
Piano/Steinway & Sons, concert grand	99,570
Shotguns/pair of James Purdy & Sons	132,117
Lawyer/established NYC firm, average hourly fee	667
Psychiatrist/Upper East Side, NYC, standard fee	249
Opera/two season tickets, Metropolitan Opera	5,982
University/Harvard, one year	33,585
Hospital VIP/Washington DC, one day	1,629
Face-lift/NYC	13,597
Spa/weekly basic cost	7,247
Champagne/Dom Perignon, case	1,604
Silverware/Kirk Steiff & Co, four-piece setting for 12	4,999
Flowers in season/weekly arrangement	7,682
Sailing yacht/Nautor Swan 112	2,125,820
School/preparatory, Groton, one-year tuition	29,363
Catered dinner for 40	6,717
Personal submarine	845,000
Shoes/men's custom-made	2,904
Automobile/Rolls Royce, Phantom VI	331,341
Dinner at La Tour Argent/Paris, per person	199
Motor yacht/Hatteras 100	4,753,481

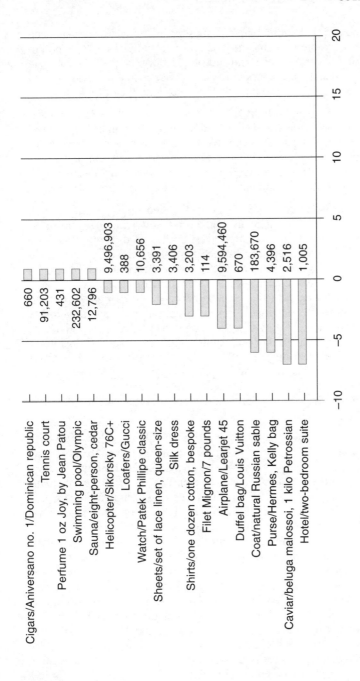

Cigars/Aniversano no. 1/Dominican republic	660
Tennis court	91,203
Perfume 1 oz Joy, by Jean Patou	431
Swimming pool/Olympic	232,602
Sauna/eight-person, cedar	12,796
Helicopter/Sikorsky 76C+	9,496,903
Loafers/Gucci	388
Watch/Patek Phillipe classic	10,656
Sheets/set of lace linen, queen-size	3,391
Silk dress	3,406
Shirts/one dozen cotton, bespoke	3,203
Filet Mignon/7 pounds	114
Airplane/Learjet 45	9,594,460
Duffel bag/Louis Vuitton	670
Coat/natural Russian sable	183,670
Purse/Hermes, Kelly bag	4,396
Caviar/beluga malossoi, 1 kilo Petrossian	2,516
Hotel/two-bedroom suite	1,005

Source: Forbes

vase fetched £25,000, more than ten times the auctioneer's estimate, and equal to an annual compound rate of return of 92%. In 1987, another Venini vase attracted a successful bid of £52,000; the pre-sale estimate had been less than half that amount. Venini vases can fetch from several hundred to several thousand pounds, depending on the design.

Another example came to light at a Geneva sale of 20th-century collectables. French and Japanese dealers bid strongly for a delicately carved glass table lamp. A Japanese dealer paid 1.58m Swiss francs (£675,000) for the lamp, originally produced commercially by Daum and Louis Majorelle less than 100 years ago. The seller had bought it 20 years before for less than £5,000, a compound annual rate of appreciation of 30%.

Art deco pottery and ceramics are becoming increasingly fashionable, valuable and affordable for many collectors. New technology inspired early 20th century designs, which were radically different from the ornate Victorian style. As an example, demand has held up for Clarice Cliff's work. She was perhaps the signature ceramics artist of the modern period, and much of her work is rare and unusual. Cliff's work came to prominence during the 1930s and now forms an important part of the history of 20th-century British ceramics. While her trademark subjects may have been traditional, with a focus on rural life, flowers and quaint cottages, the originality of her pottery lies in its unconventional geometric shapes. This striking and colourful combination of cubism and country kitchen makes her designs particularly attractive. Her output broadly comprises landscapes, geometrics and florals, with variations of design within each category. Some collectors are interested in one set of designs, others in particular items.

In 1983, a Clarice Cliff crocus sugar sifter cost about £40; by 1995, its value had risen to £150, representing a compound annual interest of 11.6%. Today, it trades at £1,200, and the compound annual interest rate has gone up to 26%. At the lower end of the scale, an *Autumn Crocus* side plate costs only £30, because it is the designer's most common pattern. However, a tea set for two in the same pattern may sell for £5,625, when six or seven years ago it could have been worth £750, representing an annual compound interest of 32%. Three years ago, Christie's sold an *Appliqué Windmill* tea set for £14,467, still short of the record for a tea set, set in Australia in 1999 when a *Lucerne* pattern set comprising a teapot, two cups and saucers, a sugar bowl, milk jug and cake plate in mint condition fetched £17,500. In 2002, a *Sunray* conical tea set sold for £11,162. In 2003, a large Cliff platter sold at Christie's for nearly £40,000, a record for Cliff. The vendor's father had bought the 18-inch dish new in 1933 for 25 shillings. Its present-day value reflects its status as one of Cliff's most unusual patterns. This highly sought-after *May Avenue* design of green and black trees in a street of red-roofed houses was produced briefly in 1932 and 1933.

Even reproductions of Cliff's work can be collectors' items. The Wedgwood Company owns Cliff's designs, and eight years ago reproduced two of the *Age of Jazz* figures, which then sold for £175 each. Now the pair may fetch more than £5,000. Then many smaller Cliff pieces have increased in value by 300% or more over the past five years. In February 1999, Christie's sold the Daniel Brodie Hogg collection for £201,699, more than double the pre-sale estimate. Among the most sought after Clarice Cliff pieces are her *Age of Jazz* figures. In March 1997, Sotheby's set a record by selling one of the figures for £12,650. The following November, Christie's sold a table centrepiece modelled as a drummer and oboe player for £13,800, double the estimate. At a Bonhams sale of Cliff's work in May 2000, an orange *Age of Jazz* dancing couple fetched £13,000, twice the estimate, despite having a chip in it.

Other pieces almost doubling their estimates included a pair of tennis vases, which made £4,200, and an example of the popular *Appliqué* pieces, a *Palermo Vase*, sold for £4,800. A record was set for a small *Viking Boat* when a *Blue Firs* boat and flower holder fetched £3,200. There was some surprise at the same sale when a *Windbells* vase, estimated at £6,000–9,000, only reached £3,000, and the orange patina tree globe was left unsold. In 2002, a rare *Appliqué Blue Lugano* charger fetched £13,000, suggesting that the popularity of Clarice Cliff continues. Another bidder paid a top price of £6,462 for a lucerne shape vase, which is only six inches high. These collectables are undoubtedly exceptional examples.

19.2 DEVELOPMENTS IN COLLECTABLES' MARKETS

19.2.1 Vintage stock certificates

Collectables with obvious appeal for the alternative investor are vintage stock and bond certificates. Enthusiasts and scripophilists may at times pay five- or six-figure prices for a rare item, as happened in 1991 when a collector laid out £70,000 for a Bank of England promise-to-pay bill, issued to back loans to the Russian Imperial government. The certificates' value lies in their historic and aesthetic appeal, and in the signatures that appear on them, not in their face value.

Certificates from the early industrial revolution are in high demand, particularly those of shipping and railways enterprises. Some collectors retain pre-communist bonds from former eastern bloc countries in the faint hope that the certificates will eventually be redeemable. They recall 1991 when the (then) Soviet government paid 54% of the face value of devalued bonds. However, the compensation settlement had a time limit.

Dealers later received a mass of certificates from owners who had missed out, causing a slump in the market for Russian bonds. The trade in vintage bonds from other pre-revolutionary regimes may be an area for speculation. Occasionally, collectors seek modern shares if they have particularly interesting or unusual designs. Printed shares are increasingly scarce because of electronic trading.

19.2.2 Rare books

Collectors have amassed books since the times of monasteries and stately home libraries. From the renaissance to the French Revolution, books were popular among readers for what was in them, not for their packaging. By the time Jane Austen's novels were entertaining England, the *nouveau riche* had begun to see books as artefacts that conferred a desired status on their owners; in line with that aspiration some buyers valued the printing and binding more than the content.

The market for collectable books is segmented. One sector is the 'first edition market', a specialised field. With some works, a book's value may depend as much on the presence and quality of its dust jacket as on its other qualities. Scott Fitzgerald's *The Great Gatsby*, for example, had a typographical error on the jacket of its first edition, but only on a few copies. With this error a copy might fetch £3,000, without it a mere £30–250. In July 1998, Christie's auctioned a first edition of Chaucer's *Canterbury Tales*. Published by William Caxton in 1477 at Westminster Abbey, it is one of only a dozen left in existence. Experts expected that the book would fetch £700,000, but it sold for £4.6m ($7.5m), a record for a printed book sold at auction. Another rare book sold at the same auction fetched £771,000 – double the estimate; *The Recuyell of the Historyes of Troye* was the first book printed in English by William Caxton at Bruges in 1474. A first edition of Kenneth Grahame's *The Wind in the Willows* sold at Sotheby's in 1998 for £44,000, three times the auctioneer's estimate. Only three copies of the book have been auctioned in the past 25 years. However, the handwritten manuscript of Marcel Proust's *Remembrance of Times Past* disappointed Christie's in June 2000 when it failed to reach the expected £1m mark, selling for £663,750.

An unusual sub-segment of this market for first editions originated with well-to-do Victorian women, who defied convention to travel through the *African Queen* hinterland of remote territories. Often alone, apart from their native bearers, garbed in long dresses and carrying umbrellas, they collected flora – and on occasion fauna – painted pictures, and proclaimed the word of God. In addition, they wrote books that became bestsellers and are now collectors' items. At least five book dealers specialise in the works of female Victorian travellers, selling first editions in fine condition for sums between £100 and £1,000.

Film versions of literary works can also stimulate interest in first editions, and the transfer from paper to celluloid can have a stunning effect on values. But not always; collectors showed little interest when a complete first edition set of J R Tolkien's *Lord of the Rings* trilogy came under the hammer at a recent Bloomsbury Book Auction. A glut of Tolkien first editions had reduced demand. On the other hand, first editions of J K Rowling's *Harry Potter* books have been breaking records. A first edition of *Harry Potter and the Philosopher's Stone* attracted a winning bid of £16,000.

One of the latest trends in collectables is the hypermoderns, ie books that have been published within the past few decades, or even the past few months. For example, John Grisham's *A Time to Kill*, his first mystery, can fetch up to £750 today: of the 5,000 printed, the publisher destroyed 3,000. An American collector recently bought a first edition of the book at a car boot sale for under $100, later selling it for $1,200. However, Peter Grogan, manager of R A Gekoski rare books in London, says that buying new releases in anticipation of future value may not guarantee a return on investment: 'There's a huge misunderstanding in the notion that first editions are worth money. Most editions are first editions because most books don't get reprinted – because they are garbage.'

Nevertheless, some writers have stood the test of time well – Lewis Carroll, C S Lewis, Dylan Thomas and Virginia Woolf are examples – and their first editions are very collectable. Other authors also remain popular. A few years ago, Phillips and Christie's compiled a shortlist of bestsellers at recent auctions. Top of the list are first editions of *The Wind in the Willows* with dust jacket (£40,000), Graham Greene's *Brighton Rock* with dust jacket (£20,000), Ian Fleming's *Casino Royale* (£5,000), Greene's first novel, *Babbling April*, and Kingsley Amis's *Lucky Jim* (each £2,760).

Notable items auctioned recently include the penultimate and previously unknown draft chapter from James Joyce's *Ulysses*, which sold in July 2001 for almost £900,000. A 120ft long scroll of tracing paper on which Jack Kerouac wrote his quintessential beat novel *On the Road* appeared at Christie's sale of printed books and manuscripts in New York in 2001. Wealthy buyers flocked to the sale, and the scroll fetched $2.46m, setting a record for a literary manuscript. A 16th century prayer book sold in 1999 for £8.5m, the most expensive illuminated manuscript ever sold at auction. The work is a masterpiece in renaissance manuscript illumination, probably published in Belgium in 1505. The *Conaro Missale*, part of the same collection, sold for £2.86m, setting a record for an Italian manuscript.

In March 2000, Christie's New York sold a copy of Audubon's *Birds of America*, a bound collection of ornithological plates published between 1827 and 1838, for £5.04m. A controversial sale of some of Jewry's most valuable and important books and manuscripts, which included one of the two copies of the Ashkenazi prayer book, fetched a total of $3.8m in New York in 1999. A sale of books from Longleat, one of the most famous stately homes in England, fetched £27m in 2002. In the sale was a 15th-century Italian manuscript of the works of Virgil, which fetched £1.2m.

Inscriptions in books by the author or a famous owner, or a relative or an influential friend of the author, can also enhance values. In 1991, Sotheby's sold a copy of the late Graham Greene's rare first novel, inscribed with a message to his wife, for £13,200. The price was double the previous record for this volume, set a year earlier. In other examples, inscriptions have increased values by even more. For example, one of four presentation copies of the first edition of *Tess of the D'Urbervilles*, inscribed by Hardy to Alfred Austin, is valued at £45,000, whereas an uninscribed first edition sold in October 1999 for £6,000.

Two rare, signed copies of the D H Lawrence novel, *Lady Chatterley's Lover* went under the hammer in 2002. It is unusual for two copies of the same book to be auctioned at the same time. Each fetched about £5,000. A first edition copy of the *Beano* was auctioned for £7,500 at the end of 2002. Its owner had placed it in a plastic folder and kept it under his sofa for more than 40 years, before putting it up for sale. This sum was exceeded when £12,100 was paid in a postal auction in March 2004. There are believed to be only nine remaining copies of the first issue of the *Beano*. Winston Churchill's first edition copy of the James Bond novel *Live and Let Die* sold for £46,000 in 2002. It was signed by the author Ian Fleming, and bore the inscription 'To Sir Winston Churchill: from whom I stole some words'.

In collectable books, as in other areas of the market, it has been works of the finest quality that have withstood downturns. As noted in chapter 18, the art market declined in the 1990s. Standard reference works, or *catalogues raisonnés*, on the other hand, have experienced little change in demand. These volumes have more than aesthetic appeal, they are in constant demand from art dealers, and can fetch four-figure sums at auction.

Rare works have also weathered recession. A book sale at Phillips raised more than £500,000, with the main attraction being manuscripts by David Garrick, the 18th century theatre luminary. Another generally successful set of collectables has been antiquarian textbooks. Christie's sale of the Loughlin collection of mainly 16th to 18th-century works on mathematics and other sciences did well for the vendors. The highest price, £280,000, was for a finely bound copy of Du Bellay's 1549 *Instructions sur le Fait de la Guerre*. A second edition of Darwin's *On the Origin of Species* now commands a five-figure sum, since the first editions have entered the six-figure domain.

The advice to collectors of rare books could easily apply to many other fields of alternative investment: 'buy the best of what you like. Rely on your own instinct, but work closely with knowledgeable dealers. Develop a collector's eye by looking at a large number of books. Browse in specialist shops. Search out auctions, fairs and even car boot sales'.

Caution is again advisable. Britain has found itself facing a problem with the illicit trade of rare books. In recent years, detectives have noticed a rise in the trafficking of such books and manuscripts, as they are valuable commodities, highly portable and often sold privately. In May 2002, an early Muslim manuscript was withdrawn from sale at Christie's after appraisers identified it as stolen property. The philosophical text had been taken from an ancient library in Konya, Anatolia. The commissioning of thefts has been particularly prevalent in the scientific works area. Two copies of Ptolemy's original works were stolen, each valued at £500,000. Works by Nicolaus Copernicus have also been targeted. In 1999, a thief stole a first edition of *Gulliver's Travels*, the Jonathan Swift classic, from a public library in Northern Ireland, which was recovered two years later in Dublin. A 1623 first folio of Shakespeare's works was among several rare manuscripts taken from Durham University's library in 1998.

19.2.3 Numismatic coins

Collectable coins have at times been almost on a par with the holding of shares and bonds. Some brokers, particularly in the US, optimistically recommended them to their clients as a substitute for stock market investments, particularly so in the lead-up to 2000, when they tried to capitalise on investors' concerns about the millennium bug. These advocates recommended numismatic coins for their portability, privacy and performance.

Authentication and grading are issues with numismatic coins. Collectors Universe Inc is a provider of authentication services to dealers and collectors of high-end collectables. It has an agreement with the Royal Mint to grade and authenticate £2 and £5 gold coins, many of which are decades old. The Mint recently shipped 600 British proof £2 and £5 gold pieces, dating from 1980 through 2003 to the Professional Coin Grading Service (PCGS) division of Collectors Universe in Newport Beach, California, which examined, graded, and sealed the coins in holders with printed inserts displaying a Union flag and the official crest of the Royal Mint. PCGS has also certified 400 gold and silver proof D-Day 60th Anniversary commemoratives struck by the French Mint, Monnaie de Paris.

To a degree, the market acceptance of a grading system has stimulated interest in coins. Agreed methods of categorising coins according to their quality help to structure the market for collectors and investors. With this help, enthusiasm for coin collecting is reviving somewhat. 'Interest in coin collecting has never been as great since the late 1960s and early 1970s,' according to Mark Rasmussen of Spinks, the coin dealers.

The heyday for coin collecting began before decimalisation in the UK. In the early 1970s, collectors examined coins they received in change to fill date-runs of denominations that were soon to vanish. The practice became almost a national obsession and, in a decade of high inflation, it was fashionable to put money into collectables, as savings in financial instruments did not pay a real return. The sharpest rise in prices for British historical coins occurred in 1973–74 when the stock market was collapsing. Although the coin market paused for breath in the first few months of 1974, it then started on a steady upward climb. Five years later prices for English coins had increased on average by 150%. 'Casual' date collectors became numismatists and began to build sets of historical coins, only to drop out of the market in the late 1970s and early 1980s. Rare coins of quality had become too costly to collect.

Before the end of the 1970s, two interrelated factors caused prices to rise further. Investment buying in the US gained impetus when buyers could invest in collectables, via retirement plans, and receive tax relief on their purchases. The Reagan administration cut out this concession in 1981. Booming bullion prices also helped. In the 1980s, silver rose to $52.50 and gold to $500 an ounce. Many coin dealers trade in bullion as an adjunct to their main business. The profits they were generating from this activity were substantial. As coin markets were buoyant, they channelled money into coin dealing. The price for US historical coins rose sharply, until almost inevitably the bubble burst; in the first half of 1983 prices fell. Those who had purchased coins as an investment became disillusioned, while many genuine numismatists had long since stopped adding to their collections. The specimens they sought were financially out of reach.

The most important determinant of value is a coin's condition, which ranges from mint to poor. An uncirculated 1887 silver crown bearing the jubilee portrait of Queen Victoria would sell for about £60. However, a coin with signs of wear on its raised surfaces would be worth only £10 and, in a poor state, £2–3, putting in question the value of coins as an investment. When hopes of monetary gain outweigh the interest in coins for their own sake, problems are likely. However, for the connoisseur, coins can tell enchanting stories and reveal a nation's history.

One enthusiast reminds audiences that coin collecting is the oldest collecting hobby, traceable to the invention of coinage in the 7th century BC. He comments: 'most people are drawn into the hobby for a variety of reasons. Pride of ownership and a desire to expand or complete a collection once started are sufficient for many collectors. For others, the profit motive is a prime incentive for collecting coins. The rest may enjoy their coin collections because they have an interest in art, history, geography or science.'

Financial traders would like coins to become respectable as the basis for investment funds they are setting up. A typical institutional scheme requires an initial tranche of capital from a group of investors – say, £50m to fund dealing in collectable coins. The essence of the plan is to acquire enough coins to appreciate over a short enough period to generate worthwhile returns. A key question is how to calculate 'worthwhile'. Some coins will gain in value; others will fall. Whatever happens, the fund has to meet its overheads, which include storage, insurance and regular valuation of the portfolio. One analyst estimates that sets of coins need to appreciate, on average, by more than 40% to give investors a 20% return. In the case of one such fund, the promoter's filings with the US Securities and Exchange Commission contend that similar types of investment vehicle have achieved returns of this figure or more, a claim that the prudent will treat with caution.

In the UK, the High Court recently wound up a British company that sold unusual gold coins to the public, but never delivered the goods. Credit First Bullion Ltd of Upper Grosvenor St, London, ran a telesales operation and secured sales for collectable gold coins for 700% of their market value. The coins offered were rare or collectable, and included American Gold Eagles. Unfortunately, the company failed to deliver the coins to the customers who had bought them. The court made the winding up order on 23 June 2004 on a petition presented by the Secretary of State for Trade and Industry, in the public interest. This followed confidential investigations by the DTI's Companies Investigations Branch.

The promise of success is echoed in fresh price records at coin auctions. An early record price paid for a coin was for an American doubloon, dating from 1793, sold in 1979 for £250,000. Rare coins have a long-established market among collectables, but rarity brings a high premium. A 1982 gold coin issued when British forces relieved the Falkland Islands sold for £2,200. It was in mint condition and was one of only 25 struck.

At a Christie's sale, an 1890 halfpenny sold for £1,380. This ordinary halfpenny is stamped with the word 'Oakley' on its obverse and is deformed by a bullet shot. Apparently, Annie Oakley, the great American sharpshooter, could hit coins thrown in the air. These were then stamped with 'Oakley' and given to the audience. In August 1999, a record for the highest price paid for a single US coin was set when an 1804 draped bust silver dollar was sold for $4.14m. The coin, from the Childs collection,

371

was once presented to the Sultan of Muscat by an agent of President Andrew Jackson, and is believed to be in excellent condition. The previous record was held by another 1804 silver dollar, which sold for $1.815m in 1987.

In 2002, investors paid an exceptional price for perhaps the world's most valuable coin, a 1933 $20 double eagle. Struck in 1933 when President Roosevelt was trying to wean America off the gold standard, these coins were never made legal tender. In the 1950s all but one were destroyed; some years later, it reappeared in the hands of King Farouk. Removed from the sale at the request of the US Treasury, but never returned to the US because of a loophole in the law, its whereabouts remained unknown, until a British coin dealer tried to sell it in 1996. After a legal battle lasting five years, the coin was finally returned to the US in 2001. It sold at auction in 2002 for $7.5m, the highest price ever paid for a single coin.

In 2003, Spink sold the Slaney collection of English coins, setting a record for English silver coins at auction. A Charles II pattern crown from 1663, the *Petition Crown*, fetched £138,000, against a pre-sale estimate of £40,000–50,000, more than double the previous record for a silver coin of £57,500. Richard Bishop, associate director of numismatic auctions at Spink said: 'This magnificent result is indicative of the strength of the market for English coins at present and of collectors' voracious appetite for fine material such as this. Of the bidders who took part in this sale, a very high proportion were collectors, rather than trade.' The sale as a whole realised more than £1m.

Over the past few years the rare coin market has also attracted a share of the controversy caused by aggressive selling practices. As noted above, some US dealers have sought to encourage investment in coins by establishing certifiable grades of quality. Associated with this is the practice of 'slabbing'. Coins graded by one of two grading houses, the numismatic guarantee corporation or the professional coin grading service, are sealed in plastic 'slabs'. However, the market in slabbed coins is not strong, and the Federal Trade Commission repeatedly indicted vendors for making false claims about the objectivity and consistency of grading.

Certification of quality, if performed consistently, could give pointers to how the market in collectables might develop. Through the American Numismatic Exchange, some dealers have sought to create their own version of the modern stock market. The exchange enables dealers to trade over a computer network. Investors can buy and sell as they wish through the network, without having to wait for auctions and sales. Critics argue that coins are not like equities; they are 'limited edition objects', so values tend to be set in a subjective way. Nor, they argue, are coins liquid assets. Investors should allow for delays in finding a buyer who will pay the 'right price' for a rare coin. On occasion such delays can be prolonged.

Advocates of the coin bourse claim that it will help to stabilise a volatile market. In theory, if such a bourse develops, it might trade in coin futures and coin options. Equally, it could conceivably extend its remit into other alternative investments. Syndicates and funds could be set up to trade in certificates backed by physical assets, hedged on the exchange. An information infrastructure could follow, as the traders and investors sought better intelligence on the fundamentals and technical performance of particular assets. These ideas may seem far-fetched, but informal coffee-house trading in the City led to the spectacular and speculative commodity, insurance and shipping markets of today. At the time, they seemed unlikely propositions.

19.2.4 Collectable cars

Classic cars have a more limited appeal, but demand remains cosmopolitan. A Porsche 959, a Ferrari F40 *Super Car* or the Bugatti *Royale* may attract bidders from almost any part of the developed world. Their chances of gain have been considerable, as are the prospects of losing money. Within a single year, 1988–89, the price of some Aston Martin DB6s rose tenfold, from £10,000 to £100,000. Prices then fell and eventually moderated to a lower 'realistic' level, at least 50% below the peak figure.

The frenetic activity in the market sprang, to some extent, from wealthy, middle-aged British enthusiasts nostalgic for their youth, or stimulated by films. A car used by James Bond in the film *Die Another Day* fetched £210,000 at auction. The tungsten silver V12 *Vanquish* was used to skid across ice, and had the ability to make itself invisible – cinematic capabilities that the buyer may not find it easy to replicate! Foreign buyers also stoked the price furnace. These buyers have not disappeared, although ageing Rolls-Royces and Bentleys still glut the market. Fondness for the highly charged sports car is undiminished, and old Ferraris, Jaguars, Maseratis and MGs continue to command high, but not always hyped, prices. The record for any car sold at auction is £6.4m for a Ferrari 250 GTO sold at auction in 1990.

The 24th annual Barrett-Jackson auction took place in Scottsdale, Arizona, in January 2004, where sales of classic and vintage cars totalled $38.5m. The auction drew a crowd of 185,000, anxious to see serious collectors and celebrities bid for rare US classics and vintage cars. Prices were high. Most of these cars may never see the tarmac. Barrett-Jackson commented: 'The collector car market has become crowded with investors, not really car lovers, but businessmen looking to diversify their stock portfolio. Vintage and collector cars have performed quite well considering crashing tech stock prices. They clearly want to see their investment go up, and driving it on the road is a sure way to see it depreciate. That's why you get to see the same car every few years, as they get traded like baseball cards, with hardly any miles put on the car.'

On the other hand, some vendors encourage buyers of classic cars to drive them. They believe that, unless it is a museum-quality machine, an ageing vehicle could benefit by being fired up to full running temperature regularly. If it costs too much to insure the car for the road, the buyer is advised to change the oil periodically, to jack up the car to protect the suspension, and take other steps such as dehumidifying the garage to prevent deterioration. According to claimed, if not acclaimed, experts, the trick is to pick the few vehicles, or to find a whole new class of collectables, that will increase in value. Some specialists believe that old vehicles can offer investment possibilities. Collector cars can be worth five- and six-figure sums. However, experts say that few vehicles are legitimate investments that can offer a hedge against inflation. A noted collector of Rolls-Royce *Silver Ghosts* warns against even this faith in rarity; he insists that it is no more than an enthusiast's market. Nonetheless, in 1997, Sotheby's sold a prewar *Silver Ghost* for £249,575.

Meanwhile, old family cars with character, for example the Volkswagen *Beetle*, the Morris Minor, the Mini-Cooper, are attracting a generation of enthusiasts willing to pay £5,000 for a model in good condition. Winston Churchill's Austin 10 sold for £66,400.

In general, demand for vintage cars is growing at the expense of old-style cars. In the 1960s, a restored Model T Ford might have sold for $12,000; today it would fetch only $7,000. A US expert in collectables, Harry Rinker, accounts for the change: 'Today's guy wants the car he used to ride in with his dad, not some classic he can't remember.'

The cost and relative scarcity of even the finest US models may put them out of reach for many car collectors. Generally, the value of these cars has stayed high but almost flat for several years. North American magazines, for example *Cars and Parts* and *Old Cars' Price Guide*, can help collectors to follow the changes in US vehicle prices. *Cars and Parts* publishes graphs every month that show the changes in collector car prices, while *Old Cars' Price Guide* gives prices for thousands of vehicles, based on condition. Advisers recommend that prospective buyers check the guide before making a purchase, and call in an appraiser. Such moves might help a buyer to avoid overpaying.

Intending purchasers of unique cars might buy through a private transaction after placing a classified advertisement in a car magazine, or from an enthusiast who belongs to a specialist automobile club. Both approaches can be risky. Some experts also believe that, when buying cars, auctions can be particularly hazardous. They argue that there may be scant opportunity to inspect the car, and they suggest that an iron will is needed to avoid being swept away by the bidding excitement.

Another simple recommendation is not to buy a car unseen. It is advice that applies equally to many other alternative investments. Skilled salesmen may give cast-iron assurances that there will never be another chance to buy a car like this again, and urge the investor to send money without delay. As a cynical commentator put it: 'Two weeks later, you will find a pile of rust on your doorstep. The chance of a lifetime comes along about once a week.'

19.2.5 Collectable wines

Wine collecting is a growing culture, which is attracting interest among people seeking to develop expertise. To help them, Christie's and Sotheby's run wine education programmes. These courses include Christie's master classes, where top-class experts present choice wines from their field of knowledge.

From an alternative investment standpoint, wine is made in fixed quantities, there are numerous vintages that allow for the accumulation of sets, and the quantities available decline over time as people drink it, with the prospect of higher prices for what is left. Many people will have one or two bottles that have been lying in the cellar or the garage for a few years. By gradually adding to the collection over the years, its value may grow. Some wine experts claim annual appreciation by up to 15%, although this is unlikely to be representative of most vintages. The truth is that wine prices are extremely variable and only a small percentage of high-quality wines will represent a sound investment. However, some French wines, for example fine vintages of Latour, have recorded an average annual appreciation of around 20% in the past 15 years. At the sale of the late Robert Maxwell's cellar, a dozen bottles of Latour 1982 sold for £800. Bidders paid around 20% above the estimate, perhaps attracted by the previous owner's notoriety.

In practice, the judgement of vintages is subjective – each vintage matures and evolves differently, with some wines improving with time and others failing to live up to expectations. Wine is of course an agricultural product, so a disastrous year can enhance the value of previous vintages. Conversely, a good series of vintages and large stocks will keep prices more or less static. Supply and demand and en premeur (before bottling) tasting reports will also affect prices. For example, American wine writer Robert Parker has a significant influence on wine prices. He produces a newsletter in which he rates the latest wines. A high rating will often lead to a high demand for a particular wine, especially for Bordeaux.

Manifestly, if the wine is destined for heirs, it is a good idea to think long-term – an investment in fine wine may take as long as 30 years to show real gains, which means storing it properly. Some organisations offer storage facilities, which can be useful, as Christie's and Sotheby's will not auction wine unless assured that it has been kept in appropriate conditions. Doris Meister, head of private wealth management at Merrill Lynch, New York, has cautioned collectors about the problems of maintaining delicate storage conditions and transporting fragile cargo. Another important factor when purchasing wine is not to buy a vintage exaggerated at the time, because it is unlikely to have such high returns in the future. Instead, the collector is advised to select wines that experts consider 'bargains now' and 'drinkable in a few years', not wines that have an immediate appeal.

Some specialists suggest that it is worth restoring wines. In one cited example, a buyer paid £425 for a double magnum of 1865 Château Lafite in 1967, and 14 years later took the bottles back to the château to have them topped up and new corks inserted. Sold at auction after a few months, lots reached £12,000 per double magnum – a growth in value of 25% pa compound. The same connoisseur believed its value in the late 1990s would be about £48,500. In February 1998, a magnum of Château Lafite 1870 fetched £9,875 at auction in Los Angeles. It originated from Glamis Castle, the late Queen Mother's family home, but had been sold to a US buyer in 1971. In June 2001, Sotheby's sold a cellar of wine for £2,659,420, making it the fourth highest grossing single-owner wine sale at auction worldwide. In May 1997, Sotheby's sold Andrew Lloyd Webber's wine collection for £3,692,821.

One approach to collecting wine is to develop a relationship with an established and reputable wine merchant, who deals with private investors. Some merchants offer tailored wine investment portfolios. A Cayman Island-based investment company, the OWC Asset Management Vintage Wine fund, registered with the Financial Services Authority, invests in a portfolio of fine Bordeaux, Burgundy, Rhône Valley and other fine wines, with the intention of generating steady, high capital growth. However, wine investment is not a well-regulated sector, and it is advisable to avoid cold-callers from unregistered dealers, as fraudsters operate in this market, as in other sectors. Another, sometimes expensive, option is the wine auction, taking into account the buyer's premium, VAT and possible delivery charges.

When making purchases it is usually advisable to buy wine by the case – the original wooden case is an important indication of a wine's provenance, although it is possible to acquire bottles of old or rare wines. Expert dealers recommend buying in parcels of three to five cases, with the option of selling to wine merchants or to private buyers.

For those keen to take a more substantial and long-term stake in the industry, an alternative is to buy a vineyard, perhaps in Burgundy,

Bordeaux or Tuscany. Lower cost vineyards are likely to be available in areas with good quality soil, such as the Loire Valley in France or Italy, Spain and Portugal. Evidently, a vineyard will call for a great deal of work to maintain, and often mean a new lifestyle. To generate returns from the wine itself and the sale of a vineyard, investors will need the right contacts. Banks such as UBS and Rothschild in France offer networking services.

19.2.6 Photographs

Imaginative photographic images can transcend the original purpose and make a photographer 'collectable'. Two main kinds are popular: the first is the 'vintage print', made for a magazine or other use at the time it was taken, and sometimes marked up for publication; the other is the 'modern print', made for sale or exhibition from an old negative, created with special care on fine paper and under the supervision of the photographer, who then signs the print. The Photographers' Gallery in London specialises in the latter. In the gallery's early days, when it sold prints from its current exhibition displayed on a trestle table, a buyer could pick up a Bill Brandt for £50. Brandt made his name as a magazine photographer in Britain in the 1930s, famously recorded the devastation of London during the blitz, and continued to capture great images up to his death in 1983. Today, the gallery print room sells Brandt prints for between £900 and £3,000.

The cost of fine photographs no doubt discourages buyers; after all, a vandal can snip the same image from books or magazines for a fraction of the cost. Nevertheless, top quality prints signed by photographers of the *Picture Post* era, for which prices start around £200, are among the Photographers Gallery's best sellers. Nostalgia is definitely 'in' with collectors. The amazing images of New York taken in 1926, just before the Wall Street crash, by Fred Zinnemann, the Hollywood film director (of *High Noon, Oklahoma!, The Day of the Jackal*), sell for £325–600. To attract new collectors, the gallery has introduced a plan for collectors called 'prime prints'. With every contemporary show it asks the photographer to prepare an edition of 50 prints of one successful image, which sell for £150 each. There is also a 'patron print scheme', by which anyone signing up as a patron receives one print free from a set of six specially made for the gallery by leading photographers.

Demand for beautifully printed photographs seems likely to increase; in Britain, there has been a steady growth in the number of collectors. Prospects in the US may be even more promising; New York has more than 150 galleries belonging to the Association of International Photography Art Dealers, a figure that has tripled since 2001. Although the association only has about 100 British members, that figure has increased tenfold since 2001. All the British dealers sell more abroad than they do in the home market, but this pattern is changing as collecting photographs becomes more popular. The signs have been positive. In May 2000, the sale of the 91-lot Craven photographic collection realised £1.4m, and set records for 19th-century British photographs. Lydia Cresswell-Jones, of Sotheby's, said at the time: 'It's a fantastically strong market at present, and there is more and more interest in buying photographs. Collectors may collect by subject, by photographer, by photographic process, or choose to buy pictures of a particular place. There is every reason to collect.'

The age of the image may also be significant. Antique photographs make fine investments, according to Niki Michelin, who sells vintage prints at the Photographers' Gallery. In her view, such prints 'are works of art, just like paintings, and prices are often massive because there are so few of these prints on the market.... They can sell for tens of thousands of pounds. But, when you compare that to what people will pay for, say, a Picasso, photographs are cheap.'

Some collectors have rushed to acquire prints by 19th-century photographers in recent years, so the prices of pictures by people in the very early years of photography are rising fast. However, experts feel that, on occasion, they might be duped into thinking they are buying an original. In reality, their purchase may be a modern reproduction, skilfully touched up in a high-tech laboratory.

In 2002, the world's oldest known photograph was sold for almost $400,000. The image, of an engraving showing a man leading a horse – made in 1825 by Nicephore Niepce, who invented the heliogravure technique. Although not strictly what would be recognised as a photograph today, as it is in essence printed ink on paper, it is the creation of the plate that is important. Niepce etched the image using light-sensitive chemicals on a metal plate, which he then transferred to paper. A collection of photographs by a Victorian pioneer of the art, the Earl of Craven, sold for £1.4m, against an expected price of between £500,000 and £700,000. The earl was a keen amateur photographer and took many pictures between 1855 and 1857, his horse-drawn darkroom allowing him to take many pictures on location.

Some of the last known pictures of the *Titanic* were sold at auction in 2003, for £14,000. The family photograph album, containing 23 pictures, belonged to a lady and her nephew who disembarked from the ship at its first port of call in Ireland. Evidently, one of the world's *Titanic* experts, Stanley Lehrer, bought the collection.

19.2.7 Sporting memorabilia

Prices of football memorabilia are rising at a high rate, and rugby is becoming more popular. Nevertheless, for the present, cricket and golf items remain the most collectable in terms of holding their value. Aficionados of cricket and golf often combine enthusiasm with a nostalgia that brings them to auctions of memorabilia. One of Bradman's personally autographed bats, or an open championship winner's accumulation of medals, can draw bids from connoisseurs, who see the purchase as a memento of past experience, a conversation piece, and an investment.

Other items, such as volumes of *Wisden*, or Joseph B Hacker's library of golf books, may attract collectors eager to complete or improve a set. As a consequence, the big auction houses – Christie's, Sotheby's and Bonhams – often hold specialist auctions of historical sporting lots. Their initiative is matched by a range of dealers, especially in the US, who will authenticate autographs of personalities and will grade and value sports collectables. Two years ago, Sotheby's sold a nearly complete run of *Wisden* cricket almanacs, from 1879–1984, for £7,920.

From the buyer's viewpoint, a drawback of cricket, for the present at least, is that its geographical coverage is not universal; spectators in the US tend to say that they do not understand it. However, the cricket world cup and similar televised events are broadening cricket's appeal. That being the case, memorabilia bought now might well go up in value, as the cosmopolitan origins of enthusiasts widen. Meanwhile, golf collectables tend to be worth more on average, and buyers across the world may pay significant amounts for sporting memorabilia of international interest. At a recent Sotheby's auction of golfing memorabilia, a silver golf medal awarded by the Musselburgh Golf Club in 1832 fetched £21,200.

The football memorabilia market, however, is providing items of the highest current value. In 2000, Sir Geoff Hurst's World Cup final shirt was sold for £91,750. Commentators suggest that the price was a blip, attributed to Hurst's hat trick, never yet equalled. None the less, in 2002 the sale of Pelé's world cup shirt brought £157,750. Perhaps not such a blip. Football memorabilia is an expanding field of collectables.

Hunting, fishing and shooting also have a broad attraction to buyers across the world. For example, shotguns in good condition by a well-known maker can be bought at auction for a few hundred pounds, and a first-class Purdey may fetch many thousands. Decoys for hunters and fishing rods can go for four-figure sums, while many enthusiasts will pay larger amounts for sporting trophies, works of art and other memorabilia. For example, a bidder paid £19,000 at a Sotheby's auction for a signed and numbered John Skeaping bronze of the 1971 Derby winner *Mill*

Reef. The item had been offered for sale by the jockey Lester Piggot, who received 50% more than the auctioneer's estimate for the collectables he put on sale in November 1998.

Sporting, and particularly angling, art has risen substantially in price in a few decades. Angling paintings show locations with an intrinsic rural charm; paintings of wild places, rivers, mountains and lakes are attractive, and often lively. Angling, however, suffers in comparison with hunting and shooting, where artists may capture even more dramatic moments. Fine angling artists whose work today commands good prices include John Raphael Smith, Francis Barlow, Henry Alken, James Pollard, Ansdell, Hardie, Barrington-Browne, Rolfe, Rowlandson and Walker. Some famous artists executed many paintings with an angling theme, most notably works by Turner, but also paintings by Zoffany, Dadd and Cruikshank.

Top auction houses usually hold bi-annual sales of sporting memorabilia, and specialists, such as David Convey, head of sports memorabilia auctions at Christie's, report that lots can sell for three times their expected price. For example, the gloves with which Cassius Clay, later Muhammad Ali, fought Henry Cooper in 1963, sold for £37,600; golfer Joseph Lloyd's US Open winner's medal, from 1897, sold for £39,950; and a collection of unpublished letters from P G Wodehouse to Billy Griffith, the Sussex and England cricketer, for £28,200.

However, most of the memorabilia sold by sportsmen themselves has tended to be for financial gain. Had past sportsmen, particularly footballers, been paid at today's levels it is less likely that these items would have reached the market. Therefore David Beckham's medals may not appear at auction in the near future, although his boots (a new pair at almost every game) continue to attract attention, with a pair worn in Manchester United's treble year fetching £14,000.

A picture of the first All Black rugby union team fetched $NZ41,000 at auction in 2003. The black and white picture, taken in 1905, displays the team's names and the scores after their tour to England, Scotland and Wales. Bidding was vigorous, and the eventual owner later revealed he would have paid up to $NZ100,000 for the item.

19.2.8 Stamps

For as long as stamps have served as a government licence to post a letter, philately has been popular, with many devotees touring events around the country and abroad in a hunt for a rare find. Granted, Rowland Hill might not have imagined that almost 160 years after he had the *Penny Black* printed, so many stamps would be issued worldwide each year. Earlier collectors had no difficulty in forming a basic international collection that reflected their interests. They had in common a curiosity about a time, place or a person that motivated them to collect stamps with a historical ambience. In those early days, philatelists collected stamps of particular periods or countries, or postal types such as airmails, postage dues and express mail stamps. With many early stamps now expensive, and a burgeoning of issues from virtually every country, few can expect to create a comprehensive set. Patience is an important trait in any philatelist. Vintage stamps may be rare, or difficult to come by in the condition that investors and collectors covet. Hunting for century-old pieces of paper in flawless condition seems like a hopeless task, but, to the collector, the wait is worthwhile. Philatelists sometimes wait decades before finding the specimen they want at a price they can afford. A rare stamp in first-class condition is a 'gem', that is, a prime investment, but for a lifetime hobbyist and stamp lover, the pleasure is in possession. Nowadays, collectors are becoming more selective. Some are turning to thematic collecting – collecting stamps that illustrate a given topic, independent of time and place.

Thematic philately attracts many collectors, who find it absorbing, if not cost-free. A truly thematic collection, whatever the topic, involves elements of frustration, elation and impatience but, like a puzzle, can come together to illustrate a novel leitmotif and form a whole. Thematic collectors think imaginatively, show how apparently disparate items interrelate, and pursue their interests. For example, David Shepherd, the cricket test umpire, comments: 'I've collected stamps ever since my childhood. I was brought up in a Post Office so that's really where the interest came from.... I'm not sure how many first issues I have in my collection, quite a few I'd say.... I like to combine both my hobbies – cricket and stamp-collecting – so I've saved a lot of cricket-oriented stamps down the years.'

Thematics have not long enjoyed respectability among serious philatelists. However, collectors today have a choice of many themes: the beasts of the fields, the birds of the air, the fish of the sea, the people who possess fame and fortune, endorsed by provenance. One US collector has a franked Martin Luther King stamp issued in 1979, and has added to its value by persuading all the members of the King family to autograph the envelope. He also has a stamp that shows the jazz musician and composer, Duke Ellington, first issued by the US Postal Service in 1986. Alongside the stamp are the autographs of all the members of his band.

Many countries no longer conform to the tradition that only people who are dead should appear on stamps. Post Offices around the world have been eager to put stamps on sale featuring stars while they are still in fashion. Britain and the US, however, have generally retained the convention. In the UK, the 160-year-old taboo on featuring living persons outside the Royal family on stamps was broken in June 2001. Stamps released on the first day of Ascot races featured the model, Erin O'Connor, who became the first living commoner to be shown on a Royal Mail stamp. Concessions were made, however, as the model was photographed in silhouette.

In parallel, the literature of topical or thematic stamp collecting is growing. The American Topical Association produces *Topical Time*. In Britain, Stanley Gibbons has several popular thematic catalogues. The British Thematic Association has the *Themescene Magazine*, and supports the yearly *Thematica* exhibition in London. Attendees include dedicated philatelists willing to research every item and write up the design of each stamp for an exhibition or a competition.

Collectors often have a wide range of reference books, catalogues and magazines, with which to authenticate stamps, covers, post and meter marks, and franked postcards. In the internet era, stamp collecting is changing its image as philatelists move into the computer age. New technology such as e-mail is unlikely to threaten stamp collecting unduly, as letters and e-mail seem to run in tandem, at least for now; add to that the fact that many collectors buy new issues. However, the Web facilitates research and exchange of information, and buying and selling online is creating a genuine international market.

Philatelic Software is a London-based company that has launched *Stampmaster GB*, a CD-Rom database of all stamps issued by the British Post Office from 1840, with pictures, the official national postal museum history and description of each stamp. 'The system should help users to build catalogues of their own collections and work out which stamps they need to complete them', says Angela Enoch for the company. 'It can also be used with thematic collecting, as can our systems for dinosaur and ball sport stamp collections.'

Admittedly, stamps are not a standard item in portfolios. Like many alternative investments, they are risky and illiquid, and prudent advisers counsel stamp collectors never to rely on realising hard cash from their hobby. Yet returns can be worthwhile. In November 1996, for example, a rare stamp, an 1855 *Yellow Treskilling* from Sweden, sold for £1.5m, a record price. That was £0.6m more than when it was on sale in 1990, representing an annual compound rate of appreciation of 9%. An 1854 Bermuda cover (its stamp still on an envelope) sold in April 1998 for £230,000. In 1980, it went for £144,000. The annual compound interest was only 2.5%. In 2002, a rare US *Pymatuning Lake Duck* stamp was discovered. *Pymatuning Duck* stamps are very 'low profile' stamps that can easily go unnoticed in a collection, as so few of the series have been discovered. Owing to its rarity, dealers have been unable to place a value on it, but vendors might receive a four- or five-figure sum.

'Globally, the stamp market is faring well, especially in Hong Kong and China,' said Robert Scott of Sotheby's stamp department a couple of years ago. According to Hugh Jefferies, editor of Gibbons *Stamp Monthly*, prices being paid at the time for scarce and desirable stamps were increasing at rates not seen since the 1970s boom. The 2000 Stanley Gibbons Great Britain *Concise Stamp Catalogue* showed significant increases in the prices of British prewar stamps as a result of collector demand rather than investment activity.

One reason for the steady rise is the influx of an ageing generation into the pastime. 'A great many 40- to 50-year-olds who had stamp albums as kids are revisiting the hobby,' said Michael Laurence, the editor and publisher of *Linn's Stamp News*. According to the US postal service, about 20 million Americans keep stamps in sets. About 550,000 are serious collectors, ie people who carefully research stamps and slowly build collections.

Price upswings now depend on collectors, in marked contrast with an artificial boom between 1979 and 1981 when investors fleeing high inflation pressed into the market. Prices soared. Then, in 1981, the US authorities barred investors from including stamps and other tangible collectables in tax-deferred retirement accounts; they were thought too risky and difficult to value. With that change and a lessening of inflation, the market collapsed. By the end of 1991, the prices of American stamps had gone down by 56% from their 1981 highs. None the less, like gold, coins and other collectables, stamps can move out of phase with stocks and other financial instruments, and might help to hedge against losses in those assets.

Some people also like stamps for other reasons, including their portability. A person can put them in a pocket 'and cross a border with no questions asked', one dealer emphasised. Profits from stamps can also be difficult for the authorities to detect. Scott of Sotheby's stated that stamp collectors can enjoy 'a great deal of anonymity', a claim once made by tax haven banks. However, the required knowledge is a hurdle in the way of profit. The philatelist has to learn about individual stamps and postal history. Details such as the cancellation or the stamp gum can affect values. High mark-ups are a factor, too. 'People in the stock market pay a commission of 2 or 3% on a buy-sell transaction', one dealer revealed. 'In stamps, it can be 100% or more. That's expensive, and it means you've got to hold for many years to cover the dealer charges.' Add the dangers of fraud and the illiquidity of this small market, and even a risk-prone investor might hesitate.

Defects can sharply increase a stamp's price. That Swedish *Treskilling*, for example, was worth £1.5m because it was wrongly printed in yellow, not the issue's standard green. In 1995, 160 out of 80 million stamps printed to honour Richard Nixon had the former president's name printed upside down and his picture off-centre. One sold at Christie's for £10,000. The odds against such a find are long, but the collector might find the search instructive.

19.2.9 Dolls, teddy bears and toys

For some collectors on the acquisitive trail, doll collecting is the passion and for a few it has become an addiction. A few specialist dealers have customers who come every week to see what new dolls are on the market. At times, visits take on an air of secrecy. 'They may not all have spouses who condone their purchases', a trader said. Another mentioned a customer who hides doll purchases under her bed until she can ease them into her collection. A few buy only with cash, so the sale will not show up on a credit card statement. Occasionally, a collector moves to a larger house simply to accommodate his collection.

A Regency doll from the early 19th century might cost around £200, but the price of one with real hair and the original dress would be nearer £1,000. Rare antique dolls often fetch thousands of pounds. Specialists advise collectors to check the texture of a bisque doll's face to ensure it is genuine; if it is smooth, it is likely to be a fake. Antique dolls should also be fairly well worn, and perhaps smell a little mouldy.

Mass production of dolls gained momentum in the early part of the 20th century. Modern dolls bought as an investment are most valuable when in pristine condition, especially the ones that are known as NRFB dolls. Translated, that means 'never removed from box'. Collectors say these dolls should be kept in storage or posed prettily on a shelf. Their value has multiplied. Rare, mint-condition *Barbies*, for example, which sold for perhaps $2 when they were introduced in 1959, are valued at more than $1,000 today, according to US dealers.

Barbie is rapidly approaching middle age, but she still queens doll collectables, especially in the US. Advisers believe that, provided an item is 'rare and of its time', it could be in demand among new century collectors. This belief is widespread. In 1996, a bidder paid £34,500 at auction for a puppet from the *Thunderbirds* science fiction series, the original Lady Penelope. With such transactions in mind, dealers and auction houses, which promote this trade, suggest that ephemeral products and packages could become collectors' 'desirables' in the 21st century, if they survive in pristine condition. They might be worth more with the makers' signatures added.

Men sometimes enter the world of dolls because their wives are doll collectors. Don Jensen, associate editor of *Doll News*, the quarterly magazine of the US United Federation of Doll Clubs, is an active member of the Lake County Doll Club of Illinois. He and his wife, Arlene, spread their collection through every room in their home, and display many dolls in a floor-to-ceiling glassed cabinet that stretches over one full wall in one room. Jensen developed an interest in the hobby partly because of his wife's interest in dolls, and partly because of their shared pleasure in antiques.

Action Man is attracting interest, perhaps because men in their thirties and forties with disposable income seek to collect the toys of their childhood. At a recent Bonhams toy sale, two early-1970s sailor *Action Man* dolls, one with HMS Renown on his hatband, the other with HMS Dreadnought, each sold for more than £100. Leigh Gotch, an expert in the field, adds: '*Action Man* dolls are a safer investment because they have not quite reached their true potential yet.' Collectors have observed that the market first began to develop in 1991, *Action Man*'s 25th anniversary. Since then, prices have appreciated by 300 to 400 per cent. With *Action Man* set to celebrate its 40th anniversary in two years, collectors expect prices to go on rising.

Collecting teddy bears has been increasing since the 1970s, so much so that the term 'arctophily' has been coined to describe the activity. The world's most popular toy has now become the most collectable toy, and the best can sell for up to £150,000. Teddy bear production began when Richard Steiff, nephew of seamstress and dressmaker, Margarete Steiff, created the very first string-jointed bear in 1902. The Steiff bear soon attracted a worldwide demand and, according to legend, began to be called 'Teddy', after US President Theodore Roosevelt. On an expedition, Roosevelt would not shoot a bear that hunters had cornered for him, and a cartoonist, Clifford Berryman, captured the moment in the *Washington Post*. A New York storeowner adopted the patronym, and labelled a toy bear in his window *Teddy's Bear* – and the name stuck.

Steiff is a German company founded by Margarete Steiff, who as a child suffered from polio, which confined her to a wheelchair. The company made the earliest toy bears at the beginning of the 20th century. With their pointed snouts, long arms and feet, early Steiff bears look much more like real bears than many teddies today. In general, Steiff bears remain the most valuable of all teddies because of their unique historical appeal and exceptionally high quality. The bear from about 1908 is the most commonly seen type of Steiff bear, and is worth £1,000 to £2,000. Typically, early Steiffs have a humped back. Later bears have less prominent humps.

Rare Steiffs, the blue and the black bears, have sold for as much as £49,500 and £22,000 respectively. A genuine Steiff bear is identifiable by its signature small button in its left ear. Another expensive bear is

Aloysius, the teddy bear from the television series *Brideshead Revisited*, for which a collector paid £50,000.

Collectors are also interested in specially designed modern bears and limited editions, which are cheaper than the pre-1914 variety. A limited edition replica of an Edwardian bear made by Steiff will cost £275. When looking for old bears, collectors are advised to check for signs of age, especially on the parts of the bear one holds. Checking deep in the leg joint should indicate the original colour of the bear's fur and again, an old bear should smell old.

As bears became popular, an increasing numbers of toy companies on both sides of the Atlantic produced them. In England, prominent companies such as Chad Valley, Merrythought, Dean's Rag Book, Chiltern and J K Farnell enjoyed considerable success with their high-quality products. Farnells, for example, supplied teddy bears to Harrods during the 1920s and reputedly made Winnie the Pooh. The angled ears and large amber glass eyes of these bears, from around 1918, are typical of this maker. A bear like this is likely to sell for between £300 and £1,300.

Baby boomers, the first generation raised on television, are now collecting many of the toys they played with as children. One of the largest collections of model soldiers auctioned fetched £125,000 in 2003. Generally, demand is high, and Christie's has in recent years organised 'TV generation and animation' auctions, which have included toy robots, *Action Man*, *GI Joe* figures, and *Barbie* dolls. Of course, popularity does not necessarily make an item collectable. 'In reality,' says Daniel Agnew, Christie's specialist in the toys and dolls department in South Kensington, 'it's often toys that weren't popular in their own time that become expensive later, since there are fewer of them'.

Dinky toys have also attracted attention in recent years, with one collection being sold for over £250,000. About £100 spent on Dinky toys in 1985 has quadrupled in value since then; three shillings and six pence in old money, spent 40 years ago would now be worth up to £500 (a 22% annual rate of compound interest). However, investing in toys can be risky. It is the condition of the toy that is the key to its value. For example a 1960s *Batmobile* might be worth £50, but as much as £500 in its original packaging. Rummaging in an old toy box might produce some rare and interesting pieces, but if they have been played with to within an inch of their lives, their highest value is likely to be sentimental.

19.2.10 Music

Some connoisseurs are confident that the largest demand in this millennium will be for early technology and craft products. Some are buying fine musical instruments. An antique dealer in the Cumbrian lakes has assembled a collection of high quality Steinway grand pianos, built from 1930 onwards and, in at least one case, rebuilt by an expert. The dealer is confident that the pianos will appreciate hugely in value over the years. Dealers in the US agree, and 1920s Steinway grand pianos, selling for about $45,000, are in demand as an investment. Bonhams auctions of grand and vertical pianos can draw buyers from across the Atlantic; when that happens, prices can be significantly higher. At the top of the market, pianos can range up to $180,000 for the most expensive – a Fazioli from Italy or a Bösendorfer from Austria.

Other musical instruments have gained in popularity in recent years among collectors and performers. The record price paid for a violin is $6m (£3.4m), for Yehudi Menuhin's Guarnerius Del Gesu. Even a mediocre Stradivarius violin will cost perhaps £600,000, but should continue to hold its value. There are thought to be about 500 Stradivarius violins left. However, many violins carry the label Stradivarius, but this does not necessarily mean the piece is an original or a fake. The label could be used to indicate the maker had modelled the piece on a Stradivarius.

In 2003, the manuscript of Beethoven's ninth symphony, complete with the composer's hand-written corrections, sold for over £2m. It had been expected to fetch up to £3m. Copyists had prepared the 575-page manuscript for Beethoven, but the thousands of scribbles and alterations he made radically increased its value.

19.2.11 Silver

Antique silver has also risen in value. For example, in the US, a pair of delicate 18th century wine coasters, estimated to be worth about $125,000, recently went to a private collector, who paid $299,500. Fine old Tiffany silver is also popular across the Atlantic. In the years after the American Civil War, Tiffany used mixed metals consisting of silver, copper and brass in crafting japanesque pitchers, vases and trays, bizarrely engraved and encrusted with an assortment of reptiles, crustaceans and insect life. Europeans bought them at the 1876 Paris exposition, and they have since become valuable. A fine piece bought for $1,000 (£625) or less in the 1970s, might easily be worth $40,000–45,000 (£27,500) today, equivalent to perhaps 13% compound a year.

In the London market, a set of 17th-century apostle spoons can now fetch up to £150,000, having gained 50% in the past three or four years. In July 1997, a single silver-gilt apostle spoon sold at Christie's for only £368. However, a St Bartholomew spoon, with a mark by Robert Tyte of Salisbury, recently went for £1,955, four times its estimate. Six years ago, the estimated value of a Henry VIII St Matthias spoon was £5,000–£8,000. Subsequently, a renowned spoon expert identified the 's' marking of William Simpson, the famous 16th century spoon manufacturer; the item fetched a remarkable £18,700. The silver spoon market comprises discerning collectors; advocates claim that these objects represent an astute longer-term investment.

At the top end of the silver market, there is a select group of multi-millionaires who bid hundreds of thousands for famous silver collections and fine pieces from the 18th century, made, for example, by De Lamerie and Thomas Germain.

At the opposite end of the market are items that sell for less than £1,000, on occasion at regular auctions run by Christie's and Bonhams. At these auctions, investors may find other silver collectables, including tea caddies and spoons, nutmeg graters and Vesta boxes. Prices of these silver collectables have risen faster than the average. Four years ago an 1830 eagle's wing tea caddy might have been worth £1,200–1,500; today it could be worth more than £10,000. A George II tea caddy spoon may have cost £300 11 years ago and £500 six years ago: now it could fetch about £900. Interest in modern silver is also increasing, particularly examples crafted by early 20th-century silversmiths such as Oscar Ramsden or Alwyn Carr.

Generally, collectors prize British silver because of its hallmark, which provides a guarantee of quality. Lorraine Turner, a silver expert from Phillips, describes the 600-year-old hallmark as the oldest kind of consumer protection for collectors. One hallmark to look out for is Paul Storr from the late 18th and early 19th centuries. Paul de Lamerie is another fine silversmith, whose pieces have fetched up to $1m. American silver has also brought high returns. A rare piece of early colonial silver set a record for American silver at auction in January 2002, when it was sold at Sotheby's, New York, for $775,750 – over twice its estimated $300,000. The entire collection of 11 lots sold for nearly three times the presale estimate of $1.3m, bringing $3,027,875. The current record price for silver sold at auction is $10.3m, for a rococo tureen made by Thomas Germain. In 1998, Sotheby's on behalf of Baron Heinrich Thyssen-Bornemiza auctioned another ornate silver soup tureen, made by Juste Aurèle Meissonnier for Louis XV, in London. It fetched $5,722,500, the second highest price yet paid for a piece of silver at auction.

When buying silver, Bonhams advises examining the object for signs of repair, splits, damage or wear, using a bright light and a good magnifying glass. A rare 1702 Queen Anne coffee urn fetched £4,000 at auction in 2002, where a similar piece had fetched £20,000 the previous year. The cause of this drop of £16,000 was that the urn's tap or spigot had been repaired.

Buying silver also creates a need to keep it in good order. Cleaning sterling silver may be as simple as washing it with a little soap and water, then drying and buffing it with a soft cloth of 100% linen or cotton. Professionals recommend buffing and polishing silver in the same direction as the manufacturer did. A magnifying glass will reveal the factory's polishing marks. Alternatively, a good way is to apply a jeweller's paste, liquid or foam. 'The art,' say antiques dealers, 'is using a polish that's relatively mild and a cloth that's very soft.' Cloths impregnated with polish can also be effective, but it is wise to avoid using the same cloth on more than one piece because the residue from one will rub off on the next.

Stored silver is best kept either behind glass, in flannel bags or in bags made from soft cloth, or wrapped in acid-free paper in acid-free, paper-lined drawers. It is imprudent to let rubber bands or plastic bags touch the collection: silver can be irrevocably harmed by contact with petroleum-based products, and plastic bags can do double damage by trapping moisture. Do not allow silver to come into contact with salt, vinegar or the juices of citrus fruits, which can be equally harmful. Expert dealers advocate bringing silver pieces out of storage from time to time: 'The more you use it, the less you have to polish it.' Finally, silver is also popular with burglars, so keep insurance valuations up to date, photograph the pieces and record any distinguishing marks or inscriptions.

19.2.12 Memorabilia generally

Memorabilia, items once belonging to famous individuals, particularly those with a royal connection, continue to gain popularity among collectors. The auction of 40,000 items from the former home of the Duke and Duchess of Windsor saw 60–90 lots snapped up per hour. As prices soared to 40 or 50 times their estimate, excitement mounted, and even a sign reading, 'Drive carefully and beware of small dogs', fetched $4,500. After just 70 seconds of frenzied bidding, the desk at which Edward VIII signed the instruments of abdication fetched $415,000. An anonymous buyer paid $2.3m for a portrait of the Duke when he was the Prince of Wales, painted by Sir Alfred Munning – almost three times the $800,000 estimate. The National Portrait Gallery acquired a portrait of the Duchess for $107,000. Appetite for the couple's belongings has not waned. Last year saw a collection of 260 letters from the Duke of Windsor to his first love, Mrs Freda Dudley Ward, sold by Christie's at auction for an impressive £34,500.

The Christie's auction of 79 dresses belonging to Diana, the Princess of Wales, raised £2m in June 1997. One dress alone fetched £136,000, which at that time was a record for an item of clothing. Even the catalogue from the original dress sale became a collector's item; auctioned for charity, one fetched £50,000 in October 1997.

In 1998, the US sale of items once belonging to President John F Kennedy raised $9m. Among the lots were Kennedy's notes and dictation from the Cuban missile crisis, and notes made during the fatal trip to Dallas in 1963. A scrap of paper with a line from his inauguration speech sold for $40,250 – almost 10 times the estimate. Kennedy's signing pens went for $48,875, his comb for $1,265 and his sunglasses for $46,000. Gold buttons from his blazer sold for $18,400, along with a photograph of him in the blazer. Despite these high prices, the sale failed to match the record $34.5m sale from the estate of Jacqueline Onassis four years earlier.

On President Kennedy's birthday in 1962, Marilyn Monroe, who was wearing a flesh-coloured silk gown adorned with 6,000 rhinestone beads and sequins, serenaded him. That *Happy Birthday Mr President* dress set the record for the most expensive dress in the world when it was sold for $1,267,500 (£760,000) by Christie's in October 1999. A platinum eternity ring given to Monroe by her second husband, the baseball star, Joe DiMaggio, went for $772,500, considerably more than the $50,000 estimate. A total of 1,500 lots, all possessions of Monroe, were in this auction, ranging from the star dress to domestic bric-à-brac. The interest in the auction was such that 75,000 people saw the previews in six cities and more than 1,200 people registered to bid. Nancy Valentino, Christie's senior vice-president, described the sale as 'probably the most lavish of the millennium'.

Sotheby's recently sold a five-page letter written by Monroe when she was 16 years old for $43,120 (£25,540). The notebook on which Paul McCartney wrote the lyrics for *Hey Jude* sold for £111,500. At the same charity sale, John Lennon's corduroy jacket fetched £9,200. At another sale in New York, Lennon's spectacles sold for $25,875, while a jacket once belonging to Elvis Presley fetched almost $60,000, four times the estimate. The charity sale of a selection of Eric Clapton's guitars in June 1999 fetched a total of £3.23m.

In April 2004, Lady Penelope's pink Rolls-Royce – from the cult television classic, *Thunderbirds* – with fully functioning steering wheel, headlamps and leather seats, fetched £80,000 at a Planet Hollywood sale of film and TV collectables. Then, in May 2004, at a toy auction in Knightsbridge, Bonhams sold a plastic replica of the same FAB 1 car, made in Hong Kong in the early 1970s, for £239. While nostalgia has led to higher prices in the market for original film and television memorabilia, there remain bargains from the 1960s and 1970s for the toy collector to hunt out at car boot and jumble sales.

19.2.13 Recent record prices for collectables

Collectables have generally continued to escape the worst effects of recession. However, prices did fall. Now, optimists and dealers see signs of recovery in trade buying, and highlight successful sales at which collectors paid spectacular prices. Books and coins, toys, glassware, ceramics, jewellery, basketball cards and Hollywood posters have continued to sustain interest. Rarity almost always attracts bidders, as do opulence, intricacy, ethnicity, authenticity and the bizarre. Recently, a collector of modern art paid £11,000 for a kitchen blind pasted with photocopies of faxed drawings by David Hockney. The seller had bought her house from David Hockney's sister, and was about to put the blind in the bin, when the previous owner called to collect mail and mentioned that the five glued-on drawings were by her brother.

In some markets for collectables, buyers' enthusiasms have led to record prices. For example, a 24-carat gold statue of *Mickey Mouse* sold earlier in 2003 for $690,000, the highest price paid for an item related to a comic character. The statue weighed about 100 lbs and stood two feet tall. The Great Western Mint had manufactured it, and Disney had provided a certificate of authenticity. In the classic car market, a May 2003 Bonham's sale in Monaco realised £3.77m, with record prices being paid for a Maserati 3500GT *Spider* and a Ferrari 275GTB/4. A month earlier, a private Italian collector paid £86,250 for a cardboard cutout of Marlene Dietrich used on the cover of the Beatles' *Sergeant Pepper* album. A collector of American furniture paid $556,000 for an 18th-century federal mahogany gentleman's secretary desk.

Perfume bottles, biscuit tins, slot machines, costumes, dolls and typewriters are items cherished as never before. In the US, memorabilia related to slavery and American historical manuscripts are fast becoming favourites. Both private buyers and museums often seek 18th-century costumes. A hoard of old master prints found inside a trunk that was home to a family of mice sold at Sotheby's for £587,952, more than twice their estimate.

In July 2004, Bonhams set world record prices with its sale of antiquities in London. An extraordinary and fragile Roman glass bowl, dating from circa AD 300, broke the world record price for a piece of glass sold at auction. A telephone bidder paid £2,646,650 for the Constable-Maxwell Cage-Cup. The piece is exceptionally fragile, cut from a single block of glass. Its probable use was as an oil lamp suspended by a collar around the rim. Another bidder paid a world record price, £534,650 for a Pre-Columbian object sold at auction – a gold figure pendant.

19.3 FUTURE DEVELOPMENTS

19.3.1 Potential areas for investment

The recovery of market values in London has revived interest at the top end of the classic car market. Quality vintage Edwardian and veteran cars may now increase in value from a reduced level. Apart from cars, collectors are currently displaying an interest in areas as diverse as 20th-century ceramics and photographic equipment. An early Leica, with its mystique of Henri Cartier-Bresson, André Kertesz and 1920s Paris, may be worth thousands in mint condition. Even the humble box camera, the 'ordinary' Kodak that sold for £3 in the 1890s, can fetch £1,200 today. The world auction record for any camera was broken three times in a sale at Sotheby's in September 2001.

Other collectables that *Antiques Roadshow* valuers favour include dolls, toys and the memorabilia of the early cinema. Dolls could fetch as much as £150,000; a 1939 German triplate *Mickey Mouse*, £12,000; and film posters, between £35 and £70,000. Collectors today tend to go for modern 'antiques', from teddy bears to comics and rock memorabilia. There is a diversity of choice to suit the taste and pocket of eclectic collectors. It might still be possible for a single enthusiast to create a sustainable market for a new collectable by writing the first textbook along the lines of Michael Bennett-Levy's work on pre-war television, and Graham Turner's fishing tackle: a collector's guide, published nine years ago.

Currently there is a large interest in all things retro. Furniture, domestic appliances and clothing are all becoming both affordable collectables and saleable items, depending on the buyer's perspective. A 60-year-old General Electric refrigerator in prime condition could fetch as much as $31,000. A GPO 300 series Bakelite telephone, with original braiding, now sells for upwards of £200. A 1980s black and tan skirt suit will sell for about £120, while a 1980s *Dior* evening dress is worth some £200. Shoes are also sought after, a pair of 1980s *Casadei* brown boots selling for £100. A 1968 Charles and Eames desk chair will fetch perhaps £650.

19.3.2 Eastern markets

Economic changes in the 1980s and 1990s created a cadre of affluent Chinese businessmen, who became active at the art and antique auctions within the country and beyond its boundaries. China's growing class of rich entrepreneurs spend their wealth on Mandarin and Cantonese antiques that they could appreciate, and believed would appreciate. Until these buyers came into the market, Chinese porcelain and jade, fine paintings and calligraphy had ebbed to the west and Japan in the backs of lorries, and in the holds, boots and cases of smugglers, traders and collectors. The tide began to turn. Local antique shops in Beijing and Shanghai found customers among the well-off, and Chinese auction houses focused on the local market. Sotheby's and Christie's now have representatives in China. However, as yet only Sotheby's holds auctions there. Both auction houses hold frequent auctions in Hong Kong.

At a Beijing sale in 1996, a Chinese businessman paid 18m yuan (£1.25m) for a seven-centuries-old painting from the northern Song dynasty. However, regulations and uncertainties constrained both traders in antiques and currency transfers, leaving the upper reaches of demand in the hands of Taiwanese and Hong Kong dealers and collectors. Also, it is difficult to assess how much of China's artistic heritage of calligraphy, paintings, porcelain and jade stays hidden in private hands. Exporting these pieces would mean bypassing laws with severe penalties that are strict in the letter if not always in their application. Pieces more than 200 years old are marked in auction catalogues to show that the regulations forbid their export. In reality, many items from local auctions soon feature in auctions or dealers' showrooms outside China. This smuggling problem might lessen as local buyers increase their wealth, confidence and cosmopolitan ventures, and the authorities relax the regulations.

Partly in anticipation of such events, a stronger demand has emerged since 1996 for Chinese artefacts at US and European auctions. Another factor is the size of the Chinese population outside China. The UK has about 149,000 Chinese, with 50,000 in London. The majority are from Hong Kong, with significant numbers from Malaysia, Vietnam and Korea. Research published in April 1997 by the Policy Studies Institute showed that the Chinese are more likely than any other group in Britain, including whites, to earn more than £500 a week.

For some collectors, furniture from China allows them 'to savour life of a cultivated genre'. Records reveal early Chinese furniture from the Shang dynasty (16th–11th centuries BC) that archaeologists found in tombs. Designs evolved from dynasty to dynasty, until styles matured in Elizabeth I's era, when the furniture makers started to use Central Asian hardwoods and shippers began to trade with China. The designs featured unique paints and woods. Experts esteem furniture made of 'light Huanghuali or yellow rosewood, and the dark zitan or purple sandalwood'. In the 1930s, sinophiles began to collect elegant pieces of Bauhaus simplicity, which remained in short supply until the 1980s, when the bootleggers increased their trade in Chinese art and antiques. Auction houses and dealers now expect to see a growing demand for these items in China and across the world.

For Asian collectors of Chinese antiques, Yuan, Ming and Qing ceramics and high-quality imperial works of art attract the most interest. Jadeite jewellery (antique or new) is another important category. Excavated porcelain produced by early dynasties has emerged recently from China, helping to change western perceptions of the scope and allure of Chinese pottery. Sotheby's devoted a week in June 1999 to Asian art sales, including many Chinese pieces, demonstrating collectors' growing interest. Meanwhile, the Chinese are generally convinced that coin and stamp prices will rise worldwide. British auctioneers predict that, in China alone, the demand for coins will increase substantially in two to three decades. In recent years, the number of Chinese stamp collectors has soared to 30m. Future investors seeking new collectables may ask: how much will they pay in Asia? The region could influence taste and force up prices.

The Chinese also want impressive coins from any source, and banknotes that were printed for China-based Dutch, German or French banks, or by the American Banknote Company or Britain's Bradbury Wilkinson, supplier of Hong Kong's paper money. Dealers predict that Chinese spending preferences will soon extend to stamps and coins of all nations. China's most expensive stamp, an 1897 overprint, was worth only £1,200 21 years ago. In May 1995, Sotheby's sold one for £143,965 at its first Hong Kong stamp sale.

Western dealers hoping to become rich in Asia have to come to terms with the region's varying taste and uncertain wealth. The Chinese are reluctant to buy excavated antiquities, second-hand jewellery or sapphires (to them blue is the colour of death). Unlike the Chinese, the Taiwanese buy western-style art, much of it, paradoxically, originating in Taiwan.

Japanese taste is the most westernised. Some western speculators have been dabbling in collectables abandoned by the Japanese, when recession struck their economy, in the hope that they will return to the same markets. These include posters by Toulouse-Lautrec, Paris school paintings, and Galle and Daum glass. Turkish money troubles have also aided speculators. Prices of the brilliant red, green and blue iznik tiles of the 16th and 17th centuries, coveted by Turks, are only slowly moving up from bargain levels.

19.4 PURCHASING COLLECTABLES

19.4.1 Strategies

Collectors need to plan their strategies. Do they intend to become experts, who gain thrills and pleasure out of the artefacts in which they collect? Or will they instead rely on dealers to feed their hobbies or their alternative investment portfolios? If the latter, the player should realise that he will miss out on the social ambience of the market, which helps to keep real enthusiasts 'in the know'. According to a 1996 survey by the US Collectables and Platemakers Guild, 'new collectors are the key trend that industry executives see shaping the future', a trend that applies equally in Europe. 'Eighty per cent of the industry executives surveyed expect company sales to increase in the short term, and new collectors coming into the marketplace are identified as the primary reason for growth.'

However, the survey also refers to the 'greying' of many 'antiques categories and some collectables categories, as one of the major developments in the antiques marketplace'. Greying implies that many collectors in a category are aged 55 or over. To sustain demand, the market needs enough entrants to replace collectors who lose interest or die. Equally, if collectors follow trends and shift their loyalty to the next hot collecting craze, a category may decline in appeal and pieces fall in value. At one time, collectors and dealers saw these shifts as part of the natural interplay of demand and supply in the antiques market. They did not worry, because they believed that everything would eventually recycle. Generally, it did until the 1990s, which demonstrated that the recycling of a collecting category is no longer a certainty, at any rate in the medium term.

Nevertheless, the Guild's researchers conclude that collecting 'is a hobby of the 'empty-nesting' years, after children have left home. With the large "baby-boomer" generation reaching 50 years old, the total number of collectors could grow rapidly'. According to the specialists, the targeting of baby boomers by the 'desirables' industry largely depends on the appeal of nostalgia for the 1960s and later pieces, but means a decline in enthusiasm for 1940s and 1950s material, especially in the toy sector. Affordability is one reason; many objects from this era are expensive. Another reason is the collecting base itself; new collectors in their fifties are seeking material from the late 1970s and 1980s.

19.4.2 Developments in methods of buying and selling

The lists of sales at the big auction houses amply demonstrate that nowadays just about anything and everything is collectable. Over a decade ago, Christopher Davidge, chief executive of Christie's, made this prediction: 'By the millennium, a majority of the lots we auction will no longer relate to the fine or decorative arts.' to some extent the move to collectables is in response to a reduction in the number of antique and art lots coming onto the market. Those that do tend to disappear into private collecting trusts and museums. Auction houses such as Sotheby's and Christie's, which once focused almost entirely on art and antiques, now cater for the collectables market, and are selling more items that are contemporary. 'There is a trend towards more unusual things being collected', says Clare Pardy, marketing manager for Axa Nordstern Art

Insurance, a specialist in the art and antiques market. Collections of keys and locks, corkscrews and textile fragments are among the items assessed by Axa Nordstern.

The normal convention is that lots should have a cycle of five years or more so that they come 'fresh' on to the market. If they are resold too soon, buyers start to cool off and even wonder what is wrong with them. However, such is the buoyancy of the art and collectables market just now, with greater numbers of collectors chasing fewer objects, that not only are prices rising, but also the turn around is much quicker. Speculators buy art, antiques and collectables and resell them quickly to new collectors – a practice termed 'flipping'. Spectacular gains can be made, especially for 'blue chip' items, but it is a risky business as the market can also dive. To avoid being stung, buyers should research an item's auction history. A sports memorabilia dealer in New York bought a *Boston Braves* ring for $5,000 and shortly afterwards offered it for sale for $10,000. An interested buyer offered him $8,800 for it, and then noticed the ring still had a sticker on it from the previous sale. The would-be buyer found out what the ring had sold for and reduced his offer to $5,300. The dealer declined.

Fairs provide another way to access many dealers at one time. These fairs range from chaotic melees in local village halls to large national events organised by trade associations. Dealers at such fairs have generally vetted goods on sale for authenticity. For example, Affordable Art Fairs bring together hundreds of dealers and galleries, offering items for less than £2,500. An advantage of buying from a dealer or at a fair is that there are few hidden costs. The collector simply pays the price on the tag. However, the dealer has a living to make, so the purchase price is perhaps 40–60 per cent higher than the price at which the dealer would immediately buy back the piece.

With the development of the Web has come the growth of online auctions, which are now big business. Sotheby's and Christie's run formal online auctions. Other online services take the form of online bazaars. With 114m registered users, eBay is the largest of over 8,000 registered online auction companies. Founded in 1995, eBay expects consolidated net revenues for 2004 to be as high as $3.185 billion. The company recorded 332.3m new listings in the second quarter of 2004, 48% higher than the 225m listings reported a year earlier These online auctions allow people to sell their own property without having to go through auction houses; also items reach a far larger market since they are advertised, viewed, bought and sold worldwide. Online auctions are generally held over a longer period of time compared with live auctions (commonly seven to 10 days) and with the extra international competition may generate relatively high bids. The online auction house is becoming more popular, and there is a burgeoning number of sites. Among these sites, eBay is still the best known, although ebid.co.uk, theauctionhouse.com and Yahoo auctions are gaining a foothold. There are also several speciality online auction houses, wine auctions being among the most popular: see, for example, auctionwineonline.com.

In practice, buyers and sellers need to beware: online auctioning has its share of tricksters; non-appearance of goods; false descriptions; auction rigging; non-appearance of payment – all practices that the reputable companies are working to discourage. Among the thousands of consumer fraud complaints the US Federal Trade Commission receives yearly, those dealing with online auction fraud consistently rank at or near the top of the list.

Most people who complain to the FTC about online auction fraud report problems with sellers who: fail to send the merchandise; send an item of lesser value than advertised; fail to deliver in a timely manner; or fail to disclose all relevant information about a product or terms of the sale. However, some buyers experience other problems, which include:

- 'Bid siphoning,' when con artists lure bidders off legitimate auction sites by offering to sell the 'same' item at a lower price. Their intent is to trick consumers into sending money without proffering the item. By going off-site, buyers lose any protection the original site may provide, such as insurance, feedback forms or guarantees.
- 'Shill bidding,' when fraudulent sellers or their 'shills' bid on sellers' items to drive up the price.
- 'Bid shielding,' when fraudulent buyers submit very high bids to discourage other bidders from competing for the same item and then retract those bids so that people they know can get the item at a lower price.

Another type of fraud occurs when sellers or buyers pose as escrow services to improperly obtain money or goods. The so-called seller puts goods up for sale on an auction website and insists that prospective buyers use a particular escrow service. Once buyers make their payment information, the escrow service does not hold the money; it goes directly to the so-called seller. The buyer never receives the promised goods, is unable to locate the seller, and, because the escrow service was part of the scheme, fails to recover any money. Most of the FTC's complaints involve sellers, but in some cases, the buyers and arrangements for payment are the focus.

Successful bidders may pay by credit card, debit card, personal cheque, cashier's cheque, money order, or cash on delivery. Credit cards may offer buyers the best protection as they allow buyers to seek recompense from the credit card issuer (also known as a 'charge back'), if the product does not arrive or is not what they ordered. Typically, sellers on business-to-person auction sites accept credit card payments. In contrast, most sellers in person-to-person auctions require a cashier's cheque or money order before they send an item. In other cases, an online payment service or an escrow service can facilitate payment.

Online payment services are popular with both buyers and sellers. They allow buyers to use a credit card or electronic bank transfer to pay sellers who may not be set up to accept credit card or electronic bank transactions. They also may protect buyers from unlawful use of their credit cards or bank accounts, because the online payment service, not the seller, holds the account information. Many sellers prefer online payment services because payment services tend to provide more security than, say, personal cheques. In online payment services, both the buyer and seller set up accounts that allow them to make or accept payments. Buyers provide payment information, such as bank account or credit card numbers, and sellers give information about where to deposit payments. To complete a transaction, the buyer tells the online payment service to direct appropriate funds to the seller. The seller then has immediate access to the funds, minus any service fee.

Online escrow services operate differently. Their primary purpose is to protect buyers and sellers from fraud. Escrow services accept and hold payment from the buyer – often an electronic wire transfer via cheque, money order or credit card – until the buyer receives and approves the merchandise. Only then do they forward the payment to the seller. The buyer pays the fee for an online escrow service – generally a percentage of the cost of the item. Online escrow services tend to be popular for high-priced items, such as computers, cars or jewellery.

In online auctions, it is important to check the arrangements for payment, and to find out who will be responsible for delivery costs and insurance. Purchasers making direct payments should use a secure server, which will display a closed padlock or a similar symbol and 'https' in the address bar. Several of the online auction companies now use a secure escrow service. The buyer sends payment to the escrow service, and the seller only receives the money when the buyer can assure the service that he or she has taken delivery of the goods.

Despite complaints of fraud, Web-based auctions remain a fun, efficient and relatively safe way to do business – given that collectors act prudently. Before bidding, it is advisable to become familiar with the auction site, and never assume that the rules of one auction site apply to another. An online tutorial on the bidding process may save frustration and disappointment later. Other precautions are to:

- Find out what protections the auction site offers buyers. Some sites provide free insurance or guarantees for items that are undelivered, not authentic or not what the seller claimed.

- Read the seller's description of the item or service, and the fine print, and scan any photographs. Look for words like 'refurbished,' 'close out', 'discontinued', or 'off-brand' – especially when shopping for computer or electronic equipment – to determine the condition of the item being auctioned.
- Try to assess the relative value of an item before bidding. Be sceptical if the price sounds too low to be realistic. 'Brick-and-mortar' stores and price comparison sites may be good for reality checks.
- Find out about the seller. Avoid doing business with sellers who are difficult to identify, especially if they try to lure the bidder off the auction site with promises of a better deal. Be aware that some fraudulent sellers may use a forged e-mail header that makes follow-up difficult, if not impossible. Obtain the seller's telephone number to provide another means of contact. Dial the number to confirm that it is correct. Some auction sites post feedback ratings of sellers based on comments by other buyers. Check them out, and bear in mind that, sometimes, the seller or 'shills' paid by the seller may be the source of favourable comments.
- Consider whether the item comes with a warranty and whether follow-up service is available if needed. Many sellers do not have the expertise or facilities to provide services for the goods they sell. If this is the case with a particular seller, the buyer, when placing a bid, is forfeiting that protection.
- Find out who pays for shipping and delivery. Generally, sellers specify the cost of shipping and give buyers the option for express delivery at an additional cost. If there is any uncertainty about shipping costs, it is advisable to check with the seller before placing a bid.
- Check on the seller's return policy. Will it be possible to return the item for a full refund if the buyer finds it unsatisfactory? In such cases, does the seller require the buyer to pay shipping costs or a restocking fee?
- E-mail or call the seller to raise any questions, and do not bid without straight and satisfactory answers to all these questions.

When bidding, it is prudent to establish a top price and stick to it. This can help ensure that the bidder secures a fair price and protection from 'shill bidding'. It is important not to bid on an item without intending to buy it. The highest bidder usually has an obligation to follow through with the transaction. Some auction sites bar 'non-paying' bidders, also known as 'deadbeats,' from future bidding. Also, it is advisable to save all transaction information – printing the seller's identification; the item description; the time, date and price of the bid; and every e-mail sent or received from the auction company or the seller.

On occasion, auctioneers split sales between online and live sales. In May 2000, Sotheby's held the third and final part of a sale of the Enid

Blyton company's *Noddy* archive. They split it between an online and a live auction 'because it was a lower value sale'. Most of the best pieces had been sold in the two previous sales. According to Sotheby's: 'sales where prices are not too high lend themselves to online auctions at this stage of the internet's development.'

Other auction sales also take place simultaneously on the floor and on the Web. One took place in April 2000 when Greg Manning Auctions held a comic book/comic art sale. The live floor auction was simulcast in real-time over the internet, so increasing bidding activity and engendering higher sale prices. Over half of the lots received internet bids from collectors worldwide. The sale exceeded pre-auction estimates by more than 40%, with many lots selling for two to five times their pre-sale estimates, setting numerous world records.

Increasingly, Web-based sales are not being restricted to lower priced and commoner items. Internet buyers are paying record prices, often for rare items. In June 2000, Sotheby's New York auctioned a copy of the *Declaration of Independence*, one of only 25 existing copies, exclusively over the Web. The estimated price was $4m–6m; it fetched $8.14m. In July 2000, eBay auctioned a Honus Wagner baseball card for $1.1m. A black leather handbag belonging to former Prime Minister Margaret Thatcher exceeded expectations when it sold for $100,000 in a charity internet auction. A recent *Observer* article reported that murder memorabilia, known as 'murderabilia', is one of the fastest-growing sectors of the collectables market. This is largely owing to the anonymity granted by internet-based services. Whereas the main auction houses, like Sotheby's and Christie's, have limited sales of historical items, for example personal belongings of notorious figures, including Al Capone and Dr Crippen, online auction companies are less restrictive. Recent items for sale online have included the bricks from the walkway where O J Simpson's wife was murdered, and even locks of Charles Manson's hair. Nevertheless, eBay has resisted pressure to remove murderabilia items from its site: 'some of the merchandise may be questionable or distasteful, but we don't want to play the role of censor', said an eBay spokesperson.

19.4.3 Predicting future collectables

Predicting what will become the collectables of the future is a tricky exercise. Paradoxically, in the design world the objects that fetch the highest prices at auction are not necessarily the best. The real 'timeless classics' of the 20th and 21st centuries are never going to fetch high prices because they have remained in production. Design failures, though, especially fiascos such as the Sinclair C5 electric car, already have rarity and curiosity value. Should environmental awareness finally put paid to the combustion engine in the coming decades, collectors may even accord 'alternative' designs pioneer status. Perhaps society's very existence 50 years hence will depend on a revolution in energy consumption, in which case disposable goods such as throwaway cameras would become 'obsolete relics of a crazy age'.

The collectables market is currently awash with various items that were produced to commemorate the new millennium. Advice from Tony Curtis of *Lyle's Price Guide* is to keep the best or the worst, as it is those items that have proved the most profitable mementoes of past celebrations. However, Sue Ryall of the Antique Collector's Club warns against buying millennium memorabilia for investment potential. 'Anyone who is collecting should buy something they like and want to live with', she said. 'Then if it goes up in value that is a bonus.' John Harvey, a director of Sotheby's, says: 'be very wary of limited editions that are mass-produced. If something is limited to 5,000, hinting that it's an investment, the likelihood is it's not going to be. Buy things of quality and things you like, if possible choosing something that is hand-crafted rather than mass-produced.' Henry Sandon, a ceramics consultant for Phillips and one of the BBC's *Antiques Roadshow* team, feels that any limited edition over 750 'is crazy and there are too many of them'.

More advances in software, information, literature, music, etc will be coming into everyone's lives via a computer screen. So how has digital recording on CD-Rom and DVD affected collecting vinyl LPs and EPs? In an article in *Record Collector*, Ted Owen is adamant that vinyl is worth collecting, particularly rare or superior quality pressings: 'If you see a rare record, buy it, whatever the price; it's still an investment and is bound to go up in value.' Condition is always critical, so storage can be a problem, even with smaller items such as records. 'The general tendency is for people to want to get rid of something just when it's at its lowest value', says the owner of *Vinyl Exchange*, a second-hand record shop in Manchester. 'We see it time and time again; troops of doleful, slightly balding men in their mid-30s whose wives have made them clear out their punk collection due to lack of space. If they could only hang on until there's no longer a glut, they might have something that other people want.'

Other possible collectable items are those that were highly popular, that no one would imagine would become items of value. In such cases keeping an item in pristine condition is the key to its value. There has also been a revival in national emblems in the wake of 11 September 2001. Sotheby's sold a collection of American flags, including a 13-star shield banner that was used during the 1789 inauguration of George Washington as president, for $1.3m in 2002.

19.4.4 Hidden costs

When buying at auction, bidders should be aware that they pay a buyer's premium (typically 10 to 15 per cent but sometimes more), as well as the hammer price. For example, if a bid for £500 is successful, the buyer actually pays £575 if the premium is 15 per cent. Sellers also pay a commission to the auction house. A purchase of a large item will also incur the costs of their delivery and insurance in transit; and, after delivery, the item will need insuring. A typical home contents policy has fairly limited cover for 'valuables'. It is worth checking the policy carefully and, if greater cover is necessary, contacting the insurer or a broker. Collectors may also need to spend extra to protect investments. There is a thriving market in stolen collectables, so the owner may have to install a higher level of home security. Certain collectables, such as furniture, will require suitable conditions of light and humidity.

19.5 TAXATION

19.5.1 Tax planning

Most alternative investments count as 'chattels' for tax purposes. Any gain made on disposal may be subject to capital gains tax, but this tax regime offers a range of reliefs, including a yearly tax-free allowance (£7,900 in the 2003–04 tax year). However, if a collector buys and sells regularly, there is a risk that the Inland Revenue might consider that he or she is carrying on a trade and may try to tax gains as income.

If purchases can satisfy the requirements of a business, for example acquisitions of furniture or wall decorations for an office, investors paying high rates of tax may obtain benefits. They may be able to offset the costs of acquisitions as legitimate business expenses, but with a corresponding liability on disposal. If, however, the chattels that form an alternative investment portfolio are not income-producing, the owners will not normally be able to secure income tax relief in relation to insurance premiums or maintenance expenses.

19.5.2 VAT

For VAT purposes, collectors' items include collections and collectors' pieces of historical, numismatic, philatelic, archaeological, palaeontological, anatomical, zoological, botanical and mineralogical interest. The quality 'of philatelic interest' should be a postage or revenue stamp, a postmark, a first-day cover, or a piece of pre-stamped stationery that has been franked – or, if unfranked, is not legal tender. Unfranked postage stamps that are valued for postage are not collectors' items, and cannot be refunded in margin schemes.

See details of VAT arrangements and sources in 18.3.3 and 18.7.5.

19.5.3 Sets of collectables

The investor may want to avoid acquiring 'a set of similar or complementary things' instead of a number of separate items that do not constitute a single set. The definition may affect future tax liabilities if the set's value would exceed capital tax thresholds, whereas the individual items would be exempt. Thus, the Revenue is of the opinion that a collection of postage stamps *per se* constitutes a single set, although in its view the stamps of one definitive or commemorative issue would not necessarily do so.

At issue is whether the acquisition of a set or sets of collectables is a mere hobby or a *bona fide* investment. Implicit in the question is whether expenses will be deductible. On balance, if the collector buys strictly for investment and capital gains, and keeps accurate records, including purchase dates, prices, provenance and current values, then it may be possible to make a case for deducting certain expenses (eg insurance, relevant publications, even travel to sales and auctions). In the majority of cases, however, the collector will be trying to create legal and tax history, in itself an expensive hobby.

When a collection is sold at auction or, after exhibition at a dealer's shop, the authorities may also be interested in the gains secured. In a case where someone has purchased collectables 'under the table', ie without a clean provenance, the Revenue may argue that the cost basis is zero. The gain would, therefore, be 100%. The advantages of documented evidence are clear. Where the authorities take the view that efforts were being made to evade payment of tax, the legal penalties can be serious, even if the action was in truth innocent.

19.6 SUITABILITY AND MECHANICS

19.6.1 Risks

Snares await buyers. Markets may be thin. Collectables can be difficult to sell quickly, and meanwhile they pay no interest. Instead they can soak up steady outlays in insurance, storage and maintenance. Repairs and restoration can also be expensive. To refurbish a good piano that a musician will want to play could cost £15,000. It might cost £60,000 to renovate a Ferrari, and only the reckless would drive it along the road. The car has a hand-formed aluminium body. If a passer-by leans against the car it can easily dent. Despite such costs and risks, enthusiasts still pay massive sums for rare vehicles. Four years ago, a 1936 Mercedes-Benz 500k roadster went at auction for £1.6m. It was not in first-class condition. According to one report, rats had eaten through the upholstery. A butcher had left it sitting in his shed, unused, for more than 30 years. Originality means a great deal with great cars.

19.6.2 Precautions

Independent advisers who specialise in collectables recommend that an investor should check carefully a dealer's reputation before deciding to employ his services. They suggest that enquiries should be pursued to find out how long the dealer has been in business, and to what professional organisations he belongs. In practice, it is also prudent to make sure that the collector fully understands what is being offered and promised.

To take numismatic coins by way of illustration, questions might be asked about a coin's grade and the backing for any guarantees. Does the dealer guarantee to buy back an investment? If so, at what price and on what terms? Are there, for example, any deductions affecting buy-back warranties? Is a service charge levied? With collectables of any value, it may be worth seeking a second opinion on quality and provenance before confirming a decision to buy. Familiarity with sales and the publications in the field will also reveal whether an asking price is in line with the market, or well above it.

Generally it is not advisable to sell collectables to the person who values them, as this presents a conflict of interest, prompting a possibly deflated valuation. Instead, the valuation should be obtained in writing, with a clear statement of the item's worth, rather than an estimate. If a piece is for sale, the valuer will usually estimate a market value below the retail price, which will include a dealer's mark-up. However, knowing a little of the market before valuation should ensure a fair assessment is given. In practice, it is also important to consult a reputable valuer. A professional who deals with valuers regularly could offer worthwhile advice, for example a trust manager or an estates lawyer.

Equally, in this market as in others, it is wise to avoid letting the marketplace dictate what to collect. Anyone can enjoy the thrill of buying low and selling high, but playing the collectables market is a reliable way to lose money. Sound advice is to join a collecting society before buying anything. There are now societies and clubs for almost every conceivable collectable. Most of these bodies publish newsletters and rosters of members with interests in common. These members usually know the reputable dealers, and can help to vet a purchase. Another judicious step is to attend specialist auctions. These events are often a good way to meet people who are knowledgeable, and to sharpen a collecting instinct. Museum curators can be very helpful people to speak to, and many larger museums hold opinion afternoons. Cataloguing a collection is also sensible, even from the very beginning, after a few purchases. The records help to keep track of purchases and sources, and the records may be useful for tax purposes. Insurance is another necessity to protect the investment, and most insurance companies demand a catalogue before they will issue a policy.

19.6.3 Other risks

Trading collectors' pieces online is gaining in popularity. The World-Wide Web offers more information on alternative investment opportunities than ever before. However, the internet is an unregulated market, and the opportunities add to the risks. Investors should be as wary of any offers as they would be about an unsolicited mail shot.

The Financial Services Authority has compared the internet with 'a galactic car-boot sale: anyone from anywhere in the world can offer anything for sale'. As with any unregulated marketplace, those with established reputations will be pitching for business alongside newcomers offering enticing deals. Investors will find false bargains, scams and frauds. Also, the Web makes it easy, and will soon make it easier, to buy and pay for goods and services from foreign organisations, almost without being aware that they have their base abroad. So, before making a purchase, a buyer needs to know about the company. Where is its base? Which authorities regulate it? Which country's laws will apply if a dispute occurs? Rights differ from place to place. For example, in some jurisdictions, when a company fails, the liquidator holds clients' assets separately, and creditors do not have access to them. In other countries, the liquidator pools all the assets, and then shares out the proceeds between the owners and creditors.

Crime adds to these risks. Sophisticated criminals are now targeting 1960s and 1970s collectables, according to the Arts and Antiques Unit in New Scotland Yard. The unit's analyses suggest that burglars are taking pieces that, a decade ago, most people would have said were junk. The *Antiques Roadshow*'s experts have told the world, including breakers and enterers, that items that fell out of fashion years ago are now back in demand, and valuable. Auction houses have detected a similar market opportunity, and have opened outlets to deal with contemporary pieces.

The Metropolitan Police enquires into art crime and manages a database of art and antiques reported stolen. Its *Bumblebee* imaging system came into operation in 1991, and now details thousands of stolen artefacts worth from £100 to £0.5m. Other European states have national art and antiques databases, and plans are in train to set up a European Union system. Britain has yet to integrate records of stolen art and antiques from police forces across the country. Yet law enforcement experts estimate that the purloining of paintings and other collectables represents a £5bn global industry, second only to narcotics in breadth and scale. In Britain alone, robbers make off with £0.5bn in such valuables each year.

The more popular a collecting field, the more likely collectors are to come across fakes. Following a three-year investigation, the FBI announced in April 2001 that 90% of US memorabilia items might be fakes. The memorabilia industry turns over $1.6bn a year.

Readers of this chapter may seek not only to protect their wealth, but also to increase it by buying rare stamps, fine wine, memorabilia or other exotic objects. Many make worthwhile gains through these alternative investments; others lose a small fortune. Vast disparities can arise in risks. Companies that offer moneymaking opportunities of this kind may claim unrealistically high rates of return; businesses and advisers regulated by the FSA would find it difficult to make similar claims.

In alternative investment markets, highly speculative activities are often loosely regulated and run by individuals or companies operating as unlicensed traders or brokers. This is the usual case in the UK, and means that:

- It is unlikely that anyone has vetted the people running the scheme to establish whether they are honest, competent and solvent.
- The company does not have to follow the special rules and codes that apply to authorised companies and help to ensure that they treat investors fairly.
- If a transaction goes wrong, no guarantees exist that anyone will look into complaints.
- If the company fails, investors have no rights to claim compensation from authorised funds, and probably no access to any other compensation arrangements.

The first step for an alternative investor is therefore to make sure that a firm is legal. UK law generally requires authorisation of firms, which formally run investment businesses. However, if such a firm has a current authorisation in another EU country, it may use its European passport to run an investment business lawfully in the UK. To operate an investment business without proper authorisation can be a criminal offence.

To check a UK business's status, contact FSA regulators and the FSA's central register (tel: 020 7929 3652). The FSA will advise enquirers to take full details of the salesperson, and to record his name, the firm's name, the full address, and the telephone and fax numbers. Equally, keeping all documents received is wise, including the envelope. If the firm is not authorised and should be, the FSA investigations department would like to know about the matter.

When a firm can trade without authorisation, the investor must rely for protection on his own efforts, preferably by going through a checklist of commonsense questions. Usually, the greater the reward, the greater the risk. If the return is so much higher than is on offer elsewhere, why is the firm letting outsiders in on it?

Is the firm seeking money for a legitimate purpose? The scams are often ingenious, and sold by experts. Illegal operators know how to take advantage of weaknesses (including greed). They also know how to exploit vulnerability. If an investor sends money to illegal operators, he is unlikely to make a profit or ever recover the money. If the money goes out of the UK, restitution is even less likely. Many firms that operate illegally either collapse or the authorities put them out of business. In these cases, investors often discover too late that all their money has gone. Sometimes, the firm took the money in high management fees; often, the firm has lost or removed all the investors' money. In any event, the sums laid out have vanished at a cost, on occasion, of people's life savings, with scant hope of compensation.

If the value of a product, and the possibility of selling it at a high price, is based on rarity, will this scarcity continue? Can those behind the firm show evidence of the expertise they claim? What is the true level of risk, and is it acceptable? If the money is lost, what will be the effect on the investor's lifestyle? What will happen to a guaranteed return, if the responsibility for delivering it lies with the firm and the firm fails? How long has it been, and will it be, in existence? The firm can only fulfil promises to buy something back if it and the money are still around.

19.7 CONCLUSION

In this field of alternative investments, the vital step is to decide whether to be an investor or a collector, or both. Those who take the trouble to understand a particular market well, and be a player, can gain the knowledge to be a specialist collector. In practice, only a limited number of people have the enthusiasm, dedication and resources to pursue the opportunities in a systematic way. As indicated, these markets for collectables are also social networks. The participants derive much pleasure from being involved in this network. Keeping in touch with fellow devotees is rewarding in the interchanges and in the exchanges.

The investor will learn quickly that he has to spend time studying the subtle connotations of hallmarks on metalwork, manufacturers' symbols on ceramics, makers' names on antique clocks, the marks of well-known furniture craftsmen, and many thousands of other characteristics that influence the attribution of collectors' pieces. Those for whom time is scarce will recognise quickly that they need to specialise, and enlist the services of a specialist. The real collectors develop a burning fervour and could scarcely stop, even if they wanted to, or were forced to by circumstances. In essence, to be a mere investor is to miss out on the social rewards and to enjoy only vicarious or second-hand advantages. But then collectables are, after all, second-hand.

SOURCES OF FURTHER INFORMATION (CHAPTERS 17–19)

Chapter 17

Why are diamonds so expensive? http://economics.uta.edu/facpages/Amacher/ Spring%202004/econ%205313%20final%20presentation.ppt

Gold Survey 2004, Goldfields Mineral Services (020 7539 7820). www.gfms.co.uk

Gold 2001: Mine Costs 1996–2005, AME Mineral Economics, GPO Box 3602 Sydney, NSW 1044 (+00 612 9262 2264). www.ame.com.au

Gold Demand Trends (quarterly), World Gold Council (020 7930 5171). www.gold.org

Gold in the Official Sector (quarterly), World Gold Council (020 7930 5171). www.gold.org

Platinum 2004, Johnson Matthey plc, New Garden House, 78 Hatton Garden, London EC1N 8JP (020 7269 8400). www.platinum.matthey.com

An analysis of the UK gold auctions 1999-2002 Vila Wetherilt, Anne (Bank of England, Monetary Instruments and Markets Division) and Young, Graham (Bank of England Foreign Exchange Division) www.bankofengland.co.uk/ qb/gold.htm

Technical Forum on the Issue of 'Conflict Diamonds', Hilton Ashton, BOE Securities, May 2000. www.boegroup.com

World Silver Survey 2004, Goldfields Mineral Services (020 7539 7820). www.gfms.co.uk

EUROPA – The European Union On-line, available from: http://europe.eu.int

De Beers, see www.debeersgroup.com

Chapter 18

The Council for Museums, Archives and Libraries, www.mla.gov.uk

Art Newspaper, TG Scott Subscriber Services, 6 Bourne Enterprise Centre, Wrotham Road, Borough Green, Kent TN15 8DG (01732 884023). www.theartnewspaper.com/

Art Sales Index 2000–2001 (33rd edition), Art Sales Index Limited (01784 451145). www.art-sales-index.com

Capital Taxation and the National Heritage, The Board of the Inland Revenue, London 1986 (amended 1988) (020 7438 6325). www. inlandrevenue.gov.uk

Capital Taxes – Relief for Heritage Assets, Capital Taxes Office, www.inland revenue.gov.uk/cto

The Death Tax, Towry Law (01753 868244). www.towrylaw.com

Picture Guide to the UK Art Market 1997, Duncan Hislop, Art Sales Index Ltd (01784 451145). www.art-sales-index.com

Sponsoring the Art: New Business Strategies for the 1990s, The Economist Intelligence Unit (020 7830 1000). www.eiu.com

Works of Art: A Basic Guide to Capital Taxation and the National Heritage, Office of Arts and Libraries, 1982 (out of print)

Works of Art in Situ: Guidelines on In Situ Offers in Lieu of Capital Taxation, Department of National Heritage, 1984 (020 7270 3000) (out of print)

Works of Art: Manuscripts and Archives. Basic information for Exemption from Capital Tax, Office of Arts & Libraries, 1991 (out of print)

Works of Art Private Treaty Sales: Guidelines from the Office of Arts and Libraries, Department of National Heritage, 1986 (020 7270 3000) (out of print)

Chapter 19

The Ephemerist (quarterly), Ephemera Society (01923 829079). www.ephemera-society.org.uk

The Guide to the Antique Shops of Britain 2004, The Old Rectory, Sessay, Thirsk, North Yorkshire YO7 3LZ

Antiques Price Guide 2003, Judith Miller, Dorling Kindersley 2003

Millers International Antique Price Guide 2004, Elizabeth Norfolk (ed), Octopus Publishing Ltd, 2–4 Heron Quays, London E14 4JP, England (020 71531 8400). www.reedbooks.co.uk

Antiques Trade Gazette, 115 Shaftesbury Avenue, London WC2H 8AD (020 7420 6600). http://www.atg-online.com

Sotheby's online, available at www.sothebys.com

Christies, available at www.christies.com

USEFUL ADDRESSES (CHAPTERS 17–19)

Arts Council of England
14 Great Peter Street
London SW1P 3NQ
Tel: 020 7333 0100
Web: www.artscouncil.org.uk

Ephemera Society
PO Box 112
Northwood, HA6 2WT
United Kingdom
Web: www.ephemera-society.
org.uk

Oriental Ceramic Society
30b Torrington Square
London WC1E 7JL
Tel: 020 7636 7985

Royal Fine Art Commission
7 St James Square
London SW1Y 4JU
Tel: 020 7960 2400

British Antique Dealers
 Association
20 Rutland Gate
London SW7 1BD
Tel: 020 7589 4128
Web: www.bada.org

Incorporated Society of Valuers
 and Auctioneers
3 Cadogan Gate
London SW1X 0AS
Tel: 020 7235 2282

Royal Academy of Arts
Burlington House
Piccadilly
London W1V 0DS
Tel: 020 7439 7438
Web: www.royalacademy.org.uk

Society of Antiquaries of
 London
Burlington House
Piccadilly
London W1J 0BE
Tel: 020 7734 0193
Web: www.sal.org.uk

Wine and Spirit Association
Five Kings House International
1 Queen's St Place
London EC4R 1XX
Tel: 020 7248 5377
Web: www.wsa.org.uk

British Antique Furniture
 Restorers' Association
The Old Rectory
Warmwell
Dorchester
Dorset DT2 8HQ
Tel: 01305 854822
Web: www.bafra.org.uk

Antiquarian Booksellers'
 Association (International)
Sackville House
40 Piccadilly
London W1J 0DR
Tel: 020 7439 3118
Web: www.abainternational.com

LAPADA – Association of Art
and Antique Dealers
535 Kings Road
London SW10 0SZ

Tel: 020 7823 3511
Web: www.lapada.co.uk

British Art Market Federation
10 Bury Street
London SW1Y 6AA

Tel: 020 7389 2148

British Thematic Association
107 Charterhouse Street
London EC1M 0PT

Invaluable
Catherine House
76 Gloucester Place
London W1U 6HJ

Tel: 020 7487 3401
Web: www.invaluable.com

Sotheby's
34-35 New Bond Street
London W1A 2AA

Tel: 020 7293 5000
Web: www.sothebys.com

Christie's
8 King Street
St James's
London SW1Y 6QT

Tel: 020 7839 9060
Web: www.christies.com

Phillips, de Pury & Company
25 Albemarle Street
London W1S 4HX

Tel: 020 7318 4010
Web: www.phillipsdepury.com

Bonhams
101 New Bond Street
London W1S 1SR

Tel: 020 7629 6602
Web: www.bonhams.co.uk

20

TAX BENEFICIAL INVESTMENTS AND SAVINGS

MIKE WILKES

PKF, Chartered Accountants

20.1 INTRODUCTION

The most important consideration of savings planning is to identify appropriate investments that offer good value and tax benefits; privileges represent only one aspect of this.

An investment that is appropriate for one person may not necessarily meet the needs of another in different circumstances. Some of the questions to ask are:

(1) How long can the savings be tied up?
(2) Are the savings for a particular purpose (eg school fees, a family wedding, retirement)?
(3) When will the money be needed?
(4) Is income required?
(5) Will fluctuations in stock market and/or property prices be such a worry that the investments become unattractive?

You may also want to strike a balance. The criteria for investing the short-term part of the portfolio should be different from the method of investing in more volatile investments on a longer-term basis. Striking the right balance is one of the hardest aspects. If savings are fairly modest, they may have to be invested on a conservative basis – and the return will reflect this. At the other extreme, high net worth individuals who have covered all their short-term requirements may deploy a proportion of capital in more risky investments that offer the prospect of a very high return.

Once these decisions have been made, the next step is to identify investments that meet the specifications and offer good value. An investment may offer good value if the managers' charges are reasonable and the tax treatment is favourable.

413

This chapter starts by looking at tax privileged investments from the standpoint of the most cautious investor who may want access to capital at short notice and who is, therefore, not well disposed towards investments that may fall in value from time to time. Then a look is taken at tax-privileged investments, which involve a degree of risk arising from fluctuations in The Stock Exchange, etc. Finally consideration is given to bank deposits and 'near cash' investments, most of which involve little or no risk but do not have a privileged treatment. Many of these investments are provided by the Government through the Department of National Savings or local authorities.

20.2 TAX PRIVILEGED INVESTMENTS

20.2.1 TESSAs

One of the government's more successful innovations were TESSAs (tax exempt special savings accounts). These were available to any individual resident in the UK and aged 18+. Although, following the introduction of ISAs, new TESSAs could not be opened after 5 April 1999, those in existence on that date could continue to run for their normal term. They could therefore run in parallel to ISAs, and on maturity the capital element could be paid into the cash component of a new ISA, and would not restrict the allowable annual subscription limit. The previous tax rules still applied to TESSAs continuing until 5 April 2004.

The investment normally ran for five years. It offered a secure return since the money had to be deposited with an authorised bank or building society and the risk of capital loss was therefore remote. The investor could withdraw his capital within the five-year period, but the tax benefits were forfeited if such withdrawals exceeded certain limits. Subject to this, the benefit of having a TESSA was that the investor received tax-free interest.

The maximum amount that could be withdrawn during the first five years without jeopardising the tax benefits was the interest credited to the account, less the savings rate of tax of 20%, which would have been deducted if the account had not enjoyed its special tax exempt status.

Example

Louise deposited £3,000 in a TESSA on 5 April 1999. In Year 1 the bank credits interest of £195. The interest has not borne any tax. Louise could withdraw £195 less 20% notional tax, ie £156.00, without affecting the account's exempt status. The remaining £3,039.00 would have continued to attract tax-free interest. However, if Louise withdraws £156.01, the bank

> would have to account to the Revenue for the tax of £39.00 and the account would thereafter be treated as an ordinary deposit account. Once five years had elapsed, Louise could have withdrawn the entire amount with no tax consequences.

There were limits on the maximum amount that could be invested in a TESSA. An individual could invest up to £3,000 in the first year and up to £1,800 each year thereafter, subject to the total not exceeding £9,000. Alternatively, an individual could have invested up to £150 per month.

Prior to 6 April 1999, the whole of the capital (up to the maximum of £9,000) of a maturing TESSA could be reinvested in a follow-up TESSA, provided the new account was opened within six months of the original account's maturity. Individuals who invested less than £9,000 in the first year of their second TESSA could continue saving over the next four years, within the usual limits for each year, subject to the overall limit of £9,000. If, however, the maximum was invested, no further investment was permitted.

An individual could not have two TESSAs at any one time. However, the above limits were applied separately for husband and wife. The terms under which banks and building societies accepted deposits for TESSAs varied. The Government regarded it as a matter of choice whether the deposit carries a rate of interest that was fixed for five years or a variable rate. TESSAs are 'portable', so investors can transfer their savings from one financial institution to another without losing tax benefits.

20.2.2 National Savings fixed-interest certificates

These are another form of investment that provides a totally tax-free return. However, the yield reflects this and so ISAs offer better value for most people.

National Savings fixed-interest certificates are either a five- or two-year investment, and offer a guaranteed fixed rate of interest. They can be encashed early, but this does involve surrendering a small amount of interest.

The current five-year issue (77th) offers a guaranteed rate of 3.65% if held to redemption, whereas the present two-year issue (27th) gives an overall net yield of 3.50%.

Once certificates have matured, they attract tax-free interest at the national extension rate (currently 2.04%) until they are redeemed.

Practical aspects

Although the certificates may be a suitable form of savings for children, children's bonus bonds (see 20.2.3) are likely to be a far more attractive proposition for small savings. They are not, however, suitable for non-taxpayers or for very short-term savings, but for the investor paying tax at the higher rate, the certificates may be appealing.

Application forms are available from most post offices and banks. Between £100 and £10,000 can be invested, plus up to £20,000 reinvestment of earlier issues that have matured.

Holdings should be reviewed from time to time, particularly since new issues may carry more attractive rates of capital appreciation than those already held. A review of holdings should certainly be made at the end of the specified period.

Any number of certificates can be cashed at one time, on at least eight working days' notice, and repayment forms are available at most post offices and banks.

20.2.3 Children's bonus bonds

As the name suggests, these bonds are designed specifically for children and are intended as longer-term savings, as the bondholder can retain the bonds up to age 21. The current issue (Issue 15) has a guaranteed tax-free return of 4.70% if held for five years. Anyone over age 16 can purchase bonds for anyone under age 16, and children under age 16 who wish to purchase bonds for themselves will have to ask a parent or guardian to sign the application form. The maximum total holding in all issues of children's bonus bonds is £1,000 per child (excluding interest and bonuses) regardless of the number of donors, and can be purchased in £25 units. Shortly before each five-year period ends, the next guaranteed interest rate and bonus is advised. No action is necessary unless it is decided to cash in the bond. Once the bondholder is over age 16, the next offer of interest rates and bonus is for whatever length of time remains until he reaches 21. The bonds can be encashed at any time, with one month's notice, but there is a loss of interest unless this is at a five-year bonus date, or at age 21.

As with savings certificates, this investment is particularly suitable for parents, as the interest is not aggregated with their own income for tax purposes, even if the growth in value produces interest in excess of £100 per annum.

20.2.4 National Savings index-linked certificates

As with National Savings certificates, these certificates are guaranteed by the Government. They cannot be sold to third parties.

There is no lower age limit for holding these certificates, although encashment is not allowed until a child reaches age seven, except in special circumstances.

If a certificate is encashed within the first year, the purchase price only is repaid. If the certificates are held for more than a year, the redemption value is equal to the original purchase price, increased in proportion to the rise in the RPI between the month of purchase and the month of redemption. In the event of a fall in the RPI, the certificates can be encashed for the original purchase price. After the death of a holder, indexation can continue for a maximum of 12 months.

They are available as a five- or a three-year investment. The current five-year issue (35th) guarantees a return above the rate of inflation for a five-year term by offering extra tax-free interest of 1.35%, as well as indexation. The amount of extra interest credited to the holding rises in each year of the life of the certificate and is itself inflation-proofed.

Similarly, the current three-year issue (8th) guarantees a return of 1.25% in addition to inflation, and like five-year issue certificates is exempt from income tax and CGT.

Certificates are suitable for individuals who do not need immediate income but are seeking protection in real terms for the amount invested. Higher rate taxpayers in this category will find the certificates particularly attractive. The investment limit here is £10,000 with a minimum of £100, in addition to holdings of all other issues of savings certificates.

Application forms are obtainable from most post offices.

Comparison with cash element ISAs

There may be circumstances where index-linked certificates could provide a better return than ISAs. Although interest rates are affected by a number of factors other than the rate of inflation, if you are pessimistic about the likely rate of inflation over the next five years, index-linked certificates can offer a low-risk alternative.

20.2.5 Premium bonds

Premium bonds are guaranteed by the Government. They cannot be sold to third parties.

417

Any person aged 16+ can buy the bonds, and a parent or legal guardian may buy bonds on behalf of a child under age 16. A bond cannot be held in the name of more than one person or of a corporate body, society, club or other association of persons. Prizes won by bonds registered in the name of a child under age 16 are paid on behalf of the child to the parent or legal guardian.

The minimum purchase for a bondholder aged 16+ is £100. Above this amount you can buy bonds in multiples of £10, up to a maximum of £20,000 per person.

Although no interest is paid, the available prize fund reflects current interest rates, and the effective interest rate is only 3.00% with effect from 1 October 2004. This equates to odds of 24,000 to 1 for each £1 bond each month. Once a bond that has been held for one clear calendar month following the month in which it was purchased it is eligible for inclusion in the regular draw for prizes from £50 to £1m. Bonds can be encashed at any time, and all prizes are totally free of UK income tax and CGT. Although the top prize may not compare favourably with potential National Lottery winnings, unlike the lottery the original stake will never be lost.

20.2.6 Personal equity plans (PEPs)

PEPs were introduced in FA 1986 to encourage wider share ownership by individuals in UK companies by offering investment tax incentives. Successive Finance Acts introduced changes that made PEPs even more attractive. PEPs were replaced by ISAs with effect from 6 April 1999, and although when the announcement was first made it was feared that existing PEPs would be severely restricted, the original proposals were revised following representations. As a result, existing PEPs can continue, almost as before, with the same tax advantages as ISAs, although no further subscriptions could be made after 5 April 1999.

Anyone who was over 18 years old and resident in the UK for tax purposes was able take out a PEP. Crown employees working overseas were deemed to be resident for this purpose. Should a planholder subsequently become non-resident, the plan can be maintained and its tax benefits preserved.

The tax benefits take the form of total exemption from CGT and income tax on the appreciation and investment income earned from equities, unit trusts and investment trusts held within the plan. However, from 6 April 2004, it will not be possible for the plan manager to reclaim the 10% credit attached to dividends from UK equities and this will certainly make the investment less attractive. A plan can be terminated at any time and the funds withdrawn without loss of the tax benefits.

There are two distinct types of plan: general plans, which have been available since the introduction of PEPs, and single company plans, which were first introduced on 1 January 1992. Single company plans allow investment only in the shares of one designated company, and are subject to an additional condition that substantially the whole of the cash subscribed to the plan, or from the realisation of plan shares, must be reinvested in plan shares within 42 days.

There is no restriction on the investment switches that can be made within the fund and no liability to income tax or CGT arises. A PEP can be transferred from one manager to another.

The cash held within the PEP can be held on deposit. The interest earned is paid gross and is exempt from tax provided it is eventually invested in plan shares or units.

Although no relief was available on the investment into the fund, the plan is virtually a gross fund in the same way as a pension fund. There is an important advantage over most pension funds in that all proceeds are tax free when drawn, whereas at least part of what emerges from a pension scheme is taxable. It is therefore a useful addition for individuals to enhance retirement benefits. The fund can be used in the same way as a pension, ie tax-free cash can be taken or the fund could be used to purchase an annuity.

PEPs are not 'no risk' investments but in the past a combination/selection of unit/investment trusts and direct investment in blue chip or 'alpha' stocks have generally produced a reasonable return where the investment was kept for between three and five years (see also Chapter 3).

20.2.7 Individual savings accounts (ISAs)

The Government issued a consultative document in December 1997 that heralded the phasing out of TESSAs and PEPs and their replacement with ISAs. Although originally it was intended to be a simple tax-saving vehicle to encourage saving by all sections of the community, the administration involved has proved to be difficult to understand, and take-up of non cash only ISAs has not been as wide as the Government had hoped.

Any UK-resident individual aged 16+ can take out a cash only ISA (although the age limit for other ISAs is 18), and all investors are exempt from income tax and CGT on the income and gains arising from investments held within the scheme. ISAs can comprise up to three separate elements: cash investments, stocks and shares, and life insurance. All three components can be provided by a single financial institution ('maxi' ISAs) or separately by different providers ('mini' ISAs). A maxi ISA provider must offer stocks and shares, and may offer cash and/or insurance. A mini ISA provider can offer one or more of the three separate components. It is only possible to invest in one mini ISA of the same type in the same tax year (eg one cash mini ISA), and similarly it is not possible to invest in a maxi ISA and a mini ISA during the same tax year.

Where an ISA contains a UK equity component, either in the stocks and shares element or to back a life insurance element, an additional 10% tax credit will be available until 5 April 2004.

The maximum annual investment, which can be made into either a maxi or a mini ISA, is £5,000, or £7,000 for the first seven years that ISAs are available (1999–2000 to 2005–06). However, the maximum investment that can be made in each individual component is different for maxi and mini ISAs, as shown below:

Maxi ISAs:	Maximum amount which can be invested	
	1999–2000 to 2005–06	*2006–07 onwards*
Stocks and shares	Up to £7,000	Up to £5,000
Cash	Up to £3,000	Up to £1,000
Insurance	Up to £1,000	Up to £1,000
Overall investment cannot exceed	£7,000	£5,000

Mini ISAs:	Maximum amount which can be invested	
	1999–2000 to 2005–06	*2006–07 onwards*
Stocks and shares	Up to £3,000	Up to £3,000
Cash	Up to £3,000	Up to £1,000
Insurance	Up to £1,000	Up to £1,000
Overall investment cannot exceed	£7,000	£5,000

Example

Anthony decides to invest in a maxi ISA on 14 July 2004. He wishes to invest £4,000 in the stocks and shares component, and £3,000 in the cash element. Because he has already invested the maximum of £7,000, he is unable to make any investment in the insurance component.

It is intended that the scheme will run for ten years, but will be reviewed after seven years to decide if any changes will be needed after the expiry of the ten-year period.

It is possible to make withdrawals from the account at any time, without loss of tax relief.

Although it is not possible to transfer shares acquired under a public offer, or on the demutualisation of a building society, as part of the annual subscription, this restriction will not apply to shares acquired from an approved profit-sharing or savings-related share option scheme. In addition, this latter transfer will not attract an immediate CGT charge.

In addition to an annual investment, it is possible to put the capital element of a maturing TESSA in a TESSA maturity cash ISA. However, no part of the interest element can be invested in an ISA, unless it falls within the normal annual limit.

Example

Marie invested £8,000 in a TESSA on 5 April 1999. This matures on 5 April 2004, and she receives a maturity cheque for £11,200. She decides to reinvest the maximum in a TESSA maturity cash ISA, in addition to a mini cash ISA. The capital element of £8,000 can be invested in a TESSA maturity cash ISA, and the annual maximum of £3,000 in a mini cash ISA. The balance of £200 can only be invested in a stocks and shares/insurance mini ISA, as the annual mini cash investment limit has already been reached.

20.2.8 Insurance policies

Insurance policies are another type of tax-privileged investment. Investors in qualifying policies are not subject to any tax on the maturity of the policy. For further discussion, see Chapter 14.

20.2.9 Friendly society investments

Friendly societies issue qualifying insurance policies and there is no tax charge for investors when such policies mature. In this respect the position is no different from policies issued by insurance companies. The difference lies in the way friendly societies are treated for tax purposes. Friendly societies are treated favourably as they are not normally subject to tax on life assurance business and this has generally enabled them to produce attractive returns.

Friendly society policies are, however, essentially a long-term investment since the surrender value can be very low where plans are cancelled or surrendered before the ten-year term has expired, as penalties tend to be heavy and frequently the charges are high.

The maximum premiums are very low. The maximum annual limit is £270, or £25 pm, but some societies do permit a lump sum investment to be made to cover the full ten-year plan. Policyholders must be between the ages of 18 and 70.

At least 50% of the underlying fund of a friendly society must be invested in narrower-range securities as defined in the Trustee Investment Act 1971. This could restrict the investment performance, but on the other hand offers a lower level of risk. All investment income and capital gains within the fund are free of all UK tax, which enhances the rate of return.

The Policyholder's Protection Act 1975 does not extend to friendly society plans and, unfortunately, there is no compensation scheme in the event of a friendly society having financial difficulties.

20.2.10 Pension policies

Personal pension policies and AVCs to approved pension schemes are among the most favourably treated of all investments. Full tax relief is available for the individual's contributions and the fund enjoys total exemption from tax. This is discussed in Chapter 15.

20.2.11 Enterprise zone property trusts

These trusts are effectively collective schemes whereby an individual acquires an interest in a portfolio of properties located in one of the designated enterprise zones. The minimum investment is usually £5,000, but unlike EIS investments (see 13.5) there is no maximum, and it is therefore possible for investors to shelter very large or exceptional income during a tax year. Investors are issued 'units' or 'shares', but in law they hold an interest in the properties as members of a syndicate.

The investment is allowable as a deduction from the investors' taxable income to the extent that the managers invest the cash raised by them to construct buildings or purchase newly constructed and unused buildings within an enterprise zone. There is usually a small part of the investment that attracts no tax relief, representing the cost of purchasing the land on which the building has been constructed. Generally this is between 7% and 15% of the total investment.

Example

Stuart invests £100,000 in an enterprise zone property trust on 3 March 2004. He has income of £75,000 that is subject to the 40% top rate.

The trust managers invest all the money raised in qualifying property before 6 April 2004. The land element is 10%. Stuart therefore receives a tax deduction of £100,000 x 90%, ie £90,000. This deduction saves him tax of £36,000 and so the net cost of the investment is £64,000.

Current yields on such investments are between 6% and 7.5% of the gross investment. The income is paid gross and is treated as rental income for the investor. The final investment return on such an investment is difficult to predict. Investors should expect to retain their units for a term of 25 years. A disposal within this term could give rise to a clawback of some or all of the income tax relief given in Year 1 (although no such clawback need arise in the case of a gift).

The yield becomes more attractive when one compares it with the net cost of the investment, after tax relief. Thus if the trust yielded 6% on the gross cost, the yield on Stuart's net cost becomes 9.7%.

These investments are tax privileged because of the relief due to the investor when he makes the investment. However, they are not risk free as the investment produces income only if the properties are fully let. In practice this risk can be minimised.

The trust managers can generally secure rental guarantees of at least two years where they buy properties from developers. Sometimes the developer offers a further guarantee that in the short term provides effectively a guaranteed income. In many cases the managers buy enterprise properties that have been 'pre-let' and this means the investor is securing a guaranteed income, usually with upward only rent reviews for a 25-year period. If good rent reviews are achieved, the capital value of the investment can be expected to appreciate.

Investors may also take a qualifying loan to acquire the units, the interest being set first against the rental income from the properties and any surplus is then available to be set off against any other Schedule A rental income for the same year. The balance of any unused interest relief is available to carry forward against rental income of future years.

In addition to the long-term nature of these investments, it is often difficult to dispose of the units as there is no established market through which units can be bought and sold. The managers do, however, offer to assist investors on a matched bargain basis.

Planning in later years

One planning possibility involving the use of these investments relies on the fact that the clawback (or 'balancing charge') need not arise on a gift. Thus, Stuart might transfer the shares in the enterprise property trust to his wife if she is not subject to the 40% rate. If she had no other income at all she would have only a small tax liability on the rents she received of £6,000 per annum.

20.3 CONCLUSION

Some of the tax benefit investments offer the prospect of outperforming inflation. The return on the cash element in an ISA might very well be 4.5% per annum or more. PEPs or ISAs invested in a range of equities should produce a comparable return over the medium to longer term. Index-linked National Savings certificates may do so, if the rate of inflation rises in the future.

The return on some of the other privileged investments looks less attractive. Where savings certificates have matured, the current rate of interest added (2.04%) may not keep pace with the rate of inflation.

The various types of deposit schemes offer a poor long-term return to anyone who cannot enjoy the income gross. They are, therefore, sensible investments for married women with little or no other income, but less attractive for a person who is subject to tax at 40%. That is not to say that these investments are not appropriate from time to time as a way of investing money short term or to secure a known commitment or liability.

21

INVESTOR PROTECTION

PETER HOWE, LLB

Barrister

21.1 INTRODUCTION

The other chapters of this book deal with the kinds of investment one might make. This chapter gives an overview of the structure of how the financial services industry is regulated. It covers:

- the need for those carrying on regulated activities as a business to be authorised under the relevant legislation and some exemptions from this requirement;
- how authorisation is obtained;
- the principles and rules which must be observed by authorised persons;
- the arrangements for the handling of complaints by investors against authorised persons and the compensation scheme which applies when authorised persons are unable to meet their liabilities;
- overseas aspects.

The chapter begins with a review of events that have occurred since the last edition of the book and ends with a look at some of the future developments that might occur.

The regulatory system today is governed by the provisions of the Financial Services and Markets Act 2000 (FSMA 2000) which replaces the Financial Services Act 1986, itself enacted following widespread concern at the collapse of a number of investment firms in the early 1980s. That legislation was based on the recommendations of the late Professor Gower who, on behalf of the Government, carried out an investigation that revealed a lack of consistency (and in some cases the absence of any controls) in the regulatory systems controlling different types of firm.

Professor Gower's approach was to recommend regulation only insofar as necessary for the protection of investors and that the regulatory structure should remain flexible so as not to impair market efficiency. The aim was to introduce a consistent regulatory structure that would produce a 'level playing field' (ie rules which do not put some firms at a competitive disadvantage compared with others). His view was that regulation should not try to do the impossible by protecting investors from their own folly but rather to prevent reasonable people from being deceived.

Finally, Professor Gower recommended self-regulation by the industry as preferable to the regulatory system in the US where the Securities Exchange Commission is a government agency. This produced a two-tier system where day-to-day regulation was undertaken by investment sector based self-regulatory organisations with overall supervision by a Securities and Investments Board.

The Labour Government became unhappy with this system and in June 1998 introduced a single integrated national financial services regulator, the Financial Services Authority (FSA), with clear and consistent objectives, accountability mechanisms and a very wide and substantial set of powers. A single regulator should provide a more efficient system better able to respond to the increase in the number of financial conglomerates and the blurring of the boundaries between financial products which has made regulation by the investment sector increasingly difficult.

21.2 HIGHLIGHTS OF LAST YEAR

21.2.1 Financial Services Authority

Treating customers fairly

The FSA issued a progress report which concluded that, despite some improvement, it was still finding examples of poor treatment of customers in retail financial services. The report emphasised the responsibility of senior management of firms to address the fair treatment of customers throughout the product life-cycle including product design, marketing, after-sales information and complaints handling. An assessment of firms' effectiveness will be checked as a part of the FSA's regular monitoring arrangements.

Consumer publications

The FSA has issued a large number of these on various subjects including with-profit bonds, long-term care insurance, mortgages, pensions and funeral plans.

Distance marketing

The Distance Marketing Directive, which aims to protect retail consumers entering into financial services contracts not sold 'face-to-face', must be implemented by October 2004 and the FSA has made rules providing for minimum specified information to be given about a financial product before contracting and giving cancellation rights. The rules include detailed conduct of business requirements for distance contracts for deposit taking. HM Treasury, which is responsible for the implementation of the directive, has also issued its final regulations effective from 31 October 2004.

Financial promotions

The FSA made changes to the rules to cover the marketing of structured capital-at-risk products (SCARPS) and the requirement to provide annual statements to customers. The FSA also warned chief executives of firms that market investment products for children of the need for clear and balanced explanations of the products and their risks, especially when making comparisons with bank or building society savings accounts.

Past performance

The FSA made new rules designed to reduce the emphasis given to past performance, strengthen the warnings to be given to reduce the link between past and future performance and to introduce standardised past performance information in all financial promotions. The new rules will only apply to funds and unit linked policies.

Projection review

The FSA issued a discussion paper on the need for a change in the information given to customers about potential future returns and charges. Proposals on this and the wider review of point of sale product disclosure will be made following consultation in early 2005.

Mortgage regulation

The FSA made final rules to regulate mortgage selling. The rules came into effect on 31 October 2004 and firms have been applying for authorisation from the FSA for what will then be a regulated activity with its own conduct of business rules.

Polarisation

The FSA announced its conclusions on the reform of polarisation last year. When the new rules apply, firms currently restricted to selling one company's products will be able to offer customers more choice. There will be restrictions on firms being able to call themselves 'independent'. Appointed representatives will still need to have a single principal but 'mere' introducers will not be restricted in this way. In February 2004 the FSA published its 'menu' proposals to inform customers concisely and up-front, of the cost of advice, whether the cost is met directly by fees or indirectly by commission or a combination of both. This document will complement the 'initial disclosure document' describing the scope and range of providers and products of the adviser.

Insurance Mediation Directive

Near final rules were published by the FSA designed to comply with the directive which becomes effective on 14 January 2005. However, because some of the rules are dependent on the rules that reform polarisation the FSA announced that the rules would all be made at the same time.

Long-term care

The FSA issued a consultative paper and policy statement with proposals to regulate those long-term care contracts that are not already regulated from 31 October 2004. All long-term care products will be regulated as 'designated investments' as opposed to insurance products.

Simplified investment products

Following the Sandler Report in 2002 both the Treasury and the FSA published consultation documents on types of simplified product which might result in a reduction in regulatory burdens provided these could be achieved without detriment to consumers. The most promising approach is one involving filtering the questions normally asked of customers to establish circumstances where the sale of 'stakeholder' products (cash ISAs, collective investment scheme/unit linked investment bond, smoothed investment fund, stakeholder pension and child trust fund in which the product specifications are stipulated by the Government) can be sold through the provision of 'basic advice'. Basic advice would still be based on the concept of suitability but would be limited to establishing the customer's broad attitude to risk, objectives and priorities. The consultation extended to September 2004 following which draft regulations were published in November 2004 to take effect in April 2005 when the simplified products are expected to be introduced.

Child Trust Funds

The FSA published its proposals for the regulation of Child Trust Funds intended to provide children with a financial asset and to develop the savings habit. There will be 'stakeholder' and 'non-stakeholder' versions of these funds and providers will have to seek both FSA and Inland Revenue approval to provide them. Children born after 31 August 2002 will automatically receive vouchers in January 2005 and will be able to make contributions from April 2005.

Money laundering

A discussion paper was issued by the FSA to stimulate debate on know your customer controls and monitoring including the desirability of adopting a risk-based approach in these areas depending on the degree of risk posed by a firm's customer, product and service profile. In a speech by the head of the FSA's financial crime section, warning was given that there is a tendency for firms to practise anti-money laundering not because they understand and support its rationale but rather because they are obliged by the rules to do it. A more targeted approach was promised in readiness for the Third Money Laundering Directive to be published by the European Commission.

The EU Financial Services Action Plan

By the end of April 2004, 38 out of 42 measures aimed at creating a single market in financial services had been adopted by the EU. The Treasury and the FSA now have the task of implementing these into UK law and over 20 such measures are likely to be implemented over the next three to four years.

21.3 BASIC FRAMEWORK

21.3.1 Financial Services and Markets Act 2000

Most of the provisions of the Act were brought into force with effect from 1 December 2001 (or N2 as known by almost everybody, although nobody seems able to explain the origin of the 'N' letter). The Act:

- makes the FSA the sole regulator of financial services and markets;
- sets out the regulatory objectives of market confidence, public awareness, the protection of consumers and the reduction of financial crime;
- states how these objectives are to be achieved;
- requires appropriate consultation with practitioners and consumers;
- prohibits the carrying on of regulated activities in the UK without appropriate authorisation or exemption from the FSA;
- controls the communication of financial promotions including advertising;
- specifies the kinds of activity which require regulation, the manner in which appropriate authorisation or exemption is obtained and how it is ended or withdrawn;
- bestows powers on the FSA to enable it to meet its objectives including the power to make rules governing the conduct of authorised firms, prohibition orders and disciplinary powers including the power to fine and publish statements of misconduct;
- establishes complaints procedures and a compensation scheme;
- contains provisions for the listing of securities and penalties for the newly defined behaviour of 'market abuse'.

The scope of the Act is much wider than the legislation it replaced. It covers banks, insurance companies, stockbrokers, investment managers and advisers, Lloyd's syndicates and those who offer advice on funeral plans. The Treasury may specify by statutory instrument the kinds of investment that are to be regulated and has already announced an intention to regulate mortgage advice, long-term care insurance and credit unions.

A key provision in the Financial Services and Markets Act 2000 (the Act) makes it a criminal offence to carry on a regulated activity in the UK unless the person concerned is authorised or exempt. A regulated activity is defined as carrying on certain activities by way of business, eg buying and selling, advising, arranging or managing 'things' which are specified investments under the Act. These include most 'paper' securities such as stocks and shares, collective investment schemes, most general, life and pension policies, gilt-edged securities, deposits and futures and options. The definition excludes real property, and alternative investments such as antiques and works of art. Most National Savings products are specifically excluded.

The Act has only minor application to the regulation of occupational pension schemes that are largely governed by trust law and other legislation. Financial services regulation is only concerned with the investment management aspects. In particular the Act requires trustees to be authorised (see 21.3.2) unless they have delegated day-to-day investment decisions to professional investment managers.

Since 1 June 1997 the provision of custody services has required authorisation.

21.3.2 Authorisation

Firms carrying on a regulated activity may obtain their authorisation from the Financial Services Authority (FSA). Those firms which were authorised under the Financial Services Act 1986 (usually as a result of membership of a self-regulatory organisation) were 'grandfathered' into the new system to save them having to re-apply for authorisation.

Certain EEA firms obtain their authorisation from the equivalent authorities in the EU member state in which the company's head office is situated. These firms do not need to seek additional authorisation under the Act although their marketing activities are subject to regulation by the FSA.

21.3.3 Exemptions

Some firms are exempted from the requirement to obtain authorisation under the Act. These include the Bank of England (except in relation to insurance business), recognised investment exchanges and clearing houses, and other bodies listed by statutory instrument in relation to specified activities.

Certain specified professions (eg solicitors and accountants) are exempt provided that any regulated activities are incidental to professional services. Again, the detailed conditions are laid down by statutory instrument.

An important category of exempt person is the appointed representative. This is an individual or firm that acts as the agent of an authorised person and for whose activities (within the limits of the authorised person's business activities) the authorised person takes legal responsibility. Although it is open to any authorised firm to appoint such representatives, the practice is most common in the case of insurance companies and firms that market life policies and collective investment schemes.

It is not possible under the Act for a firm to be both an authorised person and an appointed representative.

21.3.4 FSA Central Register

The FSA is required under the Act to maintain a public register of firms authorised to carry on investment business, including a list of authorised and recognised collective investment schemes. This Central Register permits investors as well as firms to check on the authorisation status of firms including appointed representatives. It is therefore possible to check whether such an appointed representative is the agent of a particular company.

The Central Register can be contacted by telephoning 0845 606 1234 or by using New Prestel or Telecom Gold services. The service is available through the internet, libraries and citizens' advice bureaux.

21.3.5 Authorisation criteria

In deciding whether to authorise a firm the FSA consider such matters as whether those involved in the business are fit and proper persons having the financial resources and competence to operate the business in a way which is unlikely to result in unreasonable risk to investors. In addition, the FSA has published 11 Principles (see below) that it expects all firms to observe. The breach of any principle might result in disciplinary proceedings being initiated and call into question whether the firm is fit and proper to carry on regulated activities.

The Principles

(1) Integrity

A firm must conduct its business with integrity.

(2) Skill, care and diligence

A firm must conduct its business with due skill, care and diligence.

(3) Management and control

A firm must take reasonable care to organise and control its affairs responsibly and effectively, with adequate risk management systems.

(4) Financial prudence

A firm must maintain adequate financial resources.

(5) Market conduct

A firm must observe proper standards of market conduct.

(6) Customers' interests

A firm must pay due regard to the interests of its customers and treat them fairly.

(7) Communications with clients

A firm must pay due regard to the information needs of its clients, and communicate information to them in a way which is clear, fair and not misleading.

(8) Conflicts of interest

A firm must manage conflicts of interest fairly, both between itself and its customers and between a customer and another client.

(9) Customers: relationships of trust

A firm must take reasonable care to ensure the suitability of its advice and discretionary decisions for any customer who is entitled to rely upon its judgment.

(10) Clients' assets

A firm must arrange adequate protection for clients' assets when it is responsible for them.

(11) Relations with regulators

A firm must deal with its regulators in an open and cooperative way, and must disclose to the FSA appropriately anything relating to the firm of which the FSA would reasonably expect notice.

Source: *The Financial Services Authority*

21.4 RULES AND REGULATIONS

The Act contains only the bare framework of the total investor protection legislation. The detailed rules and regulations with which authorised firms are expected to comply are contained in various statutory instruments, together with a number of 'sourcebooks' and manuals within the FSA Handbook. These include:

- the high level standards for business (including the Principles);
- prudential sourcebooks for banks, building societies, friendly societies, insurers and investment businesses;
- detailed conduct of business rules;
- manuals dealing with the authorisation of firms, their supervision, enforcement and the way in which the FSA makes decisions (including disciplinary decisions) affecting firms;
- provisions for redress, including complaints and compensation.

21.4.1 Senior management systems and controls

The FSA places great emphasis on the need for the senior management of firms to be fit and proper and to take responsibility for regulated activities. A number of 'controlled functions' has been specified by the FSA, which can only be performed by a person who has been 'approved'. These functions include the chief executive function, the director function and other functions related to compliance, money laundering reporting, investment management and investment advice. The rules require firms to establish and maintain systems and controls appropriate to its businesses and to allocate responsibility for this as one of the controlled functions. A key control function is that of apportionment and oversight, usually allocated to the firm's chief executive, which entails the allocation of all the other roles. The FSA has published seven statements of principle (similar to the principles that apply to firms themselves) which approved persons must observe, backed up by a detailed code of practice.

21.4.2 Business conduct

The detailed rules and regulations in the Conduct of Business section of the FSA Handbook cover a number of areas relating to the conduct of regulated activities by authorised persons. These include:

(1) the way in which authorised firms and their appointed representatives seek new business; and
(2) the ongoing relationships between authorised firms and their customers where such relationships exist.

433

21.4.3 Seeking business

There are detailed financial promotion rules that prohibit misleading advertisements and statements and claims that cannot be substantiated. The FSA has recently expressed concerns about advertisements which lack balance, make unrealistic claims and create unrealistic expectations. There is also concern about the use of 'small print' to provide 'key' information.

It should be remembered that the definition of a financial promotion is extremely wide and includes any inducement or invitation to engage in investment activity. It therefore includes not only promotions in newspapers or other publications but also via websites, television, radio and e-mail. What is more, it covers real-time oral presentations, meetings and telephone conversations.

Under the Act, and subject to some exceptions, only financial promotions made or approved by an authorised person are permitted and a breach of this requirement is a criminal offence.

There are rules which require authorised firms to know their customer before making a recommendation or arranging an investment transaction and to make sure that any investment that is recommended or transacted is suitable, having regard to the investor's personal and financial requirements. Poor completion of 'fact finds' (the questionnaires which intermediaries normally use to get to know their customers) have in the past been the subject of criticism by the regulator. The reasons for making a recommendation are required to be given in writing.

In the case of packaged product investments such as life assurance, pension plans and collective investment schemes, the polarisation rule requires intermediaries to disclose in a Terms of Business letter or client agreement and on business stationery whether they are independent from any particular product company, in which case the obligation is to recommend a suitable product from those available on the market or company representatives, who must recommend a suitable product from the product range of the particular company they represent.

Independent intermediaries and company representatives are permitted to make unsolicited calls (personal visits or oral communications other than at the investor's invitation) that cannot be made in relation to non-polarised investments. Investments which can be the subject of unsolicited calls normally give the investor cooling-off rights, enabling the investor to cancel an investment transaction within a reasonable period (normally 14 days) from entering into the contract. Detailed product disclosure rules are designed to provide sufficient information about the product to enable the investor to decide whether to continue with the contract.

Since 1 January 1995 product and commission disclosure rules for life companies have required a 'Key Features' document, setting out the essential elements of the product including charges and expenses, to be given to an investor before an application form is completed. The document must disclose the commission or other remuneration payable to the intermediary (whether independent or tied) and must give further important information, specific to the circumstances of the purchasing investor, about the product. The rules require life offices to use their own charges and not industry standard charges when preparing illustrations of future benefits and the clear disclosure to investors of the consequences of surrendering a policy before the end of its term or maturity. They also permit product providers to make charges that differ according to which distributor outlet is used to obtain the business. Since 1 May 1997 these rules have applied to unit trusts and other non-life assurance packaged products.

21.4.4 Customer agreements

The rules prescribe the terms of customer agreements between authorised firms and their customers including how such agreements are made, how instructions are to be communicated and how such agreements are terminated.

There are also rules requiring authorised firms to place client money in designated trust accounts to ensure that investors' money is kept separate from other money belonging to the firm. The rules provide for the payment of interest except in specified circumstances.

21.5 COMPLAINTS AND REMEDIES

21.5.1 Basic procedures

If an investor has a complaint about an authorised firm, the investor should raise the matter initially with the firm's compliance officer who is usually an employee of the firm with responsibility for ensuring that the firm complies with the rules. If the firm does not handle the complaint to the investor's satisfaction, the investor may refer the matter to the Financial Ombudsman Service and this must normally be done within six months of the date when the firm rejects the complaint.

The Ombudsman will try to resolve complaints in the most appropriate way. This may include mediation, where the Ombudsman will try to facilitate an agreement acceptable to the parties. If an investigation is necessary, he will carry this out giving the parties the opportunity to make representations and making a 'provisional assessment'. After further opportunities to make representations (which may involve a hearing) the Ombudsman will then make a written determination containing the reasons for his decision.

The Ombudsman may make a money award compensating the complainant for financial loss up to £100,000.

Referring a complaint to the Financial Ombudsman Service does not normally prevent the investor from pursuing any other legal remedies. In addition to bringing civil actions for breach of contract or negligence, the private investor is given a right, under the Act, to sue an authorised firm for any breach of the investor protection rules that causes the investor loss.

The FSA has a range of intervention powers that can be used in the interests of investor protection. These include the FSA's power to prohibit the employment of persons considered to be unfit, to apply for an injunction or restitution order where a breach is threatened or where investors have suffered loss, to restrict the business of investment firms, to restrict any dealings with a firm's assets or even to vest those assets in a trustee. These powers are in addition to the power to discipline firms and their 'approved persons' for misconduct and to impose fines.

21.5.2 Compensation scheme

Authorised firms are required to contribute a levy to a compensation scheme established by the FSA and administered by the Financial Services Compensation Scheme Ltd under which, in the event of an authorised firm going into liquidation, investors may recover up to a maximum of £48,000 if the firm is unable to meet its liabilities.

21.6 OVERSEAS ASPECTS

Overseas firms are subject to the Act if they carry on investment business in the UK. Unless an overseas company is authorised to carry on investment business in the UK, it is difficult for it to market its products and services to UK investors. It is possible for the overseas firm to promote its products and services in the UK through an authorised person.

If the investment is a recognised collective investment scheme or an insurance policy issued by a recognised insurer, which it may be if the scheme or insurer is authorised in another EU member state or in a territory designated by the Treasury (eg the Isle of Man, the Channel Islands), an authorised firm may market it freely within the UK. Although such a scheme may not be subject to the UK compensation scheme it is possible that it will be subject to a compensation scheme set up in the home country or territory concerned.

If the collective investment scheme or insurance policy is not a recognised scheme, there are severe restrictions on the extent to which it can be promoted in the UK. For example, an authorised person can promote such a scheme to established customers under the terms of a subsisting customer agreement but cannot market to investors generally.

21.7 PREVIEW OF THE YEAR AHEAD

21.7.1 FSA developments

Listing

The review of the listing rules will be completed and various EU Directives, including those on Prospectuses, Market Abuse and Transparency, implemented.

Treating customers fairly

A strengthened focus on this aspect of firms' management and controls, including firms' approaches to financial promotions and complaints handling, is emphasised. Specific measures to improve transparency and to clarify obligations of insurance companies to with-profits policyholders will be implemented.

Polarisation

Packaged products will be depolarised in early 2005.

Simplified investment products

Following consultation, draft regulations were published in November 2004 to take effect in April 2005 when simplified (stakeholder) products are expected to be introduced.

Mortgages

The new rules governing the arranging of mortgages were introduced from October 2004. The work required to implement the Credit for Consumers Directive will be carried out and, once enacted, will affect a substantial number of mortgages.

Financial services action plan

Progress will be made in implementing the various measures aimed at establishing a single European financial market.

21.8 CONCLUSION AND FUTURE DEVELOPMENTS

The Act provides the framework for the most comprehensive investor protection system ever seen in the UK or elsewhere in Europe. In the past 16 years considerable progress has been made in putting the flesh on the bare bones provided by the legislation.

Changing circumstances brought about by an innovative and competitive financial services industry as well as developments in Europe will require further adaptations of a system that needs to be responsive to such changes.

The new FSMA 2000 and the enhanced powers given to the FSA will provide added impetus to those developments. The Financial Services Action Plan (see 21.8.1) will introduce a single market in financial services in the EU in which the UK will be a major player.

21.8.1 Future developments

Looking ahead, the scope for change and future development of the regulatory system is significant. The Barcelona Summit of European ministers reinforced the aim of completing the single financial market by 2005. The benefits of such a market are thought to be a reduction in the cost to firms of capital and improved opportunties for savers to invest and diversify risk.

Although there has already been a fair amount of integration in the wholesale markets, the retail markets still differ significantly from country to country. The preferred approach of the UK is for a European system of regulation built around a set of harmonised core standards but leaving scope for individual member states to adapt the system to their own circumstances. It does seem likely though that some method will be found to ensure that such discretion is not abused and that some pan-European financial institution will be formed. It is unlikely, however, that there will be an integrated regulator for the whole of the EU in the forseeable future.

For now the Financial Services Action Plan, agreed in 1999, incorporates more than 40 separate initiatives harmonising legislation and practice. The possible adoption by the UK of the euro could provide additional impetus to the development of a single market.

Increasing resources will need to be expended on monitoring compliance, meeting the costs of the compensation scheme and financing the ongoing costs of the training and competence schemes. These expenses, have added to the competitive pressures on investment firms. The result of changes to the system following the FSMA 2000 is almost certain to increase costs for the industry, at least in the short term. Those costs, together with the opportunities created by the introduction of EMU and a single market in Europe, are likely to produce an increasing number of mergers or takeovers and a search for more cost-effective methods of securing the distribution of financial products and services. Predictions have been made that the number of banks, life companies and independent intermediaries will reduce substantially over the next few years. New methods of distribution such as the sale of more products by telephone and over the Internet will occur. The regulators have already decided to regulate mortgages and general insurance and it is possible that they will extend their reach to banking products not currently subject to the same level of control as investments under the Act. There are even signs that regulators may take an increasingly interventionist approach to the types of products sold by firms and the terms under which they are sold, including the price. In this environment new challenges will be created for the regulators as well as for those regulated. It is possible that the regulators will focus their attention on minimising the risk of fraud and other market failures instead of concentrating on the improvement of the detailed standards of industry practice. There is now some evidence that the costs of regulation, which are eventually passed on to the consumer, are actually making it uneconomic for firms to market their products to a growing sector of the community. This development conflicts with the important government aim of encouraging people to save for their own retirement rather than rely on the state.

The Act introduced a dynamic system capable of responding to change. There is little doubt that the system will be severely tested during the next few years.

USEFUL ADDRESSES

FSA (Financial Services
   Authority)
25 The North Colonnade
Canary Wharf
London E14 5HS

Tel: 020 7066 1000
Web: www.fsa.gov.uk

Investors Compensation Scheme
   Limited
c/o Financial Services
   Compensation Scheme
7th Floor Lloyds Chambers
Portspoken Street
London E1 8BN

Tel: 020 7892 7300
Web: www.fscs.org.uk

The Law Society (of England and
  Wales)
The Law Society's Hall
113 Chancery Lane
London WC2A 1PL

Tel: 020 7242 1222
Web: www.lawsoc.org.uk

The Institute of Chartered
  Accountants (in England and
  Wales)
Chartered Accountant's Hall
PO Box 433
London EC2P 2BJ

Tel: 020 7920 8100
Web: www.icaew.co.uk

Financial Ombudsman Service
South Quay Plaza
183 Marsh Wall
London E14 9SR

Tel: 020 7964 1000
Web: www.financial-
  ombudsman.org.uk

The Pensions Ombudsman
11 Belgrave Road
London SW1V 1RB

Tel: 020 7834 9144
Web: www.pensions-
  ombudsman.org.uk

INDEX